NJÁLS SAGA

A beardless man battling the forces of evil in the initial "N" introducing chapter
20 of *Njáls saga* in *Kálfalœkjarbók* (*A.M.* 133, fol.), Icelandic manuscript from
around 1300. Photo: A. Mann Nielsen.

LARS LÖNNROTH

NJÁLS SAGA

A CRITICAL INTRODUCTION

UNIVERSITY OF
CALIFORNIA
PRESS . BERKELEY, LOS ANGELES, LONDON

University of California Press
Berkeley and Los Angeles, California

University of California Press, Ltd.
London, England

For Iris, Linus, and Magnus

Contents

Preface

The work on this book started more than ten years ago, but the plan for it has changed considerably over the years as the author's views and interests have changed. Originally, my ambition was to show that *Njáls saga*, sometimes regarded as the apex of Germanic folk tradition, was actually more dependent on Christian and "learned" influences than was commonly recognized. The first result of this ambition was a series of intentionally provocative and rather overstated articles, summarized in 1965 as a Swedish doctoral thesis, *European Sources of Icelandic Saga-Writing*. Later, as a teacher of Old Norse literature at the University of California, I began to modify some of my earlier thoughts and to recognize the peculiarly Norse character of the saga as a work of art. The new thrust of my studies led to a series of articles emphasizing native tradition rather than foreign influence. As a result of this Hegelian dialectical process, my book has finally come to include a rather comprehensive introduction to the narrative tradition underlying *Njáls saga*: "native" as well as "foreign," "Germanic" as well as "Christian," "oral" as well as "literary."

Readers familiar with previous scholarship on *Njáls saga* will find that my book presents some new versions of older theories about specific problems which have been discussed many times before : "Who was the author ?," "What sources did he use ?," "How was the present text composed ?," "Why did Gunnarr return to Hlíðarendi ?," and so on. My main purpose, however, is not to solve these classical enigmas (if indeed they can be solved), but rather to provide the advanced student of Old Norse with some general guidelines which may enable him to cope with classical saga texts as a critic and literary historian without getting bogged down in too much philological detail. For this reason, I have emphasized general principles of saga tradition and saga art rather than the particular *Njála* problems, the discussion of which has been largely relegated to footnotes and to the Appendix. In its present form, my book may be said to synthezise a number of modern trends in saga scholarship: the search for a "narrative grammar" that may help us to see how stories were generated, the search for European and Christian influences on the native saga forms, and the renewed search for oral traditions as the ultimate source of the saga genre. Although *Njáls saga* is by no means typical of classical sagawriting, it is the work that most successfully and originally combines the various literary forms and ideas of thirteenth century Iceland, and thus it may serve to illustrate both the general norms and one very gifted artist's departure from them.

I had originally intended to complement my discussion of structure, style, and meaning with a series of "close readings" of select *Njála* passages such as the Burning of Njáll, the Battle of Clontarf, etc., for practically each chapter of the saga presents problems of interpretation which I was unable to deal with in the course of a general discussion. My analysis of "Gunnarr's return" at the end of Chapter IV presents one example of such close reading but I would have liked to provide the reader with more of this sort. Yet I found it impossible to do so at this time because it would have involved repeating myself and also making the book far too voluminous. I hope, however, to have provided the reader with some tools for making such close readings on his own.

The general theory of saga composition emerging from Chapter III and the conclusions of Chapters IV and V owes its origins to my contact with various friends and colleagues who were pondering structural theory and the principles of oral composition long before I started to do so myself. My greatest debt is to Carol Clover, who since 1967 helped me to change my thinking about the sagas and whose doctoral dissertation provided some of the key concepts for this book. Since my stay at Harvard in 1968, my thoughts on structure and saga composition have been much inspired through contacts with Theodore M. Andersson, Joseph Harris, and Albert B. Lord. During the final stages of my work I was also stimulated by the unexpected appearance of Richard Allen's *Fire and Iron*, a book which shares some ideas with my own, although Allen's general approach to the problems is quite different from mine.

Parts of the book were written in Sweden while I was on leave from Berkeley as a Humanities Research Professor in 1969 and 1971 and as a Guggenheim Fellow in 1971-72. Earlier versions of certain parts of Chapters III and IV have been published in *Scandinavian Studies* and *Skírnir*. For editorial help, criticism, and valuable suggestions I am indebted to Christina Allen, Theodore Andersson, Carol Clover, Patricia Conroy, Marcia Gilfillan, Gesche Kähler, John Lindow, William McClung, and Russell Schoch. Hermann Pálsson and Magnús Magnússon have generously allowed me to make free use of their translation of *Njála* for the Penguin series; in several cases I have departed from their translation in order to bring out some particular feature of the Icelandic text, and I bear the sole responsibility for any errors or awkward phrases which may have resulted from such departures.

Last but not least I should like to acknowledge my debt to Professor Einar Ólafur Sveinsson, whose long-standing authority as a *Njála* scholar I have been battling since I first started my saga studies. As the work on this book proceeded, however, I found myself agreeing more and more often with his conclusions. Although my views on *Njála* still differ from his, my respect for his scholarship and my gratitude for his teaching have increased the more I have learned about the subject.

Lars Lönnroth

Berkeley, California
May, 1974

I

Njála and Its Critics

It may seem somewhat surprising that *Njála*,* the most famous of sagas, was not printed until 1772, more than a hundred years after the rediscovery of Old Norse literature and the publication of the first saga editions. But the scholars who first occupied themselves with the sagas were antiquarians, primarily interested in collecting information about the glorious past of the Scandinavian countries,[1] and from this particular viewpoint *Njála* had little to offer. In his patriotic work on Iceland, *Crymogaea* (1609), the learned Arngrímur Jónsson presented Latin summaries of Njáll's and Gunnarr's biographies as moral examples to posterity.[2] These summaries were undoubtedly based on a manuscript of *Njála*, and we know that some other scholars in the seventeenth and eighteenth centuries also consulted such manuscripts as historical sources.[3] However, the literary "discovery" of *Njála* by the *beau monde* of Copenhagen, Uppsala, and Kristiania did

---

* Modern saga scholars, including the present author, have adopted the Icelandic habit of referring to well-known sagas by affectionate abbreviations such as *Njála* for *Njáls saga*, *Hrafnkatla* for *Hrafnkels saga*, etc.

1. There is an extensive literature about these early antiquarians. An excellent survey (with references to earlier works) may be found in the first chapter of Theodore M. Andersson's *The Problem of Icelandic Saga Origins* (New Haven and London, 1964).

2. *Bibliotheca Arnamagnaeana*, vol. 10 (1951), 134-142; cf. the comments by Jakob Benediktsson, *Bibl. Arn.*, vol. 12.

3. See, for example, Thormodus Torfaeus, *Series regum Daniae* (Copenhagen, 1705), 51; Arne Magnusson, *Brevveksling med Torfaeus*, ed. Kr. Kålund (Copenhagen, 1916), 96, 299.

not come until the nineteenth century and was then largely a product of German Romanticism and the new interest in "folk literature."[4]

Among the Icelanders, however, *Njála* was one of the most popular sagas ever since it was first written at the end of the thirteenth century. The number of early manuscripts is unusually large,[5] and the saga continued to be spread in new transcripts throughout the centuries. It also gave rise to secondary traditions in the form of local legends, ballads, rhymes (*rímur*), and proverbial sayings.[6] Quite a few of the poems and rhymes, as well as transcripts of the saga itself, have been preserved in manuscripts written during the seventeenth and eighteenth centuries, often by Icelandic clergymen and civil servants, the kind of people who would form a natural link between the narrative traditions of the island and the learned world of Copenhagen. It was therefore natural that *Njála* already would be described as "well known and famous" in the royal letter of introduction to the 1772 edition.[7]

This edition, an unusually good one for its time, was made in Copenhagen by Olavus Olavius, an Icelandic student who later became a customs officer and the author of an "economic" description of Iceland. Typically enough, the royal letter of introduction stated that *Njála* was an "historical work" and that it should be published because it could throw light on the political and legal system of early times, thereby making it possible to apply such knowledge, "insofar as it is possible," to the present time. In spite of this patriotic motivation, Olavius had to pay for the publication himself, although he seems to have been compensated for this by the wealthy Danish historian P. A. Suhm, who bought the whole edition and also paid for its subsequent translation into Latin by another Icelandic student, Jón Johnsonius (this excellent work was produced in the 1770's but not published until 1809). In addition, Suhm himself wrote an enthusiastic appraisal of *Njála* in the fourth volume of his *Critical History of Denmark*.[8]

4. On the sagas and Scandinavian Romanticism, see especially Anton Blanck, *Den nordiska renässansen i sjuttonhundratalets litteratur* (Stockholm, 1911); Jöran Mjöberg, *Drömmen om sagatiden*, I (Stockholm, 1967).

5. Cf. Einar Ól. Sveinsson, *Studies in the Manuscript Tradition of Njálssaga* (Reykjavik, 1953).

6. See especially Matthías Johannessen, *Njála í íslenzkum skáldskap* (Reykjavik, 1958), and Einar Ol. Sveinsson's footnotes to the *Njála* edition of 1954 (cf. note 39).

7. *Sagan af Niáli Þórgeirssyni ok sonvm hans*, ed. O. Olavius (Copenhagen, 1772) [hereafter cited as *Njála* (1772)].

8. The Introduction to *Historia Niali et Filiorum* (1809); P. A. Suhm, *Critisk Historie af Danmark, udi den hedenske Tid fra Odin til Gorm den gamle*, IV (Copenhagen, 1781), pp. X-XII; see also Jón Helgason's introduction to *Manuscripta Islandica*, VI (1962), pp. XVII f.

Suhm, who thus played an important role in the early history of *Njála* scholarship, was not only an antiquarian but also a novelist and a writer of short stories in the eighteenth-century rhetorical tradition.[9] He was one of the first to use Old Norse motifs in modern Scandinavian fiction, and he was definitely the first to publicly proclaim *Njála*'s importance as a work of art:

Nial's saga is in regard to its style just as good as Snorri, and in regard to its narrative technique (*Fortællingsmaaden*) superior to his, for even though it essentially contains only the story of one Icelander, yet the unknown author knows so well how to tie in other and highly important events that occurred in Denmark, Norway, Iceland, Greece; and he has so marvelously elucidated the manners and the old Icelandic judicial procedure (*saa herligen oplyset Sæderne og den gamle Islandske Procesmaade*) and yet known how to control all this and to make a whole out of it (*og dog vidst at iakttage af alt dette, at giøre eet Heelt*), that I have read few books with greater pleasure. One may justly call this saga an *Iliad* in prose, since all the incidents are the result of one female's viciousness, just as in the case of Helen.[10]

In spite of its eighteenth-century tone (note the reference to Homer and to "manners"!), this early statement contains views which are surprisingly modern: first of all, the view that the saga is to be regarded as one well-structured narrative, controlled by one artistic mind, that of "the unknown author." About a hundred years later, *Njála* would instead be described as a patchwork of originally independent short sagas, a work full of inconsistencies, loose ends, interpolations and leftovers from previous stages in the tradition. But today, critics are again coming back to Suhm's view in this respect. On the other hand, they do not share his faith in the historical authenticity of the saga, even though this faith has been amazingly persistent until comparatively recent times.

Suhm's enthusiasm for *Njála* was soon echoed by the Icelandic philologist Skúli Thorlacius in his preface to the Latin translation, where he praised *Njála*'s style and characterization, especially in the dialogue.[11] In this he has been followed by most later critics. As we shall see, they have sometimes even tended to over-emphasize such particulars as the portrayal of

9. Cf. Blanck (1911), 217-21, 238-39.

10. Suhm (1781), XI.

11. "Dictionem Nialae tot sane veneres et virtutes exornant, ut inter veteres Islandorum historiae paucas aut nullam dederis, quae hoc nomine cum Niala possit componi. Auctorem illud coarguit, non modo doctum atque disertum, sed ingeniosum quoque et mirum in characteribus ad vivum pingendis artificem, utpote qui in observando personarum decore tantae sit dexteritatis, ut verba ingenio et animo loquentis cum maxime congruant. Tantus nimirum est dictionis lepor et proprietas, ut quasi viventium colloquis interesse lector sibi videatur." (*Historia Niali*, XI.)

individual heroes, thereby neglecting the author's larger designs of structure and meaning. Like Suhm, however, Thorlacius seems to have been aware of the fact that *Njála* is not just a collection of masterly told stories and psychological portraits but a unified creation by an individual author. Following tradition from the seventeenth century, he even tried to identify this author with a well-known historical person, Sæmund the Wise, one of the first Icelandic antiquarians. But this theory about the authorship, which was to haunt *Njála* scholarship for some decades, has now been dead for a long time.

Peter Erasmus Müller, a Danish professor of Theology and later a Bishop, brought *Njála* to the attention of the literary world at large. In his *Saga-bibliothek*, published between 1817 and 1820, he gave extensive presentations in Danish of the most important sagas. Among these he declared *Njála* to be the greatest, "both in regard to the plan of the narrative and to the portrayal of characters."[12] In his view the portraits had been made "from nature," and the authenticity of the story could not be doubted. His image of *Njála* as a basically realistic work, an imitation of reality, has persisted longer than the belief in its historicity. He also set the tone for later criticism by declaring the Christian elements in the saga, especially the episode about the conversion of Iceland, to be something foreign to its nature, something not quite integrated in the narrative structure. For even though the Bishop was undoubtedly a good Christian himself, it was the Germanic, pagan and non-Christian spirit of the Viking Age which he and his contemporaries were looking for in the sagas. Later scholars were to expound the theory of a Christian intrusion or imposition upon the "basically" pagan narrative with arguments of increasing complexity and ingenuity.

By 1820 *Njála* had become regarded as one of the great Scandinavian "folk" classics by the Danish Romanticists. We know that Grundtvig, one of the leaders of the new literary movement, had made excerpts from the saga as early as 1804, and soon afterwards he appears to have transformed his experience of the work into Romantic poetry.[13] In 1821 the Romantic enthusiasm called forth a vitriolic pamphlet by Torkel Baden, a classical scholar who had translated Seneca and who was secretary to the Danish Academy of Arts. In this pamphlet—ironically entitled *Nial's Saga: The Best of All Sagas*—Baden shows himself to be a somewhat flamboyant supporter of eighteenth-century classicism against the Romanticist movement with its preference for sagas and other kinds of "folk" literature. He char-

12. *Sagabibliothek*, I (Copenhagen, 1817) 51.
13. Cf. Mjöberg (1967), 25, 73.

acterizes *Njála* as a "hotchpotch of murders and ghost stories, nothing else,"[14] refers to Gunnarr from Hlíðarendi as "that great scoundrel," and describes the saga characters in general as "undisciplined, brutal, asocial, quarrelsome and truly vicious human beings." He also expresses his contempt for its many primitive superstitions and quotes with approval "an enlightened lady" who professed that "these stories were not believed except among the common people, and this belief could manifest itself in deeds which lead to the Scaffold." In his own opinion, the only useful thing to be learned from reading the work is "a bit of legal knowledge." Otherwise, it is even worse than the tales of the Grimm brothers.

However unreasonable Baden's criticism may appear, it is still one of the most entertaining and refreshing to read, and it is interesting as a symptom of the role *Njála* played in the literary discussion of the 1820's. Obviously, Baden's indignation is not so much aimed at the saga itself as at the critics who had set it up as a model—the kind of Romanticists whom he contemptuously refers to as "German fuzzheads" (*tydske Sværmere*), people affected by what he calls "the Icelandic plague" (*den islandske Smitte*). The real reason for his attack is revealed in a pathetic passage towards the end, where he speaks with nostalgia about the good old days when people were still studying "Quintilian, the younger Pliny, Gessner and Jacob Baden" (the author's father). Today, he informs us, they are not read any more. "They have gone out of fashion. Eddas and sagas are read, translated, commented upon, and anything that takes its taste from them is counted among *the most beautiful creations of our literature*" (Baden's own italics).

Baden may have had a somewhat exaggerated impression of "the Icelandic plague" and its effects, for in fact *Njála* was not translated in full into any modern language until the 1840's.[15] The real breakthrough among the educated public occurred towards the end of the century, when the sagas found many new admirers, both among the adherents of the Naturalist school (who admired their "realism") and among the neo-Romantic Scandinavian nationalists of the 1890's (who continued to see Old Norse literature as a legacy from a glamorous pagan past). Detailed historical criticism of

14. *Nials Saga, den bedste af alle Sagaer, drøftet af Torkel Baden* (Copenhagen, 1821), 5.
15. The first Danish translation (by N. M. Petersen) was published in 1841. George Webbe Dasent's English translation was published in Edinburgh, 1861. It was followed by a German translation in 1878, a Swedish in 1879, a French and a "Landsmål" Norwegian in 1896. (See Einar Ól. Sveinsson's edition of 1954, p. CLIX f. for a complete list.) It should be noted, however, that *selections* from *Njála* were available in numerous works during the nineteenth century, and many educated readers probably knew the saga only from such selections. It should also be noted that the Swedes and the Norwegians could easily use a Danish translation before they had their own translation.

Njála started only in the 1870's, when Konráð Gíslason made a new, very thorough, and in many respects still unsurpassed edition, based on a large number of manuscripts,[16] while Guðbrandur Vigfússon began the scholarly research aimed at determining *Njála*'s age, sources, and place of origin, thereby introducing a discussion that has ever since dominated the scholarly study of the saga.

Before going into this learned discussion, however, we should note the appearance in 1855 of an excellent essay about *Njála* by the Danish poet Carsten Hauch.[17] This essay, based on a series of lectures at the University of Kiel, can be regarded both as an answer to Baden's attack and as a departure from the conventional nineteenth-century interpretation of the sagas. Hauch is the first critic to analyse *Njála* in some detail as a truly literary creation (*et virkeligt Digt*) illustrating "how the spirit of revenge is defeated by the spirit of Christianity" (465). In contrast to Müller and his followers, he saw the Christian elements, especially the Conversion episode, as belonging to the very essence of the narrative. According to his interpretation, the conversion introduces "the very element which alone may bring about a satisfying ending" (436). To support this view, Hauch tried to demonstrate how the unknown author had built up his story in symmetrical patterns which not only are effective artistically but also point towards a Christian moral. It should follow from this analysis that the whole structure of the story is determined less by the "objective" facts of history than by the author's artistic and religious vision, but this is a conclusion Hauch himself did not emphasize. Instead, he was satisfied to show that the saga can be read not *only* as history but *also* as a sort of didactic novel.

Guðbrandur Vigfússon, professor at Oxford and one of the great pioneers of modern saga research, was the first to break away openly from the historical naiveté of Müller and his generation. He seems to have shared Hauch's basic views about the meaning and structure of the saga. In the commanding survey of Icelandic literature which introduced his edition of *Sturlunga saga* (Oxford, 1878), he described *Njála* as "the Saga of Law par excellence" and maintained that "the lesson it teaches is of a Divine retribution, and that evil brings its own reward in spite of all that human wisdom and courage, even innocence, can do to oppose it" (p. xlii). He also stated clearly that the saga "is certainly to be taken as a whole and

16. *Njála udgivet efter gamle Håndskrifter at Det Kongelige Nordiske Oldskrift-selskab,* I (Copenhagen, 1875) ; A second volume with important contributions to the textual criticism by Konráð Gíslason, Jón Þorkelsson et. al., was published in 1889.

17. "Inledning til Forelæsninger over Njals saga og flere med den beslægtede Sagaer" in *Afhandlinger og æsthetiske Betragtninger* (Copenhagen, 1855), 411-67.

ascribed to one man," although it consists of three parts which are only "loosely connected" (pp. xlii-xliv).

Vigfússon's most important contributions to the study of *Njála* were his dating of the saga and his theory about the author and his sources. After having studied the language, chronology, placenames, and genealogies of the saga, he had reached the conclusion that it was "the work of a lawyer,— living in the far East of Iceland" at some time between 1230 and 1280. He saw this author as a man who "deals freely with his facts" and makes use of various older sources to suit his own purpose, not only oral narratives but also genealogical lists, "law scrolls and law manuals" and probably also a lost *Gunnars saga*, which had been incorporated with the material about Njáll and his sons (the original *Njáls saga*).

Some of these conclusions, which clearly at the time represented a considerable advancement of scholarship, he had already reported in a private letter to his German colleague Konrad von Maurer in the beginning of the 1860's.[18] It appears indeed likely that Maurer—an expert in legal history and one of the first to apply German *Quellenkritik* to the study of sagas— had influenced Vigfússon to take a more critical look at these matters. Maurer himself had used *Njála* as an historical source (and found it wanting) already in the 1850's, and he later encouraged further research into its dating and general background, especially its relation to the written laws of Iceland.[19] These two men, Maurer and Vigfússon, can thus be said to have started a new and more scientific era in the history of *Njála* scholarship.

Yet it was these two men who planted the seed of a doctrine which (though partly sound) would eventually prove a stumbling block to any serious analysis of *Njála* as a work of art: the doctrine that the saga received its present form through a deliberate combination of older "sources," written or oral. Doctrines of this sort were exceedingly common at the time in any discussion of the "folk" epic. Some decades earlier, Karl Lachmann had presented his so-called *Lieder-theorie*, according to which the Homeric epics had originated out of several independent short songs. Lachmann himself also applied his theory to the *Nibelungenlied*, and it was soon applied to other works as well.[20] It is not unlikely that this way of thinking had influenced N. M.

18. Published by Þorleifur Bjarnason under the title "Rök um aldur Njálu" in *Skírnir* (1922), 147-53.

19. See Maurer's introduction to Lehmann-Carolsfeld, *Die Njálssage* (cf. note 23, below). It should be noted, however, that Guðbrandur Vigfússon had already, in 1856, pointed out certain grave chronological errors in *Njála* (*Safn til sögu Islands*, I, 418).

20. See, for example, Sir John Myres, *Homer and his Critics* (London, 1958), 90-91; J. A. Davison, "The Homeric Question," *A Companion to Homer*, ed. A. Wace and F.

Petersen, the first Danish translator of *Njála*, who (in a survey of Old
Norse literature published in the 1860's) stated that "the whole design"
of the longer sagas (*Hele deres anlæg*) "shows that they have first been told
in the form of shorter sections, and that the individual parts have later
been joined by art to a unified whole."[21] The classical methods of textual
criticism and *Quellenkritik* further encouraged the kind of interpretation
that would soon reduce the "unified whole" to a mere compilation of earlier
material.

This was exactly what happened when the followers of Vigfússon and
Maurer started to scrutinize *Njála* in all its details. In 1878, Oscar Brenner,
one of Mauer's students, published a comparative study of all the various
accounts in the sagas of the conversion of the Icelanders. One of his conclusions was that the Conversion episode in *Njála* was an interpolation in
the main text from an older written source, related to (but not identical
with) the famous *Íslendingabók* of Ari the Wise.[22] Five years later, in 1883,
two other students of Maurer's, Karl Lehmann and Hans Schnorr von
Carolsfeld, presented the results of a much more extensive study of *Njála*
and its sources, especially its legal sources.[23] On the first page of this very
solid and impressive work, the authors declared that their intention was
not to discuss the many good qualities of *Njála* as a work of art but rather
to study its "shortcomings" in order to arrive at conclusions about its age.
The "shortcomings" were mainly various minor inconsistencies and factual
mistakes in the descriptions of legal procedure. From such mistakes Lehmann
and Carolsfeld concluded that the author of *Njála* had been rather ignorant
about the ancient laws of Iceland; in some cases he had compiled his knowledge from the written laws of the later thirteenth century, and the saga
could therefore not have received its present form before that time.

But Lehmann and Carolsfeld also found several other "shortcomings"
in the narrative structure which they used to argue that the saga had incorporated material from sources other than the law scrolls—sources they
thought of as being, at least in part, alien to the true nature of the saga.[24]
Thus they tried to prove that the episode about the Battle of Clontarf at

Stubbings (London, 1962), 249-50. The connection between the Homeric analysts and
the *þáttr* theorists was noted by Th. Andersson, 61.

21. *Bidrag til den oldnordiske Litteraturs Historie* (Copenhagen, 1866), 220.

22. *Über die Kristni Saga* (München, 1878), 61-62.

23. *Die Njálssage insbesondere in ihren juristischen Bestandtheilen. Ein kritischer
Beitrag zur altnordischen Rechts- un Literaturgeschichte* (Berlin, 1883).

24. Note especially the appendices entitled "Über fremde Bestandtheile der Njála"
and "Anachronismen. Geographische Fehler. Unebenheiten in der Composition," *op.
cit.*, 139-60, 166-71.

the end of *Njála* (an episode full of Christian miracles) was based on a lost *Brjáns saga*, which had been copied more or less mechanically by an interpolator and which also had been used as a source by the author of *Þorsteins saga Síðu-Hallssonar*. Finally, they gave additional support to the theories about lost sources already advanced by Vigfússon and Brenner. The end result of their investigation was that the present *Njála* came about through the combination of (a) a lost *Gunnars saga*, (b) a lost *Njáls saga*, (c) written laws, (d) a lost saga about the conversion (*Kristni þáttr*), (e) a lost *Brjáns saga*, and (f) lost genealogical sources.

Lehmann and Carolsfeld have been criticized for their narrow analytical approach, but it cannot be denied that their main results have stood up well against attacks by later critics and are now, with several minor modifications, accepted. More details have been added to their theories about the individual lost sources, their origin, age, and relations to other sources, lost or still extant.[25] Only the theory about the combination of *Njáls saga* and *Gunnars saga* can now be said to be obsolete.

But however valuable their contribution was, their methods obviously tended to obscure the *function* that each individual episode has in *Njála*, regardless of origin and dependence on earlier sources. Yet their theories could be combined with a more synthetic and structural approach only a few years later in a dissertation by the Swedish poet A. U. Bååth,[26] a translator of *Njála* and one of the leading representatives of the "Literary Eighties" in Scandinavia. The gist of this dissertation can be regarded as a further elaboration of the general ideas expressed by Lachmann, N. M. Petersen, and the Homeric "analysts": by a series of examples, the author tried to show that all the long family sagas had originated out of short stories, socalled *þættir*, which had been joined together by the thirteenth century authors.

Unlike many other analysts, Bååth concerned himself with the actual composition of the sagas, not only with the origin of their components. His most important conclusion in regard to the composition was that the idea of Fate held the individual episodes together through a system of anticipatory techniques: omens, premonitions, prophetic dreams, etc. The structural unity was, in his opinion, directly dependent on the importance of its fatalistic element: the more "fate" introduced by the author, the better he would succeed in keeping the *þættir* together. *Njála* in his analysis represents the height of success in this respect: it is both the best-

---

25. For bibliographical references (esp. concerning *Kristni þáttr*, *Brjáns saga*, and the legal sources) see Sveinsson's Preface to *Njála* (1954), ch. 3 (cf. note 39 below).

26. *Studier öfver kompositionen i några isländska ättesagor* (Lund, 1885).

structured and the most fatalistic of all sagas. Accepting Vigfússon's, Lehmann's, and Carolsfeld's theories about the lost sources, he divided the saga into an even larger number of components in the form of *þættir*, and yet he was able to maintain that "the author has had such a command over his material that he wrote down his first line having the last line within his vision" (pp. 159-60). In accord with this view, Bååth followed Hauch in assigning an important function to the Conversion episode and to other Christian elements in the saga (pp. 144-46). In his opinion, the only episode that falls outside the natural scope of the narrative is the one about the Battle of Clontarf, which he (following Lehmann-Carolsfeld) regarded as an interpolation (pp. 158-59).

Bååth's *þáttr* theory was later criticized by the great Germanist Andreas Heusler, and today it is seldom referred to in discussions about the origin of the sagas.[27] Many later critics have also disagreed with his views concerning the function of the Conversion and the Clontarf episodes. On the other hand, they have generally accepted his analysis of the structure, especially his way of dividing the saga into episodes held together by various techniques of anticipation. But very little has actually been said about such matters since Bååth's time, and his own structural analysis is in fact rather brief and schematic. On the whole, the historical problems of origin (especially the questions of the sources) have continued to engage the scholars more than the problems of structure and narrative technique.

During the 1880s and 1890s, scholars, critics, and poets concerned themselves with *Njála* several times[28]—this was the period when the sagas were at the height of their popularity among the Scandinavian reading public—but nothing essentially new was said about the saga as a whole before 1898, when Finnur Jónsson published the second volume of his *Literary History*,[29] thereby establishing himself as the leading figure within saga studies in Scandinavia (a position which he vigorously held for several decades). A hearty and explosive man, one of the greatest philologists of his generation, Finnur Jónsson was also one of the most ardent believers in the historicity

27. "Die Anfänge der isländischen Saga," *Abhandlungen der K. Preuss. Akad. d. Wiss., Phil.-Hist. Classe* (1913). See also Th. Andersson (1964), 61-64.

28. Among the critical appraisals of *Njála* from this period we may mention Wilhelm Goetz, *Die Nialssaga ein Epos und das germanische Heidenthum in seinen Ausklängen im Norden* (Berlin, 1885) and especially W. P. Ker, *Epic and Romance* (London, 1897), 252 f. See also Vilhjálmur Finsen, *Om den oprindelige Ordning af nogle af den islandske Fristats Institutioner* (Copenhagen, 1888), 100-101. Concerning the influence of *Njála* on the poetry and fiction of the eighties and nineties, cf. Matthías Johannessen (1958); Mjöberg, II (1968).

29. *Den oldnorske og oldislandske Litteraturs Historie,* II: 1 (Copenhagen, 1898), 525-47.

of the "classical" sagas which he thought of as having been written from oral tradition already around 1200 or earlier. He saw these sagas as the very incarnation of realism and of a certain secular rationalistc spirit which he personally loved and felt to be specifically Norse. Elements of fantasy, piety, or rhetoric he tended to dismiss as signs of decadence, artificiality (*forkunstling*), and unhealthy foreign influences. Sagas containing many such elements he declared to be either late or interpolated. He had grown up in Iceland with the best sagas always around him, and *Njála* seems to have been one of his favorites, except for its religious passages, especially the Conversion and the Clontarf episodes. In his literary history—still an indispensable work, full of immense learning—he reported that he had "known a child" (evidently himself) who had read *Njála* "ten times at the age of ten" (547).

It was natural that such a man would protest against some of Lehmann's and Carolsfeld's theories, especially their contention that the saga as a whole was late and untrustworthy as an historical source. On the other hand, it was also natural that he would gladly accept the idea that the Conversion and the Clontarf episodes were interpolations. By adopting theories about such interpolations and adaptations, he could in fact defend the "genuine" and "original" saga as a model of realism and reliability. In a series of learned contributions, including a new and useful edition of *Njála*, he scrutinized the text again along these general lines.[30] Since his own philological principles were—in spite of all polemics—rather similar to those of Lehmann's and Carolsfeld's, he had no difficulties in accepting "inconsistencies" and other "shortcomings" as conclusive proof of multiple authorship. In this fashion he managed to add a few ingredients to the brew of lost sources and interpolations already concocted by his German colleagues: a lost *Lýtings þáttr* among other little bits and ends. The predictable result of his analysis was that the present *Njála* is ultimately based on two good, realistic, unchristian sagas from around 1200, i.e., the lost *Gunnars saga* and the lost *Njáls saga* already hypothesized by Vigfússon; later in the thirteenth century, these sagas were presumably combined and adapted together with various other material. The final version of this theory, which Finnur Jónsson presented in the introduction to his edition and in the revised second edition of his *Literary History*, attributed *Gunnars saga* to the man who made this adaptation, but it still did not accept him as the "real" author of the "real" *Njáls saga*.

---

30. "Om Njála," *Aarbøger for nordisk Oldkyndighed og Historie*, 19:2 (1904), 89-166; *Brennu-Njálssaga* (*Altnordische Saga-Bibliothek*, 13, Halle, 1908), XIII-XLVI; *Den oldnorske og oldislandske Litteraturs Historie*, 2nd edition, vol. 2 (1923), 519-40.

Since the 1930's it has been *comme il faut* among Old Norse scholars to criticize Finnur Jónsson, but the influence he exercised on his contemporaries was considerable and is still noticeable in modern handbooks. His views on *Njála* became an obstacle to any further advancement of the discussion about the structure, meaning, and art of the saga. Instead, a good deal of scholarly energy was wasted on attempts to find evidence for and against its historicity. Archeological excavations were made at Bergþórshváll, and the meager findings were used to verify the story about the fire.[31] The personalities of Hallgerðr and Skarpheðinn were seriously analyzed and "explained," as if their historical existence were beyond any reasonable doubt and could be separated from their literary existence in the saga. It is symptomatic that the brilliant Norwegian novelist Hans E. Kinck, a man who should have known better, wrote a celebrated essay entitled "A few things about the family saga: characters it did not understand" (1916).[32] The thesis of this essay is that the Icelandic storytellers did not really grasp all the psychological complexities of the remarkable men and women they were trying to portray. *Njála*, Kinck's prime example, is accused of having misrepresented Hallgerðr, actually a tragic and brutally treated lady and not the evil *femme fatale* the saga makes her out to be. With a similar kind of logic, Skarpheðinn's famous grin is interpreted by Kinck as a sign of a serious psychoneurosis, unfortunately misunderstood by the medieval Icelanders themselves. This whole line of thinking is about as meaningful as the well-known scholastic debates about Hamlet's activities in Wittenberg, his former associations with Rosencrantz and Guildenstern, etc. (Kinck was not the first author to defend Hallgerðr against the "evidence" of the saga; this had been done several times in Icelandic *rímur* and skaldic verses since the beginning of the eighteenth-century; the most famous defense, which led to a series of versified attacks from other poets, was composed by the folk poet Sigurður Breiðfjörd.)[33]

An essay about Gunnarr of Hlíðarendi by the Icelander Sigurður Guðmundsson which appeared shortly afterwards[34] is similar to Kinck's in its point of view even though it is based on a closer study of the saga and is clearly aimed at establishing its literary and unhistorical character against the most naive believers in its historicity. Its author said little about the narrative art and meaning of *Njála* that had not been said before (by Hauch,

31. Cf. *Árbók hins íslenzka fornleifafélags* (Reykjavik, 1951-52); Sveinsson's Preface to *Njála* (1954), ch. 1.

32. *Til Gerhard Gran 9. des. 1916*; republished in the collections *Mange slags kunst* (Oslo, 1921) and *Sagaenes ånd og skikkelser* (Oslo, 1951).

33. Cf. Johannessen (1958), 18-24, 37-67.

34. "Gunnar á Hlíðarenda," *Skírnir* (1918), 63-88, 221-251.

Bååth, and others), and he spent all too much time demonstrating that the saga had "idealized" the real Gunnarr's personality and heroic deeds—a thesis which should not have been in need of demonstration at this stage in the development of scholarship. His form of historical criticism, which pre-supposes that the saga is somehow "basically" historical even though it contains elements of fiction, should have appeared harmless enough even to such authorities as Finnur Jónsson. One is therefore slightly amazed to find Sigurður Guðmundsson suggesting, in a postscript to his essay, that his views had been met with strong disapproval because of their radicalism when presented in lecture form at the University of Iceland. But it should always be remembered that the popular faith in the veracity of the sagas has been—and still is—surprisingly strong in Iceland.

The first scholar to break new grounds after the appearance of Finnur Jónsson was Andreas Heusler, professor in Berlin and Basel and undoubtedly the greatest Germanist of his time: a brilliant stylist and one of the few to combine philological learning with a critical sense of history and the gift to understand literature. Unfortunately, his contribution to the study of *Njála* was mainly limited to a brief introduction in his own German trans-lation of the saga,[35] but practically everything he said in these few pages deserves to be read by later critics.

Unlike most of his contemporaries, Heusler did not accept the theories about interpolations, although he did accept the idea that the author of *Njála* had used older traditions concerning Gunnarr and Njáll, which had been available to him "probably as two separate works and in written form" (17). He also believed that the Conversion and the Clontarf episodes were based on earlier written sources which the author himself had incorporated in his text, although their function in the narrative was slight. To explain such seemingly unwarranted inclusions, Heusler referred to what he called the author's *Stoffreude* (5), i.e., his delight in storytelling regardless of the consequences for the overall structure.

But in spite of his concessions to the "analytic" theory, Heusler regarded *Njála* as essentially one unified literary work, created by one man, a Christian author living at the end of the thirteenth century, well versed in the heroic narrative traditions of his country but also familiar with at least certain aspects of the clerical and chivalric culture of medieval Europe. Christian and pagan elements had been combined into a sort of Romantic and nostalgic apotheosis of the Saga Age. In consequence of this interpretation, Heusler warned against overstressing the naturalism of the saga:

35. *Die Geschichte vom weisen Njal, Thule,* IV (Jena, 1914).

One does not understand our artist if one only emphasizes his realistic profile. In the bottom of his heart, he is an idealist who wants to express edifying ideas (*erhebende Gesinnungen verkörpern*). But the fact that he is an Icelander and schooled in the sagas—much less in the Bible and the Romances—saves him from any moralizing distortion (*rettet ihn von jener traktätchenhaften Schwarzweissmanier*) (13).

Although Heusler seems to have shared at least some of the naturalistic literary prejudices of his time (for example when he speaks of *Schwarzweissmanier* or when he, elsewhere, reproaches the author for not having understood "feminine nature" in his portrayal of the female characters) he is nevertheless one of the first to appreciate the stylized technique of the saga. Among other things, he issued a much-needed warning against psychologizing about individal saga characters. Hallgerðr is no Hedda Gabler, but rather the stereotyped, proud, and revenge-seeking Valkyrie-type so frequently found in Germanic tradition. Gunnarr is "Siegfried in an Icelandic farmer's costume" (12). On the whole, Heusler laid the grounds for a more precise analysis of *Njála's* style by briefly discussing some of its typical formulae, stereotyped motifs, and rhetorical devices and the way they are used in the narrative to heighten suspense, prepare the audience for a dramatic climax, etc. A technical dissection of this sort could not easily be made as long as the sagas were thought to be a more or less direct imitation of nature.

Thirteen years later the stereotyped motifs and literary conventions of *Njála* were finally studied on a much larger scale in a Dutch dissertation by Anna Cornelia Kersbergen.[36] The main object of her study, however, was not so much to explain the art of the saga but rather to arrive at new conclusions about its sources, original components, and literary models. It was, in other words, a contribution to the debate of Finnur Jónsson and Lehmann-Carolsfeld, even though Kersbergen's methods were different. By studying the repeated treatment of conventional motifs in the saga, she hoped to measure its unity and determine to what extent it could be regarded as one man's creation. By hunting for parallels in other sagas, she also hoped to determine which of them had influenced the author, so that *Njála* could be placed within a specific literary tradition.

Kersbergen's definition of a "literary motif" seems to have been liberal enough to include almost anything from a general concept or idea (which can be expressed in a multitude of ways) to a stereotyped scene with stock characters and conventional formulae, allowing very little individual variation. This tends to make her analysis somewhat imprecise, but her catalogue of motifs (organized in a few broad categories such as "Domestic Motifs,"

---

36. *Litteraire Motieven in de Njála* (Rotterdam, 1927).

"Motifs from Public Life," etc.) is still useful, and her study of recurrent scenes and situations within the saga has provided new arguments in favor of its basic unity, even though she herself never openly departed from the current "analytic" theories about *Njáls saga* and *Gunnars saga*. Her contention that the author of *Njála* was influenced by a large number of earlier written sagas has also been accepted by most later critics, even though there is some variation in the opinions as to which these sagas were.

In her willingness to interpret literary parallels as evidence of direct influence, Kersbergen is representative of the new trends of saga scholarship during the 1920s and 1930s. To Heusler and Finnur Jónsson and their generation, it was self-evident that sagas on the whole were based on oral traditions, even though they believed that written sources had been used in the composition of *Njála* in its present form. But to the new generation, which followed the lead of such older scholars as Maurer and B. M. Ólsen, and which soon established itself at the University of Iceland under Sigurður Nordal's leadership, the family saga was interpreted as essentially a thirteenth-century genre, formed by literary "schools" of writers who used oral traditions only as a kind of raw material for their creations. As a consequence of this so-called "book-prose" theory, it became natural to see practically *all* important correspondences between *Njála* and earlier works as a result of written influences, not as a result of their common dependency on oral traditions. At the same time, however, the adherents of the book-prose theory strongly emphasized the artistic unity and individuality of each saga—and particularly of *Njála*.[37]

The new trends are specifically associated with the name of Einar Ólafur Sveinsson, Nordal's successor at the University of Iceland and today the unquestioned authority on *Njála*—so much so, in fact, that few remember the considerable work that was done by his many eminent predecessors. Even so, Sveinsson's contribution is weighty and impressive. It started with the dissertation *Um Njálu* (Reykjavík, 1933), in which he again took up the problem of the sources in all its details, arguing against the theories of interpolations and the supposed combination of *Gunnars saga* and *Njáls saga*. Ten years later, he also published a book on the art of Njála, *Á Njálsbúð: Bók um mikið listaverk* (Reykjavik, 1943),[38] in which he elaborated the observations of Hauch, Bååth, and Heusler in greater detail,

---

37. Cf. Th. Andersson (1964), 65-81.

38. Translated into Norwegian in a slightly revised form by L. Holm-Olsen under the title *Njåls saga: Kunstverket* (Bergen-Oslo, 1959). An English adaptation by Paul Schach has now appeared under the title *Njáls saga: A Literary Masterpiece* (Lincoln, Nebraska, 1971). Cf. my review in *Scandinavica*, 11, May 1972, 48-49.

adding important observations of his own and integrating all this into a very personal interpretation of the saga as a whole and of its unknown author. After ten more years, he published his *Studies in the Manuscript Tradition of Njáls saga* (Reykjavík, 1953), in which he enlarged and improved upon the earlier textual studies by Konráð Gíslason, Jón Þorkelsson, and Lehmann-Carolsfeld. The main results of these three books were summarized and to some extent modified in his much-quoted introduction to the *Íslenzk Fornrit* edition of *Njála* (1954).[39]

It is difficult to give a succinct and fair presentation of Sveinsson's contributions because they encompass so many different aspects of the saga. While correcting and elaborating the results of previous scholars, he has also tried to harmonize their divergent views in a way that may be characterized as prudent and tolerant but also as somewhat eclectic. With Bååth he regards *Njála* as a perfectly unified whole, but he also agrees with Heusler's theory that only the author's *Stoffreude* could have prompted him to include the Conversion and the Clontarf episodes. He agrees with Kersbergen and Heusler about the use of stereotyped motifs and stock characters, but he also regards the saga as a model of realism. He agrees with Hauch and others on the importance of Christian didacticism in the saga, but he also insists that it contains important layers of pagan and secular thinking, basically irreconcilable with the Christian faith but coexisting with it in a "dynamic relationship." He defends the old notion that the saga is based on oral traditions, and at least to some extent on historical facts—and yet he argues that large portions are created by the thirteenth-century author as pure invention or as imitations of various literary models.

In his interpretation of the author's role, however, Sveinsson shows himself most clearly to be a member of the new "Icelandic School."[40] To him the saga is primarily the expression of one individual's soul, a man torn between the religious and political forces of his time—an Icelandic patriot, well versed in the pagan and secular traditions of his country but also attracted by the ideas of the Church. As we can see, this is a more romantic version of the author as described by Heusler. According to Sveinsson, *Njála*'s author has created his own saga and has spoken to us in his own words (except for the Clontarf and Conversion episodes), but in doing so he has

---

39. *Brennu-Njáls saga*: Einar Ól. Sveinsson gaf út (Islenzk Fornrit, XII). This edition will be referred to as *Njála* (1954) in later footnotes. It has served as our basic text throughout this study, except in a few cases when it has been necessary to quote variant readings which only appear in Konráð Gíslason's edition, *Njála* (1875).

40. See especially his introduction to *Njála* (1954), pp. C-CXII, and his most recent statement on the sagawriter's "Ideas and Ideals" in *Njáls saga; A Literary Masterpiece*, 181-210.

been influenced not only by oral traditions but also by a whole library of written works: *Laxdœla saga* and a number of other family sagas, *Brjáns saga, *Kristni þáttr, and also some religious and chivalric works such as the *Dialogues* of Gregory the Great and *Alexanders saga*, a Norse translation of Gautier de Chatillon's Latin poem *Alexandreis*. In spite of all this learning, Sveinsson is convinced that the author was a layman, not a priest. His interpretation tends to make us visualize the unknown author of *Njála* as a sort of Icelandic Dr. Faustus, a learned but secular humanist living somewhere in the Southeast of Iceland and expressing his grand but inconsistent vision of man and the world to rid himself of the inconsistencies of his own soul.

Considering all the speculations about the author which not only Einar Ólafur Sveinsson but also other Icelandic scholars have indulged in, it is hardly surprising that this problem would be taken up on a large scale by another Icelander, Barði Guðmundsson. In a series of articles, later published in book form,[41] Barði Guðmundsson tried to prove that the author was a certain well-known chieftain, Þorvarðr Þórarinsson, one of the most powerful men in Iceland during the latter half of the thirteenth century. He furthermore tried to prove that the whole saga was a kind of *roman à clef* containing numerous allusions to characters and events in the Sturlung Age. His arguments have been sternly rejected by Sveinsson,[42] and it must be admitted that they are often more fanciful than really convincing. Nevertheless, Barði Guðmundsson's studies deserve attention as the only serious attempt to place *Njála* in some kind of social context.

While this attempt is normally regarded as an interesting curiosity, Einar Ólafur Sveinsson's views on *Njála* have been accepted almost without any reservations in such works as Sigurður Nordal's, Jan de Vries', and Stefán Einarsson's literary histories,[43] in Peter Hallberg's *The Icelandic Saga*,[44] in Bjarni Guðnason's article on *Njála* in *Kulturhistorisk Leksikon for Nordisk Middelalder*,[45] and in the introductions to the two most recent English translations.[46] And there are only timid hints of minor disagreement

---

41. *Höfundur Njálu* (Reykjavik, 1958).
42. Cf. *Njála* (1954), pp. CVII-CXI, CXIV. A more appreciative view of Barði Guðmundsson's contributions may be found in P. Hallberg's "Nyare studier i den isländska sagan," *Edda* (1953).
43. S. Nordal, "Sagalitteraturen," *Nordisk kultur*, VIII B (Uppsala, 1953), 259-61; J. de Vries, *Altnordische Literaturgeschichte*, 2nd ed., vol. II (Berlin, 1967), 450-63; S. Einarsson, *History of Icelandic Literature* (New York, 1957), 146-48.
44. Trans. by Paul Schach (Lincoln, Nebraska, 1962), 131-36.
45. Vol. 12, 1967, 318-22.
46. *Njáls saga*, trans. by C. F. Bayerschmidt and L. M. Hollander (New York, 1955), 1-15; *Njal's saga*, trans. by M. Magnússon and H. Pálsson (Penguin Classics, 1960), 9-31.

in two excellent recent essays on *Njála* by I. R. Maxwell[47] and Denton Fox.[48] In both essays, structure and meaning are discussed according to modern critical principles developed in the Anglo-Saxon countries. Very few references are made to the problem of the sources. Efforts are made to explain the relationship between the individual episodes and to integrate apparent digressions (particularly the Conversion and Clontarf episodes) into the saga as a whole. In many respects these contributions are similar to Hauch's and Bååth's, although their authors go further in stressing parallels and subtle correspondences within the narrative, and in emphasizing the Christian ideas as the controlling and decisive elements in the structure. But in spite of their many virtues, these essays have so far not had any influence on the "Icelandic School."

In his dissertation of 1964, however, Theodore M. Andersson delivered a frontal attack on the current book-prose theories of the "Icelandic School," and especially on Einar Ólafur Sveinsson's theories about *Njála's* relations to earlier sagas.[49] According to Andersson, most of the parallels used by Kersbergen and Sveinsson to prove literary influences actually prove nothing of the sort. In the cases where "the same" story is told differently in *Njála* and in some other saga, it is often more reasonable to believe that both are based on oral tradition than to believe that one saga influenced the other. Andersson also issued a warning against "hypothetical written sources, which are no more susceptible of proof and no less an article of dogma than oral tradition, the indemonstrability of which has been so firmly impressed upon us by the adherents of bookprose" (103). Although this line of reasoning can be found already in works by such adherents of "free-prose" as Andreas Heusler and Knut Liestøl, it clearly needed to be expressed again, and was also rather well received in the scholarly journals. But so far nobody has drawn the logical conclusions of Andersson's criticism in a discussion of *Njála* as a whole.[50]

Three years later, Andersson published another book on the structure and narrative art of the family sagas.[51] In this study he tried to show that

---

It is the latter of these two modern translations that we have usually quoted in our own English renditions of the *Njála* text.

47. "Pattern in *Njáls saga*," *Saga-Book of the Viking Society*, 15 (1957-61), 17-47.

48. "*Njáls saga* and the Western Literary Tradition," *Comparative Literature*, 15 (1963), 289-310.

49. Andersson (1964), 95-103.

50. See, however, Heimir Pálsson, "Rittengsl Laxdælu og Njálu," *Mímir*, 6 (1967), 5-16.

51. *The Icelandic Family Saga; An Analytic Reading* (Cambridge, Mass., 1967). *Njála* is specifically discussed on pp. 291-307.

all such sagas are built up around a revenge conflict which is normally presented in six stages: 1) Introduction (presentation of characters, etc.); 2) The conflict is introduced; 3) Climax (a major clash between the feuding parties); 4) Revenge (the wronged party takes it out on the enemy); 5) Reconciliation (usually in the form of a legal settlement at a Thing meeting); and 6) Aftermath (usually consisting in a brief report on the later destinies of the main characters and their descendents). This pattern, which Andersson regarded as a legacy from heroic poetry and from oral tradition in general, he found repeated twice in *Njála*: first in chapters 1-81 (corresponding to the *Gunnars saga assumed by previous scholars), then in chapters 82-159 (roughly equivalent to *Njáls saga). Since the Conversion and Clontarf episodes cannot be fitted into this scheme, they are declared to be digressions. Also in this respect, Andersson thus returns to the ideas of a much earlier generation. But his structural analysis of *Njála* cannot be accepted without serious reservations.[52]

The most recent and "modern" study of the saga is an American dissertation by Richard M. Allen, *Fire and Iron: Critical Approaches to Njáls saga*.[53] Allen follows Theodore Andersson in emphasizing the saga's structural heritage from oral tradition. At the same time, he emphasizes the Christian patterns in the saga to an unusual extent. On one hand, he makes an attempt to analyze *Njála* as built up of various stereotyped narrative elements developed in native storytelling long before the introduction of Christian literature in Iceland. On the other hand, he finds subtle theological meanings in many places where previous critics have found nothing but straight narrative.

Although Allen never openly criticizes Sveinsson and the Icelandic School, his "critical approaches" are very different from theirs and are in the same general tradition as the earlier articles by Fox and Maxwell. Like these authors, Allen avoids discussing the problem of sources and influences in any detail; instead he concentrates on trying to demonstrate "intrinsic" literary patterns and the unity of *Njála* as a work of art. In so doing, he has sought inspiration from such modern critical autorities as Erich Auerbach, Northrop Frye, C. G. Jung, and Wayne Booth. He also makes a laudable attempt to relate the saga to Western literary tradition as a whole. Scandinavian saga scholars could learn much about critical approaches from Allen's stimulating exposition, but it is unfortunately too sketchy to serve as a reliable guide to the problems of literary history, and some of its generalisations can be very easily criticized. Because of his ambition to mediate

52. Cf. my review in *Speculum*, 43 (1968), 115-19.
53. University of Pittsburgh Press (Pittsburg, Penn., 1971.)

between all conflicting schools of thought, Allen also tends to be unnecessarily vague and ambivalent in his attitude to some of the major problems presented by the text. Such criticism, however, should not prevent us from appreciating his many brilliant suggestions or the theoretical models for structural analysis he has introduced in the discussion. On several points he has anticipated my own conclusions concerning the literary art of Njála.[54]

The center of gravity in Njála scholarship has gradually been "moving west" (as does the saga itself in its first chapter!): from Denmark, Sweden, and Germany it has been transferred to Iceland and is recently drifting toward the United States. This development has been paralleled by a similar trend in public opinion. In Germany and Scandinavia the general interest in the sagas has been decreasing during this century, especially after the last war and among intellectuals, who have often associated sagas with conservative ideals and an outmoded form of nationalism. In Iceland, on the other hand, the sagas are still felt to be an important part of the national heritage, and they were often cited during the country's recent struggle for political independence, a struggle in which scholars of the Icelandic School have often been actively involved. During recent years, Njála has found many new readers in America, especially after it was made available in a modern paperback edition.[55] Apparently, this new popularity in the Western hemisphere is part of a general trend among American college students to rediscover "folk" literature, mythology, and early epic narratives.

SUMMARY AND CONCLUSION

As can be seen from our survey,[56] the problems of the historicity, the sources, and the original components of Njála have dominated scholarly interest until quite recently. The problems of meaning, structure, and artistic technique have, for the most part, been scrutinized only in relation to the problems of origin. Although several divergent—and often contradictory—views have been advanced on such matters, they have seldom been con-

---

54. For a detailed discussion of Allen's book, see my review in Speculum, 48 (1973). A more negative opinion was expressed by R. I. Page in Scandinavica, 11 (1972), 149-51; a more positive one by Theodore Andersson in JEGP, 71 (1972), 100-104.

55. Cf. note 46.

56. It should be noted that our survey is by no means complete; particular aspects of Njála have been treated in a number of works which have not been mentioned here but will be referred to in later chapters. The studies mentioned in this first chapter may, however, be considered the most important and representative among the studies devoted specifically to Njála.

fronted with each other and discussed in detail. Many scholars seem to have felt that a literary interpretation—in contrast to philological and historical studies—is something personal and subjective which should not be dissected with scholarly arguments.

It has thus largely been left to the reader's discretion whether he wants to interpret the saga as a unified whole or as a collection of episodes; as an "objective" narrative about pagan heroes or as a piece of Christian didacticism; as an epitome of realism or as a highly stylized narrative loaded with symbolism. Yet, these are questions, I think, that can be discussed in a rational manner—if we decide how to use such terms as "unity," "objectivity," "realism," etc.

It would perhaps be tempting to the "new" critical mind to simply ignore the whole problem of the sources, but I think it would be a mistake to do so. This classical problem is still relevant and open to new interpretations, as is suggested by Andersson's criticism of Einar Ólafur Sveinsson. Only by forming *some* opinion about the author's sources can we fully appreciate his own artistic contribution.

It seems to me less important, however, to determine the precise sources of *Njála* than to determine its place within the *general* narrative tradition of Iceland and of Medieval Europe. This is a task that still remains, although a brilliant beginning has been made in the studies by Heusler, Kersbergen, and Einar Ólafur Sveinsson. What seems to me especially important at the present time is to show *Njála*'s relations to the foreign traditions of romance, hagiography, and chronicle, genres which have obviously influenced its author but ar still unduly neglected by Old Norse scholars. But even though the native, Germanic tradition has been studied much more intensively, there are many more characteristics of *Njála* that need to be explained in the light of existing conventions in the "domestic" genres, not only in the so-called "family sagas" but also in kings' sagas, mythical-heroic sagas, and Eddic poetry. The aim of comparative studies should not be to register isolated "influences" but rather to establish the "literary grammar" of *Njála*: the conventional rules which govern its genre and which must have been more familiar to the first audience than they are to us.

Just as the genre is more important than any individual source, the general social context is more important than any individual author. Also in this area it may be possible to arrive at some new insights in the light of recent studies of the social structure and the modes of literary production in thirteenth-century Iceland. Even more essential, however, is the information that can be derived from the saga itself about its original audience. Tracing the social norms and the literary expectations of the audience is a task closely related to the "esthetic" discussion of structure and narrative technique. No literary work of art, least of all a medieval one, can in fact be analyzed without analyzing, at least to some extent, its audience.

In accordance wih these guidelines, we shall begin our study with the plot and its immediate sources (chapter II). We shall then proceed to define the "literary grammar" which the author took over from earlier sagas (chapter III). Then we shall see how the traditional material was reshaped by the author's "clerical mind" and influenced by foreign literary patterns (chapter IV). We shall finally widen our scope by describing the social context in which the saga was produced (chapter V).

Results of certain special investigations (of a somewhat technical nature) have been presented in appendix form at the end of the book.

II

The Plot and Its Sources

1. MAIN PARTS AND EPISODES

In spite of its name, *Njála* is not primarily the biography of Njáll, as Suhm thought,[1] nor is it a chronicle about one particular area in Iceland, as Thorlacius and Bååth have argued.[2] Its scope is both wider and narrower than ordinary biographies or chronicles. It is a story about a series of conflicts, or—as Einar Ólafur Sveinsson puts it—"a network of events"[3] which primarily engages certain chieftain families in Southwestern Iceland around the year 1000. But the story extends its tentacles to other times, places, and families, often very far away from the principal center of action. Both the setting and the characters continuously shift throughout the saga, although the conflicts are basically the same and the chain of causality remains unbroken.

While there is thus continuity in the narrative, it can nevertheless be divided into two main parts, roughly corresponding to the **Gunnars saga* and the **Njáls saga* hypothesized by an earlier generation of scholars. The first part is introduced by a semi-independent narrative which we may call the "Prologue." This Prologue, as well as the two main sections, may be further divided into episodes and chapters as follows[4]:

1. Suhm (1781), 11.
2. Thorlacius in his introduction to the Latin version of *Njála* (1809), pp. iii-iv; Bååth (1885), 90.
3. "Saga af atburðafléttu," Sveinsson (1943), 40.
4. Cf. Bååth (1885), 91 f.; Andersson (1967), 298; Heusler (1914), 1-5; Maxwell (1957), 23 f. I am following the traditional chapter division in order to facilitate references to

I.   *Prologue* (chapters 1-17)
1. Hrútr and Unnr (chapters 1-8)
2. Hallgerðr's marriages (chapters 9-17)

II. *"Gunnarr's saga"* (chapters 18-99)
1. Introduction (chapters 18-34)
   A) The recovery of Unnr's dowry (chapters 18-24)
   B) Gunnarr's travels and marriage (chapters 25-34)
2. The feud between Hallgerðr and Bergþóra (chapters 35-45)
3. The feud with Otkell (chapters 46-56)
4. The feud with Egill and Starkaðr (chapters 57-66)
5. The feud with the two Þorgeirrs (chapters 67-74)
6. Gunnarr's fall (chapters 75-81)
7. The feud between Þráinn and the sons of Njáll (chapters 82-99)
   A) The fall of Þráinn (chapters 82-94)
   B) The rise of Hǫskuldr Þráinsson (chapters 95-97)
   C) The death of Hǫskuldr Njálsson and the final reconciliation (chapters 97 A - 99)

III. *"Njáll's saga"*
1. The Conversion of Iceland and its results (chapters 100-107)
2. The murder of Hǫskuldr Þráinsson (chapters 108-112)
3. The attempted settlement with Flosi (chapters 113-123)
4. The Burning of Njáll (chapters 124-132)
5. Lawsuit against the Burners (chapters 133-145)
6. Kári's revenge and the final reconciliation (chapters 146-159)
   A) The feud between Kári and Flosi in Iceland (chapters 146-152)
   B) Continuation of the feud abroad (chapters 153-158)
   C) Reconciliation (chapter 159)

Such an outline can give only a vague idea of the real structure. To perceive this structure, it is necessary to summarize the main action in each episode and to note the most important connective links between them. It is also necessary to understand the relative independence of the episodes and the relation they bear to the structure of the saga as a whole.

The Prologue begins with the presentation of two prominent chieftain families, so far unrelated and living in different parts of Iceland. One is the

---

the standard editions. My structural analysis is, however, based on a revised version of the traditional chapter division, presented in my article "Structural Divisions in the *Njála* Manuscripts," *Arkiv för nordisk filologi,* 90 (1975). Readers who wish to check my argument concerning principal parts and episodes may therefore be referred to this article, originally planned as an appendix to this book.

family of Mǫrðr Fiddle, whose daughter Unnr will later play a prominent role. The other is the family of Hǫskuldr Dalakollsson, whose daughter Hallgerðr turns out to be one of the main forces of evil in the first half of the saga. This role is foreshadowed by an ominous prophecy at the end of the first chapter: she is said by her uncle to have "thief's eyes."

The two families continue to dominate the foreground throughout the Prologue. Its first episode (I:1) centers around Hǫskuldr's half-brother Hrútr, who marries Unnr after various adventures on his travels abroad. The marriage ends in divorce because Hrútr—as a result of a curse put on him by his former mistress, the Queen of Norway—cannot satisfy his wife in bed. Unnr moves back to her father, who unsuccessfully tries to regain the dowry from his son-in-law.

At this point the narrator takes leave of Hrútr and Unnr with the words: "And this is the end of the episode of Hrútr and Mǫrðr."[5] He now turns to Hallgerðr, whose unfortunate marriages are pictured in the second episode of the Prologue. She first marries a certain Þorvaldr, whom she makes unhappy through her excessive pride and prodigality. When he slaps her face, she brings about his death by letting her private hatchet man, Þjóstólfr, kill him. A settlement is arranged between her family and that of Þorvaldr, but when she marries another man, Glúmr, the same disastrous pattern is repeated: Hallgerðr is slapped after a quarrel, and Þjóstólfr promptly kills the husband. Again, a settlement is arranged, and Hallgerðr—like Unnr in the previous episode—is available for marriage.

"Gunnarr's saga" begins with the introduction of Gunnarr of Hlíðarendi, whose heroic struggle constitutes the main theme of the following episodes. As a close relative of Unnr and as the third husband of Hallgerðr, Gunnarr is the point of contact where the two narrative strands of the Prologue finally meet.[6] His first heroic deed is the recovery of Unnr's dowry from Hrútr; this episode (II:1 A) can thus be said to continue the episode about Hrútr's marriage (I:1). The second episode (II:1 B), dealing primarily with Gunnarr's early adventures abroad, ends with his and Hallgerðr's wedding in chapter 34.

---

5. Chapter 8: "ok er nú lokit þætti þeira Marðar". Cf. the variants and Sveinsson's comment in *Njála* (1954), 29, note 2. *Reykjabók* has the alternative reading *þrættum* for *þætti*, but this must be a secondary variant, even though it has been accepted as the main text in early editions. For the meaning of *þáttr* in ON, cf. Lönnroth, *Scripta Islandica*, 15 (1964), 19-21.

6. Cf. Maxwell (1957), 27: "The function of chapter 18 is to group the two women together at the end, as at the beginning: they are the two strands to be taken up in Gunnar's story."

The most important function of these introductory episodes is to present (at last) the main characters of the saga. Apart from Gunnarr himself, there is Njáll, who from now on plays his role as the wise counsellor in every important crisis; Gunnarr's brother Kolskeggr, who appears as the hero's able assistant; the sons of Njáll who in "Gunnarr's saga" play subsidiary roles but who will later succeed Gunnarr as the main heroes; Valgarðr grái, who marries Unnr and will later appear as one of the villains together with his son Mǫrðr; Þráinn Sigfússon, a kinsman of Gunnarr's, who is also to play an ominous role. All these characters are pictured as guests at Gunnarr's and Hallgerðr's wedding, the ideal occasion at which to survey the scene and the actors before the main action starts.

In the rest of "Gunnarr's saga" we learn of the various feuds in which Gunnarr is involved against his will at the instigation of Hallgerðr, Mǫrðr, and other evil members of the community. These feuds gradually lead to his destruction in the last episode (II:6).

The feud between Hallgerðr and Njáll's wife Bergþóra (II:2) starts with a petty quarrel about seating arrangements at a party, but it soon escalates when Hallgerðr sends a slave to kill one of Bergþóra's slaves. Bergþóra retaliates by having one of her men kill the slayer, and so the feud continues until both households are threatened by annihilation because of the belligerent and increasingly irreconcilable matrons. Their husbands try to make peace through legal settlements, which are always broken by the women and their various henchmen. Although the friendship between Gunnarr and Njáll is thus severely tested, it remains constant and is finally even strengthened through a settlement in chapter 45. One lasting result of the feud, however, is the hostility between Þráinn Sigfússon and the sons of Njáll (cf. II:7).[7]

The feud with Otkell (II:3) is also instigated by Hallgerðr, although it is made worse through the evil machinations of Mǫrðr and Skammkell. During a severe famine, Hallgerðr sends a slave to steal food in the house of Otkell, a wealthy farmer who has already refused to sell provisions to her husband. She thereby fulfills the prophecy about "thief's eyes" (I:1), and she also involves Gunnarr in a conflict not only with Otkell and his evil adviser, Skammkell, but also with their two influential protectors, the chieftains Gizurr the White and Geirr goði. After hearing about the theft, Gunnarr slaps Hallgerðr's face, as did her two earlier husbands (cf. I:2). We thus anticipate Gunnarr's destruction at this point, but at presant he is still rather successful. Since Otkell refuses to accept any atonement, a

---

7. Cf. Maxwell, 30 f.: "It is the killing of Þórðr that divides the sons of Sigfúss and of Njáll, and later on this is to be the fundamental division."

battle cannot be avoided. Gunnarr finally kills Otkell and Skammkell, and he manages to arrange a settlement with the chieftains through the clever mediations of Njáll, who predicts that he will remain victorious unless he kills twice within the same family; there is a clear connection between this episode and the Prologue exposition of Hallgerðr's early years.

The feud with the brothers-in-law Egill and Starkaðr (II:4) starts with a *hestavíg* ("horse-fight"), a kind of traditional Icelandic tournament, at which Gunnarr's horse is wounded by Þorgeirr, son of Starkaðr. Eventually, an ambush is arranged for Gunnarr, but he and Kolskeggr manage to kill fourteen assailants, including Egill. As usual, the episode ends with a scene at the Allthing, where Njáll helps Gunnarr to reach a settlement and to win the legal battles against his adversaries, who are advised by Mǫrðr, Njall's evil counterpart.

The feud with the two Þorgeirrs (II:5), the sons of Starkaðr and Otkell, can be regarded as an outgrowth of both of the preceding episodes. Influenced by Mǫrðr, the two Þorgeirrs join forces to avenge the dishonor inflicted by Gunnarr upon their respective families. It is now important that Gunnarr avoid killing Þorgeirr Otkelsson, since this will involve killing twice in the same line (cf. Njáll's prophecy, II:3). But this, of course, cannot be avoided when he is attacked and seriously provoked by his adversaries. After this slaying, Gunnarr is finally convicted at the Allthing—in spite of Njáll's efforts to free him. He will have to spend three years in exile or become an outlaw in his own country.

Gunnarr's fall and the revenge taken for him (II:6) are described in the most celebrated and climactic episode of "Gunnarr's saga." On his way to the ship that is to carry him away from Iceland, Gunnarr decides that he does not want to leave. In spite of Kolskeggr's warnings, he returns to his farm, where he is soon attacked by Gizurr the White, Geirr goði, Mǫrðr, Starkaðr, Þorgeirr Starkaðarson, and other enemies. After a truly heroic defense, Gunnarr is finally defeated, primarily because Hallgerðr refuses to give him a strand of her long hair so that he can repair his broken bow. This refusal represents her revenge for the slap (cf. II:3). After Gunnarr's death, his ghost appears to his son Hǫgni and to Njáll's son Skarpheðinn, who then take revenge on some of Gunnarr's slayers.

At this point several important characters, including Hǫgni and Kolskeggr, are dropped "out of the saga," and it is clear that an important section of the narrative has been concluded. But there is still one episode left (II:6) which should probably be interpreted as the end of "Gunnarr's saga" and not—as most critics have thought—as the beginning of the second part,

"Njáll's saga" proper.[8] This episode centers around a feud between Gunnarr's kinsman Þráinn and the sons of Njáll—a feud that does not end
until both Þráinn and one of the sons have been destroyed.

It starts with the arrival of Þráinn and the Njáll sons in Norway. A new
villain, Hrappr, is introduced, and we are told how this man committed
crimes in Norway until he finally had to flee from the wrath of Earl Hákon.
We then hear of the fugitive's arrival at the port of Hlaðir, where he tries
to persuade both Þráinn and the sons of Njáll to take him away to Iceland.
The sons of Njáll refuse, but Þráinn accepts after Hrappr bribes him. Later,
the sons of Njáll are attacked by the Earl, who suspects them of having
conspired with Þráinn to help the fugitive. When they finally come back
to Iceland, they ask Þráinn for compensation but are given only insults
by members of his household, which includes both Hallgerðr and Hrappr
(who has become her lover). In retaliation, Hrappr and Þráinn are both
killed, in a dramatic confrontation which parallels the fall of Gunnarr
(Þráinn is pictured as the heir of Gunnarr in several important respects).

Hallgerðr now disappears from the narrative. Njáll tries to atone for the
slaying by adopting Þráinn's young son, Hǫskuldr, whom he then fosters to
become one of Iceland's greatest chieftains. Another kinsman of Þráinn,
Lýtingr, is not satisfied with this atonement, however, and kills Njáll's
illegitimate son, who is also called Hǫskuldr. The other sons of Njáll retaliate
by killing some of Lýtingr's kinsmen. (This is the so-called *Lýtings þáttr*,
which Finnur Jónsson regarded as a separate story incorporated into *Njála*.[9])
Both Njáll and Hǫskuldr Þráinsson—who is now generally referred to as
"Hǫskuldr Hvítaness priest"—are eager to build a lasting settlement, and
they succeed in doing this despite some grumbling from Skarpheðinn.
Chapter 99, which appears to conclude "Gunnarr's saga," ends with this
important observation: "Now it should be said that they kept this settlement thereafter" (255).[10]

The remaining half of the saga—"Njáll's saga" proper—is introduced
by an unusually large and lavishly decorated chapter initial in several old
manuscripts which at this point clearly reflect a major division in the
author's own text.[11]

There is now a shift in the ethical climate of the saga. The second part
has a unity of its own: a slower pace and a less episodic structure.[12] It

8. See note 11 below.
9. Cf. Sveinsson (1933), 50-65.
10. For a more detailed analysis of this conclusion, see Chapter III, note 23.
11. See Lönnroth, *ANF* 90 (1975), 70.
12. Cf. Heusler (1914), 3: "Der zweite Hauptteil, die Njalsgeschichte im engern Sinne,

centers around one single feud which arises out of a new conflict between the sons of Njáll and Hǫskuldr Hvítaness priest.[13] This conflict is described in much greater detail than any of the previous ones and in such a manner that the entire first part (including both the Prologue and "Gunnarr's saga") may be regarded as a gigantic prelude to it. This section of the saga is even more difficult to divide into separate and distinct episodes, but it may nevertheless be divided into several stages.

The first stage (III:1) is represented by the Conversion of Iceland, which lays the ground for the later development (cf. below, p. 142). The pagan Earl Hákon is killed and the Christian King Óláfr Tryggvason succeeds him. A German missionary, Þangbrandr, is sent to Iceland and meets with many difficulties before the new faith (and Christian law) is finally introduced at the Allthing. The family of Njáll as well as Hǫskuldr and his kinsmen— among whom Síðu-Hallr and Flosi now emerge as the most important— all work to promote Þangbrandr's cause, but the old villains, Mǫrðr and Valgarðr, work against it. After the victory of the Christians, the results of the new faith are shown, as Ámundi, a blind son of Hǫskuldr Njálsson, miraculously gets his sight back for the few moments he needs to slay the evil Lýtingr. Valgarðr in a rage destroys crosses and other Christian symbols, but dies shortly afterwards. Before his death, however, he advises his son Mǫrðr to sow hostility between Hǫskuldr and the sons of Njáll in the hope that Hǫskuldr will be destroyed so that Mǫrðr will gain more power in his district.

This malicious plan is carried out in the second stage of the narrative (III:2). Hǫskuldr shows his nobility by refusing to listen to Mǫrðr's evil slandering of the sons of Njáll, but Skarpheðinn and his brothers are less immune against such underhanded tactics. They soon become convinced that Hǫskuldr is conspiring against them, and they finally murder their innocent foster brother in an unusually brutal manner, when he is not able to defend himself. This murder is pictured as a major tragedy, the crime that leads inevitably to the fall of Njáll's family. Hǫskuldr's widow, Hildigunnr, finds the dead body. She saves her husband's bloodied cloak for the future.

The attempts to reconcile the sons of Njáll with Hǫskuldr's family (III:3) end in disaster. Hildigunnr incites her kinsman Flosi to seek revenge by throwing the bloodied cloak over his head. Flosi nevertheless tries to seek

---

hat die epische Einheitlichkeit einer Novelle und wäre insoweit zu vergleichen etwa mit der Saga Hawards oder der des Goden Hrafnkel."

13. See chapter III, note 23.

justice by peaceful means at the Allthing; but when a settlement seems close at hand, he and Skarpheðinn become involved in an argument, insults are exchanged, and Flosi finally refuses to accept any monetary compensation for the killing.

The feud is climaxed in the Burning of Njáll and his household (III:4), an event pictured in minute detail and preceded by several portents. We learn of Flosi's careful plans for an attack on the houses at Bergþórshváll, Njáll's home. We also learn of the activities at Bergþórshváll as the attack is under way. Finally, the confrontation is described, Flosi's decision to burn down the house is dramatized, and we follow each of the leading members of the household as they perish in the flames: Njáll, Bergþóra, all the sons, and various other people. Only one man, Kári, a son-in-law of Njáll, manages to get away.

The lawsuit against the Burners (III:5) is described with a wealth of legalistic detail. The major protagonists in this episode are the leading lawyers: Eyjólfr, who handles the defense of Flosi and the Burners, and Þorhallr Ásgrímsson, who is the leading counsel of the plaintiff, Kári and his family. When the lawsuit fails, Þorhallr attacks the Burners, and a gigantic battle breaks out at the Allthing. After the battle, a settlement is finally arranged, mainly because Síðu-Hallr, one of the leading chieftains on Flosi's side, renounces his claim for compensation, even though his own son has been killed in the battle. He thereby sets an example of peaceful moderation for the others. But Kári remains irreconcilable.

Kári's revenge (III:6) is carried out in several successive confrontations with the Burners, whom he relentlessly persecutes both in Iceland and abroad. In Iceland, he is assisted by Bjǫrn hvíti, a mock-heroic peasant who provides one of the few elements of comic relief in the saga. As Flosi leaves Iceland with his men, after having been sentenced to exile by the Allthing, Kári follows after him to Orkney, where he slays one of the Burners. While Flosi is still in Orkney, some of his men follow the Earl of Orkney to Ireland, where they take part in the Battle of Clontarf against the pious King Brian. The Irish are victorious and fifteen of the Burners are killed. After this battle—the concluding *presto agitato* of *Njála*, as Einar Ólafur Sveinsson calls it[14]—both Kári and Flosi go to Rome and receive absolution for their sins. Upon their return to Iceland, they finally become reconciled, and Kári marries Hildigunnr, the widow of Hǫskuldr Þráinsson. The saga ends with a report on Flosi's death and a list of Kári's descendants.

14. Sveinsson (1933), 76.

2. CONTINUITY

As can be seen from this plot summary, several episodes, especially in the first half of the saga, have a fairly unified structure of their own. These "independent" episodes (e.g., II:2-5) normally begin with an extensive presentation of new characters, followed by the introduction of new reasons for conflict. Further on, there is normally some kind of violent clash between feuding parties, often followed by revenge and a more or less temporary settlement at the Allthing. The narrator then drops some of the characters – often by means of the well-known formula "he is now out of the saga" – before proceeding to the next episode.

It is thus important to recognize what Maxwell has termed "the principle of the integrity of episodes";[15] the structure of these episodes can sometimes (not always) be analyzed according to the six-point scheme suggested by Theodore Andersson (cf. above, p. 19, and below, p. 69).

On the other hand, it is also important to recognize the continuity of events, especially in the second half of the saga. In many cases there is also an indirect continuity between episodes that are separated by several chapters: old narrative strands are taken up again; characters reappear after having been out of the story for some time; old feuds suddenly break out again, and so on.[16] Examples of this indirect continuity are provided by the episode of Hrútr and Unnr (I:1), which is continued in the episode of Unnr's dowry (II:1 A), and the episode of Hallgerðr's marriages (I:2), which is continued in the episode of the feud with Otkell (II:3).

Apart from this continuity of the action, the saga is held together by a series of structural devices, which will be discussed in further detail in later chapters. Among these devices are the various techniques of anticipation, which Bååth associated with the Old Norse belief in an impersonal Fate, governing all events: dreams, omens, prophecies, visions, and other portents that foreshadow later events and thus direct the reader's attention to them before they have actually occurred.[17] The portent and its fulfillment are often separated by several episodes. An example is provided by the prophecy about Hallgerðr's "thief's eyes" (I:1), which is not completely fulfilled until

15. Maxwell (1957), 25.

16. Cf. Sveinsson (1943), 40: "Fyrsta orsök er ekki ein, heldur margar, sundurlausar og óskyldar . . . Þær sjúga næringu sína úr jarðvegi sínum eins og rætur, þær þróast og vaxa, og áður en vitað er, hafa þær skotið sprotum, sem koma niður víðs fjarri upptökum sínum og eru tvinnaðar saman við aðra, óskylda atburði og koma þá af stað nýrri atburðarás, sem aftur fær nýja stefnu og innihald af öðrum óskyldum og sakleysislegum atburðum." Cf. Schach's translation (1971), 54.

17. Cf. Bååth (1885), 160; Sveinsson (1943), 41-42.

the Otkell episode (II:3). Some portents control very large sections of the saga in such a way that the reader is constantly reminded of them. Right after the Burning of Njáll, for example, we hear of a dream in which Flosi sees a giant calling out the names of several Burners, who are all destined to die. We are reminded of this dream every time a new Burner is killed in the exact order predicted by the giant.

Another common device, noted especially by Maxwell and Fox, consists in the use of parallel situations and parallel characters.[18] By this I refer to the fact that the same dramatic patterns are often repeated, even though the names of characters and localities may differ, so that we get a distinct feeling of recurrence. Each of Hallgerðr's three husbands, for example, goes through the same series of experiences. And there are several important similarities between the adventures of Hrútr, Gunnarr, Þráinn, Kári, and the sons of Njáll. Some of these similarities may be unintentional and may simply reflect the fact that the author is following traditional, stereotyped patterns of narration. In other cases, however, the parallels are clearly intended, and the reader's attention is drawn to them by means of direct comparisons in the text – for example, between the death of Gunnarr and the death of Njáll and his sons.

Finally, there is a remarkable consistency in the author's point of view, rhetoric, and ideas, and this consistency sets him apart from most other sagawriters. The individual episodes are subordinated to a metaphysical scheme, a sort of historical philosophy, which will be discussed in a later chapter.

It is hardly surprising, however, that *Njála* has been described *both* as a highly unified narrative *and* as a series of independent episodes. These descriptions are in fact not mutually exclusive. Our immediate concern will be to determine *how* independent the episodes were originally, i.e., before the writing of *Njála*, and to what extent the present overall structure may be considered the author's own. In order to determine this, we shall have to reexamine the evidence from other sources concerning the events and characters of our saga.

3. TRADITIONAL BASIS OF THE EPISODES

The problem of the author's relationship to earlier traditions has been discussed in detail by Einar Ólafur Sveinsson and several of his predecessors (cf. Chapter I). The relevant sources are also quoted at length in Sveinsson's

---

18. Cf. Maxwell (1957), 26 f.; Fox (1963), 295, 308.

1954 edition,[19] to which the reader may be referred once and for all. Our present survey will be concerned only with the most important documents that have been claimed as evidence that the story, or stories, told in *Njála* were known to the Icelanders in either oral or written form before our author began his creative work.

There is no indication in any early source that the story *as a whole* was familiar before the saga was written. All suggested sources pertain only to isolated events and isolated characters. The weightiest evidence, consisting of genealogies and information about special individuals, has been compiled from *Landnámabók*, the Icelandic "Book of Settlement," first written in the twelfth century but now available only in thirteenth century redactions.[20] Other references and parallel texts have been sought in *Laxdœla saga, Eyrbyggja saga, Kristni saga, Íslendingabók* of Ari the Wise, *Orkneyinga saga, Þorsteins saga Síðu-Hallssonar*, and other sagas which have been shown to be either earlier than *Njála* or based on traditions which are, at least to some extent, independent of the *Njála* text. Some important references are also to be found in the Icelandic Annals, although these are generally so late that we cannot always be certain that their information is not derived from our saga itself. This is even more true of the various sayings and local traditions collected in comparatively recent times, traditions referring to the wisdom of Njáll, the prowess of Gunnarr, etc. We shall, on the whole, disregard the latter kind of evidence and stick to the early texts.

In cases where these texts fail us, however, we shall use evidence from *Njála* itself in trying to show that a particular episode was known in an earlier form. This is permissible under certain conditions, e.g., when the author of *Njála* explicitly refers to earlier traditions, or when he implicitly presupposes knowledge about such traditions among his audience. In some cases, a tradition is also testified by skaldic verses quoted in the text which appear older than the surrounding prose. At times, it is also possible to perceive narrative structures in the saga which are alien to the author's overall designs, and which seem to reflect an earlier stage in the tradition. It was largely by means of such "inconsistencies" that Lehmann and Carolsfeld tried to prove that the author had used a great number of lost sources (cf. pp. 8-9), and although they clearly went too far in their conclusions—as Einar Ólafur Sveinsson convincingly showed—it must be admitted that their method *may* be valid in certain cases. Their major mistake was in not analysing the structure sufficiently before going on to theorize about the sources.

19. Pp. IX-LX; see also Sveinsson (1933), 67-219.
20. The relationship between *Landnámabók* and individual sagas has been discussed in Jón Jóhannesson's *Gerðir Landnámabókar* (Reykjavík, 1941).

The early parallel texts of *Njála* usually differ from our saga in numerous details concerning major events and characters, and they are also widely different from each other. Each one of them contributes only a small part of the story, rarely covering more than a single episode. Several episodes have no parallels at all. These facts in themselves suggest that the overall structure is primarily the work of the author, while some of the individual episodes may have existed earlier in some form. To this extent, there is undoubtedly something to be said in favor of Bååth's *þáttr* theory (cf. Chapter I). But we cannot on these grounds exclude the possibility that some episodes belonged together in an early tradition; nor can we exclude the possibility that some of the undocumented episodes were invented by the author himself.

However, the episodes most obviously based on an earlier tradition are those which stand most easily on their own as narratives within the saga. Episodes that function primarily as structural links to other episodes do not seem to have as strong a basis in tradition, and they are therefore more likely to have been invented, or at least handled very freely, by the author.

The following episodes in *Njála* are the ones that can be shown to have been based on earlier traditions. I list the best documented episodes first:

1. The Conversion of Iceland (III:1)
2. The Battle of Clontarf (III:6B)
3. The Fall of Gunnarr (II:6)
4. The Burning of Njáll (III:4)
5. The Battle of the Allthing, following the Law-suit against the Burners (III:5)
6. Gunnar's feud with Otkell (II:3)
7. The feud with Egill and Starkaðr (II:4)
8. Hrútr and Unnr (I:1)
9. Hallgerðr's marriages I:2

1-2. The Clontarf and the Conversion episodes are the only ones now generally assumed to be based on lost written sagas. (This assumption will be discussed in the Appendix.) Both episodes have several close parallels in sources known to be independent of *Njála*, and their traditional bases are thus beyond reasonable doubt. Their traditional nature is also evident from the saga itself, which at these points quotes several skaldic verses and refers to characters and incidents without any apparent function in the saga as a whole. As we shall see, however, both episodes do have important functions, even though they include a certain amount of superfluous material.

3. Gunnarr's death[21] is referred to in *Landnámabók, Eyrbyggja saga* (written before 1250) and in a poem called *Islendingadrápa*, probably composed in the twelfth century.[22] The event is also mentioned in some verses quoted in the saga itself. Several of these sources agree that he fell defending his house against a large number of enemies. Some of them also mention that Gunnarr wounded sixteen men and killed two before he died. According to *Landnámabók*, he was assisted by one man, a tradition clearly at variance with our saga. In *Eyrbyggja*, there is a reference to an incident during Gunnarr's last defense which is described also in our saga: he is said to have shot at his enemies with one of their own arrows. But the account of this incident is at variance with *Njála*. Hallgerðr's long hair is mentioned in *Landnáma*, which may suggest that the story of her refusal to lend Gunnarr a strand of it was known in popular tradition.

In any case, it is evident that both she and Gunnarr were familiar to Icelanders in the thirteenth century, and the name of Gunnarr must have been specifically associated with traditions about his last heroic stand and his skill as a bowman.

4. The Burning of Njáll (*Njálsbrenna*)[23] is mentioned in the Icelandic Annals and in *Landnámabók*. There are also references to the fire in skaldic verses which are generally held to be older than the saga. In the Prose Edda (written around 1230) a skaldic stanza is attributed to "Burned Njáll" (*Brennu-Njáll*), a name that clearly presupposes knowledge of the fire. The same conclusion can be drawn from the names *Brennu-Kári, Brennu-Flosi,* and *Sviðu-Kári*, which appear in *Landnáma* and other early sources. We can thus be certain that Njáll, Kári, and Flosi were all familiar before the writing of the saga, and they must all have been specifically associated with stories about the great fire at Bergþórshváll.

On the other hand, there is nothing to indicate that either Hǫskuldr Þráinsson or Skarpheðinn Njálsson were known before *Njála*. The feud leading up to the fire, therefore, cannot be shown to have any traditional basis. The association between Gunnarr and Njáll, one of the most important features of our saga, is also conspicuously absent from all early documents and sagas, a fact that lends some support to the old theories about Gunnarr and Njáll as the heroes of two separate sagas joined together by the author.[24]

---

21. Cf. Sveinsson *Njála* (1954), pp. xxviii-xxxiv.

22. See in particular Jónas Kristjánsson's "*Islendingadrápa* and Oral Tradition," *Second International Saga Conference, Reykjavik, August 1-8, 1973*.

23. Cf. Sveinsson, *Njála* (1954), pp. IX-XVIII.

24. See, for example, Bååth (1885), 130-31.

5.   The Battle of the Allthing[25] is mentioned in the Annals, but it is not
associated with the Burning of Njáll or the lawsuit against the Burners.
In *Gunnlaugs saga Ormstungu* (usually thought to have been written at the
end of the thirteenth century), there is a reference to the Thingmeeting
"after the Burning of Njáll," but this information may well be derived
from *Njála* itself. On the other hand, the text of *Njála* at this point suggests
that the narrative has a firm traditional basis, not necessarily in its account
of the lawsuit against the Burners, but definitely in the story about the
ensuing battle at the Allthing. Like the Conversion and the Clontarf episodes, this is a story full of names, incidents, and skaldic verses with no immediate bearing on the main plot. At one point the narrator makes the
remark that even more things happened at this battle, although they have
not been reported (*En þó at hér sé sagt frá nǫkkurum atburðum, þá eru hinir
þó miklu fleiri, er menn hafa engar sagnir frá*, 404). Much of the information
seems aimed at an audience interested in the event as such, regardless of
its connection with the story of Njáll.

6.   Gunnarr's battle with Otkell and Skamkell[26] is mentioned in *Landnáma*, where it is immediately followed by the report on Gunnarr's last
stand and death. The story of Hallgerðr's theft from Otkell is connected –
as we have already seen – with the story of Hallgerðr's marriages (cf. below).

7.   Egill's ambush for Gunnarr[27] is also mentioned in *Landnáma*, in a
version quite different from that of *Njála*. The list of men who are said to
have participated in the attack is only partly similar. Nothing is said in
this context about Starkaðr, Mǫrðr, Otkell, the two Þorgeirrs, or any other
of Gunnarr's principal enemies. The ambush is reported as an isolated event.

It is particularly significant that the two Þorgeirrs are totally absent
from *Landnáma* and other early sources since these namesakes constitute
the most important link between the Otkell episode, the Egill episode, and
the story of Gunnarr's death. This may indicate that they have been invented by the author in order to unify the heterogeneous traditions about
Gunnarr's struggles.

8.   Hrútr appears as a prominent hero in *Laxdœla saga* (probably written
before 1250) and in other sagas as well, although their accounts differ from
that of *Njála* on several important points.[28] His marriage to Unnr is referred
to in both *Landnáma* and *Laxdœla*, and the latter source also mentions the

25. Cf. Sveinsson, *Njála* (1954), p. XVIII.
26. Cf. Sveinsson, *Njála* (1954), p. XXIV.
27. Cf. Sveinsson, *Njála* (1954), p. XXIV.
28. Cf. Sveinsson (1933), 112-15; Andersson (1964), 100-102; Sveinsson, *Njála* (1954),
pp. 6-7, 29 (notes).

divorce, which is said to have led to the" conflict between the people from Laxdale and the people from Fljótshlíð" (deilur þeira Laxdœla ok Fljótshlíðinga). These words apparently refer to the conflict over Unnr's dowry (Njála, chapters 6-8, 18-24), but there is nothing to indicate that the author of this remark associated this conflict with Gunnarr or Njáll.

9. Hallgerðr's marriages are not referred to in any sources earlier than Njála, and the names of her two earliest husbands are not found elsewhere. It is nevertheless obvious that she herself must have been a fairly well-known character, since she is mentioned in both Landnáma and Laxdœla under the name of Hallgerðr Langbrók or Snúinbrók, i.e., "Hallgerðr with the long [or twisted] breeches," a name that also occurs in Njála.[29] Since a woman in Iceland could be outlawed for wearing breeches,[30] we have to assume that the name is intended to be derogatory, even though the author of Njála explains it by simply referring to her height: "she was a beautiful, tall woman, and hence she was called Langbrók" (chapter 9).[31] It seems much more likely that she received her name because she was reputed to "wear the pants" in the family and because of her harsh, unfeminine nature, which is repeatedly demonstrated in the stories about her marriages. In any case, the variant Snúinbrók ("twisted breeches"), which occurs in one of the Landnáma redactions, can have nothing to do with sheer size.

We may conclude that the author of Njála used a series of traditional stories about specific characters and events, often corresponding to one episode in our saga, although some traditions apparently covered more than that. Some of the episodes may well have been joined together in larger narrative blocks before the writing of the saga, even when this is not apparent from the available sources. It is possible, for example, that a single oral saga about Gunnarr and Hallgerðr existed at an early date, in spite of the fact that the early documents refer to each of them separately. But the saga as a whole is much too complex, and contains all too many separate elements, to have existed as an entity before our saga was written. The overall structure, and the connective links between the episodes, must then be ascribed to the author, i.e., to the man who wrote or dictated the text.

Although our author may well have thought of himself as a writer of nonfiction, essentially faithful to older traditions, he obviously had to use

---

29. Sveinsson, Njála (1954), xxxi f.; Cf. 6-7, 29.

30. Cf. Laxdœla saga, ch. 35; Grágás, ch. 155: "Ef konur geraz svá afsiða at þær ganga í karlfǫtum . . . þá varðar þat fiorbaugsgarð." (Ed. V. Finsen, II, 1852, 47).

31. This explanation is also accepted by Einar Ólafur Sveinsson in Njála (1954), 29, note 3.

his imagination considerably in order to fill in all the gaps in the tradition and make all the separate elements fit together. We may expect him to use his imagination most freely in passages where motives are provided for the main actions and the episodes are joined together by various means. At such points we may also expect him to draw most heavily on general literary motifs and borrowings from unrelated works.

A good example is provided by the story of Flosi's dream, in which the giant calls out the names of the Burners who are soon to die. As we have seen, this dream controls the structure of the last third of the saga (chapters 133-159), although it does not contribute to the main action and is therefore in itself likely to be a product of the author's own structural inventiveness. In this case, we may indeed be rather certain that this is so because Einar Ólafur Sveinsson has shown that the dream is closely modeled on a dream in the *Dialogues* of St. Gregory the Great—a work that is unlikely to have influenced traditional storytelling at an early date.[32]

Kersbergen's inventory of stereotyped literary motifs in *Njála* further confirms this general interpretation of the relation between tradition and literary authorship. As Kersbergen herself points out, such stereotyped motifs have a tendency to occur at precisely those points where the narrative seems to lack any kind of historical basis.[33]

As could be expected, our author is most faithful to earlier traditions when he is dealing with major historical events, presumably wellknown to his audience, such as the conversion of Iceland, the Battle of Clontarf, or the Battle at the Allthing. At such points there is a density of factual information which interferes with the overall design of the narrative. I do not believe it is correct to explain the superfluous material by referring to the author's *Stoffreude*, as Heusler and, following him, Einar Ólafur Sveinsson have done. It seems more likely that the author included this material because he felt he had to—out of respect for his audience. The fact that the narrative is especially dense and concentrated in these passages indicates that the author did not want to dwell on these events more than was strictly necessary.

When writing about the Death of Gunnarr or the Burning of Njáll, the author also had to respect earlier traditions, but in these cases he expands rather than concentrates, elaborating his story in numerous ways. In such episodes, we may really speak of *Stoffreude*—a joy in sheer storytelling, heightened by the importance of these events in the overall structure.

---

32. Cf. Sveinsson (1943), 10-11, 171; Schach's transl., 14-16, 205-206; see also Dag Strömbäck, "Some Remarks on Learned and Novelistic Elements in the Icelandic Sagas," *Nordica et Anglica: Studies in Honor of Stéfan Einarsson* (1968), 140 f.

33. Cf. Kersbergen (1927), 183-85.

Because these were not public events of major historical importance, as the conversion was, he probably was more ready to use his own imagination.

We may compare the work of our author with that of an architect designing a house. Tradition and the demands of the public largely determine what should be in the house, and certain sections leave very little room for innovation. Other sections, however, and the overall design are left to the architect, even though he may often have to compromise his basic vision to make room for all the things that are felt to "belong."

4. NATURE OF THE SOURCES

In what form, then, did our author find his traditional material? Ever since Lehmann and Carolsfeld, no one has doubted that he used written sources as well as oral traditions. Some say he copied certain of these sources out of earlier manuscripts. If we may believe Jan de Vries, whose views are both representative and recently expressed, the author of *Njála* had access to a whole library of earlier sagas which he consulted as he was writing his own work.[34] Even Theodore Andersson, who in general substitutes oral traditions for written sources, tends to accept Lehmann-Carolsfeld's and Einar Ólafur Sveinsson's theories about a lost *Kristni þáttr* and a lost *Brjáns saga* in addition to law scrolls and written genealogies.[35]

Such theories are supported primarily by two arguments: 1) there are parallels between certain sections of *Njála* (the Clontarf and Conversion episodes, the legal sections, etc.) and other preserved texts (the account of the conversion in Ari fróði's *Islendingabók*, the account of the Clontarf battle in *Þorsteins saga Síðu-Hallssonar*, the genealogies of *Landnámabók*, the laws of *Grágás* and *Járnsíða*, etc.), and 2) there are differences between such sections of *Njála* and the saga as a whole (stylistic and linguistic variation; factual and ideological inconsistencies, etc.).

But are the parallels close enough to exclude any possibility other than written (as opposed to oral) sources? We may also ask if the stylistic, linguistic, and ideological variations are great enough to warrant the con-

---

34. "Gerade ein Werk wie die Njála zeigt uns deutlich, was alles am Schreibtisch des Verfassers hinzugekommen ist, ja dass erst bei der Niederschrift die Saga ihre Gestalt bekommen hat. Dass die Njáls saga schon voraussetzt, dass der Verfasser eine nicht so ganz kleine Bibliothek zu seiner Verfügung gehabt hat, lässt sich leicht nachweisen," de Vries (1967), 452.

35. "Good evidence was produced long ago by Lehmann and Schnorr von Carolsfeld to support the view that *Njála*'s author used written laws. That he used written genealogies, a written *Kristni þáttr*, and perhaps a written *Brjáns saga* is not improbable," Andersson (1964), 103.

clusion that *Njála* contains sections not formulated by our author but simply transcribed by him from earlier manuscripts. Finally, we may ask if there is any evidence outside of *Njála* that these "lost works" ever existed.

An argument along these lines will be presented in the Appendix, but the general conclusions must be given at this point. As I hope to have shown, the theory about lost sources rests on a series of false or dubious assumptions. There is no reason to believe that there was either a **Kristni þáttr* or a **Brjáns saga*. On the contrary, there is much evidence that the author of *Njála* himself composed the Conversion and the Clontarf episodes in his own narrative idiom and style. And, even though he was probably familiar with written genealogies and lawscrolls, there is no evidence that he used such works when writing *Njála*. It is entirely possible that all (or practically all) of the older tradition used in the saga reached its author in oral form only.

By saying this, I certainly do not want to deny that the author of *Njála* had read many sagas and other texts as well. As we shall see in later chapters, he was unusually well versed in both native and foreign literary traditions. He may well have consulted manuscripts during the preparation of his own work. But whatever learning he possessed seems to have been perfectly "internalized"—there are no clear examples of direct quotations, except in cases when the quotes are likely to have been memorized and transmitted to *Njála* without the help of written notes or manuscripts. The "borrowed" material (which is indeed considerable) is so well integrated with the rest that it can hardly be separated from the author's "own" contributions. We are dealing with an artist who writes his own saga with the ease and fluency of an experienced storyteller, not an academic pedant making excerpts from "sources." We need only compare the text of *Njála* with a medieval scholastic treatise to see the immense difference in this respect.

Nevertheless, there are passages in *Njála* which *may* leave an impression of being adapted or mechanically transcribed from earlier works—these are primarily certain genealogical name-lists, legal formulas, and a few obscure references to otherwise unknown persons and events. To a modern reader, such passages have little meaning and do not fit well into the narrative structure. But we must always remember that they had a significance for an Icelandic audience. Genealogy, history, and law constituted the very essence of institutionalized oral tradition. A narrator could draw on a considerable amount of tradition, knowledge, and memorized formulae; he could also presuppose a good deal of knowledge among his listeneres about such matters; he would not have to spell everything out for them, and he could count on their interest in the facts as such (see below, chapter V).

It is thus not surprising that he occasionally rattled off an "irrelevant" list of facts with no apparent function in the narrative.

There are examples of such "irrelevancies" not only in the Clontarf and Conversion episodes but also in the introductions of practically all the most important characters (whose ancestors are faithfully recorded, even when they do not play a role in the narrative), in the description of major Thing meetings (where legal details are recorded to an extent completely unwarranted to modern readers), and in the accounts of the major historical events, where even the least important incidents are felt to "belong" (Introduction of the Fifth Court, the conversion of Iceland, the Battle of Clontarf, etc.). There has been a tendency among scholars to suspect a lost written source behind every such passage; it would seem more appropriate to regard them as unusually well founded in oral traditions (which may, of course, occasionally have been recorded in writing even before the composition of *Njála*).

But we do not need to commit ourselves to any free-prose theory concerning the origin of *Njála*. Suffice it to say that its plot was built up of traditional material which existed in some form before the writing of the saga, but that the material was then thoroughly transformed by the author to suit his particular idiom, style, ideology, and artistic vision. We may thus conclude that even though the *plot* was traditional, the *saga* was not; it was an individual literary creation.

III

The Language of Tradition

1. INTRODUCTION

The composition of *Njála* was governed by a set of narrative conventions established long before the saga was written. Our author had heard (or read) so many tales that he was able to use the language of earlier sagas freely without having to depend on any particular saga, or even a particular genre. For although most of the narrative and stylistic patterns of *Njála* are characteristic of native sagas (and probably were derived from oral tradition), some traits either are original or were derived from foreign genres (chronicles, romances, saints' lives). Even though the author habitually uses traditional clichés, he often combines them with great ingenuity to achieve new effects. In order to appreciate the originality of his composition we must first analyze its standard ingredients.

In this chapter we shall primarily consider ingredients taken over from native sagas ("foreign" patterns will be treated in the following chapter). First, the author's use of a traditional system of composition in which smaller narrative "building blocks" are combined into larger units according to established rules. Second, the system of stock characters and stock settings inherited from the traditional "world" of sagas. Third, stereotyped patterns of action in which these characters appear. Finally, we shall make an inventory of typical saga techniques for manipulating audience reactions and expressing the author's sympathies and antipathies in the presentation of his material.

2. THE BUILDING BLOCKS

The hierarchy of compositional units

It has been emphasized recently that orally composed literature follows a "literary grammar" of its own. This is especially true of epic poetry, where the verse lines are often "improvised" by the epic singer. In order to compose during his performance, the artist uses a system of formulaic building blocks which can be easily and rapidly combined. As Milman Parry and Albert Lord have shown, the epic singers of Yugoslavia use *formulas* as their basic unit: fixed combinations of words frequently used to express the same conventional idea and always found in the same metrical position, Formulas are combined into larger blocks called *themes*: stereotyped clusters of formulas which may in their turn be combined into still larger but equally conventional patterns, resulting in an epic composition governed by traditional laws.[1]

Attempts have been made to show that Old Norse literature follows similar laws of composition, which could then be regarded as a heritage from oral tradition.[2] The oral-formulaic theory cannot, however, be applied to sagas without considerable modification. Unlike the epic singer of Yugoslavia, the saga-writer was not bound by metrical rules or by the necessity of composing his story at high speed in front of an audience. He did not have to rely solely on "prefabricated" material. Even when composing a traditional scene, such as a trial or a shipboard fight, he could avoid formulas and introduce new motifs and unusual expressions. The author of *Njála* took great advantage of this freedom, especially at the "highest" level of his composition. Although he used traditional phrases and motifs, his way of combining episodes into a complete saga is unique.

I shall here propose a taxonomic hierarchy of concepts for analyzing saga structure, largely inspired by Richard Allen and Carol Clover, even though my terminology differs from theirs on some points.[3] At the top of

1. See especially Albert B. Lord, *The Singer of Tales* (Cambridge, Mass., 1960). For an excellent survey of the discussion about the oral-formulaic theory, see Michael Curschmann, "Oral Poetry in Mediaeval English, French and German Literature: Some Notes on Recent Research," *Speculum*, 42 (1967), 36-52.

2. See in particular R. Scholes and R. Kellogg, *The Nature of Narrative* (New York, 1966), 17-56, 303-11; L. Lönnroth, "*Hjálmar's Death-Song* and the Delivery of Eddic Poetry," *Speculum*, 46 (1971), 1-20; R. Allen, *Fire and Iron* (1971), 57-94; C. Clover, "Scene in Saga Composition," *Arkiv för nordisk filologi*, 89 (1974), 57-83. Long before the oral-formulaic theories became known among Old Norse scholars, Knut Liestøl had argued that the formulas in the sagas were a heritage from oral tradition. See his *The Origin of Icelandic Family Sagas* (Oslo, 1930), 26-32.

3. Cf. Allen (1971), 71-74; Clover (1974), 58.

the hierarchy are the semi-independent episodes, *þættir*, discussed in Chapter II. These can be divided into chapters, which in turn may be divided into *segments*: discrete smaller units of narrative which may consist of either a dramatic "scene" (including dialogue) or a "description" (like the introduction of a new character). Segments may be considered the atoms of saga narrative, for they cannot be further broken down into discrete and well-rounded units of narrative.[4] From a purely syntactic standpoint, however, the segments may be said to consist of sentences, which may be broken down into clauses or phrases. All these categories refer to *form*, not content.

A *formula*, on the other hand, is a particular kind of phrase associated with a particular type of content. It is a frequently recurring sequence of words which may be used in the construction of *stock scenes* and *stock descriptions*, i.e., segments associated with a particular type of traditional content. But a formula may also have other functions, and it is by no means a necessary ingredient in any type of segment. Likewise, stock scenes and stock descriptions may often be used in the construction of a "typical *þáttr*" or a "typical chapter," but they are not necessarily present.

In accordance with common usage, I shall reserve the term *motif* exclusively for *units of content*, such as "a battle," "a feud," "a shipboard fight," or "a hero's travels abroad." Such units may be expressed in various forms within the composition and are thus not necessarily tied to a particular formula or a particular type of structural entity such as a scenic segment or a *þáttr*. We may nevertheless say that there are certain formulas, stock scenes, "typical" *þættir*, etc. which are always tied to particular motifs.

For example, the motif of "a hero's travels abroad" may be expressed in the simple formula X *fór utan*, "X went abroad"; it may also be expressed in the well-known stock scene of an Icelandic traveler being presented at the court in Norway; finally, it may be said to constitute the main theme of a very large and important group of traditional *þættir* found primarily in the Kings' Sagas. The motif may be used to define this type of *þáttr* as well as the stockscene and to some extent the formula (even though it is not necessarily used about a *hero*'s travel), but the *þáttr*, scene, or formula cannot be used to define the motif.

---

4. The key function of scenic segments in saga composition has been particularly emphasized by Clover (1974) and by M. C. van den Toorn, "Zur Struktur der Saga," *ANF*, 73 (1958), 140-68. The most detailed analysis of scenic components and the way they are used in traditional saga narrative may be found in Clover's unpublished dissertation, "*Njáls saga, The Legendary Saga of St. Óláfr*, and *Runzevals Þáttr*: A Structural Comparison" (University of California, Berkeley, 1972).

Formulas

Formulas in *Njála* may be divided into three broad categories. The first of these consists of commonplaces for presenting recurrent but fairly trivial motifs such as a ride to the Allthing ("They now ride to the Allthing") or the introduction of characters ("A man was called X, the son of Y, the son of Z; he lived at farm X; he was wise and well liked"). Although the most common, these are the least obtrusive types of formula in the sagas. They are found frequently in transitions to more dramatic incidents, but they may occasionally be found in the middle of highly dramatic stock scenes (*ok varð þat hans bani,* i.e. "that was the end of him," etc.).

A second category consists of "transition formulas,"[5] used to call our attention to sceneshifts and other changes in the structure. Among the most common are *Nú er þar til máls at taka* ("Now we shall talk about," "Now we shall turn to)", *Nú er at segja frá X* ("Now this is to be said about X"), and . . . *ok er X ór sǫgunni* ("and X is now out of the saga," i.e., not to be mentioned again). Sometimes a single word, such as *Nú* ("Now") or *Síðan* ("Then") may serve the same function. Although there are few such "transition formulas," they are important as a kind of cement between the larger building blocks.

A third category consists of proverbs, legal formulas, and figurative statements made directly by characters: "Cold are the counsels of women," "Our land must be built by Law," etc. This is the most heavily emphasized type of formula in the saga, but it is not a standard element. It is used only sparingly, but it frequently sets the tone for the narrative. We shall have more to say about it under the heading of "Rhetoric."

Scenes

A *scene* in *Njála* may be defined as a discrete narrative segment presenting a dramatic situation. It normally consists of a brief dialogue, introduced by some narrative lines which define the setting and the situation. After the dialogue more narrative lines may conclude the scene before a transition (often expressed in a "transition formula" such as *Nú er þar til máls at taka*) to a new scene or to a longer narrative passage.

As an example we may take the following passage from the beginning of chapter 2:[6]

5. Cf. Clover (1974), 62.

6. The same example is used by Allen (1971), 64, but his analysis is open to some criticism; cf. R. I. Page's review in *Scandinavica*, 11 (1972), 150-51, and P. Schach's review in *Scandinavian Studies*, 44 (1972), 559. The traditional nature of this scene was demonstrated by Kersbergen (1927), 106-08, where several parallels from other sagas are cited.

Þat var einu hverju sinni, at þeir brœðr riðu til alþingis, Hǫskuldr ok Hrútr; þar var fjǫlmenni mikit. Þá rœddi Hǫskuldr við Hrút: "Þat vilda ek, bróðir, at þú bœttir rád þitt ok bæðir þér konu." Hrútr segir: "Lengi hefir mér þat í hug verit, ok hefir mér þó tvennt um sýnzk. En nú vil ek gera at þínu skapi, eða hvar skulu vit á leita?" Hǫskuldr svaraði: "Hér eru nú hǫfðingjar margir á þingi, ok er gott um at velja, en þó hefi ek í einum stað á stofnat fyrir þína hǫnd. Kona heitir Unnr ok er dóttir Marðar gígju, ins vitrasta manns, ok er hann hér á þingi ok svá dóttir hans, ok mátt þú nú sjá hana, ef þu vill."
Ok annan dag eptir, er menn gengu til lǫgréttu, sá þeir konur úti hjá Rangæingabúð . . . .
(It happened once that the two brothers, Hǫskuldr and Hrútr, rode to the Allthing. There was a large attendance. Then Hǫskuldr said to Hrútr: "I would like you to look to your future, brother, and find yourself a wife." "I have been in two minds about it for a long time," replied Hrútr. "But now I will do as you wish. Where should we turn our attention?" "There are many chieftains here at the Allthing," said Hǫskuldr, "and we have a wide choice. But I have already decided on a match for you, a woman called Unnr; she is the daughter of Mǫrðr Fiddle, a very wise man. He is here at the Allthing now and his daughter is with him, so you can see her if you wish."
Next day, as people were going to the Lawcourt, they saw some women outside the Rangriver booth . . . .)

The situation in this scene recurs several times in *Njála* and in many earlier sagas: a man suggests to his kinsman that it is time to get married; the kinsman is hesitant but prepared to accept good counsel; the name of the prospective bride is advanced, and the scene closes with the expectation that the "bartering for the bride" will soon begin. The setting for the conversation is equally conventional: a meeting at the Allthing. We may therefore characterize this as a *stock scene*.

Formulas appear at several places in the passage, but especially at the beginning and the end. First, we find a transition formula (*Þat var einu hverju sinni*), followed by a formulaic description of arrival at the Allthing meeting (*þeir brœðr riðu til alþingis . . . þar var fjǫlmenni mikit*). Saga characters typically "ride" to these meetings, which typically are crowded. Thus such "information" is merely a conventional introduction; the audience is not supposed to pay any particular attention to the means of transportation or the number of people present at the meeting (as they might very well have done if the narrator had said that the brothers "walked" or "hurried," or that the meeting was "poorly attended").

With the beginning of the dialogue, however, the knowledgeable reader begins to pay more attention. The theme of bride-bartering is a conventional one but not as conventional as the arrival at a Thing meeting; and the narrator has emphasized the importance of the conversation not only through his use of dialogue but also by letting Hrútr and Hǫskuldr speak in unusual and "poetic" phrases: "*at þú bœttir ráð þitt ok bæðir þér konu*" (note the use of alliteration !), "*Lengi hefir mér þat í hug verit, ok hefir mér þó tvennt um sýnzk.*" Although such phrases may contain formulaic elements, there are no exact equivalents in parallel scenes from other sagas. They can thus not be counted among the "prefabricated material" for presenting this type of scene.

Other ingredients in the dialogue are more obviously formulaic, e.g., *Þat vilda ek, bróðir* (a similar dialogue in *Laxdœla saga* begins with the same phrase),[7] and *Kona heitir Unnr ok er dóttir Marðar gígju* (the usual formula for introducing a new character). The transition to the following scene is just as stereotyped as its beginning: *Ok annan dag eptir, er menn gengu til lǫgrettu* . . . (a typical way of introducing a scene at the Allthing). Here again the narrator ignores the "personal touch" and falls back on the conventional mechanisms of saga narrative, until he is ready to present another dramatic "high point."

Although the scene with Hǫskuldr and Hrútr may be characterized as a stock scene with many traditional parallels, it can not be defined as a "cluster of formulas," composed according to the stereotyped patterns Parry and Lord found in Yugoslav epic poetry. Instead, the stock scenes in *Njála* are based on a general motif patter, or *Gestalt*,[8] combined with verbal commonplaces and transition formulas but allowing the author the freedom to use his "own words," especially at the dramatic high points. Many scenes cannot be characterized as stock scenes since the situations they convey have no close parallels elsewhere.

Certain scenes however, may be characterized as "individual stock scenes"; they are repeated within *Njála* itself but are not found elsewhere. We may speak also of "individual formulas," i.e., phrases which the author of *Njála* uses repeatedly but which are rare in other sagas. Such scenes and phrases are of particular use in describing the personality of the author or the difference between *Njála* and other works of the same genre. But in this chapter we are primarily interested in stock scenes and formulas which can be attested from sagas other than *Njála* itself.

Among the most characteristic stock scenes in *Njála* are the following: 1) a hero is presented at a foreign court and accepted as one of the king's

---

7. See Kersbergen (1927), *loc. cit.*

8. The concept of the "Gestalt" has been used in M. N. Nagler's interesting article, "Towards a generative view of the oral formula," *TAPh.A*, 98 (1967), 269-311, in which the author presents a new interpretation of the relationship between "originality" and "traditional elements" in Homer.

men; 2) a woman goads her kinsman to take revenge on her enemy by suggesting that he is a coward if he does not; 3) a man encounters his enemy and kills him; 4) two heroes exchange boasts and insults at a feast or at the Allthing; 5) a woman encounters her kinsman (or lover) as he is coming back with a bloodied weapon after having killed his enemy; 6) two heroes make a settlement at the Allthing; 7) a man visits a kinsman or neighbor to solicit his support before a meeting at the Allthing; and 8) somebody tells another person about an ominous dream.

Each of these stock scenes has its rules and recurrent formulas in addition to using general conventions for scenic presentation. Several of these rules may be traced far back in Germanic tradition. For example, the nucleus of the stock scene of a woman goading her kinsman to take revenge may be found in the very earliest Eddic poetry.[9] In other cases the rules must have developed between the "saga age" and tirtheenth century sagawriting. But we must also assume that each sagawriter, including the author of *Njála*, could generate his own rules from the preceding ones and thus construct unprecedented scenes still felt to be "within saga tradition." The analogy of transformational grammar may be helpful when trying to understand the composition of sagas.[10]

Descriptions

Alongside the traditional scenes, we also find narrative *descriptions*,[11] which possess a similar structural unity and are used as building blocks by the author of *Njála*. The presentations of new characters may serve as an example. Some of these are very highly formulaic, such as this from chapter 41:

Sigmundr hét maðr; hann var Lambason, Sighvats sonar ins rauða. Hann var farmaðr mikill, kurteiss maðr ok vænn, mikill ok sterkr. Hann var metnaðarmaðr mikill ok skáld gott ok at flestum íþróttum vel búinn, hávaðamaðr mikill, spottsamr ok ódæll. Hann kom út austr í Hornafirði. Skjǫldr hét félagi hans; hann var sænskr maðr ok illr viðreignar. Þeir fingu sér hesta ok riðu . . . .
(There was a man called Sigmundr, the son of Lambi, the son of Sighvatr the Red. He was a great traveler, well bred and handsome, tall and strong. He carried himself arrogantly, was a good poet and was proficient at most sports, but he was rowdy and sarcastic and a difficult man to get on with. He returned to Iceland, landing in Hornafjord in the east. His companion was called Skjǫldr, a man from Sweden, most unpleasant. They got themselves horses and rode . . . .)

9. See Rolf Heller's chapter on "Die Hetzerin" in *Die literarische Darstellung der Frau in der Isländersagas* (Halle, 1958), 98-122; also: Wolf (1965), 109-147.

10. This analogy is further explored by Nagler (1967) although with reference to Homer, not to the sagas.

11. Cf. Allen (1971), 33 ("passages of sheer fact)".

The beginning of a narrative segment is marked here by the frequently used phrase X *hét maðr*, a kind of transition formula which also contains necessary information. Next is the obligatory genealogy, which may be long or short depending on the status of the character and the information available to the author. Here Sigmundr's appearance and character are described in conventional phrases found throughout saga portraits of typical troublemakers: *mikill ok sterkr, skáld gott, hávaðamaðr mikill, spottsamr ok óðæll*, etc. One of the adjectives used to describe Sigmundr is a French loanword (*kurteiss*, from French *courtois*), but it had become conventional in saga portraits by the end of the thirteenth century.

Had Sigmundr lived on a farm in Iceland, we would expect some formulaic words about this farm and the other people who lived in it with thim, but since he is presented as a traveller from abroad, the narrator instead tells us where he landed and with whom. Equally conventional words about Sigmundr's companion—another stereotyped troublemaker—concludes the presentation. The next sentence (*Þeir fingu sér hesta ok riðu*, etc.) may be regarded as the beginning of a new segment and a stock scene: the arrival of troublemakers at a peaceful farm (Hlíðarendi).

The Combination of Segments

Descriptions and scenes thus constitute the segments of a normal chapter. The first chapter of *Njála* has three segments. The first (beginning with the formulaic *Mǫrðr hét maðr*) presents Mǫrðr Fiddle and his family. The second—heralded by an unusual transition phrase: *Nú víkr sǫgunni vestr til Breiðafjarðardala*—presents Hǫskuldr Dala-Kollsson and his family. Both segments are conventional: genealogies, formulaic words of character-ization, and so on. But the third segment, introduced by the formula *Þat var einu hverju sinni*, presents a scene traditional only in a general sense, for its motif is highly original, even though the presentation follows the general conventions for a saga scene. I am of course referring to the famous scene in which Hrútr comments on Hallgerðr's "thief's eyes," a scene un-precedented in saga literature. The chapter thus includes both traditional and untraditional elements.

Most chapters in *Njála* can be similarly divided into discrete segments as can chapters in many earlier sagas, although our author is more consistent and deliberate in his employment of these building blocks, which probably served as important elements in oral saga composition. Narrative segments are distinguishable in early saga manuscripts, even though their beginnings are rarely marked on the written page except where they coincide with the beginning of a new chapter. And unlike the chapter division, the segment division has no precise equivalent in the foreign literature which influenced the sagawriters. Certain stock scenes and stock descriptions may, however, have been influenced by narrative conventions in foreign genres (this will be further discussed in Chapter IV).

Expansion and contraction

One characteristic of the narrative segment is that it appears in both "expanded" and "contracted" versions. The presentation of a new character may be lengthened through extensive genealogies, characterizing adjectives, etc., but it may easily be (and often is) abbreviated into a few lines. A stock scene may dwell on incidentals and allow the characters to express themselves in long, articulate sentences (particularly in the presentation of highly dramatic events); but the narrator also may cut the scene to its essentials, present part of the dialogue in summarized form, or omit it altogether.[12]

An example of a "contracted" chapter segment in *Njála* is the following, from chapter 101, which deals with the missionary Þangbrandr and his travels around Iceland to convert the farmers and win their support at the next Allthing meeting:

Þaðan fóru þeir till Fellshverfis ok gistu at Kálfafelli. Þar bjó Kolr Þorsteinsson, frændi Halls, ok tók hann við trú ok hjú hans ǫll.
(From there they went to the Fell District and stayed at Kálfafell. Kolr
Þorsteinsson lived there, a kinsman of Hallr. Kolr and his household took
the new faith.)

Here the author is not particularly interested in dwelling on the incidentals of the visit. He wants only to tell the most basic facts before he hurries on to report about Þangbrandr's next visit (that report is equally brief and employs the same formulas: *Þaðan fóru þeir* . . . *Þar bjó*, etc.)

But a similar situation is pictured with much more detail in chapter 134, which deals with Flosi's visits at various farms to win people's support after the Burning of Njáll:

Þaðan fóru þeir á Valþjófsstaði. Þar bjó Sǫrli Brodd-Helgason, bróðir
Bjarna; hann átti Þórdísi, dóttur Guðmundar ins ríka af Mǫðruvǫllum.
Þeir hǫfðu þar góðar viðtǫkur. Ok um morgininn vakti Flosi til við Sǫrla,
at hann mundi ríða til þings með honum, ok bauð honum fé til. "Eigi
veit ek þat," segir hann, "meðan ek veit eigi, hvaðan Guðmundr inn ríki,
mágr minn, stendr at, því at ek ætla honum at veita, hvaðan sem hann
stendr at." Flosi mælti: "Finn ek þat á svǫrum þínum, at þú hefir kvánríki."
Síðan stóð Flosi upp ok bað taka klæði þeira ok vápn; fóru þeir þá í braut
ok fengu þar enga liðveizlu.

---

12. Cf. Heusler's remarks on "Ausführlichkeit" and the variation between "dünnen Bericht" and "geschaute Auftritte" in *Die Altgermanische Dichtung* (Potsdam 1943) 225-227. The subject is discussed in more detail by Clover (1974), 59-61.

(From there they went to Valþjófstead. Sǫrli Brodd-Helgason lived there, the brother of Bjarni; he was married to Þórdís, the daughter of Guðmundr the Powerful of Mǫðruvellir. Flosi and his men were well received there. And the following morning, Flosi sounded Sǫrli about accompanying him to the Allthing, and offered to pay him for it. "I cannot say," replied Sǫrli, "until I know whose side my father-in-law, Guðmundr the Powerful, is taking, for I shall be supporting him whatever side he is on." "I can see from your replies that you are under woman's rule here," said Flosi. He rose to his feet and told his men to take their clothes and weapons. Then they left, without having received any support.)

The passage begins with the same formulas as the first one: *Þaðan fóru þeir . . . Þar bjó . . . .* But here the farmer and his family are given a fuller presentation and a dramatic scene is built between the proud helpseeker and his cowardly host (another traditional motif). The author has moved beyond the stage of "just wanting to tell the basic facts"; he wants his audience to "see" the scene and to achieve this result has to be more circumstantial.

But he can be even more circumstantial. This is how he presents Flosi's visit at the next farm:

Fóru þeir fyrir neðan Lagarfljót ok um heiði til Njarðvíkr. Þar bjuggu brœdr tveir, Þorkell fullspakr ok Þorvaldr; þeir váru synir Ketils þryms, Þiðranda sonar ins spaka, Ketils sonar þryms, Þóris sonar Þiðranda. Móðir þeira Þorkels fullspaks ok Þorvalds var Yngvildr, dóttir Þorkels fullspaks. Flosi hafði þar góðar viðtǫkur. Hann sagði þeim deili á um ørendi sín ok bað þá liðveizlu, en þeir synjuðu, áðr hann gaf þrjár merkr silfrs hvárum þeira til liðveizlu; þá játuðu þeir at veita Flosa. Yngvildr, móðir þeira, var hjá stǫdd; hon grét, er hon heyrði, er þeir hétu alþingisferðinni. Þorkell mælti: "Hví grætr þú, móðir?" Hon svarar: "Mik dreymði, at Þorvaldr, bróðir þinn, væri í rauðum kyrtli, ok þótti mér svá þrǫngr vera sem saumaðr væri at honum; mér þótti hann ok vera í rauðum hosum undir ok vafit at vándum dreglum. Mér þótti illt á at sjá at honum var svá óhœgt, en ek mátta ekki at gera." Þeir hlógu at ok kváðu vera loklausu ok sǫgðu geip hennar ekki skyldu standa fyrir þingreið sinni. Flosi þakkaði þeim vel ok fór þaðan . . . .

(They went down along the lower end of Lagarwater and over the Heath to Njarðvik. Two brothers lived there, Þorkell the Sage and Þorvaldr, the sons of Ketill Þrymr, the son of Þiðrandi the Wise, the son of Ketill Þrymr, the son of Þórir Þiðrandi. The mother of Þorkell the Sage and Þorvaldr was Yngvildr, the daughter of Þorkell the Sage. Flosi was well received there. He told them his mission, and asked for their support; at first they refused, and only finally agreed to help him when he had given them three marks of silver each. Yngvildr, their mother, was present, and when she heard them promise to ride to the Allthing she started weeping. "Why do you weep mother?" asked Þorkell. "I dreamed " she replied "that your brother Þorvaldr was wearing a red tunic and this tunic was so tight that it looked as if he had been sewn into it. He was also wearing red hose

bound with shabby tapes. I was distressed to see him looking so uncom-
fortable but I could not do anything to help him." They laughed and called
it nonsense and said that her babblings would not stop them riding to the
Allthing. Flosi thanked them warmly and left . . . .)

Again, we notice formulas that occur in the previous quotations: *fóru þeir . . .
Þar bjuggu . . .* (names followed by genealogy) *. . . hafði þar góðar viðtǫkur.*
And the errand is the same as before: to ask for support, *liðveizla*, in return
for economic compensation. Again, the dealings between the visitor and
his host(s) are telescoped in a brief, dramatic scene. But each stage has
been pictured with more details: the road to the farm is more thoroughly
described, the genealogy is longer, the information about economic compensation more precise, the final dramatic scene more carefully staged and
developed. The author here has focused less on the actual negotiations than
on the incident immediately following: Yngvildr's ominous story about the
dream, which evidently is intended to prepare the audience for Þorvaldr's
death. This use of a dream is another common device in traditional saga
narrative. Its presence signals that this visit is an unusually important one,
requiring a fuller and more circumstantial treatment. The basic narrative
segment has been expanded almost to its limit.

For when a segment has been expanded too far, it breaks up into two or
more separate units. In this case, the presentation of the farmers is so detailed that it could well have been a separate segment before Flosi's visit.
The author could have done this by beginning: "There were two brothers
called Þorkell and Þorvaldr" (beginning of the first segment); Flosi's visit
(the second segment) could have begun with a transition formula: "It now
happened that Flosi and his men went to the farm of Þorkell and Þorvaldr,"
etc. He could even have made the scene with the mother into a third se-
ment by closing the negotiation scene with a phrase like: "Flosi thanked
them for their support and prepared to leave," followed by something like:
"It now happened that their mother, Yngvildr, stood by weeping," etc.
In fact, this is a technique which sagawriters often use near the climax of
an episode, e.g., the Burning of Njáll or the Death of Gunnarr. Theodore
Andersson has called this technique *staging*, "a deceleration of pace, a magni-
fying of detail, and a dwelling on incidentals in order to focus the central
event one last time and enhance its importance."[13]

The narrative segment is thus a flexible unit which cannot be defined in
terms of its motifs (like "visit to a farm to gain support" or "bartering for
the bride"), since the same content may be either telescoped into one sentence or expanded into a series of presentations and scenes. In some cases,

13. Andersson (1967), 54.

it is difficult to determine where one segment ends and another begins, for the author is inconsistent in his use of transition formulas and other devices for marking structural divisions. But, on the whole, narrative segments in *Njála* are easy to distinguish, and they provide excellent opportunities for studying the author's method of composition.

Segmental Sequences

Stock scenes and stock descriptions have a tendency to appear in predictable sequences. A scene of "proposing a match to a kinsman" (cf. above) may thus be expected to precede a scene of "asking for the bride's hand." "Heroes leaving home to fight the enemy" will precede "fight with the enemy," which will be followed by "homecoming of the heroes." Predictable sequences will be further discussed under "Action Patterns" (below, p. 68). It may be possible to define the typical episode, or *þáttr*, as a string of typical segments in a certain order: first the conventional presentation of new characters, then a group of segments introducing a conflict between two families or parties—and so on (cf. below, p. 69; also above, p. 19, for Theodore Andersson's "six-point scheme" for analyzing saga structure).

Chapters

It is much more difficult to determine general rules for the structure of a saga chapter. Unlike the narrative segment and the *þáttr*, the chapter as a unit is clearly of foreign origin and the sagawriters did not always accomodate it. Chapter divisions are notoriously inconsistent in many saga manuscripts. The only rule that all sagawriters followed was to start a chapter at the beginning of a new segment, particularly if it is introduced by an obvious transition formula such as *Nú er þar til máls at taka* or *Litlu síðar*. But there are often several segments in each chapter and it is often impossible to determine why the sagawriter (or scribe) introduced his chapter division before one particular segment instead of another one. In many sagas, the divisions—indicated in the medieval fashion by a large initial and/or rubric—serve more as a table of contents than as a guide to structure: the rubrics function as signposts for a reader leafing through the manuscript in order to find a particular incident.[14] One feels in such cases that the chapter divisions were superimposed on a more "natural" structure of scenes, descriptions, and *þættir*. It should be noted that while the word *þáttr* refers to a "strand" within the story itself (a story which may have existed quite independent of saga manuscripts), the word *kapítuli* (from

---

14. Cf. Allen (1971), 23, and L. Lönnroth, "Structural Divisions in the *Njála* Manuscripts," *ANF*, 90 (1975).

Latin *capitulum*) originally referred to the "head" of the chapter in a manuscript, i.e., to a visible "thing" on a page, not to a structural element in narrative composition.

Yet the author of *Njála* usually treats the chapter as a structural unit guided
by rules which probably developed as a result of foreign influence on sagawriters in the later thirteenth century. His main principles are: each chapter
should either give an extensive introduction of new characters (e.g., chapters
19, 20, 46) or present a new course of action (e.g., the killing of a man, a
lawsuit, a journey from Iceland to Norway, and so on). Although the original
chapter rubrics cannot be safely reconstructed, we may assume they were
similar to those found in the extant manuscripts and that they probably
named new characters or a new course of action, e.g., "About Gunnarr,"
"About Njáll," "The Slaying of Þráinn," etc. The chapter thus begins either
with a "presentation" segment (*Maðr hét* . . ., etc.) or with a segment in
which a new course of action is introduced; in the latter case the chapter
will normally conclude with a segment that completes the action and reports
its immediate results (the man to be killed has either died or saved his life,
the lawsuit has been either lost or won, the travellers to Norway have either
arrived safely or given up their goal, and so on). In some cases, however,
the author may end the chapter before the action has been completed so
that he can switch to a new scene with a new setting and new characters.
This is often done to heighten suspense in such highly dramatic passages
as the Death of Gunnarr: one chapter describes the preparations of Gunnarr's enemies until the barking of his dog is about to wake the hero. At
this point there is a chapter division followed by a scene in which Gunnarr
wakes up, and we are then told of his actions to defend himself. This
chapter ends when Gunnarr has been killed—his course of action has failed
and that of his enemies has succeeded.

Problems of Composition

More could be said about the rules governing the author's use of traditional
structural elements, but this should suffice as a general introduction. To
what extent was it possible for him to follow these rules and yet subordinate
them to his overall design? This is something only a few sagawriters ever
managed to do; many developed traditional episodes and stock scenes as
if they were ends in themselves. These writers would, for example, repeat
twenty times that their heroes were "received well" and "given good gifts"
each time they visited someone even though the visits are insignificant
and uninteresting to the saga as a whole. A force of habit, strengthened
by the conventional expectations of the audience, encouraged the inclusion

of unnecessary details. This is a weakness inherent in all oral literature and in many written works based on oral tradition.

Although the author of *Njála* is more in command of his saga than most other sagawriters, he too suffers from this weakness.[15] He is often much more circumstantial in his treatment of conventional motifs than is warranted by his own "blueprint" for the saga. Subordinate characters are often introduced with long genealogies. Actions easily summarized are presented in dramatic scenes as if the whole plot depended on them.

The digressive mechanisms may be seen at work in the episode of Hrútr and Unnr (I:1). The main function of this episode is to explain the feud over Unnr's dowry, which later leads to Gunnarr's first heroic deed and his first contact with Hallgerðr's family (cf. above, p. 25). But the "explanation" has become so circumstantial through the introduction of standard motifs that the episode seems a self-contained narrative with little relation to the saga as a whole. Hrútr's marriage proposal and his agreement with Unnr's father about the dowry are described with a wealth of detail. The narrator next follows Hrútr on his long journey abroad, which leads to his betrayal of Unnr and to Gunnhildr's curse on their marriage. Although the curse may initiate the feud about the dowry, it can hardly motivate the full reporting of Hrútr's travels, which take up chapters 3 to 6 of the saga. In these chapters, the author seems to depart from his preconceived plan in picturing Hrútr as a hero in his own right. His adventures are described according to an "action pattern" (to be analyzed below), inherited from tradition, which may have lured the author off his main track.

To summarize, we may say that the "literary grammar" learned from earlier sagas probably made the composition of *Njála* easier, but it also gave rise to inconsistencies and to the inclusion of material that seems superfluous to modern readers. For the "grammatical rules" were not in themselves consistent. Rules pertaining to the composition of a stock scene might conflict with rules pertaining to the composition of an episode, or with rules pertaining to the saga as a whole; and it was not always easy to achieve a smooth compromise. But the most important effect of traditional saga composition was that it limited the "world" that sagawriters could portray.

3. WORLD

World and Language

The action in *Njála* takes place in Iceland (and in some other parts of Northern Europe) during the so-called Saga Age: a period of about one

---

15. Cf. Heusler's introduction to his Thule translation (1914), 14-15.

hundred years between the middle of the tenth century and the middle of the eleventh century. But the "world" of the saga is not defined by its historical setting. The term "world" is used here in the sense of "world picture": a system for interpreting the actual world so that its heterogeneous mass of data is reduced to simple categories, opposing "forces," and symbols for human values and beliefs. Old Norse mythology may be said to provide a world in this sense, and part of it has survived in the sagas.

It has often been observed that our world picture is dependent on our language, and this is no less true of the saga. The formulas and stock scenes discussed in the previous section determined the sagawriter's concept of a typical hero, a typical meeting at the Allthing, or a typical bloodfeud. Or perhaps we should say that his world picture determined his selection of formulas and stock scenes. Whichever came first, "world" or "literary grammar," they are dependent on each other. To illustrate this in more detail, we may say that the stock scene of "woman goading her man to take revenge" (cf. above, p. 48) helped shape the saga image of Old Norse women as exceedingly strong, proud, and vengeful, an image which is part of the "saga world." At the same time, such an image may have given rise to the extremely popular "goading scenes."

Images

The term "image" refers not to a particular motif or action pattern but to a whole set of ideas and expectations associated with particular types of characters, places, and objects. The saga image of Strong Woman is formed not only by the "goading scenes" but also by other recurrent pattern—for example, by scenes in which a woman receives the message of her lover's death with apparent indifference. On the other hand, a single motif may contribute to the forming of several different images: thus a "goading scene" builds up not only the image of Strong Woman but also the image of Gullible Man, easily prompted by woman to prove his manhood by rash and violent action. The combination of such images in a saga helps to constitute its "world."

While a motif (expressed in a formula, stock scene, etc.) appears in a temporal sequence, an image appears as part of the "total picture" of the saga. A systematic description of the saga world would include the most important images, especially of stock characters, standard objects, and typical settings, plus an explanation of how they are related to each other. An historical study would trace the origins and the development of each image and explain how they were combined.

Our attempt to describe the traditional saga world, as known to the author of Njála, will aim only at a very general and schematic presentation of basic features.[16] Some of these features may be considered "universal" since they appear in heroic literature all over the world. Other features are more sepcifically "Germanic," while still others have been derived from non-Germanic sources known to the early sagawriters. To make the relationships clearer, we shall sometimes provide analogies from early Germanic myths and legends. These analogies should not imply that the world of sagas was necessarily derived from such myths and legends, although this may often have been true.

Topographical Structure of the Saga World

One way to picture the saga world is as a system of concentric circles, where the daylight falls clearly on the inner circles, gradually fading into darkness towards the periphery.[17] In the center are the heroes and their families, Icelandic farmers from the "Saga age" surrounded by servants, slaves, and other household members. At some distance from this center are various neighbors, allies, and kinsmen with *their* families and households, some loyal to the hero, others indifferent or hostile. Further away is the Allthing, where conflicts are mediated and Icelandic public opinion is formed on all major events. Still further out, at a considerable distance from Iceland, are the foreign Scandinavian courts (especially the Norwegian court), often visited by saga heroes during their travels abroad. As long as the characters move within these circles, most sagas maintain an impression of, "realism."

But still further out, towards the periphery, sagas tell of more exotic places such as Miklagard (Constantinople), Holmgard (Novgorod), or the open sea of viking adventures—strange places where reality is mixed with fancy. Supernatural and fantastic elements (fights with berserks and trolls,

16. The best general introduction is still V. Grønbech, *The Culture of the Teutons*, translated by W. Worster, vols. 1-3 (London and Copenhagen, 1931). The Danish original: *Vor Folkeæt i Oldtiden*, 2nd revised edition (Copenhagen, 1955). The layman is recommended to consult this work for further information about "Honor," "Luck," "Fate," "Kinship" and other key concepts in the Old Norse *Lebensanschauung*, but he should be aware of the fact that many of Grønbech's theories are speculative and outdated. Later, more critical studies, intended for the specialist, include Walter Gehl's *Ruhm und Ehre bei den Nordgermanen* (Berlin, 1937); *Der germanische Schicksalsglaube* (Berlin, 1939); Walter Bætke, *Christliches Lehngut in der Sagareligion* (Berlin, 1951). In addition there is a large number of publications devoted to some more limited aspect of the saga world, e.g., A. Gödecke, *Die Darstellung der Gemütsbewegungen in der Isländischen Familiensaga* (Hamburg, 1933), and A. Hruby, *Zur Technik der isländischen Saga. Die Kategorien ihrer Personencharacteristik* (Wien, 1929).

17. Cf. Roman Ingarden's discussion of "Orientierungsraum" and "Orientierungszentrum," *Das literarische Kunstwerk*, 3rd edition (Tübingen, 1965), 243-46.

magic spells, etc.) increase as the hero gets further from home. This tendency is unusually strong in the sagas, where life at the home farm appears rather prosaic while life in foreign countries is usually presented as strange, adventurous, and romantic.

Within Iceland, but outside its established community of more or less law-abiding citizens, the saga reader may encounter supernatural and demonic forces: sorcerers, witches, berserks, giants, and fetches. But even when these forces are close to the geographical center of the saga, they are conveyed as if perceived from a distance: some of them appear only in dreams and visions; others appear in the "real" world, but so briefly and mysteriously that one cannot always be certain of their true identity. These supernatural inhabitants of Iceland may be compared to the marvels of far-away countries, which are also seen through a sort of mythical haze. These marvels all belong, in a sense, and regardless of their geographical location, to that outer circle at the periphery of the saga world.

Furthest away from home and "reality," are members of the Old Nores Pantheon, such as Odin or Thor; they are usually absent from the so-called family sagas, even though they may appear in dreams or in skaldic verses spoken by saga characters. Fate, however, is often represented as an impersonal force working behind the visible scene of action. Fate may be said to dominate the "outermost circle" of many sagas about the pagan era; beyond it is nothing, before the arrival of the Christian God.

The Social Structure

Within these concentric circles, the saga characters move in patterns determined by their social and dramatic roles. The most important *social* roles may be arranged in these two hierarchies:

A. *Society at large*: King, earl (*jarl*), chieftain (*goði*), large freeholder (*stór-bóndi*), small farmer, peasant (*smábóndi*).
B. *The family household*: Father, mother, oldest son, younger sons, daughters; servants with responsibilities as overseer, foster-father, etc.; other free servants; slaves (*prælar*).

These two social hierarchies are seen from the standpoint of the leading Icelandic families, usually large freeholders and chieftains. This point is important, for the hierarchies would have been quite different from the standpoint of a slave or a visitor from abroad. It is also important to remember that the social roles are seen in relation to specific types of dramatic events: feuds, viking adventures, confrontations at the Allthing, etc. If the subject matter had been different, society would also have appeared differently.

The home of the main characters and the most typical scene of action in a family saga is thus a fairly large farm in Iceland, occupied by a reasonably wealthy family with slaves and free servants. The farm itself is described only when details of its location and appearance are necessary for the understanding of the action. In many cases, the narrator assumes that his audience knows not only generally about such farms but also about specific localities, especially the homes of very prominent men.[18]

And "normal" activities on the farm are also described only when they have a bearing on the main action (e.g., when a servant is killed while bringing home the sheep). In the few cases where daily life is pictured in more detail, the activities are usually conveyed in a "typical" and stylized manner: the father sits in his High Seat, the young sons sharpen their weapons, the women prepare food, etc. Usually members of the household are shown in more dramatic situations: receiving messages about new assaults, preparing to take revenge on the enemy, listening to ominous prophecies, and so on.

The effect of such dramatic scenes is to present the family (and the clan of which it forms a part) as a tightly knit social unit, in which each member has a duty to help the others and to defend the collective honor. Young sons are expected to take arms against members of other clans in order to avenge the death of a kinsman or other violations of the family's rights. Mothers and daughters are expected to goad them on if they seem reluctant. Fathers are expected to help their sons achieve victory by giving good counsel and by working in their favor at the Allthing meetings. Servants and slaves are expected to sacrifice themselves for their masters in these conflicts.

Loyalty within the family is a necessity because the world outside is hostile and there is no strong central authority to enforce the law. The power of kings, earls, and chieftains is limited to their small areas and is dependent on the loyalty of their followers, who may easily desert them. The Allthing is often both corrupt and powerless. The outcome of a trial or a settlement is largely dependent on bargains, manipulations, bribes, threats, and legal tricks. One of the most common stock scenes at the Allthing is of people visiting Things booths between sessions to make deals and solicit support. Often enough, violence breaks out at the meeting.

At the King's court there is more romance but even less security than at the Allthing. The King sits in his hall surrounded by beer-drinking warriors as the Icelandic visitor arrives to have his heroic valor tested. Evil royal advisers and beautiful but dangerous women lurk behind the throne. Mar-

---

18. On the landscape, cf. Allen (1971), 35; Paul Schach, "Anticipatory Literary Setting in the Old Icelandic Sagas," *Scandinavian Studies*, 27 (1955), 1-13.

velous gifts and great honor may be gained in this place of splendor and glamour, but the perilous sea must be traversed to reach it, and viking berserks may appear as challengers even in the royal hall itself.

It is thus no wonder that Fate often appears as the supreme ruler, even though members of the clan may do their best to avoid inpending disasters. Enemies are everywhere, some of them human, some of them subhuman, beastly, and demonic: ghosts, witches practising *seiðr* (an Old Norse variety of black magic), sometimes a troll or a giant. Agents of Fate, such as fetches and other strange creatures, appear in dreams and visions warning of catastrophies, but there is little recourse except to stoicly prepare to meet death bravely. Human laws and human wisdom are of little use on a lonely farm threatened by the entire universe. A lucky person (*gæfumaðr*) may survive and prosper; but most are persecuted by bad luck (*ógæfa*), which affects their kinsmen as well as themselves.

Yet the family is morally obliged to show hospitality and generosity to visiting strangers and to follow the decisions of the Allthing which are compatible with law and honor. This obligation is necessary for if others did not respect it, the result would be total anarchy. This also means that each family member must show restraint and moderation in his dealings with others, must respect alliances with other clans and take care not to involve his own kinsmen in unnecessary feuds. Peaceful settlements are preferable to violent confrontations as long as the actions of the enemy have not passed a certain limit.

A major problem facing saga characters is to determine this limit. Some have an inflated notion of what their honor requires; their impetuous behavior may endanger the welfare of the whole clan. Others are too slow to take action against an aggressor because they do not value their own honor enough; such members also are a nuisance to their kinsmen. The "best" members of the family are those who know exactly what their honor is worth at any specific time, which requires luck as well as courage, wisdom and moderation. Honor must be carefully measured and well invested, and bad luck can diminish its value.

The "actual" honor of the family, like the honor of its individual members, is dependent on social status and strength: a wealthy chieftain family has more than a poor farmer's family, a king has more than a chieftain, a farmer more than a slave, a father (normally) more than his young son. But honor as well as luck is also dependent on ability and willingness to fulfill the obligations to one's own kind and to society at large. The obligations increase with the social status: a chieftain is expected to show more courage, restraint, generosity, and wisdom than an ordinary farmer; a slave (whose low status excludes him from honor) can hardly be expected to be anything but foolish and cowardly, in spite of his formal obligations to his master.

This rather complex "honor system," which dominates the characterization and the whole saga world, is shown in the economic compensation used where a settlement is negotiated between families. The size of the fines is a measurement of honor. It always costs more to kill a chieftain than a slave, but a "good" slave is worth more than a "bad" one. And while it may be very expensive to kill a "bad" chieftain, it is practically impossible to compensate for the killing of a chieftain who has fulfilled all his obligations. In such cases, a settlement can rarely be achieved before revenge has been taken on the killer or on his family.

For the killing of the actual culprit is not sufficient if his victim had more honor and status; this is often the case in sagas. Revenge must then be taken on one of the culprit's kinsmen who possesses the same amount of honor, and it matters little whether or not this kinsman had taken part in the feud. This is the only way in which the balance of power between leading families can be maintained: the family is responsible for the actions of each member.

This is, then, the system out of which a saga conflict normally develops, and it is in this context that we should view the characterization of saga characters as "wise," "lucky," "honorable," "impetuous," "proud," etc. *Wise*, for example, means primarily "wise in his judgment of feud situations"; *impetuous* means "tending to involve himself in unnecessary feuds." This perspective clearly limits the psychology of the sagas; people are pictured almost exclusively in a very specific type of human hebavior. We never learn, for example, whether a saga character was a tender lover, an absent-minded philosopher, or a bad cook—such matters are simply outside the scope of the narrative.

Roles and Stock Characters

Within the saga feuds, we may distinguish the following common dramatic roles (which sometimes overlap): 1) The Hero, 2) The "Prima Donna," 3) The Wise Counselor 4) The Comrade-at-arms, 5) The Villain, 6) The Villain's Helper, 7) The Messenger, 8) The Witness, 9) The Agent of Fate, 10) The Judge or Arbitrator.[19]

The Hero and his Comrade-at-arms actively fight in the feud and carry the main sympathies of narrator and audience. The Wise Counselor is a

---

19. There is no good general study of roles and stock characters in the sagas, but some of my generalizations on this subject (especially on stock characters such as the "Siegfried type," the "Grettir type" and the "Brynhildr type") are borne out by the material presented in works such as Hruby (1929), Heller (1958), and my own "Kroppen som själens spegel—ett motiv i de isländska sagorna," *Lychnos*, 1963-64.

nonfighting protagonist also pictured with sympathy who participates primarily through his counsels and Allthing manipulations. The Villain and the Villain's Helper usually initiate the conflicts and work against the interest of the Hero, although they may well be his kinsmen and thus "officially" on his side (on the Villain's function as Instigator of Feuds, cf. below, p. 76). The Judge or Arbitrator passes judgment on the feud; Messengers and Witnesses spread information about it in the community; Agents of Fate predict its further development. The Prima Donna, finally, is both an object of feuding and an active participant who goads her men on to battle; she may work in the interests of either the Hero or the Villain.

Heroes and Villains often appear on both sides in a saga feud. The same character may be the Hero in one part of the saga and the Villain in another, the Comrade-at-arms in a third part, and so on. This has prompted many critics to proclaim the sagas as "realistic." In fact the characters and their roles are generally stereotyped, but saga conflicts are more complex than those in most other epic works, mainly because of the intricacies of the "honor system" and because of the double loyalty which every clan member has to his clan and to society at large. A person who appears on the "good" side today may be forced by his kinsmen to appear on the "bad" side tomorrow. And a change in fortunes may relegate a Hero to a more subordinate role, or advance a subordinate character to the status of Hero.

The young Hero, who grows up on the farm, often belongs to one of two main categories: the Siegfried type or the Grettir type. The Siegfried type is blond, handsome, generous, lucky, friendly, usually well-balanced, and popular with most kinds of people. This is the sort of person who follows the law of restraint and moderation in preferring peaceful settlements to revenge which may endanger his kinsmen; but he is also able to strike hard when honor is at stake. The Grettir type is more homely in appearance or even ugly, heavy, usually dark or red-haired, sarcastic, impetuous, and difficult to get along with, persecuted by bad luck, often outlawed from the community, but noble in his suffering and frequently a good poet. This sort of person is so concerned with honor that he easily forgets the law of restraint and moderation, thereby involving his family in feuds even though a settlement should have been possible. While the Siegfried type rarely can be a Villain, a Grettir type occasionally may appear in this role—but most of the time he is doing more good than harm. Often these two heroic types are contrasted within the same saga: Egill and his brother Þórólfr in *Egils saga*, Jǫkull and his brother Þorsteinn in *Vatnsdœla*, etc.

The Prima Donna is practically always a strong, active, immensely proud, and sometimes beautiful woman who may be devoted to her own family and to the Hero but who may turn against him when her honor has been slighted. She thus may be both a Heroine and an accomplice of the Villain, or indeed even the Villain; she may play all these roles within the same saga: Brynhildr in *Vǫlsunga saga*, Guðrún in *Laxdœla saga*, etc. In this respect the leading women of the sagas differ markedly from the leading women of medieval Romance, who generally play more passive, "feminine" roles, mainly as objects of the hero's quest. When coupled with a hero of the Siegfried type, the Icelandic Prima Donna tends to be particularly vengeful and destructive (as witnessed again by Brynhildr and Guðrún), and her general role is important in providing an effective contrast to the hero. When coupled with a problematic Grettir type or with a Wise Counselor, she tends to remain in the background as a loyal partner. On the mythical plane, these women have their counterparts in the valkyries and in goddesses such as Freyja or Frigg. Their literary history may be traced back to the earliest Germanic poems and legends.

The Wise Counselor is an important father figure, often a chieftain, some one with great authority in the community. In some sagas, he may be more important than any young hero, and he often takes an active part in the feuds through his counsels and cunning manipulations. He may or may not have supernatural powers, but there is always something slightly mysterious about him. On the mythical plane his equivalent is Odin himself. In the sagas, he appears in various guises: as Snorri goði in *Eyrbyggja*, Gestr Oddleifsson in *Laxdœla*, Þorsteinn Egilsson in *Gunnlaugs saga*, etc. Occasionally we learn about earlier stages of his career, when he appeared as a Young Hero, but in most cases he seems to have been born old and wise.

The Comrade-at-arms is an accomplice of the Hero who may become a hero himself, especially if his social status is high. If his social status is low he will usually play a subordinate and sometimes comic role. His main function is to provide a contrast to the Hero: he is wise if the Hero is foolish, calm and cautious if the Hero is impetuous, dark if the Hero is blond, and so forth. His role is not associated with any particular stock character, but many stock characters may appear in his role, for example, the Grettir type, the Siegfried type, the Foolish Slave, and the Loyal Servant.

The Villain's role may also be filled by a large variety of stock characters. We have already described the vengeful Prima Donna type. Other common villains are the Loki type and the Berserk type. The Loki type is a sly manipulator who makes others accomplish his shameful deeds. He rarely partakes in battle but uses slander and deceit to start feuds between former friends and allies. His cunning and legal knowledge may at times be used for a good purpose, so that his role merges with that of the Wise Counselor (note the similarities between Loki and Odin in the mythology). And he may be treated with respect by the narrator if his status is sufficiently high. If his social status is low he will be treated with contempt as an envious and despicable small-time operator (cf. *Hœnsa-Þóris saga*).

The Berserk type, on the other hand, is brutal, noisy, impetuous, and rather foolish; sometimes he is a real berserk, who bites his shield-rim, howls like a dog, and becomes invulnerable to all weapons in his berserk fits; this is most common in mythical-heroic sagas and in episodes dealing with viking travels abroad. In the feud episodes of family sagas, he is usually pictured as a mere roughneck without any supernatural powers. He is frequently characterized as *ójafnaðarmaðr* or *hávaðamaðr*, i.e., as a person wpo bullies others, makes trouble, and is impossible to get along with. Such persons bring bad luck (*ógæfa*) to the community and may become outlawed—just like the Grettir type, with whom they invite comparison.

Even further away from the community of law-abiding citizens, a hero may encounter still more frightening adversaries: the ghost, the giant, and and other supernatural ogres; the witch and sorcerer, who practice the form of black magic known as *seiðr*.

The Villain's Helper is often lower in social rank than the Villain. He may be a Foolish Slave, ugly and cowardly. He may be a thug of the Berserk type, known as an *ójafnaðarmaðr*. But he may also be an honorable young man of good family who has been tricked and goaded by a vengeful Prima Donna or by a cunning Loki type. This character is often contrasted to the Villain in much the same way as the Comrade-at-arms is contrasted to the Hero. Both of these Helper figures may often be regarded as extensions of their respective "master."

The Messenger's role is minor and unobtrusive, yet important to the plot. Messengers channel information between two combattants, two feuding families, etc. They are sometimes sent out for this specific purpose. At other times they act on their own, for example in spreading slander and dissent. The gossiping beggarwomen who tell Hallgerðr about Njáll's family (chapter 44) are examples of this type. Such beggarwomen appear in other sagas as well, but the author of *Njála* uses them particularly often. In some other sagas the Foolish Slave type serves the same function, which is evidently thought of as suited for members of the lower classes. In most cases the Messenger is not characterized at all, except perhaps as a "shepherd" or a "slave"; he is merely an instrument for the news that he brings. The narrator makes frequent use of him in scenes intended to show how events pictured in an earlier scene (at Farm A) became known to other people (at Farm B).

The Witness has a role similar to that of the Messenger in that he is important mostly because of the information he conveys. He is more passive and generally even less individualized than the Messenger. He may, for example, be a farmer who happens to observe an ominous portert and later makes his observations known to the community. In chapter 125 of *Njála* we learn of a certain Hildiglúmr who went out one night shortly before the Burning of Njáll and saw a black man with a torch riding across the sky, putting fire to the landscape. Hildiglúmr's only function in the saga is to serve as witness to this mysterious portent.

Agents of Fate are supernatural beings, such as the Black Rider, which appear before important confrontations, usually to warn about a death. Most commonly they appear in dreams or visions and carry a mysterious aura. There is a large variety of such creatures, including fetches (*fylgjur*), giants, and various kinds of beasts.

The Judge or Arbitrator, finally, plays a role similar to that of the Wise Councelor but one more neutral and less involved in the main action. He mediates between feuding parties and pronounces verdicts. When played by an individual, the man is naturally of considerable status: a king, earl, lawspeaker, or chieftain. But this role may also be played by a collective: the Allthing as a decision-making body of men, or the community at large. Although the role is rarely individualized, it is important and is functioning every time we hear that a character was "popular" or "thought to have come well out of this dealing" or "condemned by all for this deed."

Our model for analyzing roles and stock characters is naturally very schematic and it may not be suitable for *all* family sagas. Our main points, however, are that it should be suitable for analyzing *Njála* and that it can be derived from various earlier sagas as part of a traditional heritage.

It should be obvious to a reader of *Njála* that Gunnarr is a hero of the Siegfried type, Skarpheðinn is a "problematic" hero of the Grettir type, Njáll is a Wise Counselor and Hallgerðr is a Prima Donna of the Brynhildr type. Many other important characters in the saga can be classified according to our model, but this does not mean that all of them can or that the author has not individualized them to a considerable extent. A typologic classification of saga characters cannot describe them completely but it may help to show the traditional patterns more clearly. With such reservations in mind, we present the following diagram showing the roles and character types of some personalities within *Njála*:

Heroes:	*Comrades-at-arms:*
Gunnarr (Siegfried type)	Kolskeggr
Skarpheðinn (Grettir type)	Helgi, Grímr, Kári
Hrútr	
Hǫskuldr Þráinsson	
Flosi (Primarily Siegfried type)	
Kári	Bjǫrn of Mǫrk

Wise Counselors:	Heroes counselled:
Njáll (Odin type)	Gunnarr, Skarpheðinn
Síðu-Hallr	Flosi
Þórhallr Ásgrímsson	Kári

Prima Donnas:	Male partners:
Hallgerðr (Brynhildr type)	Gunnarr, Þorvaldr, Glúmr
Bergþóra (Frigg type)	Njáll
Unnr	Hrútr, Valgarðr
Hildigunnr	Hǫskuldr, Kári

Villains:	Helpers of the Villain:
Hallgerðr (Brynhildr type)	Þjóstolfr (Berserk type)
Mǫrðr (Loki type)	Otkell
Hrappr (Berserk type)	Þráinn

Messengers:	Messages delivered between:
The Beggar Women of chapter 44	Bergþórshváll and Hlíðarendi
The Shepherd of chapter 45	Skarpheðinn and Hallgerðr

Witnesses:	Observed Agents of Fate:
Hildiglúmr of chapter 125	The Black Rider
Dǫrruðr of chapter 157	The Weaving Valkyries

Judges:	Judging over:
The Allthing (as a collective body of men)	Most of the family feuds
Þorgeirr Ljósvetningagoði of chapter 105	The Conflict between Christians and pagans at the Allthing in year 1000
Skapti Þóroddsson of chapter 142	The legal dispute between Eyjólfr and Þórhallr at the Allthing after the Burning of Njáll

Some of these characters of course, appear in several roles within the saga and their personalities sometimes change as a result. An extreme example of such role-shifting is Hrútr, who is first presented as a "moderate" Siegfried type, "a handsome man, big and strong, a good warrior and well-balanced in temper, the wisest of man, tough in his dealings with his enemies but a good negotiator in large conflicts" (*Vænn maðr, mikill ok sterkr, vígr vel ok hógværr í skapi, manna vitrastr, harðráðr við óvini sína, en tillagagóðr inna stærri mála;* chapter 1). Consistent with this presentation, he appears in the Hero's role for several chapters; and he is contrasted to his brother Hǫskuldr, who is made to appear more foolish and less heroic. But later in the saga, when he is matched against Mǫrðr Fiddle and Gunnarr in the conflict over the dowry, he becomes almost a Villain of the Berserk type, bullying people by challenging them to *hólmganga*, and is justly defeated by Njáll's wise counsels (chapters 8, 21-24).

Yet it is not a question of psychological "development," for Hrútr appears in a typically heroic role as late as chapter 17 (where he defeats Þjóstólfr,

Hallgerðr's henchman). The varying situations are what force him to play varying roles. His situation is most drastically changed after the introduction of an even greater hero, Gunnarr, who was evidently pitted against him traditionally (cf. Chapter II). As long as Hrútr occupies the center of attention, he can live up to his heroic image; but when Gunnarr forces him toward the periphery, his image is transformed.

A character's role and image will shift more often the more subordinate he is to the main plot. As a matter of fact, most characters in *Njála* are not very clearly defined and can be used for different purposes in different parts of the saga. Hrútr's brother Hǫskuldr, for example, may appear somewhat foolish and naive when contrasted to Hrútr in chapter 1 (the scene with Hallgerðr's "thief's eyes"). In the very next scene, at the beginning of chapter 2, however, he appears prudent when counselling his brother about marriage. In later scenes, he is used as a somewhat reluctant accomplice of the Villain or as a mere passive witness. The roles of Gunnarr, Njáll, or Hallgerðr are much more predictable; their images are clearer and more consistent. Yet Gunnarr, for example, makes a different impression when he appears with Njáll than when he appears with Hallgerðr. In the first case, the contrast is that between a bewildered young Hero and his Wise Counselor; in the second case, the contrast is that between a wise and moderate man and an impetuous, hateful woman.

It is such contrasts, or "oppositions," which determine our view of saga characters and their world. We will here list some of the most important oppositions, which will be referred to in our later analysis of the saga. Since the various oppositions are closely related to each other, they can be presented in a system of headings and subheadings:

Honor-Dishonor
Hero-Villain
High Status - Low Status
Retaliation - Cowardly Retreat

Wisdom and Moderation - Impetuous Pursuit of Honor
Wise Counselor (Njáll) - Hero (Gunnarr, Skarpheðinn)
Sigfried type (Gunnarr) - Grettir type (Skarpheðinn)
Leading Man (Gunnarr) - Leading Woman (Hallgerðr)

Security - Danger
The Family - The World Outside
Life on the Farm - Viking Travels Abroad
Settlement - Revenge
Wise Counselors - Agents of Fate
Heroes - Villains
Prosperous Community - Outlawry
Good Luck - Bad Luck

The Law - Lawbreakers
Natural World - Supernatural World

High Status - Low Status
King - Icelandic Traveler
Chieftain - Small Landholder
Farmer - Slave (etc.)

Good Luck - Bad Luck
Siegfried type - Grettir type
Hero - Villain
Prosperous Community - Outlawry
Honor - Dishonor
Retaliation - Cowardly Retreat
Victory - Defeat

Cunning - Foolishness
Wise Counselor - Grettir type
Loki type - Berserk type
Good Luck - Bad Luck

Such categories could be multiplied almost indefinitely. But these should serve at least as our general introduction to the traditional literary world of *Njála*.

4. ACTION PATTERNS

The action patterns within a saga plot both determine and are determined by the saga "world." They are also dependent on the stock scenes and other traditional building blocks of saga composition (cf. above, p. 53). We may nevertheless study these action patterns in isolation, for the same action pattern may be filled with many different combinations of motifs, stock scenes, stock characters, etc.[20]

Njála may be said to contain a succession of more or less traditional action patterns woven into a large system. These patterns must be analyzed before we can judge the system as a whole.

There are two basic types of action patterns, both of which are repeated several times within *Njála* and are also found in many other sagas. The first of these, which corresponds to Theodore Andersson's six-point scheme,[21]

20. Concerning action patterns in traditional narrative, see Vladimir Propp, *Morphology of the Folktale*, translated by Laurence Scott, revised by Louis A. Wagner, 2nd edition (Austin, Texas and London, 1968). The latest Russian edition, *Morfologiya skazki* (Moscow, 1969), contains an excellent appendix by Professor E. M. Meletinsky, surveying the international discussion about Propp's structuralism.

21. Andersson (1967), 3-30, 291-306; Andersson appears to have reached his conclusions about saga structure without being influenced by Propp, but their approaches are similar.

I shall call the Feud Pattern. The second, which is somewhat less important, I shall call the Travel Pattern.[22]

The Feud Pattern

The Feud Pattern emerges from a previous state of balance in the relationship between two families. A cause for conflict is presented, and the feud breaks out as members of one family commit a punitive act against members of another family. This first punitive act consist of a lawsuit or a physical assault. Attempts may be made to settle the conflict, but the feud usually escalates by means of increasingly serious acts of revenge from both sides until there is a major confrontation, the climax of the episode. This climax may be followed by new revenge acts, but eventually a final settlement restores the peace and balance between the two feuding parties. Hostilities may break out again later, but only with a new cause for conflict, usually involving some new character or characters.

It is difficult to predict how long a feud will last or how many separate acts of revenge it will contain. It is also difficult to predict which acts will be discribed in dramatic detail (thus constituting the "climax") and which will be merely summarized. As a rule, however, the climax of a short feud comes near the end, while it is closer to the middle of a very long feud story, where it is always followed by more acts of revenge, some of which may be almost as dramatic as the climax. In view of these considerations, this modified version of Theodore Andersson's six-point scheme may be found useful:

1. Introduction.
2. Cause for Conflict (Balance disturbed).
3. First punitive act plus X-number of revenge acts leading up to:
4. Climax (The Major Confrontation).
5. More revenge acts (optional).
6. Final settlement (Balance restored).

Defined in this way, the Feud Pattern appears once within each of the following *Njála* episodes or episode clusters:

I:I plus II:1A The feud over Unnr's dowry.
II:2 The feud between Hallgerðr and Bergþóra.
II:3 Gunnarr's feud with Otkell.

---

22. See Joseph C. Harris, "Genre and Narrative Structure in Some *Islendinga Þættir*," *Scandinavian Studies*, 44 (1972); Harris, who refers to Propp, Andersson, and other modern structualists, has confined his study to short, semi-independent stories, found in the *Konunga sǫgur*, about Icelanders visiting the Norwegian court. In my own analysis of travel episodes in *Njála* I have used Harris' structural scheme with some minor modifications.

II:4 Gunnarr's feud with Starkaðr and Egill.

II:5-6 Gunnarr's feud with the two Þorgeirrs followed by G's banishment
and death and the revenge taken for him.

II:7 Þráinn's feud with the sons of Njáll.

III:2-6 The feud after the murder of Hǫskuldr Þráinsson.[23]

Each feud may be analyzed as a kind of game, in which each act of retaliation (lawsuit, ambush, etc.) represents a "move."[24] For each such move,
one of the two feüding parties "gains points." For example, if Family A
kills a slave belonging to Family B, this represents a moderate gain for Family A and a corresponding loss for Family B. The balance may be restored
if Family A agrees to pay an appropriate sum of money to Family B. It
may also be restored if Family B kills a slave belonging to Family A. But
B may also gain more than it lost by killing a higher ranking member of
A, by forcing A to pay an unreasonably large sum of money in compensation,
or by making some other move to deprive Family A of honor, lives, or property.

The game ends not with a victory for either side but with the restoration
of balance. Before that happens, however, one of the two families will have
made an unusually drastic move which results in an *almost* complete victory

23. According to Theodore M. Andersson (1967), 291-307, the Feud Pattern appears
only twice in *Njála*: 1. chapters 1-81, and 2. chapters 82-159. The episodic nature of
chapters 1-81 ("Prologue" plus "Gunnarr's Saga") has been demonstrated above, in our
Chapter II; it is also in general accordance with Bååth's analysis, which is more careful
than Andersson's on this point. My interpretation of II: 5-6 and III: 2-6 as separate
feuds is more debatable, but it may be supported by the following arguments: 1) Chapter
66, which I regard as the conclusion of the Starkaðr/Egill episode, ends with almost
exactly the same phrases as chapter 56, which is clearly the end of the Otkell episode.
Cf. "Reið Gunnarr heim af þingi . . . ok fekk af ina mestu sæmð. Sitr nú heima í sæmð
sinni" (56). "Reið Gunnarr heim af þingi ok sitr nú kyrrt; en þó ǫfunduðu mótstǫðumenn
hans mjǫk hans sæmð" (66). In both cases, the following chapter makes a "new start" at a
later time, presenting new characters as main protagonists, even though it must be admitted
that there is more continuity between chapters 66 and 67 than between chapters 56 and
57. 2) Chapter 99, which I regard as the conclusion of the Þráinn episode and of the entire
"Gunnarr's saga" (cf. above, Chapter II), ends with the following words about the settlement between Þráinn's kinsmen and the sons of Njáll: "Nú er at segja fra því, at þessi
sætt helzk með þeim," indicating that a complete reconciliation has taken place. When
the hostilities start again, several years later, this is clearly a new feud. My analysis of
the chapter divisions (ANF 90, 1975) and the plot structure (Chapter II) also shows
that there is a very important break in the narrative structure between Chapters 99 and
100. 3) The Battle of Knafahólar (chapters 61-63) and the Death of Þráinn (chapter 92)
are both built up as major events, each constituting the climax of a previous conflict.
They would lose this status if they were regarded merely as preludes to the Death of
Gunnarr and the Burning of Njáll, respectively.

24. For this analogue I am indebted to Carol Clover.

and which constitutes the climax. The more serious this move is for the losing party, the more difficult it is to achieve a final settlement. The Burning of Njáll and his household thus requires a series of acts of revenge before the balance can be restored.

The Travel Pattern

The Travel Pattern appears in *Njála* as a digressive strand within or between feud episodes. Unlike the Feud Pattern, the Travel Pattern centers on the adventures of one hero (or one unified group of heroes). The hero leaves Iceland to win fame and is presented at the Norwegian Court, where he is honored by the King or the earl. His valor is tested at this visit and/or in encounters with vikings of the Berserk type, and he finally passes all heroic tests and returns safely and with honor to Iceland. Such a Travel Pattern appears four times in *Njála*:[25]

Chapters 2-6. Hrútr's travels; part of feud episode I:1.
Chapters 29-32. Gunnarr's travels episode II:1B; interlude between feud episodes II:1A and II:2.
Chapters 75, 82, 88. Þráinn's travels, presented in portions, episodes II:6 and II:7.
Chapters 75, 83-86, 89-90. The travels of Helgi and Grímr Njálsson, presented in portions, episodes II:6 and II:7.

Schematically, the Travel Pattern in *Njála* may be represented as follows:

1. Departure (*Útanferð*).
2. A series of tests, including court visit and viking adventures.
3. Homecoming (*Útkoma*).

Filling the Pattern: Gunnarr's Travels

Let us next see how both the Feud Pattern and the Travel Pattern are filled out with stock characters, stock scenes, and other traditional elements. Because much of this standard material has already been catalogued by Kersbergen and other authors, our main task will be to see how it functions in the structure.

We shall begin with the Travel Pattern, which is easier to analyze, and take as our example the episode of Gunnarr's travels abroad. This episode begins in chapter 28 with the arrival in Iceland of Hallvarðr hvíti, a Norwegian who asks Gunnarr to go with him on his ship to foreign countries; but Gunnarr does not want to answer (end of first narrative segment). Gunnarr then visits Njáll and asks his advice; Njáll consents to take care of

---

25. Other examples in Kersbergen (1927), ch. V ("Motieven uit het leven in het buitenland").

his friend's property if he goes abroad (end of second narrative segment). In the next scene, the Norwegian again asks Gunnarr to come with him, and Gunnarr consents (end of third narrative segment). Here the chapter ends with the expectation that Gunnarr definitely will go; Hallvarðr's mission has succeeded.

As Kersbergen has shown,[26] there are close parallels to this chapter in *Finnboga saga*, *Víga-Glúms saga*, *Ljósvetninga saga*, and *Bjarnar saga Hitdœlakappa*. The Norwegian visitor is a stock character used to motivate the hero's departure (he functions partly as a Messenger, partly as a Comrade-at-arms); the hero's consultation with a Wise Counselor before leaving is traditional; the concern about property is a stereotyped motif which appears also in the story of Hrútr's *útanferð*. In other sagas we find different ingredients at this stage: for example, the hero is eager to go but his father will not let him (*Gunnlaugs saga*, *Grettis saga*); before leaving, he obtains an old family weapon (*Grettis saga*; several mythical-heroic sagas); he is not *persuaded* by a Norwegian to go but rather *persuades* some Norwegian to take him with him. In some cases he has a particular reason to leave: for example, he wants to visit his kinsmen in Norway in order to collect an inheritance (Hrútr, Egill Skalla-Grímsson, and others). All of these elements are common variables with one invariable function: to motivate the Hero's *útanferð*.

In the next chapter (29), Gunnarr and his brother Kolskeggr arrive in Norway as passengers on Hallvarðr's ship (first narrative segment). Here the narrator inserts a standard presentation of the Norwegian ruler, in this case Earl Hákon (second narrative segment). Next is a stock scene in which Hallvarðr suggests to Gunnarr that he go to visit the earl; but Gunnarr does not yet feel worthy of such a visit because he has not proved his heroic valor (third narrative segment).

This sequence is very typical for the beginning of the second stage, in which the Hero is to be tested. Compare the following sequences of travel episodes from two other sagas and from chapter 2 of *Njála*:

A. *Gunnlaugs saga, chapters 5-6*: 1) Gunnlaugr arrives in Norway on Auðunn's ship. 2) Presentation of the Norwegian ruler, Earl Eiríkr. 3) Gunnlaugr goes with Auðunn to see the earl.

B. *Víga-Glúms saga, chapter 2*: 1) Glúmr arrives in Norway on Hreiðarr's ship. 2) Hreiðarr suggests a visit to the Norwegian ruler, King Hákon (who is now presented), but Glúmr does not yet feel that he is worthy of such a visit.

---

26. Kersbergen (1927), 119.

C. *Njála*, *chapter 2*: 1) Hrútr arrives in Norway on Qzzurr's ship. 2) Presentation of the Norwegian ruler, King Haraldr. 3) Queen Gunnhildr sends out a servant to invite Hrútr to the court. 4) Qzzurr advises Hrútr to go.

Each segment may of course be more or less expanded and more or less formulaic, and the sequence may be made longer or shorter through the addition or omission of a segment. (Note that the "presentation segment" is missing from the *Glúma* sequence, while the Hrútr sequence has a new segment in Queen Gunnhildr's invitation to the hero). But the basic structure remains the same.

We may next expect a presentation at the court. But Gunnarr first goes out on his obligatory viking expedition, which takes up the rest of chapters 29, 30, and 31. The expedition is conveyed in stock scenes in which Gunnarr and Kolskeggr fight two pairs of viking brothers (Berserk types). Kersbergen has found a wealth of parallels in other family sagas and in mythical-heroic sagas.[27]

The first viking pair is presented in a dialogue between two of Gunnrar's companions, Hallvarðr and Qlvir:

... "hefi ek spurt, at ófriðr er kominn í ána; ok veit ek eigi, hvárt þit komizk í braut." "Hverir eru þar komnir?" segir Hallvarðr. "Brœðr tveir," segir Olvir; "heitir annarr Vandill, en annarr Karl, synir Snæúlfs ins gamla ór Gautlandi austan." (pp. 76-77)
("I have heard that trouble has come to the river, and I don't know if you can get away." "Who has come?" said Hallvarðr. "Two brothers," said Qlvir, "one is called Vandill, the other Karl, sons of Snæúlfr the Old from the East, in Gautland.")

The second viking pair is similarly presented in a dialogue between Gunnarr and Tófi:

... "herskip liggja hér qðrum megin undir nesinu, ok mun ek segja þér, hverir fyrir ráða. Þar ráða fyrir brœdr tveir; heitir annarr Hallgrímr, en annarr Kolskeggr. Þá veit ek mesta orrostumenn." (pp. 79-80)
("There are battleships lying on the other side of the ness, and I will tell you under whose command they are. Two brothers command them; one is called Hallgrímr, the other Kolskeggr. I know them both to be fierce fighters.")

Both encounters follow the same pattern: Gunnarr and his men catch sight of the ships; they are attacked, and a stereotyped shipboard fight follows, ending with the hero's victory.

After having passed his tests and gained *fé ok frami* ("property and honor"), Gunnarr makes his obligatory court visit. He first visits King Haraldr

---

27. Kersbergen (1927), 143-145; cf. Sveinsson (1933), 149.

Gormsson of Denmark, who *tók við honum vel ok setti hann it næsta sér* ("received him well and placed him next to his High Seat") and comments: *"Svá virðisk mér sem óviða muni þinn jafningi fásk"* ("It seems to me that your equal will not be found easily"). Such phrases belong to the stock scene of "a hero's presentation at the court," and some motifs introduced here are equally conventional: the hero asserts himself in contests against the King's men; in appreciation of his valor, the King offers him valuable gifts. The same general pattern is repeated when Gunnarr returns to Norway and visits Earl Hákon. In this second visit, there is another common motif: the hero has a romance with one of the noblest ladies at the court—Bergljót, Earl Hákon's kinswoman (cf. Hrútr and Queen Gunnhildr; Kjartan and In-gibjǫrg in *Laxdœla*).[28]

At the beginning of chapter 32 comes Gunnarr's *útkoma* to Iceland. After two viking adventures and two honorable court visits, Gunnarr has passed through his initiation stage and is now a hero of the first rank. The departure from Earl Hákon forms the subject of another stock scene, in which the earl gives the hero provisions for his journey. After the journey itself is described in a few factual words, his homecoming is concluded with the following symptomatic remark: *Þeir váru blíðir við heimamenn sína, ok hafði ekki vaxit dramb þeira* ("They"—Gunnarr and Kolskeggr—"were friendly to their people at home, and they had not become more conceited").

With this final comment (which is more typical of the *Njála* author than of saga tradition in general) the Travel Pattern has run its course. But the episode is not yet over, for the homecoming immediately leads to Gunnarr's wooing of Hallgerðr and their subsequent marriage (chapters 32-34). This transition is also traditional, for the homecoming is frequently the beginning of various erotic complications: the hero either marries a woman who has been waiting for him, or arrives just in time to see somebody else marry her (cf. Hrútr and Unnr in *Njála*, Gunnlaugr and Helga in *Gunnlaugs saga*, Kjartan and Guðrún in *Laxdœla*, etc.).[29] Disregarding such continuation, and concentrating on the actual travel story we may use the following scheme to represent its structure:

1. *Útanferð*   Hero at home with his people.
                                 Norwegian visitor makes an offer.
                                 Wise Counselor advises Hero to go.
                                 Hero goes to Norway.

28. Cf. Kersbergen (1927), 120-128.

29. This pattern has been discussed by Bjarni Einarsson in *Skáldasögur* (Reykjavík, 1961) and by Thomas Bredsdorff, *Kaos og kærlighed* (Haslev, 1971).

2. *"Tests"*	He rejects offer of court visit.
1st Viking Adventure	He defeats two Berserk types.
2nd Viking Adventure	He defeats two Berserk types.
1st Court Visit	He is honored, receives gifts.
2nd Court Visit	He is honored, receives gifts, possibility of noble marriage.
3. *Útkoma*	He takes leave of his benefactor. He returns to his people.

Although this structure may be varied slightly and contains many different motifs, it is still representative of the Travel Pattern in several sagas. To what extent may the pattern be said to conform to social realities and to what extent is it "purely literary"?

Many young Icelanders must, of course, have travelled to Norway, both in the Saga Age and in the Sturlung Age. In particular members of leading chieftain families evidently visited the Norwegian and the Danish courts, where they sometimes were honored by the kings. In the early days, some of them must have taken part in viking expeditions and fought sea battles against other vikings—exploits they probably described to their families. To this extent, the Travel Pattern may be said to conform to history.

Yet there is not much "realism" in Gunnarr's travel adventures (or, for that matter, in Hrútr's or Gunnlaugr's). Almost everything is stylized and "typical": the Hero's valor, the King's generosity and admiration, the brutal belligerence of the viking adversaries, the marvelous battle feats, and so on. There would have been very few surprises to an Icelandic audience; the enjoyment of such a story probably came in recognizing a well-known narrative structure and in measuring this particular hero against the many other heroes who passed similar tests. Each listener would have in mind both the Travel Pattern and a number of traditional ideas of life abroad. A storyteller could count on this and thus would not have to spell out matters in detail—a few hints would be enough.

Thus it is never explicitly said that Gunnarr's initial refusal to visit Earl Hákon is motivated by his desire to win fame as a viking before he is presented at the court. But this can be safely assumed from the context and from parallels in other sagas.[30] And even though his adversaries in the sea battles are never explicitly characterized, any one accustomed to saga style would immediately recognize them as foul villains of the Berserk type. A thirteenth-century audience may well have regarded Gunnarr's battles with them as

---

30. Cf. Sveinsson's footnote in *Njála* (1954), 75. There is a good parallel in *Víga-Glúms saga*, chapter 2, where Glúmr declares that he does not want to visit the king ("Vanfærr em ek at fylgja konungum").

historical facts; if so, history itself must have been determined by literary conventions.

Filling the Pattern: Feud Openings

Compared with the Travel Pattern, the Feud Pattern is more complex and has more variables. This is why feud episodes generally seem more realistic than travel episodes. It is also natural that the feuds seem more real because their setting is "closer to home"; the feud actions generally take place in Iceland, within the "inner circles" of the saga world. Yet one may still distinguish some general principles for the introduction of stock characters and stock scenes in feud patterns.

Feud episodes vary most in their second stage, i.e., the Cause for Conflict. The nature of the cause largely determines the nature of the whole feud, i.e., what kind of characters and scenes will appear in it. We therefore shall first study the causes.

In a sense, there are many causes for each feud, but usually one particular incident is presented as the *upphaf* or "origin".[31] Usually, one character is presented as chiefly responsible for the strife, even though other characters may share the responsibility. This character will be called the Instigator or *Upphafsmaðr* (note the Old Norse saying: *Sá veldr mestu er upphafinu veldr*: "That person is most responsible who is responsible for the beginning," i.e., the beginning of a feud or a quarrel). In *Njáls saga*, there are four main types of Instigators, all traditional villains in saga literature: the destructive Prima Donna, the cunning Loki type, the impetuous Berserk type or *hávaða-maðr*, and (in one case) the ungenerous miser. At least one of these types appears at the beginning of each feud episode; several of them may appear later.

The causes for conflict in the seven major feuds of *Njála* may be summarized as follows:

1. *The feud over Unnr's dowry*: After having been betrothed to Unnr, Hrútr goes abroad and is seduced by Queen Gunnhildr, who puts a spell on him so that later he cannot consummate his marriage. Result: Unnr divorces Hrútr and claims her dowry back (feud starts). Instigator: Gunnhildr (Destructive Prima Donna).

2. *The feud between Hallgerðr and Bergþóra*: Hallgerðr feels dishonored by Bergþóra's seating arrangements at a feast, and a quarrel begins between

---

31. On causality in *Njála*, cf. Sveinsson (1943), 40; (1970), 54-55; also, Clover, *op. cit.* What we have called "Cause for Conflict" corresponds to the term "Veranlassung" in Richard Heinzel (1880), 34-36. I have found Heinzel's listing of such "Veranlassungen" extremely useful. Some of them are also discussed by Andersscn (1967), 12-16 (here they are termed "irritants").

the two women. Result: Hallgerðr sends a slave to kill one of Bergþóra's slaves (feud starts). Instigator: Hallgerðr (Destructive Prima Donna).

3. *Gunnarr's feud with Otkell*: During a famine, Otkell refuses to sell hay and other provisions to Gunnarr, even though he is offered an excellent bargain. Result: Hallgerðr sends a slave to steal from Otkell (feud starts). First Instigator: Otkell (Ungenerous Miser). Second Instigator: Hallgerðr (Destructive Prima Donna).

4. *Gunnarr's feud with Starkaðr and Egill*: At a horse-match (*hestavíg*), the sons of Starkaðr and Egill run berserk and attack Gunnar and his horse against the rules. Result: Gunnarr strikes one of them unconscious (feud starts). Instigators: the sons of Starkaðr and Egill (Impetuous *Há-vaðamenn*).

5. *Gunnarr's feud with the two Þorgeirrs*: Þorgeirr Starkaðarson, not content with the outcome of the previous feud, is advised by Mǫrðr to involve Gunnarr in a feud with Þorgeirr Otkelsson, whose death will inevitably lead to Gunnarr's downfall. Result: everything happens as planned by Mǫrðr. Instigator: Mǫrðr (Loki type), in cooperation with Þorgeirr Starkaðarson (*Hávaðamaðr*).

6. *Þráinn's feud with the sons of Njáll*: During his stay in Norway, Þráinn hides a fugitive killer, Víga-Hrappr, from Earl Hákon and later brings him to Iceland under his protection. Earl Hákon punishes the sons of Njáll for Hrapp's escape because of their association with Þráinn. Result: the sons of Njáll demand compensation from Þráinn but receive only insults from Hrappr and his new mistress, Hallgerðr. Instigator: Hrappr (*Hávaða-maðr*), assisted by Þráinn and Hallgerðr.

7. *The major final feud*: Mǫrðr makes the sons of Njáll believe that Hǫskuldr Þráinnsson is plotting against their lives. Result: they kill Hǫskudr, even though Njáll had advised them not to believe Mǫrðr. Instigator: Mǫrðr (Loki type), assisted by the sons of Njáll.

All of these feud openings have analogues in other sagas. Some of them, such as the horse-match leading to Gunnarr's feud with Starkaðr and Egill, have so many close parallels elsewhere that they may be regarded as stereotyped motifs.[32] Other openings, such as the refused hay bargain at the beginning of the Otkell episode, have at least one very close analogue in sagas earlier than *Njála*.[33] In each of the feud episodes, the author's exposition

---

32. For parallels and analogues see in particular Kersbergen (1927), 73-74, 87-88, 96, 120-26; Heinzel (1880), 34-36.

33. On the refused hay-bargain, see Kersbergen (1927), 72-73; Sveinsson (1933), 140-141. Kersbergen, Sveinsson, and other scholars have drawn the conclusion that the author of *Njála* borrowed the motif from *Hænsa-Þóris saga*. This is possible but by no means certain; cf. our Appendix.

thus appears to be ruled by convention, and in most cases the further development of action is determined by the author's choice of conventional opening, just as a chessplayer's game is determined by his initial choice of "Queen's Gambit" rather than a "Sicilian" or "French" opening.

The analogy with chessplaying may also help to explain the author's use of stock characters to develop the plot once the feud has started. If, for example, he makes much use of his Wise Counselors, we may expect the feud to be largely a battle of wits fought with lawsuits at the Allthing, with various clever manipulations. If, on the other hand, he makes use of young militant Heroes, impetuous *Hávaðamenn*, and vengeful Prima Donnas, we may expect the feud to be violent and bloody. The scene of action will be a battlefield rather than a court of law. Most saga feuds contain both types of punitive actions, but the proportions may vary considerably. It would be extremely complicated, perhaps impossible, to formulate exact rules for the combination of court scenes, battle scenes, goading scenes, and so on, in various types of feud stories within *Njála* and other sagas.

Filling the Pattern; A Feud Reaches Climax

This holds true particularly of the early stages of the feud. The closer we come to its climax, or "endgame," the easier it is to predict what motifs will appear and in what order. As Theodore Andersson has shown, the climax almost invariably is a major battle in which at least one major character is killed. This battle is preceded by omens and warnings to the characters who will soon die. There is often a goading scene as the attacking warriors leave their home. The most important character who is about to die normally belongs to the side which is attacked and the narrator normally focuses his attention on him as the attackers are on their way. The scene then shifts between victim and attackers before the battle begins. During the battle, which is described blow by blow, there is a good deal of heroic posturing, with memorable "last words" uttered by the dying warriors. After the battle, there is sometimes a "necrology," a brief eulogizing comment on the main victim's death. Finally, the warriors return home and report to their kinsmen.[34]

As an example we may take the story of Þráinn's death, the climax of his feud with the sons of Njáll. The story is full of well-known motifs arranged in predictable sequences. Beginning in chapter 92, it consists of the following narrative segments:

---

34. Cf. Andersson (1967), 16-18, 49-64. For a more detailed analysis of scenic patterning in such climactic accounts. see Clover (1972).

1. *Victim leaves home.* Runólfr í Dal invites Þráinn to his farm. Þráinn leaves home with his men. On their way they help some beggar women over Markarfljótr River.

    (Cf. Runólfr's invitation to Otkell before the First Rangár Battle, chapters 52-53; Ásgrímr's invitation to Gunnarr before the Battle of Knafahólar, chapter 60. Another parallel in *Laxdœla*, chapter 47: Kjartan leaves home, meets Þorhalla málga, a "messenger role" corresponding to the beggar women in *Njála*.)

2. *First scene of warning and foreshadowing.* They arrive and stay with Runólfr for two days. Þráinn is advised by his host to make peace with the sons of Njáll, but Þráinn refuses. Runólfr then predicts that Þráinn will die.

    (Cf. Runólfr's warning to Otkell at the end of chapter 53.)

3. *Second scene of warning and foreshadowing.* Þráinn leaves Runólfr, stays with Ketill ór Mǫrk for two days, then returns to Runólfr and announces his intention to ride home the same day. Runólfr advises him not to go because there may be dangers on his way, but Þráinn does not want to be a coward.

    (Cf. Kolskeggr's warning to Gunnarr at the end of chapter 60 and Ásgrímr's warning at the beginning of chapter 61; parallels from several other sagas have been collected by Kersbergen, p. 75. Also: *Laxdœla*, chapter 48 (Death of Kjartan).)

4. *New chapter: the attackers are informed and goaded.* The beggar women arrive at Bergþórshváll and inform Bergþóra about Þráinn's ride. She has a secret conversation with her sons.

    (Cf. the beggar women who act as informers before Sigmundr's death, chapter 44; the shepherd playing the same role before the First Rangár Battle, beginning of chapter 54. Þórhalla málga in the same role before the death of Kjartan, *Laxdœla*, chapter 47. Parallels from other sagas listed by Kersbergen, pp. 68-70.)

5. *The attackers leave home.* Njáll wakes up on the morning that Þráinn is preparing to ride home. He has heard a noise from Skarpheðinn's axe and he now finds his sons fully armed. They tell their father that they are going out to look for some sheep. Njáll reminds them that they have said this before when they planned to kill people. The sons leave and place themselves where they can see Þráinn and his men leave Runólfr.

    (Cf. the parallel scene before the slaying of Sigmundr, chapter 44: the conversation between Gunnarr and his mother before the First Rangár Battle, chapter 54. The sheep searching motif: cf. *Droplaugarsona saga*, chapter 3. Kersbergen, pp. 74-75.)

6. *Sceneshift: the Victim's last moments.* Þráinn and his men begin their ride home. They see shields gleaming in the sun and change their route, proceeding towards the river.

   (Cf. the sceneshifting before the Burning of Njáll, chapters 127-129. The Discovered Ambush Motif appears at the Battle of Knafahólar, chapter 62, where Kolskeggr sees the spears of the enemy. Another parallel is *Laxdœla*, chapter 49 (Death of Kjartan).)

7. *New sceneshift: the attackers approach the victim.* The sons of Njáll understand that their ambush has been spotted. They rush down to the other side of the river.

   (Cf. the sceneshifting in chapters 127-129 and in several others sagas, e.g., *Laxdœla*. chapters 48-49, *Heiðarvíga*, chapter 25-27.)

8. *New sceneshift: the victim's last moments.* Þráinn and his men stop and discuss what the sons of Njáll may have in mind. Þráinn takes off his cape and helmet.

   (Cf. the parallels mentioned above and other examples of scene-shifting in Theodore Andersson's *The Icelandic Family Saga*, pp. 57-60.)

9. *The Attack, Battle, Fall of Victim.* Skarpheðinn's shoe-buckle bursts and he is left behind his brothers. After he has tied his shoe, he runs past all the others, leaps over the river, glides on the ice, and buries his axe in Þráinn's head, no longer covered by the helmet. There is a major battle in which both Þráinn and Hrappr are killed. As Helgi cuts off Hrappr's arm, Hrappr congratulates him on having destroyed an arm that has brought death to many men. After their victory, the sons of Njáll grant safe conduct to the surviving members of Þráinn's party.

   (The shoe motif: Kersbergen, pp. 76-77. The frozen river: Kersbergen, p. 77. Battle motifs and battle formulas: Kersbergen, pp. 75-76. Hrappr's "last words": cf. Andersson, pp. 62-64, on "posturing".)

10. *Homecoming of the attackers.* The sons of Njáll return home to their father, who predicts that this will lead to the death of one of his sons (Hǫskuldr Njálsson, as it later turns out).

    (Cf. Njáll's reaction after the killing of Hǫskuldr Þráinsson, chapter 111. Predictions of this kind are, of course, common in the sagas.)

11. *Homecoming of the victim.* Þráinn's dead body is brought home and buried in a mound.

    (A very common ending throughout Germanic tradition; cf. *Beowulf* and numerous mythical-heroic sagas, as well as the classical family sagas.)

As indicated by the parallels, each segment consists of elements that had been used in earlier sagas. The arrangement of the segments is also largely conventional: victim leaves home; victim is warned; the sceneshifts to the attackers as a new chapter is started; attackers leave home; sceneshifts back to the victim, and so on. At this particular point, the Feud Pattern appears as predictable as the Travel Pattern in the episode of Gunnarr's adventures abroad. Understandably, the death of Þráinn has some of its closest parallels in other chapters that form the climax of feud episodes within *Njála* itself: chapters 44-45 (death of Sigmundr and Skjǫldr; climax of the episode of the feud between Hallgerðr and Bergþóra); chapters 53-54 (death of Otkell; climax of the Otkell episode); chapters 60-63 (death of Hjǫrtr, Gunnarr's younger brother; climax of the Starkaðr/Egill episode); chapters 76-77 (death of Gunnarr; climax of "Gunnarr's saga"); chapters 123-132 (Burning of Njáll; climax of the last major feud and of *Njála* as a whole). Some of the parallels (e.g., the sheep-searching motif as the attackers leave home before the death of Þráinn and before the death of Sigmundr and Skjǫldr) were clearly intended by the author, but many of them must have resulted from his unconscious habits of composition, formed by listenening to sagas and then applying what he learned in his own creative work. There are, as we shall see, individual touches among these habits, but most of them have been adopted from earlier Icelandic storytellers.

Conclusion

It would certainly be possible to explore the Feud Pattern's various stock motifs in further detail—for example, by studying the methods used to introduce the feuding parties, escalate the feud before the climax, and prepare the final settlement. But what we have said should suffice to show the basic pattern and emphasize the fact that the traditional motifs, catalogued by Kersbergen and others, must be related to this pattern before their significance can be understood. Motifs in *Njála* are not just "borrowed" individually from various sources; they are adopted as parts of a general structural heritage which determined what kind of events the author could present and in what order he could present them.

In our analyses of the Feud Pattern and the Travel Pattern, we have chosen to follow Propp in regarding the individual motifs as variables used to fill the constant structural functions (or "slots") within each pattern. But there is no great difference in frequency between some variables and the constant factors, in spite of the fact that a feud episode clearly needs a cause for conflict (constant factor) even more than it needs fights or foreshadowings (variable motifs). In actual saga practice, several motifs—battles, dreams, ect.—are frequent enough to be considered inherent in traditional action patterns. And the patterns may even be said to "carry with them," as a potential, less frequent motifs which, although they may appear in only a few sagas, have a set function within the structure as soon as they do appear (e.g., the gossipy beggar women acting as messengers in several feud episodes).

But the action patterns were connected not only with particular sets of traditional motifs, stock characters, stock scenes, etc. but also with a particular type of rhetoric used to manipulate audience reactions. This will be our next subject.

5. RHETORIC

The classical sagas, especially the "family sagas," are generally regarded as the very opposite of anything homiletic, rhetorical, or moralistic. They stand out as the ultimate examples of "objective" narrative, where events are calmly presented as they were seen and heard by reliable men, without any value judgment or comment by the narrator. The reader can easily assume that there is no message or moral at all, simply a story to be told.[35]

Yet each saga also manages to convey the idea that certain ethical norms exist, against which both characters and actions can be measured. Critics have no difficulty identifying heroes and villains in terms of values implied in the sagas themselves.[36] Our impression of "objectivity," then, must at least in part be illusory. If we look more closely at the narrative technique inherent in the action patterns and structural components, we discover a variety of traditional devices whereby the narrator leads us to accept his point of view.

Before making this study, we may consider briefly some meanings of "objectivity" when applied to narrative. Wayne Booth, who has discussed this problem in *The Rhetoric of Fiction*,[37] distinguishes three kinds of ob-

---

35. The "objectivity" of the sagas is stressed by most critics, e.g. Hallberg (1962) and Andersson (1967). My own analysis of saga rhetoric started out as a reaction against Andersson's views (cf. my review in *Speculum*, 43, 1968, 115-119) and was then presented as a separate article, "Rhetorical Persuasion in the Sagas," *Scandinavian Studies*, 42 (1970), 157-189. The section on rhetoric in the present book is a revised version of this article. Later, Andersson modified his views in "The Displacement of the Heroic Ideal in the Family Sagas," *Speculum*, 45 (1970), 575-593. And my own views were supported by Richard Allen (1971) in his chapter on "The Rhetoric of *Njáls saga*," 95-127.

36. The classical work on the ethical norms of the saga is still Grønbech's *The Culture of the Teutons* (London and Copenhagen, 1931). More recent works include M. C. Van den Toorn, *Ethics and Moral in Icelandic Saga Literature* (Assen, 1955), and Hermann Pálsson, *Siðfræði Hrafnkels sögu* (Reykjavík, 1967).

37. (Chicago, 1961). My general indebtedness to Booth should be obvious enough, even without specific references.

jectivity: "neutrality," "impartiality," and "impassibilité." These terms may be borrowed for our purpose. "Neutrality" describes an uncommitted attitude, possible only in a purely scientific work; it can hardly be used in even the most factual narrative, for the very selection of facts and the emphasis put upon them implies a certain amount of commitment. "Impartiality," on the other hand, means giving a fair and equal hearing to all participants in the presentation of a dispute or conflict, even though the narrator may be committed to one side or person. "Impassibilité," finally, means an emotional restraint in the narrator's treatment of his subject matter; it is primarily this quality, rather than actual neutrality or impartiality, which makes a story appear "cool" and "detached." The most insidious kind of propaganda often seems "objective" in this sense, although it is clearly neither neutral nor impartial.

These definitions may differ slightly from Booth's but are sufficient for our purpose. Tc these should be added a fourth kind of objectivity which might be called "empiricism" and which is generally acknowledged to be of special importance in the sagas. "Empiricism" describes facts in the manner in which they were observed and separates such observed facts from the conclusions that may be drawn from them. It is the kind of description, in short, that we expect from a good witness in a criminal case. In a fictional narrative, there is an impression of empiricism (and hence credibility) when the narrator presents scenes and situations directly—without speaking *about* them or interpreting their significance. The impression of empiricism is even greater when the narrator also refers to specific witnesses or when he claims to be ignorant of facts for a lack of witnesses. This quality, however, also may be found in works which are in fact meant to influence our values and emotions.

When impartiality, impassibilité, and empiricism all appear in a text, it contains a maximum of "formal" objectivity. Most saga critics would probably agree that this is the kind of objectivity found in the sagas. They would not insist that sagas are "neutral" or uncommitted to any cause or value. They also would probably agree that all sagas contain elements of rhetorical persuasion, if we mean thereby any technique or device of narrative which tends to control audience reactions.

Such techniques are not necessarily conscious ones. The Icelandic saga-writers and storytellers may have felt that they were "just telling a story," even when they were in fact manipulating the sympathies of their audience. Insofar as their stories were based on a long tradition, it would be quite natural for them to be unconscious of expressing any personal bias. And in some cases their personal values may actually have differed from those expressed in their stories. For example, as Christians they may have disapproved of certain pagan heroes, but tradition required them to picture these heroes favorably.

Because of this possible dichotomy between the ethics of the author and the ethics of his saga, we shall regard the "narrator," not the "author," as responsible for the rhetorical persuasion exerted by the saga text. "Narrator" refers not to an historical person (like the author of *Njála*) but to a fictitious "will behind the stage." Such a narrator may be the product of several "authors" or storytellers who have related a saga over several generations.

The rhetorical techniques in *Njála* differ in different sections of the narrative. We shall here deal primarily with the techniques used within a typical feud episode: the introduction of characters, the development of conflict, and the confrontation ending with a settlement.

Rhetoric of the Introduction

In his presentation of characters, the narrator establishes the basic set of values for his episode. Although the tone of these presentations is generally sober and factual, many judgments are made which violate the principle of impassibilité: *Hann var slœgr ok illgjarn* ("He was insidious and malicious;" chapter 46); *Manna kurteisastr var hann, harðgǫrr í ǫllu, fémildr ok stilltr vel, vinfastr ok vinavandr* ("He was the most courteous of men [cf. French *courtois*], tough, generous and calm, loyal to his friends and careful in choosing them;" chapter 19). Notice that the second, positive statement emphasizes calm and restraint. Such praise naturally reflects on the narrator as a man of maturity and wisdom who would not judge people lightly; this in turn gives authority and credibility to the judgments he makes. They probably will remain in the reader's mind throughout the saga.

As we can see from the second example, a panegyrical description may also be emphasized by superlatives (*kurteisastr*) and by euphonic effects such as alliteration and assonance (*VINfastr ok VINa Vandr, fémILDR ok stILLTR vel*).[38] This method of eulogizing characters, which is at least partly influenced by foreign literature (cf. below, pp. 118-120), is used more often and with greater elaboration in *Njála* than in most other sagas. The portrait of Njáll's eldest son, Skarpheðinn, for example, may be presented as poetry or prose:

Han var *m*ikill *ma*ðr vexti ok styrkr,	(He was a big and strong man, a good
*ví*gr *v*el,	warrior,
*s*yndr sem *s*elr,	swimming as a seal,
manna fóthvatastr,	swiftest among runners,
skjótráðr ok ǫruggr,	quick-witted and brave,

38. See my article "Det litterära porträttet i latinsk historiografi och isländsk sagaskrivning—en komparativ studie," *Acta Philologica Scandinavica*, 27 (1965).

gagnorðr ok skjótorðr,
en þó lǫngum vel stilltr
Hann var jarpr á hár
ok sveipr í hárinu,
eygðr vel,
fǫlleitr ok skarpleitr,
liðr á nefi
ok lá hátt tanngarðrinn,
munnljótr nǫkkut
ok þo manna hermannligastr.

articulate and fluent of speech,
but mostly restrained.
He was brown-headed
with curly hair,
he had goodlooking eyes,
pale skin and sharp features,
a crooked nose
and a protruding jaw;
his mouth was somewhat ugly,
and yet he looked the most gallant
of men.)

Here, as in most other cases, an exaggerated eulogy is checked by such realistic details as an ugly mouth. Nevertheless, the heavy display of sonorous effects makes it clear to the audience that Skarpheðinn is one of the greatest heroes of the saga. Such effects, however, are rarely found in other sections of the narrative; even in the introductions they are used sparingly.

Often the narrator presents even his major characters with ironic understatements and subtle hints. About the great skald and warrior Egill Skallagrímsson, the hero of *Egils saga*, it is said: *hann var brátt málugr ok orðviss ; heldr var hann illr viðreignar, er hann var í leikum með ǫðrum ungmennum* ("He was an early talker and fluent of speech; he was rather tough to get along with when playing with other youngsters": *Egils saga*, chapter 31). There is no reason to regard such statements as less expressive of the narrator's opinions than the examples given in the preceding paragraphs. An experienced reader would understand that a character so described must turn out to be a very difficult person indeed! Actually it is quite likely that such underhanded, apparently noncommittal presentation is more effective than the most impassioned advocacy. Few things can make us more certain that a character is a raving maniac than a discreet hint from the narrator that he was "somewhat difficult to deal with when things did not go his way," or something similar.

But there are even more indirect ways of conditioning an audience's reaction to a character. One way is to present him with the outward characteristics of a conventionel hero or a villain. Blond and beautiful persons will generally turn out to be good; dark and ugly persons generally turn out to be, at best, problematic.[39] Especially when used with other types of information, references to such characteristics are effective on a more or less subconscious level. There can be no doubt, for example, that the following

---

39. I have discussed this type of relationship between personality and physical appearance in "Kroppen som själens spegel—ett motiv i de isländska sagorna," Lönnroth (1963-4).

presentation tends to prejudice the audience strongly against the described person:

Bróðir hafði verit kristinn maðr ok messudjákn at vígslu, en hann hafði kastat trú sinni ok gǫrzk guðníðingr ok blótaði heiðnar vættir ok var allra manna fjǫlkunnigastr. Hann hafði herbúnað þann, er eigi bitu járn á; hann var bæði mikill ok sterkr ok hafði hár svá mikit, at hann vafði undir belti sér; þat var svart.

("Bróðir had been a Christian and a deacon, but he had cast away his faith and become an apostate and was making sacrifices to heathen spirits and was very skilled at magic. He had a mailcoat which iron could not penetrate; he was both big and strong and had so much hair that he could tuck it under his belt; the hair was black"; chapter 155).

The information about Bróðir's faith and magic practices is enough to prejudice a Christian audience, but the mention of his mailcoat and long black hair provides the most effective blow to his reputation. Invulnerability in the sagas is generally a characteristic of berserkers and trolls. And the prejudice against dark and long-haired people seems to run very deep in Germanic tradition. Suffice it to say here that the literary portraits of the sagas draw heavily upon such imagery.

Very often the narrator characterizes a person by telling what others thought about him: a hero is said to be *vinsæll*, popular, while a villain is said to be *óvinsæll*, not well liked. A great chieftain can be respectfully introduced by saying, that *engir þóttu lǫgligir dómar dœmðir, nema hann væri við* ("nobody considered a verdict valid if he were not present;" chapter 1). A beautiful but wicked queen can be discreetly deprecated by saying that *Þat er mál manna, at henni hafi allt verit illa gefit, þat er henni var sjálf-rátt*, ("people have said about her that she was ill endowed in everything that she herself had any influence over"; chapter 154).

Most effective, although sparingly used, is the method of presenting a whole dramatic scene in which a new and especially an important character is presented through the reactions of others. A famous example of this occurs in chapter 1, where Hrútr comments on Hallgerðr's "thief's eyes," thereby establishing her as one of the most villainous characters of the saga: *Œrit fǫgr er mær sjá, ok munu margir þess gjalda; en hitt veit ek eigi, hvaðan þjófsaugu eru komin í ættir várar* ("The girl is beautiful enough, and many men will pay for it. But I don't know how the thief's eyes got into our family"). Many factors give tremendous authority to this ominous prediction. First of all, Hrútr himself has already been presented as *manna vitrastr*, the wisest of men, so we immediately accept him as a spokesman of the narrator. Second, his words are given special emphasis by concluding the scene and the chapter. Third, the narrator says that the words aroused the father's anger, and this information can only confirm that the uncle has indeed hit the nail on the head.

The last example shows that the persuasion depends not only on what is said, but also on the way it is presented. Matters the narrator wants stressed and especially remembered by his audience are often expressed in direct rather than indirect speech, are the "last words" of a scene, chapter, or episode, and are presented with more details and retarding elements than other, less important information. In many cases this is a flagrant breach of "impartiality." The heroes of *Njáls saga* are generally presented in greater detail than their adversaries, and they always get the "last word," even though the personalities and last words of their adversaries may be as relevant to an impartial understanding of the conflict. Characters who do think that Hallgerðr is good—such as her father—are not allowed to express their views as freely and directly to the audience, although it is true that they are generally given a hearing in order to create an impression that minimal requirements of impartiality have been met.

Much depends, of course, on *what kind* of actions and statements the narrator uses to represent either side. When the villainous Valgarðr grái is shown desecrating Christian crosses and other sacred symbols (chapter 107), we need no special lecturing to understand that this is not a good man. In fact, we tend to let our shock at the blasphemy influence our judgment about the conflict between Njáll's sons and Hǫskuldr which develops in the chapters immediately following (108-109)—a conflict instigated by Valgarðr's even more villainous son, Mǫrðr. Even though it would seem that the father's behavior is irrelevant to a fair judgment of his son, the narrator easily establishes guilt by association, for most of us are susceptible to such arguments as "like father, like son," and "by their fruits ye shall know them." Likewise, the narrator strongly suggests that we should believe in Gunnarr's cause when he shows us his hero giving food to the starving (chapter 47) or making such noble statements as "I don't know if I am less brave than other men because I am less eager to kill" (chapter 54), even though the noble words and actions may be irrelevant to a fair judgment of his conflict with his enemies.

Usually it is not necessary to employ such drastic contrasts. To boost the hero's cause it is often quite enough to show him in everyday situations with which the audience can identify: eating, sleeping, being surrounded by children, working on the farm, etc. This method is much practiced in the sagas, as is the corresponding method of depicting villains' lives as alien to a "normal" social existence. Although the hero Gunnarr and the villain Mǫrðr are both farmers, only Gunnarr is ever *seen* at his farm, and we get better insights into his family life. When attention focuses on Mǫrðr, he is usually working a crooked scheme, far from his home. This makes it almost impossible for us to see him as anything but an alien intruder, even had he not been presented as a villain from the start.

Rhetoric in the Development of Conflict

The method of steering the sympathies and the expectations of the audience by sheer emphasis and narrative techniques becomes more important as the narrator develops the conflict. At this stage, he also makes use of value judgments and emotive reactions to the incidents he conveys and thus provides a running commentary to his story. The major differences are that the comments are now seldom made by the narrator directly: they come mostly from his spokesmen within the narrative, and they refer not so much to *characters* as to *specific actions or events*.

Often the spokesmen are anonymous representatives of the community at large—"the people,"—whose favorable or unfavorable responses are registered at Thing meetings or private gatherings. A typical episode may conclude with the observation that "Gunnarr was thought to have come well out of this dealing" (cf. Chapter II), or "This slaying was ill spoken of"—we have already seen an example of this in the quoted passage from *Droplaugarsona saga*. There is rarely a hint of conflict between this public opinion and the narrator's own views, or between public opinion and the views the narrator expects his audience to have. "Good" and "bad" can be identified almost completely with what the community approves or disapproves.

Instead of referring to public opinion, the narrator may also use some particularly wise member of the community as his main spokesman—the technique already demonstrated in the introduction of Hallgerðr. As we know, there are several Wise Counselors in *Njála*, the most important, of course, being Njáll himself. His personality dominates the saga, but his role is essentially passive. Most of the time he functions as a Greek chorus, commenting, warning, expressing approval and disapproval, prophesying about the future. That he is known to be endowed with second sight gives the highest possible authority to his words. Similar characters are found also in other sagas, e.g., Gestr Oddleifsson in *Laxdœla saga*. Such men are often said to be great lawyers as well, i.e., they are especially competent to interpret the norms of the community, which are also the norms of the narrator. The saga narrator's admiration for legal expertise is a natural result of his basic conformism and support of community norms and values.

The wise community spokesmen within the narrative tend to state their views in brief but succinct speeches, where they can make use of legal quotations, proverbs, and other kinds of generalized statements often highlighted by their more rhetorical form.[40] In contrast to most speeches in medieval narratives, the eloquence is extremely elliptic, but it is hardly less expressive. In a confrontation scene with his adversaries at the Allthing, for example, Njáll makes effective use of a well-known Norse *sententia: Með lǫgum skal land várt byggja en með ólǫgum eyða,* ("Our land must be built with law or laid waste with lawlessness"; chapter 70). This reference to an acknowledged and respected principle lends credibility to the speaker's cause. At the same time, such rhetoric may help establish a moral, even though it is not directly expressed by the narrator himself. This is especially true in *Njáls saga,* where we find an unusually large number of aphoristic statements in the dialogue, particularly in counsels, speeches, and prophecies pronounced by Njáll and other wise men. Most of the proverbs and aphorisms, although frequently having the form of factual observations about life, emphasize such social values as respect for the law, patience, restraint, peacefulness, and correct procedure: *skamma stund verðr hǫnd hǫggvi fegin,* ("the blow makes the hand happy for a short while only"; chapter 42), *Kemsk, þó at seint fari* ("Even the slow mover arrives"; chapter 44), *ef sundr skipt er lǫgunum, þá mun ok sundr skipt friðinum* ("If the law falls apart, the peace falls apart, "; chapter 105), etc. Villains and unwise persons never talk in this way.

The use of prophecy to establish values is also worthy of note. Very often Njáll and other Wise Counselors express the narrator's approval or disapproval by saying that it will have good or bad *results* (predictions which are always fulfilled). This gives an impression of pragmatism, but we also get the feeling that there is justice in the course of history: "crime doesn't pay." Both these aspects of Old Norse ideology are clearly present in the concept of "luck" (*gæfa, gipta, hamingja*). A man who is described as a "lucky man" (*gæfumaðr*) is one whose actions turn out well, both for himself and for others, and who therefore deserves admiration; such a man is always pictured as good and noble. A man described as an "unlucky man" (*ógæfumaðr*), on the other hand, is pictured either as a scoundrel or as a noble man who has gone wrong—there is a definite relationship between morality and worldly success.

Thus, predictions by authoritative spokesmen of the narrator that this or that character will be lucky or unlucky are important clues to the ethics of the saga. When in *Njála* Hrappr asks other characters for protection

---

40. Collections of proverbs from the sagas have been made by Finnur Jónsson, H. Gering, and K. Vrátny in *Arkiv för nordisk filologi,* vols. 30, 32-33 (1914-1917). The classic work on Old Norse law as it appears in the sagas is A. Heusler, *Das Strafrecht der Isländersagas* (Leipzig, 1911). So far, however, very little has been said about the function of proverbs and legal quotations in their narrative context.

from his enemies (chapter 88), we need only hear that he is considered "un-lucky" to understand right away that this man should be avoided at all costs: indeed, he turns out to be a singularly unpleasant person who finally brings disaster to the whole community. Likewise, when Skarpheðinn is suddenly treated as an "unlucky man" by the Thing community after his killing of Hǫskuldr (chapter 119), we know what a horrible mistake the killing was—the classical "tragic mistake" of the hero.

Dreams and visions can be used to create empathy.[41] Agents of Fate in a saga dream (or vision) warn the dreamer of a coming disaster. The signi-ficance of the dream is often explained by a Wise Counselor, who thus adds his stature as a prophet to the authority exerted by the dream itself. The effect is not only to prepare the audience for events later in the narrative, but also to inspire fear and pity; the audience knows that the dream (vision) will come true in a terrifying manner, which places the dreamer in a tragic light, especially if he understands that he is doomed and accepts the impending disaster stoically. As an example, we may take a narrative segment from the feud between Hallgerðr and Bergþóra, in which the narrator builds up sympathy for one of Bergþóra's agents, Þórðr leysingjasonr:

It happened once that Njáll and Þórðr were sitting outdoors. There was a goat which used to roam about the home-meadow, and no one was al-lowed to drive it away. Þórðr said, "This is very strange" (*Undarliga bregðr nú við*). "What do you see that seems to you so strange?" asked Njáll. "The goat seems to be lying in the hollow there, drenched in blood," replied Þórðr. Njáll said there was no goat and nothing else either. "What is it then?" said Þórðr. "You must be doomed to die" (*Þú munt vera maðr feigr*), said Njáll, "and you have seen your own fetch (*munt þú sét hafa fylgju þína*), so be on your guard!" "That will not help me much if that is to be my fate" (*Ekki mun mér þat stoða . . . ef mér er þat ætlat*), said Þórðr.

(chapter 41)

The peaceful setting makes the audience feel at home with Þórðr when the Agent of Fate suddenly appears to him. As the fetch is a manifestation of a person's soul, there is here a mysterious identification between Agent of Fate and Dreamer (or rather Visionary, since Þórðr appears to be fully awake). The bloodied goat is a symbol of the friendly old servant soon to be sacrificed in the ruthless feud between the women. Yet there is no great display of emotion or dramatic action. The conversation between Þórðr and his Wise Counselor, Njáll, who is also his master, sounds calm, factual, and unhurried, even though it is absolutely clear both to Þórðr and to the

---

41. On dreams in the sagas, see M. Haeckel, *Die Darstellung und Funktion des Traumes in der isländischen Familiensaga* (Hamburg, 1934), and G. D. Kelchner, *Dreams in Old Norse literature and their affinities in folklore* (Cambridge, 1935).

audience that he will soon be killed. His laconic reaction to Njáll's terrifying prediction raises him in our esteem. Crooks and cowards do not have such visions, and they never anticipate their own death with such tranquility.

In the sagas most clearly influenced by foreign hagiography, the dreams and visions are sometimes miracles indicating divine judgment. This was of course an especially potent means of persuasion for a Christian audience in the Middle Ages, and we find it used rather often in *Njála*. In the description of the Battle of Clontarf for example, we are told of various miracles (blood rains, the ground opening up so that Hell could be seen, etc.), all of which indicate that God is on King Brian's side against the Norse vikings. Although such miracles are dependent on hagiographic tradition, there are other kinds of miracles and omens which are part of a pre-Christian, Germanic legacy. Þórðr's fetch, for example, belongs to this category. There are others which are more similar to Christian miracles in that they presuppose a superhuman will (not just an impersonal Fate) steering the course of events. For example, when Skarpheðinn and Hǫgni go to take revenge on the slayers of Gunnarr (chapter 79), the narrator points out that two ravens followed them all the way. And we know from the Edda that this was a good omen in pagan times, the ravens being Odin's own birds. Here their appearance stresses the righteousness of Skarpheðinn's and Hǫgni's revenge.

But, it is not always necessary to use miracles to suggest that some great power is working behind the stage, helping good people against bad people. The beginning of the Conversion episode provides an interesting example:

A change of rulers had taken place in Norway. Earl Hákon had died and Óláfr Tryggvason had taken his place. Earl Hákon had met his death at the hands of the slave Karkr, who cut the earl's throat at Rimul in Gaulardale.

At the same time it was learned that there had been a change of faith in Norway. The old faith had been discarded and King Óláfr had Christianized the eastern lands also: the Shetlands, the Orkneys, and the Faroe Islands.

Njáll heard many people say that it was a great wickedness to give up the old faith, but he answered: "It seems to me that the new faith is much better, and happy he who accepts it (*sá mun sæll, er þann fær heldr*). If those who preach it come here I shall do all I can to further it."

He often went by himself and mumbled (*hann fór opt frá ǫðrum mǫnnum ok þuldi, einn saman*). (chapter 100)

The indoctrination *for* the new faith and *against* the old one is present already in the first lines, where the disgraceful death of the last pagan ruler is contrasted to the success of the new and Christian king. Both Earl Hákon and King Óláfr were of course wellknown to an Old Icelandic audience, which would probably associate the first of these men with evil, black magic, and "bad luck," and the latter with great heroism, nobility, and "good luck."

The death of Hákon and the shift of rulers is explained as follows in *Heimskringla*, the most authoritative of all sagas of the kings of Norway: "The main reason for it was that the time had come when heathen sacrifices and those who took part in them would be condemned (*at fyrirdœmask skyldi blótskaprinn ok blótmenninir*), but instead came Holy Faith and True Religion" (*en i stað kom heilǫg trúa ok réttir siðir*) (*Óláfs saga Tryggvasonar*, chapter 50). This interpretation, which accords with the Augustinian idea of God's plan for human history (cf. Chapter IV), is presumably shared by the narrator of *Njála*, although he is less explicit.

The next piece of information, about the adverse reaction to Christianity by "many people," would normally cast a shadow of doubt upon the new faith, but in this case we know also that it had strong support in the Norse community. What finally settles the matter in favor of the Christians is that the pagan argument is presented anonymously and indirectly, while the counterargument is given in direct quotation—and as the "last word"— from the greatest authority among all characters of the saga. His prediction that Christianity will bring happiness (here roughly equivalent with "luck") to its converts, will be accepted immediately by anyone acquainted with his second sight. The wisdom of the prediction is further emphasized through its gnomic form (*sá mun sæll, er þann fær heldr*). And the final comment about the "mumbling," strange as it is, further underlines Njáll's contact with the supernatural, and hence his credibility.

The passage shows how a new conflict may be presented in the saga after the main characters have been introduced. The Conversion episode is, of course, atypical in that it pictures not a normal family feud but a great struggle between Good and Evil. In most feud episodes, the narrator remains uncommitted to either side, but invariably he builds a moral contrast between "good" and "bad" members of each side. The bad members are the Troublemakers, the Instigators of Strife. An example is chapter 44, where Gunnarr's restraint and nobility are contrasted to the meanness and belligerence of Hallgerðr and his kinsman Sigmundr. Here the audience knows from the introductory presentations and from previous incidents that Gunnarr is good and Hallgerðr and Sigmundr are bad; this chapter emphasizes the difference.

The chapter begins (in the modern editions, not in the original text) with Gunnarr's admonition to Sigmundr after he had paid compensation at the Thing for Þórðr leysingjasonr, whom Sigmundr had slain at Hallgerðr's instigation:

"You are a man of worse fortune than I thought (*Meiri ertú ógiptumaðr en ek ætlaða*) and you are using your talents to do evil. But I have nevertheless settled your conflict with Njáll and his sons, and now you had better not snap for any more flies. You are not my kind of man; you treat people with insults and scorn, but that is not may way. You get on well with Hallgerðr because you two are more similar."

We are then told (indirect speech only!) that Sigmundr has promised to follow Gunnarr's advice more often. At this point (note the importance of the chapter division!), we are told that some beggar women—characterized as "gossipy" and "slanderous"; the typical Messengers of *Njála*, repeatedly used to spread dissent between families—arrived at Gunnarr's home after having previously been at Njáll's. A conversation between Hallgerðr and the beggar women concerns the present activities of the Njáll family. We expect this conversation to be highly slanderous, and we are not disappointed. Their dialogue is climaxed by Hallgerðr's suggestion that Sigmundr compose an insulting poem calling Njáll a "beardless old man" and his sons "dung-beardlings."

That he would gladly do, he said, and right away he recited three or four stanzas, and they were all slanderous.

"You are a pet to do as I tell you," Hallgerðr said (*'Gersimi ert þú,' sagði Hallgerðr, 'hversu þú ert mer eptirlátr'*).

Then Gunnarr came in. He had been standing outside the women's room and heard everything. All were very startled when they saw him, and they were silent, but before there had been a lot of laughter.

Gunnarr was very furious, and he said to Sigmundr: "Mindless are you, and you do not care about good advice, when you are insulting the sons of Njáll and, what is even worse, Njáll himself, after all the harm you have done to them before. I predict that this will be the end of you. But if anybody repeats your verses, he shall have to leave this house and lose my friendship in addition."

But they were all so scared of him that nobody dared to repeat the insults. Then he went away. (chapter 44)

The effect of this scene at least partly depends on the fact that Sigmundr is never quoted directly, not even his unfortunate verses, while Gunnarr is quoted in such a way that his words have the strongest possible authority. His initial characterization of Sigmundr as a man who insults people and gets on too well with Hallgerðr, is immediately shown to be true; and Sigmundr's initial vow to behave is immediately shown to have no weight whatsoever. Hence, Hallgerðr's praise of Sigmundr as *gersimi* stands out as deeply ironic. The fear Gunnarr causes by his sudden appearance bears witness to the bad conscience of everybody present. Although the insults to Njáll and his sons seem rather innocent (we have, of course, no way of knowing if they appeared worse in Sigmundr's poetic version), we are therefore prepared to accept Gunnarr's fury as perfectly legitimate. We may even applaud his restraint in not using stronger language in his concluding speech, which, after all, deals the final blow to poor Sigmundr by predicting (quite rightly, as it turns out) that he will be killed as a result of his foolish verses! The audience, in any case, is likely to feel that there is not much more to be said after such a speech.

A modern writer could easily have told the same story in such a way as to make Hallgerðr and Sigmundr appear as thoroughly charming and witty, the beggar women folksy and lovable, and Gunnarr as a priggish bore who insists on spoiling innocent fun. That such a change of perspective is possible indicates that the narrator has played a trick on us by portraying Gunnarr as a shining white figure amidst a crowd of shady and despicable characters. The trick is played primarily by sheer narrative technique, i.e., by selecting and emphasizing the appropriate details in the appropriate order. There is a faint hint of direct commentary only in the introduction of the beggar women (the only place where the principle of impassibilité is not strictly adhered to). On the other hand, indirect commentary—by Gunnarr—plays a very important role, although it has to be supported by the context to acquire its full authority.

Rhetoric of the Climax

As the narrator approaches the climax of his story, dramatic presentation gradually takes the place of both direct and indirect commentary. This is only natural, for we are by now thoroughly persuaded and need only to have our prejudices confirmed in scenes that are as moving and as vivid as possible. To a great extent this is done by expanding the narrative segments through the technique which Theodore Andersson has called "staging" (cf. above, p. 52). As *Njála* moves towards the great fire, where Njáll and his sons are finally to perish, staging is increasingly employed: Njáll's household is shown, as it were, in cinematic close-ups, which serve not only to further the action but also to strengthen the reader's empathy with the heroes. We are told, for example, of their last meal together, when Njáll's wife lets everyone have the food he likes best (chapter 127). We are also told of various portents and prophetic dreams that foreshadow the impending doom (chapter 124). The setting shifts rapidly back and forth between Njáll's home and the approaching burners (chapter 128). As the end nears, the narrative focuses a last time on each of the most important members of Njáll's family (chapters 129).

Two staging techniques deserve special attention. First, the narrator increases or decreases sympathy for a character simply by changing the focus or perspective. A good example is the treatment of Skarpheðinn. At first he is pictured in the center of events, but when he decides to slay the noble Hǫskuldr, the attention immediately shifts to the victim and remains there until well after the killing. Skarpheðinn is suddenly seen only from afar—from the viewpoint of the slain man and his widow—and in the process he loses a good deal of our sympathy. Later, just before his own death, he regains sympathy by being shown again at close range. Some critics have felt that his killing of Hǫskuldr is not suffiently motivated,[42] but such criticism misses the point: the killing *should* appear senseless in order to make Skarpheðinn fall low in the eyes of the audience. To make his motives understandable by showing him closeup at this point would be to let him off too easily.

A second technique is the use of pastoral and demonic imagery to set the stage for the catastrophic climaxes. Pastoral images—fields on a sunny day, a peaceful meal at the farm, a sheepfold in the summer, etc.—may be used to make the life of the heroes appear in an especially idyllic light before the catastrophe hits them. On the other hand, demonic images—blood and fire, darkness, blizzards, wolves, horrible monsters, etc.—may be used to picture the catastrophe itself and to create the appropriate mood of fear and pity.[43] Sometimes this is done by transcending our "normal" reality, most prominently in the dreams and other premonitions that prepare us for the climax: Njáll sees his house full of blood before the great fire (chapter 127); someone sees a black man riding a grey horse across the sky, carrying a burning torch in his hand which lights the sky (chapter 125). When set against the normal, everyday world of the heroes, such visions seem to give their lives a higher significance, as if they were gods, as if the forces that threaten hem were set loose by all the demons of the underworld.

Usually, however, the demonic and pastoral images are less obtrusive and are used only within a framework of meticulous realism. Pastoral sheepfolds or demonic blizzards are introduced as perfectly natural ingredients in the landscape, and they usually have a definite function within the plot. Icelandic saga narrators do not fill their stories with incidental details and descriptive ornamentation *just* to set the mood. If, for example, they place a hero against the background of a sheepfold, it is not merely to show him as a pastoral and peaceful person but to prepare for an action, usually a fight. By choosing the right setting, and by focusing on it at the right moment, the narrator nevertheless may also manipulate sympathies and antipathies. A good example is provided by the story of Hǫskuldr's death, which is said to have taken place on an early spring morning:

---

42. E.g. Sigurður Nordal in *Nordisk kultur*, 8 B (1953), 259.

43. Concerning the use of pastoral and demonic imagery, cf. Northrop Frye, *Anatomy of Criticism* (College edition, Atheneum, 1965), 141-158.

The weather was fine and the sun was up. At this time Hǫskuldr Hvitaness priest woke up. He dressed and put on the cloak that Flosi had given him. He took a basket full of grain and a sword in his other hand and went out on his field to sow (*hann tók kornkippu ok sverð i aðra hǫnd ok ferr til gerðis sins ok sár niðr korninu*). Skarpheðinn and his companions had agreed they should all use their weapons against him. Skarpheðinn rushed up from behind the fence, but when Hǫskuldr saw him he wanted to turn away. Then Skarpheðinn ran at him and said: "Don't bother to take to your heels, Hvítaness priest" (*"Hirð eigi þú at hopa á hæl, Hvítanessgoðinn"*)—and struck him with his axe. The blow hit his head, and Hǫskuldr sank down on his knees. He said this: "May God help me and forgive you!" Then they all attacked him and cut him down (*Hljópu þeir þá at honum allir ok unnu á honum*). (chapter 111)

Clearly, this is the death of a martyr! The effect is achieved primarily through a skillful use of pastoral stageprops as a setting for a revolting display of brutality. As Peter Hallberg aptly puts it: "The entire situation of the peaceful sowing of grain in the early morning affords a touching contrast to the blackness of the atrocious deed. It is as though the very light of day were concentrated into a resplendent nimbus about the figure of Hǫskuldr."[44] Most of the pastoral details (the weather, the cloak, the basket full of grain, etc.) are indicental to the story and could easily have been left out. But, presented so naturally and discreetly as part of the setting, they are never felt to be superfluous. The inexperienced reader will not notice that the narrator is deliberately creating a medieval *passio*, or description of martyrdom!

It is interesting to compare the killing of Hǫskuldr to the killing of Kolr Þorsteinsson, a minor character who had participated in the burning of Njáll's house and afterwards talked scornfully of the victims. The hero Kári attacks this man just as he is about to make a business transaction in a British port:

This morning Kári came to the city. He came to the place where Kolr was counting his silver. Kári recognized him. Then he attacked him with his sword drawn and chopped off his head while he was counting, and the head said "ten" as it fell off (*Síðan hljóp Kári til hans með sverð brugðit ok hjó á hálsinn, en hann taldi silfrit, ok nefndi hǫfuðit tíu, er af fauk bolnum*).

(chapter 158)

In *this* case we are obviously meant to be amused rather than moved and shocked, although the deed in itself is analogous, and there is no overt editorializing in either case. How, then, should we account for the difference in effect? First, the victims are very different in stature. Second, the situations are significantly different: being killed while counting money

44. Hallberg (1962), 112.

abroad somehow appears less atrocious than being killed while sowing grain on one's own land, and it is definitely more dignified and moving to die with a prayer than with a trivial utterance about property. Third, the killing seems somewhat less brutal in the latter case, since it is done more quickly and in a neater way and by only one man. The most important difference, however, lies in the staging, which is more elaborate in the first case, involving careful preparations and foreshadowings, a fairly extensive dwelling on incidental details of the setting, and a solemn, almost biblical tone. The killing of Kolr, on the other hand, is told so swiftly and abruptly that there is no time at all to feel sorry for the victim. It is the suddenness of the whole incident, rather than anything else, which makes it comic instead of tragic.

Rhetoric of the Conclusion

Directly after a hero has been killed, the narrator often sums up the personality in a commentary resembling the introductory presentations. These final characterizations, which Theodore Andersson calls "necrologies,"[45] may to some extent be dependent on the Latin convention of inserting eulogies at the end of biographies.[46] The saga necrologies, however, are generally more concise and less florid than their Latin counterparts. In most cases, the narrator avoids committing himself openly, and instead refers to the consensus of public opinion: "*People thought* he was a great loss because he had been a great chieftain and a popular man"; "*It is generally said* that Glúmr was the greatest chieftain in Eyjafjǫrðr for twenty years, and for another twenty years no one was more than his equal. *It is also said* that Glúmr was the best warrior this country has seen." There is indeed a very thin line between such "factual" statements and direct editorializing, which also does occur in a few instances: "Skúta's death came as no surprise to many people. *And yet it is only fair to say* that he was wise and every bit a man, and many were no better than his equals, though they were outstanding men."[47] The effects on the audience are probably similar in all three cases.

The examples given so far are fairly typical of the restrained, matter-of-fact saga tone, even though they express a high degree of praise and are more florid in style than most saga passages. In some cases, however, the tone of the necrology becomes much more eulogistic through the use of quotations from skaldic poems about the dead hero. This is done after the death of

---

45. Andersson (1967), 60-62. Cf. above, p. 78.

46. Cf. "Det litterära porträttet" (1965), 80-81, 86-87.

47. All these examples have been borrowed from Andersson (1967), 60-62. The italics are my own.

Gunnarr in *Njála* (chapter 77), for example, and it is repeatedly done in *Heimskringla* towards the end of a king's biography. The narrator merely gives the quotation, without lengthy introductions or elaborations: "The skald So-and-so has said this about his death"—no further comment is necessary.

Sometimes the necrology will be spoken (occasionally in verse, but more often in prose) by one of the "wise" characters of the saga. After the death of Hǫskuldr, for example, Njáll says that he would rather have lost two of his own sons (chapter 111). Gizurr the White, makes this remark over Gunnarr's dead body: "We have now slain a great chief, and it hasn't been easy; his memory will last as long as man lives in this country" (*Mikinn ǫldung hǫfu vér nú at velli lagit, ok hefir oss erfitt veitt, ok mun hans vǫrn uppi, meðan landit er byggt*; chapter 77). Note the poetic, slightly archaic tone and the use of alliteration: *velli, veitt, vǫrn*. A more subtle form of necrology is implied in the words uttered by Hǫskuldr's widow upon finding her husband's dead body: "This would have been a manly deed if it had been done by one man only" (chapter 112). Here, as in so many other cases, the staging gives the words a greater impact; we have previously been told how the young widow woke up in her bed, after having an ominous dream and missing her husband by her side. She has gone out to find him, full of dark premonitions. Her worst fears have now come true and we would of course expect her to break down completely. This makes her understated comment the more sublime and thus increases not only her own but also Hǫskuldr's stature, even after his death.

When the hero survives his struggles, the narrator usually takes leave of him by telling of his final reconciliation with his enemies, adding a few words about his later life and his descendants. The last thing we hear of Gunnarr's noble brother, Kolskeggr, for example, is that he had a dream that made him go to Denmark, become a Christian, and later settle in Constantinople as a "knight of God" in the Varangian guard (chapter 81). And the last we hear of the two bitter antagonists Flosi and Kári is how they went to Rome as pilgrims, were absolved from sin, and fell in each other's arms when they met again in Iceland (chapters 158). The Christian tone is more prominent in these concluding sections, as if the narrator were anxious to dispel any idea that his story might be regarded as impious. Conversions and pilgrimages, often referred to, serve at least partly to legitimize the not-so-Christian exploits that went before.

The listing of descendants, especially if wellknown and respected, also can serve as an effective booster of the hero. One respects a notable ancestor, and a notable man will reflect splendor on his offspring. No one, of course, wants to be the descendant of a villain.

A few sagas (but not *Njála*) end with a reflective comparative comment on some of its most prominent heroes and their families—a sort of extended version of the necrology. Thus *Vatnsdœla saga* says of its last hero, Þorkell Krafla, that

"he was rightly considered (*hann þótti, sem var*) a great chieftain and a very lucky man (*mikill giptumaðr*) and most similar to the older chieftains of Vatnsdalr, such as Þorsteinn and Ingimundr; but Þorkell had that edge over them, that he had the right faith and loved his God and prepared for his death in the most Christian manner" (*at hann var réttrúaðr maðr ok elskaði guð ok bjósk mjǫk kristilega við dauða sínum*). (chapter 47)

Forms of Persuasion; A Retrospective Survey

The rhetorical techniques of the saga can be divided into three broad categories: *commentary, stylistic variation* and *staging*.

"Commentary" is any expression of opinion, whether made directly by the narrator himself ("editorializing") or indirectly through his spokesmen. By "stylistic variation" I refer to such devices as using a heightened or a solemn language when speaking of heroes while using a more straight-forward and "vulgar" language when speaking of less important characters. The term "staging," finally, here refers not only to the specific technique used to dramatize the climax of a feud story (cf. above, p. 94) but to the entire process whereby an author determines: a) which motifs and narrative segments to use in the presentation of an event; b) the order in which to present these motifs and segments; c) the relative emphasis put upon them through the use of "showing" versus "telling," direct versus indirect speech, detailed description versus passing reference.

With such an admittedly wide definition of "staging," it is obviously the most important method used in conditioning the minds of the saga audience, for it occurs in almost every phase of the narrative while the other methods are used much less. Heroes, for example, in comparison with their adversaries, are presented in greater detail, are quoted more often, always get the "last word," have their most attractive features stressed, and are shown in situations with which the audience can identify. And if there is a conflict between two different opinions within the story—for example between paganism and Christianity—the more accepted, respectable view always receives more exposure and a more attractive presentation. The use of conscious or unconscious symbolism in the presentation of physical features is noteworthy: the blackness of the villain's hair, for example, or the placing of a hero against an idyllic background. Dreams, visions, and miracles can also testify to the goodness or wickedness of men. All of this amounts to a high degree of partiality, to a semi-mythical transformation of reality in almost every saga episode. It is sometimes difficult to see this, partly because of the restraint in the use of emotive language, and partly because heroes are often evenly distributed in a conflict, so that the significant contrast is not so much between feuding parties as between factions *within* each party.

Indirect commentary is an important supplement to staging, used especially during the early development of a conflict or at the end of an episode. The comments are made either by "people" in general, or by selected spokesmen of the established community values; they usually refer either to a character's status within that community ("Gunnarr was a popular man") or to the outcome of a specific action ("The killing was ill spoken of"). A more generalized indirect comment is provided by proverbs, legal quotations, and prophecies. The function of prophecy is thus *both* to prepare the audience for future events *and* to indicate the ethical value of the object of the prophecy. The same double function is often present in other types of foreshadowings, such as dreams and miraculous omens. Such supernatural happenings can thus be regarded not only as part of the staging but as a special kind of indirect commentary—the "comments" being made either by God or by some other metaphysical power behind the stage.

Direct commentary (editorializing) and stylistic variation seem to be used much less than either staging or indirect commentary. When they *are* used, it is frequently in combination, e.g., an important comment will be further emphasized by a more elevated style. This occurs primarily in the presentation segments at the beginning of an episode. A heightening of style also occurs in proverbial expressions and quotations from law and poetry spoken by characters within the story, especially if they are spokesmen of the narrator (e.g., Njáll). Both the editorializing and the heightened language violate the basic saga principle of impassibilité, and they are both, as we shall see, influenced by other genres (by skaldic poetry, and by the rhetoric of foreign biographies and saints' lives). Although these methods seem foreign to the saga, and although they have been neglected by critics, they nevertheless may play an important role in the formation of our sympathies, especially since the passages in which they are used stand out against the calm, even flow of factual narration.

The saga narrator shows a remarkable restraint in his use of *all* these techniques and devices, compared to most medieval authors and also to most modern novelists. Not only is he frugal in his use of editorializing and emotional expressions, but the indirect comments of his spokesmen will also be brief and restrained. He will use his emotive staging effects discreetly and never in a way that interrupts the continuous flow of action. Once the reader has become used to this restraint, however, he may be as strongly

affected by one dry prose line from *Njála* as by several passionate excla-
mations in a poem of the *Sturm und Drang* variety. This does not mean,
of course, that sagas are either better or worse than romantic poems, or
that their emotional impact is either stronger or weaker—it is merely that
the literary language is different.

6. *NJÁLA* AND SAGA TRADITION: SOME GENERAL CONCLUSIONS

We have surveyed a large number of traditional saga elements and narrative
techniques used by the author of *Njála* and by many of his colleagues among
thirteenth-century sagawriters. Our survey is far from exhaustive, but a
few general conclusions may perhaps be stated.

First of all, the narrative technique of *Njála* is firmly rooted in Old
Norse tradition. Although some of the techniques exemplified in this chapter
may have been influenced by the author's reading of foreign literature (in
translation or in the original), most of them must have developed in Iceland,
or at any rate within the North Germanic language area. It would otherwise be difficult to explain why the saga world, the action patterns, the
basic building blocks of composition, and most of the rhetorical devices are
so much different from what we find in other European narratives from the
same period. It also seems probable that the narrative conventions developed largely in oral storytelling before the first sagas were committed to
vellum, for we find them in saga manuscripts at such an early date that they
could hardly have had time to develop between the introduction of writing
and the composition of "classical" sagas such as *Njála*. Although some sagas,
such as *Heiðarvíga saga* or *Reykdœla saga*, have a more primitive and stereotyped appearance than *Njála*, which is unusually sophisticated and "literary,"
their basic technique is the same and bespeaks their common origin in the
oral saga.

This fact must be recognized even by scholars (like the present writer)
who think that the Christian and continental influences on thirteenth-
century sagawriters have been strongly underestimated. As Heusler, Theodore Andersson, and several others have pointed out, this same fact should
be recognized by the "Icelandic School," whose members often explained
parallels in the sagas by literary borrowings among sagawriters, and who
then, on the basis of such alleged borrowings, established a saga chronology
to show the development of the classical saga as literary (as opposed to a
folklore) phenomenon. As indicated by the studies of the oral-formulaic
school, it appears more natural to assume that most saga parallels resulted
from the influence of the same oral tradition over a long period on saga-

writers who could use similar motifs and techniques without necessarily reading any manuscripts produced by their colleagues.

We also may conclude that although saga style appears more "realistic" than the style of medieval romances or saints' lives, it only represents reality in a limited sense. Not only is the saga world peopled by stock characters and supernatural forces, its very shape is determined by a set of action patterns, filled in with stock motifs and narrative segments according to rules. In this respect, the saga is reminisent of the folktale, as studied by Propp, or the oral epic, as studied by Parry and Lord. Furthermore, the values of the narrator are clearly expressed in the narrative patterns, even though sagas would seem "objective" and "factual" to a reader coming from the more heightened rhetoric of some other medieval genres.

What ultimately determines the ethical climate of a saga, however, is not so much the style as the arrangement of narrative segments and episodes. Each structural combination has its own implied "moral." A typical sequence of battle scenes teaches us to fight and die like a hero. The Feud Pattern itself may be said to teach us that family honor should be bravely defended, even though a peaceful settlement is preferred to violent acts of revenge (this "moral" is of course not only expressed in the structure but also frequently pronounced by the narrator's spokesmen in "indirect commentary"). Likewise, the Travel Pattern implies that young men of good family should go abroad, be honored at foreign courts, and prove their valor in viking adventures. By combining such episodic patterns into even larger and more complicated structures, the narrator (willingly or unwillingly) delivers a sermon which may be regarded as the "message" of the saga as a whole.

What then is the message of *Njála*? In order to see this, it is necessary to analyze not only its traditional ingredients and conventional patterns but also what the author has done to them. Specifically, we have to take a closer look at the overall structure which forges all the more or less traditional segments and episodes together into one large epic. This overall structure is unique in saga literature. It may to some extent have been inspired by certain earlier family sagas, but it appears to have been more deeply influenced by biblical myth and by the author's own Christian philosophy, as we shall see in our next chapter.

Very long sagas probably did not exist in the oral tradition as complete narrative units, only as a succession of episodes which could be arranged very differently by different storytellers. It was therefore natural that sagawriters would turn to foreign models or, alternatively, create their own models when faced with the task of building large narrative structures like *Njála* out of the old and comparatively simple feud patterns and travel patterns. It was also natural that they would include individual motifs and techniques from foreign literature once the narrative tradition of the Icelanders had made contact with the Christian culture of Europe.

The sagawriters did not have to import foreign rules for the construction of smaller units such as a battle scene, a goading scene, or even an entire feud episode. They did not have to learn abroad how to make the audience feel antipathy for a treacherous Loki figure or sympathy for a Siegfried figure fighting his last battle. They could use the old motifs and narrative rules which they had inherited from their ancestors; this was a heritage strong enough to resist many foreign influences even when the sagawriters were familiar with foreign literature. Their native literary grammar was too ingrown to be radically changed, but it could be modified and refined to suit new and more sophisticated literary interests, fostered by clerical minds of the thirteenth-century. This process will now be the object of our study.

IV

The Clerical Mind

1. INTRODUCTION

Njála was written when Iceland had been officially Christian for almost 300 years. Literacy had arrived through priests versed in the Latin culture of medieval Europe, and the art of writing was practiced mostly by servants of the Icelandic and Norwegian church. Although oral traditions from pagan times would never have been recorded unless clerical minds had taken an active interest in such matters, it took time for native tales and legends to be committed to vellum. The earliest Icelandic manuscripts contain no family sagas but a wealth of saints' lives, homilies, and theological treatises. When sagas were finally written in the thirteenth century, they competed with other secular genres, which clerics introduced from abroad at the instigation of the Norwegian court and of courtly romances, French heroic epics (*chansons de geste*), and Latin historiography. All these secular foreign genres were incorporated in the so-called *riddarasǫgur* ("sagas of Knights") which gradually merged with the indigenous forms of narrative.

In the past, scholars have generally maintained that the foreign genres had little influence on the "classical" Icelandic sagawriters of the thirteenth century except in encouraging them to preserve their native tradition in writing. Family sagas that reveal obvious influence from romances and saints' lives have often been considered "late" or "interpolated," representing a decline in the "genuine" and "pure" sagawriting of the Sturlung Age. During recent years, however, there has been a strong reaction against this traditional view of the sagas. Unsuccessful attempts have been made to derive the genre of family sagas from foreign sources. But most modern scholars now agree that the classical sagas, in their present written form, combine folklore material from native tradition with a fairly strong element from medieval Christian literature and *Lebensanschauung*.[1]

The problem is to define this foreign element. It does not much concern style and language, except in a few sagas. The basic action patterns and stock characters are also on the whole, of native origin. The foreign influence thus should be sought in the overall composition of individual sagas and in the religious philosophy which underlies some of the greatest among them, particularly *Njála*.

The mixture of "foreign" and "native" is different in different sagas, both in amount and kind. While *Heiðarvíga saga* is a pure feud story with rather few Christian overtones, *Laxdœla saga* is a combination of traditional feud and travel tales mixed with French chivalry and motifs from the saints' lives. *Grettis saga* contains heroic legends and folktales rooted in Germanic pagan tradition, but one episode (the so-called *Spesar þáttr*) is influenced by the conventions of romance and hagiography. *Fóstbrœðra saga*, on the other hand, has the general appearance of a "native" saga, but here and there we find digressions into medieval theology—digressions written in a high-flown rhetoric, influenced by Latin syntax, and very much different from the regular saga style that dominates the narrative. Such variations indicate that foreign influence is a problem that concerns the individual saga-writer rather than the saga genre as a whole.

Some sagawriters were better educated than others. To the extent that they were well versed in foreign literature and theological concepts, they probably had received some formal clerical training; but this does not necessarily mean that they were priests or monks. Even a layman in thirteenth-century Iceland may have had a "clerical mind" in the broad sense we are using in this chapter: a mind formed by the Christian culture of medieval Europe (cf. Chapter V).

But, regardless of how much Christian education a sagawriter had in fact received, he may in the actual *writing* of his saga have been more or less influenced by what he knew. Some would perhaps offer a traditional story as told by uneducated farmers, in which case the foreign and Christian influence on the story would probably be rather slight, even though the writer himself may have been both pious and learned. Other writers would try to make the native tradition conform to their own Christian thinking and to literary patterns they had absorbed from clerical writings. In such

1. For a convenient survey of the discussion about foreign influence, cf. Mattias Tveitane, "Europeisk påvirkning på den norrøne sagalitteraturen. Noen synspunkter," *Edda*, LXIX (1969), 73-95.

a case we can say that their "clerical minds" took over the work and made the saga different from a "genuine," "native" saga.

It is, therefore, difficult to generalize about the clerical or Christian component in family sagas as Richard Allen has tried to do in a stimulating chapter of his book on *Njála* ("Saga Style: Christian Context and Epic Background"). Allen suggests very persuasively that "in the sagas we have a genre based on the stuff of Germanic legend and tradition, observed and set down by men possessed of a Christian sensibility but free from religious tendentiousness."[2] Because of its diplomatic vagueness, this statement may appear acceptable to almost everybody, but, in fact, it says both too much and too little. Allen's own interpretation of *Njála* as a Christian work is hardly compatible with the idea that its author was "free from religious tendentiousness." And Allen's analysis of saga style *in general* contains nothing to convince the reader that the genre as a whole was created by "men possessed of a Christian sensibility."

Allen thus tends to regard the genre as too homogeneous. Our interpretation will emphasize the clerical patterns in *Njála* even more strongly than he or any previous critic has done, but we certainly do not want to maintain that all these patterns are typical of the family saga. On the other hand, we have chosen to present the "foreign" elements and the Christian ideology of *Njála* against a very wide background of comparative material from other sagas, saints' lives, romances, and theological works known to the Icelanders in the later thirteenth century. It may be felt that we have included matters of limited value for the understanding of sagas as living works of art. But we are dealing with an author who seems much more sophisticated than he cares to reveal and who uses the native forms of saga narrative in a highly unusual manner. Thus, while a survey of the clerical thinking of his time may not illuminate the "esthetic surface" of his creation, it should help us to understand how he shaped his traditional material.

In the next section of this chapter, we shall discuss the influence of "clerical style" on the author's language and narrative technique; we shall also discuss influences of specific foreign works or genres. We shall then, in the following section, widen our scope by discussing our author's Christian theology in relation to the native concepts of Fate and Fortune inherent in the traditional "saga world." Next, we shall attempt to explain his attitude to pagan society, pagan law, and the Germanic "ethics of revenge." Finally, we shall analyse in some detail the famous incident of Gunnarr's

2. Allen (1971), 46. For a discussion of Allen's theories about saga style and Christianity, see the conclusion of this chapter.

return to Hlíðarendi to illustrate the clerical "reinterpretation" of tradition which we have found to be characteristic of this particular author's method.

2. CLERICAL STYLE AND FOREIGN INFLUENCE

"Clerical style" and clerical thinking

In discussions of Old Norse prose, "saga style" is distinguished from the "clerical style" used in the "foreign" prose genres (romances, saints' lives, etc.).[3] The concept of "clerical style" may seem unduly wide: romances and saints' lives are indeed very different, and it is obvious that the Norse clerics who adapted these foreign genres for their native audience had different stylistic ideals.[4] Yet it may be permissible, within certain limits, to speak of one "clerical style" that appears frequently both in *riddarasǫgur* and in various types of religious prose written in Iceland and Norway during the "classical" period of sagawriting (around 1220-1280).

This style, which provides a striking contrast to saga style, is obviously influenced by Latin prose (even in Norse translations of French poetry !). Among its characteristic features are, for example: an involved sentence structure; a frequent use of adjectives, appositions, and participal constructions; and a predilection for alliteration, assonance, and various rhythmic effects, particularly at the end of a sentence. Rhetorical devices such as metaphor, simile, and antithesis are also used more often then in the native "language of tradition." But a technical description of this kind cannot explain the essential difference, which is one of "content" rather than of "form." For the clerical style expresses a mode of thinking and experiencing entirely different from that of the traditional Icelandic saga. In order to see this, we shall consider a scene from *Alexanders saga*, an Icelandic prose adaption of a Latin twelfth century epic by a French poet, Gautier de Châtillon; the Icelandic version is attributed to Bishop Brandr Jónsson and was probably written about twenty years before *Njála*. The scene pictures Alexander, the young prince of Macedonia, after he has learned that King Darius of Persia is demanding a humiliating tribute from his father:

3. See, in particular, M. Nygaard, *Norrøn Syntax* (Kristiania, 1905) and "Den lærde stil i den norrøne prosa," in *Sproglig-historiske studier tilegnede C. R. Unger* (Kristiania, 1897).

4. Distinctions can also be made between "clerical styles" from different time periods— for example, between the comparatively simple style of saints' lives translated in the twelfth century and the extremely florid and artificial style ("den florissante stil") of certain Icelandic clerics in the fourteenth century; cf. Ole Widding, *Norrøn fortællekunst* (1965), 132-136; M. Tveitane, *Den lærde stil. Oversætterprosa i den norrøne versjonen av Vitæ Patrum* (Bergen, 1968), 129-131.

Oc sva æddiz hann nu þegar akafliga imot Dario konunge er scattinn let heimta af fauðor hans, oc neytir i hugenum vapna sinna með snarpligom ahlaupom, sem þa er leons hvelpr ser hiortinn fyrir ser, er hann hefir eigi tekit afl sitt, en tenn ero sva litlar at hann ma eigi bita, þo hellir hann ut bloði hiartarins með huginum at hann mege eigi með taunnunom; hann er þa oc seinn a fæti, en þo er vilinn skiotr til arøðesens. Alexander hafði oc litið afl at vinna sva stort sem honom bio i hug. En leons akefð hafðe hann ser i hiarta með dirfð alldri meiri.

Nu bar sva til at Aristotiles meistare hans oc fostrfaðer hafði gengit ut af herbergi sino, þar er hann hafði gort eina boc af iðrott þeire er dialectica heitir a latino, en þretoboc er kolloð a norøno. Þat matti oc sia a honom hverso mikla stund hann hafði lagt a boc þa er hann hafði þa saman sett, oc hverso litt hann hafði meðan annars gætt: hann var rufinn oc oþveginn, magr oc bleikr í andlite. Oc er hann sa Alexandrum fostrson sinn þrutinn af mikille reíði þeire er eigi matte leynaz fyrir brugðnu oc bloðrauðo litar apte, þa spurðe hann eptir vandliga hver soc til vere sva sollinnar reíði. Hann gerði sva sem hlyðnom lærisveini byriar við sinn meistara, fellr a kne fyrir honom oc drepr niðr haufðeno, oc svarar sva af miklom moðe: "Þungt þycke mer þat at faðer minn elligamall scal lyðskylldr rangligom kraufom Darij konungs, oc þar með allt fostrland mitt." Oc þar matti hann þa ecki fleira um tala, þviat þesso nest kom gratr upp, sa er nackvat sva bra til bernsconnar, oc vara sa af litlo scape, oc með þvi minkar hann þa fyrst i stað sina reíðe. (*Alexanders saga*, ed. Finnur Jónsson, pp. 3-4)[5]

5. The quotation is a free translation of the following lines from the Latin poem, edited by Migne in *Patrologia Latina*, CCIX, col. 463 ff.:

Qualiter Hyrcanis si forte leunculus arvis
Cornibus elatos videt ire ad pabula cervos,
Cui nondum totos descendit robur in armos,
Nec pede firmus adhuc, nec dentibus asper aduncis
Palpitat, et vacuum ferit improba lingua palatum,
Effunditque prius animo, quam dente cruorem,
Pigritiamque pedum redimit matura voluntas.
Sic puer effrenus totus bacchatur in arma,
Invalidusque manu gerit alto corde leonem,
Et præceps teneros audacia prævenit annos.
   Forte macer, pallens, incompto crine magister
Nec facies studio male respondebat, apertis
Exierat thalamis, ubi nuper corpore toto
Perfécto logices, pugiles armarat elenchos.
O quam difficile est studium non prodere vultu!
Livida nocturnam sapiebant ora lucernam,
Seque maritabat tenui discrimine pellis
Ossibus in vultu, partesque effusa per omnes
Articulos manuum macies jejuna premebat;
Nulla repellebat a pelle parenthesis ossa:
Nam vehemens studii macie labor afficit artus,
Et molem carnis, et quod cibus educat extra,
Interior sibi sumit homo, fomenta laboris.

(And he is now filled with such a mighty fury against King Darius for having sent people to collect the tribute from his father, and he is, in his own imagination, taking arms for a bold attack, as when a lion's cub, before he has yet grown strong, sees a hart in front of him while his teeth are still so small that he cannot bite, but yet he empties the blood from the heart of the prey with his mind since he cannot do it with his teeth; and although he is slow on his feet, his will is quick to set forth. Thus Alexander had not enough strength to accomplish the great deeds that dwelled in his mind, but in his heart he had the courage of a lion with a boldness far greater than his age.

Now it so happened that Aristotle, his tutor and guardian, had left his room, where he had been writing a book about the art that is called *Dialectica* in Latin; this is called "The Book of Argumentation" in Norse. One could see from his appearance how much he had worked on this book that he had written, and how little he had cared about other things in the meantime. For he was ruffled and unwashed, and his face was thin and pale. And when he saw Alexander, his foster-son, swelled up in a rage so great that it could not be concealed, because his face had changed color and become red as blood, he asked him with care to give him the reason for such a swelling fury. Alexander then did as befits an obedient pupil in the presence of his teacher—he fell on his knees in front of him and bowed his head and answered with great sorrow: "It seems to me sad that my aged father shall be forced to obey the unjust demands of King Darius, and with him also my whole country." And he could not speak more words than these, for now his tears came flowing, more because of his childishness than because of any cowardly feelings, and in this way he first of all diminished his fury.)

The basic situation presented here is very common also in the native sagas: a young hero, eager to take revenge on his father's enemy, consults his Wise Counselor. But the quoted presentation is completely different. A native saga would emphasize action and dialogue, while here the emphasis is on psychology and morals. The narrator is eager to tell us what goes on in Alexander's mind. It is the *inner* drama that is important: the uproar of the passions, pictured as if they were independent "forces" seeking to dominate the personality. The perspective is openly didactic in a way that is alien to Icelandic saga tradition: the narrator holds up Alexander as a model

---

Ergo ubi flammato vidit Philippida vultu,
Accusabat enim occultam rubor igneus iram,
Flagitat, unde animus incanduit, unde doloris
Materiam traxit? quæ tanta efferbuit ira?
Ille sui reverens faciem monitoris, ocellos
Supplice dejecit vultu, pronusque sedentis
Affusus genibus, senium lugere parentis
Oppressum imperio Darii, patriamque jacentem
Conqueritur lacrymans, lacrymisque exaggerat iras . . .

(*Alexandreis*, vv. 59-90)

for his audience, explaining, analyzing, and moralizing like a preacher, so that there can be no doubt about the point that he is trying to make. *Alexanders saga* is similar to a hagiographic *vita* in that it is meant as a lesson on virtue and vice, even though its hero is a pagan prince with the virtues of a medieval knight, not a Christian martyr or confessor (note, however, that his tutor, Aristotle, embodies the ascetic ideals of a scholastic monk!).

At the same time, the scene has a wealth of descriptive detail which does not further the action but appeals to the senses in a way also uncommon in the native sagas. Alexander is "red as blood," while Aristotle is pale and looks "ruffled and unwashed." Alexander's gestures are flamboyantly expressive: he falls on his knees, his words are drowned in tears. And the parallel with the young lion and the hart is a visual image to be admired in its own right. Such graphic but exaggerated descriptions are especially frequent in the *riddarasǫgur*, in which the beauty of a lady, the splendor of a palace, or the ugliness of a villain are often portrayed in striking colors that would seem out of place both in hagiography and in classical family sagas. But these visual images are used primarily to dramatize mental states and mental reactions: the eulogized description of a beautiful woman, for example, emphasizes the attraction that the hero feels for her. The descriptions of Alexander and Aristotle in our quotation emphasizes the youthful agony of the former and the asceticism of the latter: their bodies mirror their souls.

In its presentation of characters, the clerical style reveals a theoretical and scholastic sophistication which must have seemed very strange to an Icelandic saga audience. For in a genuine native saga, such as *Heiðarvíga* or *Reykdœla*, all characters are primarily stock characters functioning within a conventional action pattern; their "inner" life is rudimentary, at most. They undergo no struggles within their souls.

Still, it was only natural that some sagawriters would attempt more "profound" characterization by applying a clerical perspective to the Icelandic saga heroes. This was done in an extremely unskillful but interesting manner by the author of *Fóstbrœðra saga*, whose style invites comparison to that of *Njála*.

Fóstbrœðra centers around Þorgeirr Hávarson, a customary Norse strong and silent hero, not as well individualized as the heroes of *Njála*. At the beginning of the saga, Þorgeirr's father is killed—a common motif, treated in conventional saga style and leading to an equally common motif, the hero's revenge on his father's slayer. It is usual to report how the son first received the news about his father's death, but the author of *Fostbrœðra* elaborates this in a way that completely violates "objective" saga rhetoric (cf. the passage from *Alexanders saga*):

Ok er Þorgeirr spurði víg fǫður síns, þá brá honum ekki við þá tíðenda sǫgn. Eigi roðnaði hann, því at eigi rann honum reiði í hǫrund; eigi bliknaði hann, því at honum lagði eigi heipt í brjóst; eigi blánaði hann, því at honum rann eigi í bein reiði, heldr brá hann sér engan veg við tíðenda sǫgnina, því at eigi var hjarta hans sem fóarn í fugli; eigi var þat blóðfullt, svá at þat skylfi af hræzlu, heldr var þat hert af inum hæsta hǫfuðsmið í ǫllum hvatleik. (*Fóstbr.*, chapter 2)

And when Þorgeirr heard about his father's death, he did not show any reaction to these tidings. He did not blush, for wrath did not run in his skin; nor did he become pale, for hate did not dwell in his chest; nor did he become black, for wrath did not run in his bones. No, he did not show any reaction to these tidings, for his heart was not like a bird's gizzard; it was not filled with blood so that it trembled in fear, for it was hardened in boldness by the highest heavenly smith.)

This, again, is a clear example of clerical style: alliterations and rhythmic effects, metaphor and antithesis, complicated sentence structure, and so on. The analytic and didactic perspective is the same as in *Alexanders saga*. We are to see Þorgeirr's body as a mirror of his soul and to understand his reaction in terms of "forces" influencing the human psyche and ultimately derived from God. (Metaphors such as "the highest heavenly smith" were often used in clerical writings of the Middle Ages to emphasize the similarity between God and the human craftsman.)[6] The description of Þorgeirr's heart (cf. Alexander's heart in the quotation from *Alexanders saga*!) appears to come both from Icelandic folk tradition and from learned speculation about the "nature of man."[7] But obviously the "learned" and "clerical" thinking has determined the peculiar shift of style.

The author was unable to integrate his clerical learning with the native saga traditions about Þorgeirr, and the result is rather heterogeneous. The saga is badly structured, full of "loose ends." In several places, the author seems naive and ignorant of the native language of tradition.

Let us now see what the author of *Njála* can do with the saga motifs used by the author of *Fóstbrœðra*. This is how *Njála* reports the reaction of Þórhallr Ásgrímsson to the death of *Njáll*:

Þórhallr Ásgrímsson was so upset when he was told that Njáll, his foster-father, was dead and burned in his home, that his whole body swelled up (*hann prútnaði allr*) and a stream of blood came out of each ear (*ok blóðbogi stóð ór hvárritveggju hlustinni*), and it could not be stopped until he fell unconscious. Then he stood up and said that he had behaved in an unmanly fashion: "I would like to avenge this on those who burned him." People

---

6. Cf. E. R. Curtius, *Europäische Literatur* . . . (7th ed., 1969), 527-529.

7. Cf. Lönnroth (1963-64), 44-48; Jónas Kristjánsson, *Um Fóstbrœðrasögu* (Reykjavik, 1972), 247.

said that nobody would blame him for what had happened, but he said that nobody could stop people from talking. (chapter 132)

Here the style is that of the traditional Icelandic saga: perfectly dry, empirical and "objective." The narrator shows us a scene but does not comment on it. Yet the scene has no precedent in the native tradition, and its psychology is "clerical" rather than typical of sagas: Þórhallr's spectacular and strange behavior is evidently meant to signal a violent inner conflict, one his will cannot control. Blood coming out of the ears suggests that the author of Njála was familiar with medieval medical theory; the stream of blood may be a sign that the sudden fury has caused Þórhallr's gall fluid to seek its "natural" exit through his ears (according to Hauksbók, the gall fluid would then appear as "red blood").[8] In any case, the struggle within Þórhallr is still more in the spirit of Alexanders saga than the almost inhuman coolness of Þorgeirr in Fóstbrœðra.

Þórhallr's inner struggle has important consequences. After his "unmanly" fit of passion, he carefully begins to prepare the lawsuit against the Burners of Njáll, and while doing so, an ugly boil empts on his leg. (This boil may also be interpreted as a result of his turbulent humors, which clerical minds believed to cause such infirmities.)[9] In connection with the growing boil,

8. This interpretation was first presented (with fewer reservations) by Lönnroth (1963-64), 49-50. P. Hallberg has justly objected that no medieval Latin treatise on the humoral system explicitly refers to blood streaming through the ears as a symptom of wrath. According to Hallberg, the medieval theory of "natural purgation of the gall fluid through the ears" should probably be understood to mean that the gall fluid left the body in the form of ear wax or purulent discharges from the ears (Samlaren, 1965, 170). This is probably quite correct. But any thirteenth-century Icelander familiar with the Norse version of this theory, presented in Um natturu mannzins ok blodi (Hauksbók), must have thought that the gall fluid was indeed supposed to come out through the ears in the form of "red blood." For in this brief thirteenth-century treatise on "The Nature of Man and His Blood," we find the following description of the four humors and their "natural exits" in the body: "Vari er i hofði mannz, bloð i lifr, rauða bloð i galli, suarta bloð i millti. Hvert þessarra luta hefir ok sinn vtgang ok andar tak: rauða bloð at eyrum, suarta bloð at augum, rett bloð at nosum, enn vari at munni" (Hauksbók, ed. Finnur Jónsson, 181-182). It seems to me most probable that this specific version of the humoral theory was known to the author of Njála (and possibly even to his audience), for it appears difficult to explain Þórhallr's curious and quite unprecedented reaction as pure artistic exaggeration "in baroque style" (as Sveinsson and Hallberg have tried to do; cf. Hallberg loc. cit.). The author of Njála may not be a realist, but he does not use such "baroque" effects without good reason.

9. Cf. Lönnroth (1963-64), 50. Hallberg does not accept this interpretation either since he does not consider it necessary for the understanding of the passage and since boils were quite common in the Middle Ages (Samlaren, 1965, 170). But boils are not very common in traditional sagas, and in this case the boil motif is presented in a way that is quite unique: in the context of an unusually sophisticated psychological characterization.

Þórhallr is characterized as "quiet in speech but yet quick-tempered" (*vel orðstilltr ok þó bráðskapaðr*; chapter 135), which further emphasizes inner conflict. His friends later notice that "his face was as red as blood and big hail stones came out of his eyes; he asked them to give him his spear" (chapter 141). Still later, when Þórhallr is told that the lawsuit has been lost, he pierces the boil with his spear so that blood and matter gush out of the wound, whereupon he strides quickly out of his booth and slays one of his enemies, thereby provoking the major battle at the Allthing (chapter 145). His passions have finally defeated his self-control.

The author of *Njála* evidently wants his audience to consider that a hero who becomes a slave to his passions destroys the chance of a peaceful settlement. Although this "moral" may be compatible with the ethics inherent in traditional sagas, it is at least partly inspired by the author's "clerical mind." Even in *Fóstbrœðra*, the idea of a struggle between will and passion plays a far less important role—not because the author of *Fóstbrœðra* did not care about such ideas, for his "clerical" digressions show that he did, but because he was not skilled enough to let his Christian ideas animate the heroic legends which he had inherited from earlier generations. In spite of these digressions and other departures from saga style, he probably presents oral tradition in a "rawer" form than the author of *Njála* ever does.

Thus, though the author of *Njála* generally uses traditional saga language, he gives a new twist to the old motifs and narrative techniques by integrating them with the clerical thinking of his time. The integration is so successful that it is difficult to know which specific romances, saints' lives, or theological writings he was familiar with. Yet we can say with certainty that he knew the style of such works.[10]

Clerical Style in Njála

At times his style does give him away. When Njáll speaks at the Allthing about his sorrow after Hoskuldr's death, he says: "it seemed to me that the sweetest light of my eyes had been turned out" (*þótti mér sløkkt it sœtasta*

Our "humoral" interpretation of the motif may explain why this is so. It is also quite probable, however, that the motif should be related to the indigenous Icelandic belief that a person's body "swells up" from too much sorrow (see, for example, *Guðrúnarkviða* I). At any rate, there is more subtle thinking behind this passage than we usually expect from a saga and, to this extent, it may be said to be indicative of the author's "clerical mind."

10. Cf. Heusler (1914), 17. Peter Foote has put it this way: "The author of *Njála saga* must have known much translated romance and ecclesiastical literature . . .-yet, he writes *Njáls saga*" (*The Pseudo-Turpin Chronicle in Iceland*, 1959, p. V).

ljós augna minna). This is not saga language. As Sveinsson has shown, the expression emanates from the Vulgate.[11] David uses the same metaphor when he feels estranged from God: "even the light of my eyes has left me" (*lux oculorum meorum etiam ipsa non est mecum*; Psalms 37.11). In medieval hagiography, the phrase is used particularly when a parent mourns the loss of a beloved and saintly child. *"Heu heu me fili ut quid te misimus peregrinari lumen oculorum nostrorum!"* exclaims old Tobit about his lost son in the Book of Tobit (10.4). *"Heu me, lumen oculorum meorum!"* cries the mother of Saint Alexis. *"Filia mea dulcissima Juliana, lux oculorum meorum!"* sobs the father of Saint Juliana, and an Anglo-Saxon poet who translated these sobs used words extremely similar to Njáll's:

> Ðu eart dohtor min   seo dyreste
> ond seo *sweteste*   in sefan minum,
> ange for eorþan,   *minra eagna leoht*,
> Iuliana!
> (You are my daughter, the dearest and
> sweetest to my heart, my only one in the
> world, light of my eyes, Juliana!)
>   (*Juliana*, vv. 93-96; italics added)

None of these mourning scenes appear to have been translated into Icelandic before *Njála* was written, and the Anglo-Saxon poem could hardly have been known in Iceland; thus it is quite likely that our author took the phrase directly from the Latin tradition. What makes this borrowing particularly significant is the clear association between the metaphor ("sweetest light of my eyes") and the Hǫskuldr motif. For Hǫskuldr is pictured as a saint, and his death is portrayed as a medieval *passio*. When his foster-father, Njáll, speaks about him in this way, the hagiographic pattern is further emphasized.

At the beginning of chapter 116, Hildigunnr greets Flosi with another phrase that seems strangely out of style: "my heart rejoices at your arrival" (*er fegit hjarta mitt tilkvámu þinni*). Again we seem to hear an echo of the style used in the Vulgate and in later medieval prose: *laetatum est cor meum in adventu tuo*.[12] To an Icelandic audience this must have sounded almost blasphemic, spoken by a vengeful Prima Donna type about to send her visitor out either to kill or to be killed (the traditional Goading Scene). The effect, however, is superb and, obviously, quite deliberate; Hildigunnr's sweet biblical cajoling makes her seem both alluring and terrifying, a veritable Judas greeting her master with a kiss. A few moments later, her true emotions are revealed as she throws the bloodied cloak over Flosi's

---

11. Cf. Sveinsson (1933), 339-40; *Njála* (1954), 309 (note).
12. Cf. Sveinsson (1943), 21 (English transl., 1971, p. 31).

head and appeals to his "manhood" as well as to "all the virtues of your Christ" to make him seek revenge. Flosi's bitter and very traditional Icelandic comment, "Cold are the counsels of women," provides an effective contrast to the literary, non-Icelandic, and quite insincere "warmth" of Hildigunnr's greeting.

When Flosi somewhat later (chapter 124) decides to take the revenge Hildigunnr had asked for, he says to his men: "We shall ride to Bergþórshváll with all our forces and fall upon the sons of Njáll with fire and iron, and we shall not leave until they are all dead" (*skulu vér ríða til Bergþórshváls með ǫllu liðinu ok sœkja Njálssonu með eldi ok járni ok ganga eigi fyrr frá en þeir eru allir dauðir*). The formula "fire and iron" (*eldr ok járn*) is used twice in Old Norse poetry, but was used more commonly in Latin prose (*flamma et ferrum* or *ferrum et flamma*) to describe military destruction.[13] Theodoricus Monachus, the author of a Latin history of Norway, quotes Hugh of St. Victor as saying that the Northmen broke into France and "everything was laid waste by iron and fire" (*Northmanni de Scythia inferiori egressi, classe advecti Gallias intrantesque per Sequanam fluvium omnia depopulati sunt ferro et flamma*).[14] The formula here conveys a particularly terrifying military destruction, threatening all of Christianity and ordained by God. In a similar context, the phrase *ignis et gladius* is used in Pseudo-Turpin's *Historia Karoli Magni et Rotholandi*, a fictitious chronicle translated into Icelandic in the early thirteenth century and later incorporated in *Karlamagnús saga* (around 1250). When Charlemagne reproaches the heathen King Agolandus for destroying his country and persecuting the Christians, he says, in the Icelandic translation: *Mínar borgir hefir þú niðr brotit ok kastala ok eydd lönd mín með eldi ok járni* ("You have destroyed my cities and castles and laid my countries waste with fire and iron"; cf. the Latin original: *Meas urbes et castella destruxisti, totamque terram igne et gladio vastasti*).[15]

Flosi's speech to his men before attacking Bergþórshváll appears to reflect this "clerical" usage of the "fire and iron" formula. The grim intensity of his words is more characteristic of clerical prose than of saga style. He speaks as a man fulfilling a destructive mission within the Christian world order—a mission similar to that of the Northmen as pictured by Hugh of St. Victor, or to King Agolandus as pictured by Pseudo-Turpin. This becomes evident later, when Flosi says to his men as they are about to begin

---

13. Cf. *Lexicon Poeticum*, 328; *Thesaurus Linguæ Latinæ*, VI, col. 585, 866.

14. *Monumenta Historica Norvegiæ*, 4. The parallel has been noted by Clover (1972).

15. *Karlamagnús saga*, ed. Unger, 273; *Historia Karoli Magni et Rotholandi*, ed. Meredith-Jones, 130; on the Icelandic tradition, cf. Peter Foote (1959).

the burning of Bergþórshváll: "We now have two choices and neither is good; one is to leave and that will be our death; the other is to burn them in their house, and that will be a heavy responsibility before God, since we are Christians ourselves. Yet, that is what we shall do" (. . . *er þat þó stór ábyrgð fyrir guði, er vér erum kristnir sjálfir. En þó munu vér þat bragðs taka*). And we later learn that the burning has cleansed Njáll's family from the sin of killing Hǫskuldr; Flosi is used as God's tool in an act of divine retribution (cf. below, pp. 131-132). It is thus natural that Flosi's language is "clerical" directly before the Burning of Njáll.

As these examples indicate, the author's clerical mind is most evident in his language where the native saga language cannot express the ideas and emotions he wants to convey. Occasionally, he will use a foreign loanword, e.g., *panzari* (mailcoat, German *Panzer*), *leó* (lion, Latin *leo*), *náttúra* (nature, Latin *natura*), *próba* (investigate, inquire in a legal case, Latin *probare*), *púta* (whore, French *putain*), *kurteiss* (French *courtois*), *jústa* (a kind of vessel, used to measure liquids, from Latin *justa mensura*), and a few others.[16] Although his usage of such words shows him to be a well-educated man (his usage of *próba*, for example, suggests the sophistication of a lawyer),[17] he uses them sparingly and only to convey concepts that were not present in his native language. The very idea of a "whore," for example, was alien to native thinking: prostitution did not exist in Iceland, and sexual attitudes were liberal even after the conversion. It is thus both anachronistic and a violation of saga style (but typical of his own "clerical mind") to let Skarpheðinn in chapter 91 accuse Hallgerðr of being a whore, *púta*. But *púta* is certainly the right word, for by various subtle means the author has managed to present Hallgerðr in such a way that the audience must see her not only as a traditional Norse Prima Donna but also as the Seductive Bad Woman known to the Christian Middle Ages (cf. below, p. 160).

Influence from Riddara Sǫgur

The influence of religious prose is naturally most apparent in sections dealing with specifically Christian motifs (miracles, the conversion of the Icelanders, etc.). Romance is most influential in descriptive sections that picture the heroes in a chivalric splendor, which is alien to native tradition: for example, gilded mailcoats, belts of silver, scarlet cloaks, silk jackets, decorated shields, etc. As noted above, these visual details aid in the

16. Fischer, *Die Lehnwörter*, 110-111; Cf. Lehmann-Carolsfeld (1883), 3.

17. Cf. Sveinsson, *Njála* (1954), 161, note 3; *Alexanders saga* uses *próba* in very much the same way as *Njála*. A few other family sagas also use that term but in a more general and vulgar sense ("try" or "test").

psychological characterization. The sons of Njáll are thus described as they leave their home to attack Þráinn:

Skarpheðinn var fremstr ok var í blám stakki ok hafði torguskjold ok øxi sína reidda um oxl. Næst honum gekk Kári; hann hafði silkitreyju ok hjálm gyldan, skjold ok var dreginn á leó. Næst honom gekk Helgi. Hann hafði rauðan kyrtil ok hjálm ok rauðan skjold ok markaðr á hjortr. Allir váru þeir í litklæðum. (chapter 92)

(Skarpheðinn came first, dressed in a blue jacket and carrying a round shield, with his axe hoisted on his shoulder. Kári came after him, dressed in a silk jacket and a gilded helmet; a lion was painted on his shield. After him came Helgi dressed in a red tunic and a helmet and carrying a red shield decorated with a hart. They all wore colored clothing.)

Needless to say, the description is completely anachronistic; Icelandic farmers did not dress like this in the tenth century (not even when they went out to slay a neighbor.) Such decorated shields belong to chivalric customs that were not introduced in Scandinavia until the thirteenth century. It is not certain that the author of *Njála* had even seen any people dressed like this in his own time. The origin of the description should be sought in passages like the following from *Þiðreks saga af Bern*:

Heimir inn mikilláti hefir . . . skjold bláan ok á markaðr hestr með bleikum lit . . . Hornbogi jarl hafði skjold ok alla herneskju með brúnum lit; á hans vápnum var markaðr haukr af gulli . . . . Fasold inn stoltzi hefir skjold ok alla herneskju sem gull ok markat á león með rauðu . . . . Gunnarr konungr hefir alla herneskju hvíta sem silfr ok er ámarkað hans skildi orn ein ok króna á hofði. [18]

(Helmir the Haughty had . . . a blue shield decorated with a horse in yellow . . . . Earl Hornbogi had his shield and all of his armor colored in brown; a golden hawk was painted on his weapons . . . . Fasold the Proud had his shield and all of his armor colored like gold and decorated with a red lion . . . . All of King Gunnarr's armor was white as silver and his shield was decorated with a crowned eagle.)

Þiðreks saga also explains the symbolic meaning of the colors and the shield decorations: the lion signifies courage, the blue color signifies "a cold breast and a cruel heart," etc. Explanations of this kind are typical of "clerical style," but they would seem out of place in *Njála*. Yet, the author of *Njála* may well have had such symbolic meanings in mind. It is appropriate, for example that Skarpheðinn, who is more cruel, scornful, and problematic than his brothers, is shown in the color that signifies "a cold breast and a cruel heart," while his more gentle brother Helgi is shown wearing red clothes and carrying a picture of a hart, a gentle and peaceful animal, on his shield. It also seems appropriate that Kári, whose role and

18. *Þiðriks saga af Bern*, ed. H. Bertelsen, 328, 332, 336-37, 342.

character are most reminiscent of chivalric heroes in *riddarasǫgur*, should be dressed in gold and silk and have a lion painted on his shield.

Even if such symbolism was not intended, the colorful images arrest the flow of action in order to let us *see* the heroes and think about their characters, status, and relationship to each other precisely when they are leaving home to fight a dangerous battle. This close-up technique may be considered part of the traditional "staging" before climactic events in the sagas. Yet the author's borrowings from the romance tradition have added a new dimension to the characterization, making it more subtle and individualized than in traditional Icelandic feud stories.

Some introductory presentations of characters in *Njála* are also clearly influenced by the literary portraits of *riddarasǫgur*. This can be seen if we compare, for example, the portrait of Gunnarr to portraits of similar heroes in other texts. Let us begin by comparing Gunnarr's portrait to that of Þórólfr Skallagrímsson in *Egils saga*, another traditional Icelandic hero of the "Siegfried type":

A. Hann (Gunnarr) var vænn at yfirliti ok ljóslitaðr, réttnefjaðr ok hafit upp framanvert, bláeygr ok snareygr ok roði í kinnunum; hárit mikit, gult, ok fór vel. Manna kurteisastr var hann, harðgǫrr í ǫllu, fémildr ok stilltr vel, vinfastr ok vinavandr; hann var vel auðigr at fé. (*Njála*, chapter 19)

(He was a handsome man, with fair skin and a straight nose, slightly tilted at the tip, had keen blue eyes, red cheeks, thick flaxen hair which suited him well. He was a most refined man, fearless, generous, eventempered, faithful to his friends and careful in choosing them; he was a very prosperous man.)

B. Var Þórólfr manna vænstr ok gǫrviligastr; hann var líkr móðurfrændum sínum, gleðimaðr mikill, ǫrr ok ákafamaðr mikill í ǫllu ok inn mesti kappsmaðr; var hann vinsæll af ǫllum mǫnnum. (*Eg.*, chapter 1)

(Þórólfr was a most handsome and accomplished man; he resembled his kinsmen on his mother's side, very cheerful, swift and eager in all his undertakings and a great warrior; he was well liked by everybody.)

The description of Þórólfr is typical of a "presentation segment" in a traditional family saga. It is hardly a "portrait" since it does not present any clear visual image. The narrator merely defines the hero's relation to his family ("like his kinsmen on his mother's side") and to the community at large ("cheerful . . . well liked"). The presentation is conventional, with no striking details. It is also completely unromantic and unpoetic. Introductions in oral sagas were probably of this kind—brief, rapid, and colorless, leading quickly to the action.

The portrait of Gunnarr, however, clearly appeals to the senses, and is much more detailed (our quotation actually represents only a small part of the introduction, which also describes his family relations, his various talents as a warrior, etc.). The visual image of the hero is to be admired as a separate work of art. While there are several "realistic" details ("a straight nose, slightly tilted at the tip," etc.), the tone is eulogistic and romantic (note the use of alliteration and assonance!), and the overall impression is that of a chivalric ideal: a beautiful soul in a beautiful body, "a most refined man."

The technique is very similar in portraits such as that of Hector in *Trójumannasaga* (a romantic adaptation of the Troy legend) or King Gunnarr in *Þiðreks saga*:

C. Ector . . . var blestr í máli, hvítr á hárslit, hrokkinhárr ok nǫkkut skjálgr, sterkligr ok stórlimaðr með tiguligu yfirbragði, hygginn ok hógværr, mildr ok mjúklátr, ǫrr ok ástsæll við alla sína menn ok hin mesta kempa í ǫllum bardǫgum. (*Trójumanna saga*)[19]

(Ector . . . was lisping in his speech, his hair was white and curly; his eyes squinted somewhat; he was strong and had large limbs and a noble appearance; he was prudent and gentle, mild and meek, generous and adored by all his men and the greatest of warriors in all battles.)

D. Gunnarr konungr var ljóshárr ok breiðleitr, ljóst skegg ok skammt, herðibreiðr, ljóslitaðr ok háligr at ǫllum vexti, sýndum kurteiss, sterkr ok allgóðr riddari ok haukligr er hann sat á sínum hesti, ok vel kann hann á sínum hesti við skjǫld ok sverð ok skot. Hann er áræðismaðr mikill, frækn ok óforsjáll, grimmr, glaðr ok mildr af fé, auðtryggr við vini sína, talhlýðinn, góðr drengr, harðr við sína óvini. (*Þiðreks saga*, chapter 289)

(King Gunnarr was blond and broadfaced had a blond and short beard, broad shoulders, bright skin and a stately appearance; he was refined, strong and was an excellent horseman, looking like a hawk when he sat on his horse, skillful with shield, sword and arrow while riding. He was a very brave man, grim, bold and uncautious, credulous, a good warrior, cruel to his enemies.)

Although such portraits in the translated *riddarasǫgur* are undoubtedly influenced by the native saga tradition, they are naturally even more determined by their foreign originals. The portrait of Hector is thus ultimately derived from the following description in Dares Phrygius' *Historia de excidio Trojae*: (*Dares ait se vidisse*) *Hectorem blaesum, candidum, crispum, strabum, pernicibus membris, vultu venerabili, barbatum, decentem, bellicosum, animo magno, in civibus clementem, dignum, amore aptum.*[20] Portraits of this kind are frequent in Late Latin prose, and they were elaborated to fit the chivalric ideals of French romance in works such as Benoit de Saint Maure's *Roman de Troie*. This is how Benoit presents Hector:

19. The text of the portrait is reconstructed in my article "Det litterära porträttet," *APhS*, 27 (1965), 110.

20. Dares, *Historia de excidio Trojae*, ed. Meister, 15.

De pris toz homes sormontot,
Mais un sol petit baubeiot.
D'andous les ieuz borgnes esteit,
Mais point ne li mesaveneit.
Chief ot blont e cresp, blanche char,
E si n'aveit cure d'eschar.
Cors ot bien fait e forniz membres
Mais il nes aveit mie tendres . . .
. . . Sol proëce li remaneit
E li frans cuers, quil somoneit
De toz jorz faire come ber.[21]

(In honor he surpassed everybody, even though he stuttered a little.
Both his eyes squinted, but it did not bother him. His head was blond and
curly, his skin fair; he had no fear of scorn. His body was well formed with
muscular limbs, not weak . . . . His prowess alone kept him up, and his
stout heart, which always made him act like a knight.)

Norse writers of *riddarasǫgur* apparently constructed their portraits of
chivalric heroes by mixing together elements from both Latin and French
tradition with the "presentation segment" of their own native sagas.[22] In
dwelling on such detailed descriptions, often to the detriment of the action,
they were probably inspired by clerical ideas about "the body as a mirror of
the soul." In one of the Old Norse tracts on "the nature of man," we thus
find detailed explanations of the relationship between human physiognomy
and character:

En þeir, er með bjǫrtu blóði skína ok blandit meðr litlum roða, eru blíðir
í viðrmæli ok léttir . . . . En hvítr skinnslitr ok nǫkkut rjóðr segir styrka
menn ok hugfulla . . . . Svartr skinnslitr ok blandinn meðr litlum bláma
synir hryggva menn ok í lunderni þunga . . . . Rauðlitaðir menn með
blǫnduðum dǫkktum lit eru djarfir ok til reiði skjótir, etc.[23]
(Those who shine with bright blood and mixed with a little red are mild
in speech and easy-going . . . . White skin, somewhat blushing, is characteristic of strong and thoughtful men . . . . Black skin, mixed with blue,
is characteristic of anxious and depressed people . . . . Men with red and
somewhat dark skin are bold and easily angered, etc.)

We shall never know the extent to which the author of *Njála* was familiar
with such theories. The influence of clerical style in *Njála* is not obtrusive.
It is present merely as an undertone, as bright imported threads are woven
into a rustic, home-made fabric. Yet we suggest that the weaver knew
more about the continental fashions than he cared to show in his work.

---

21. Benoit de Sainte Maure, *Le Roman de Troie*, ed. Constans, vol. I, 277-78.
22. Cf. Lönnroth, "Det litterära porträttet" (1965).
23. *Alfræði íslenzk*, III, ed. Kålund, 97-98, 103; Cf. Lönnroth (1963-64), 38-43.

Specific Foreign Models

Some specific works of foreign origin have been proposed as models for particular scenes or incidents in *Njála*. Let us examine briefly each of these possible cases of literary borrowing.

First there is Saint Gregory's *Dialogues*, composed in the sixth century and extremely popular among the clergy throughout the Middle Ages; it is one of the Latin texts first translated into Old Norse—the earliest Icelandic manuscript dates from about 1200.

The *Dialogues* is a theological tract used to teach the fundamentals of Christian ethics; its form is that of a conversation between Gregory and one of his students, Peter. The student asks questions, and his master answers them by providing a series of edifying *exempla* from the lives of pious men and women. The stories are often concluded with a "moral" or some observation on Christian doctrine, giving rise to new questions and new stories. This technique is common in medieval didactic works and was imitated in the Icelandic *Prose Edda* and the Norwegian *Konungs skuggsjá*.

One of Gregory's *exempla*, which illustrates the relation between man's free will and God's predetermination, tells about Anastasius, a monk who dreamed that he heard a voice coming out of a mountain near his monastery. The voice called his name and that of several other monks, then paused before calling the name of still another monk. This dream meant that the monks were destined to die very soon and in the order in which they had been called, the last of them somewhat later than the others (as indicated by the pause). But one young monk whose name had *not* been called asked Anastasius to pray for him, so that he would also be called away with the others. Anastasius' prayer was heard, and the young monk died with the others. Gregory's conclusion: human life is governed by God's plan, but man may still exert his free will to a certain extent—even though Anastasius' prayer had, in fact, been included in the plan from the beginning!

As Sveinsson has shown,[24] this *exemplum* must have inspired the story of Flosi's dream in chapter 133. In this dream Flosi sees a giant coming out of the mountain Lómagnúpr, not far from his home. The giant calls out the names of Flosi's companions who participated in he Burning of Njáll, and he pauses between some of the names. Here also, the men are doomed to die in the order in which they are called, each pause signifying time between the deaths.

Although there are very few verbal similarities between the two stories, their basic structure and meaning are the same. No other parallels have

---

24. Sveinsson (1943), 10-11, 171. English trans. (1971), 14-15, 205-206. See also Strömbäck (1968), 140 f.

been found, either in the sagas or elsewhere, and we know that the *Dialogues* must have been read and studied often in thirteenth century Iceland, so it is indeed possible that the author of *Njála* knew the work in its entirety. It is also possible that he had heard the story of Anastasius read as an isolated *exemplum* or told second-hand in some secular context. Anecdotes from the *Dialogues* may well have drifted into popular tradition several years before the writing of *Njála*. To *prove* that our author had read Saint Gregory is, therefore, impossible.

Yet the *Dialogues* may be considered an extremely likely source, not only for the story of Flosi's dream but also for the entire clerical philosophy of *Njála*, including the Augustinian ideas about free will and predestination, the concept of the human soul as ridden by ignoble passions, and so on. We shall, therefore, use the *Dialogues* now and then to provide parallels and illustrations of our author's "clerical mind."

Another work which he *may* have known is *Placidus saga* (*Vita Eustachii*), a hagiographic *píslarsaga* (*passio*) translated into Old Norse around 1200 and popular enough to have inspired a skaldic poem, *Plácítúsdrápa*. The hero of this legend is a noble Roman officer who was converted to the Christian faith during the reign of Trajan and was then tested by God. Placidus remained forever patient and placid as he lost his wealth, his wife, and his two sons. At the end of his life, he found his family again, and they were all happily martyred together, none of them wishing to worship pagan idols. They were first exposed to a lion, but the noble beast refused to eat them. They were then placed together in a "brazen ox" (*eiruxi*), a sort of large oven, in which they burned to death. But their dead bodies were untouched by the fire and left "white as snow"—a sure sign of holiness.

This story is evidently similar to the scene in *Njála* where the dead bodies of Njáll, Bergþóra, and their grandson are found untouched by the fire under the skin of an ox. In this case only Njáll himself is shining and bright enough to be among God's martyrs. But the parallel is still obvious, and it is strengthened by the fact that Njáll's behavior and attitude before his death is reminiscent of Placidus in suffering his ordeals. The appearance of an "ox" in both texts (the "brazen ox" and the "ox-skin") suggests a further connection between the stories. We cannot be certain that the author of *Njála* had read our present text of *Placidus saga*. We may, however, be certain that he knew at least some hagiographic tales of this general type.[25]

It has been suggested that he knew *Þiðreks saga*, mainly because of a parallel between its chapter 200 and chapter 69 of *Njála* (the description of

25. Cf. Lönnroth (1963-64), 32. The text of *Placidus saga* is found in *Heilagra manna sögur*, ed. Unger, 193-203.

Gunnarr's sleeping enemies).[26] Parallels in the descriptions of armor in the two sagas have been noted above (p. 117), but the similarities are so general that we can assume no direct influence. Besides, Þiðreks saga is a very large collection of stories which were probably known to people in bits and pieces, so that the author of Njála may well have picked up isolated motifs from it without knowing the whole work.

The case for direct influence is stronger in Alexanders saga, a work we have already used to illustrate "clerical style." Einar Ólafur Sveinsson first discovered a close parallel between a key scene in Alexander's biography and the most famous scene in Gunnarr's life: the one where he sees the "beautiful slopes" and decides to return to Hlíðarendi. There are other parallels as well,[27] but since the most important of them will be discussed in a later section of this chapter, we shall here merely say that even though we cannot prove that our author had read it, he probably did know Alexanders saga in some form or other. Alexanders saga is attributed to Bishop Brandr Jónsson, a prominent member of the so-called Svínfellinga family, who traced his descent from Flosi and was active in the area of Iceland where Njála is known to have been written, evidently by a man who had close connection with Bishop Brandr's family (cf. Chapter 5). Our author may, in fact, have had easy access to the Bishop's original manuscript of Alexanders saga, which was probably written shortly before Njála.

Yet it is futile to speculate about the books contained in our author's library. In his relation to clerical and chivalric literature of the Middle Ages, he stands as free and independent as he does in his relation to native saga tradition. He does not copy from "sources" but uses from memory whatever fits his own plan: to write a saga that incorporates both the traditional style of sagas and Christian values and ideas. We shall hence forth discuss his "clerical" thinking with only incidental concern for specific literary influences.

3. GOD'S PLAN AND THE ÓGÆFA

Augustinian Theology in Iceland

In Augustinian theology, which dominated the clerical minds of the Middle Ages, history is seen as a continuous feud between God and the devil. Both use man to carry out their designs. The struggle is enacted in each human

26. Cf. Marina Mundt, "Observations on the Influence of Þiðriks saga on Icelandic Saga-Writing," a paper delivered at the First International Saga Conference in Edinburgh, 1971.

27. Cf. Sveinsson, Njála (1954), p. xxxvi; Lönnroth, "Hetjurnar líta bleika akra: Athuganir á Njáls sögu og Alexanders sögu," Skírnir, 144 (1970), 12-30.

heart as well as in the political arena. The main representatives of God on earth are the chosen martyrs and confessors, the inspired prophets, and the rightful kings blessed by divine grace and supported by loyal, law-abiding citizens; these are the people who strive for justice and peace and the attainment of Heaven. They must constantly defend themselves against the sin in their own souls and against the ubiquitous emissaries of the devil: sorcerers, idolators, heretics, evil spirits, seducers, disrupters of the peace, and unjust rulers who set themselves up against the divine kingdom and attract a large following among the foolish and the sinful. Just wars must be fought against such forces of evil, and the Church is therefore militant rather than pacific.[28]

To an Augustinian mind in Iceland, the Good Christian Chieftain would correspond to the rightful kings of biblical and European history, while the Evil Chieftain would correspond to the unjust ruler. The worshippers of Odin and Thor were identified as idolators, and the practitioners of *seiðr* and other forms of pagan witchcraft were looked upon as close allies of Hell. Among the earliest Norse Christians, on the other hand, one would look for prophets, martyrs, and chosen warriors of Christ. In order to see this kind of theology at work, we need only to take a look at any of the *biskupasǫgur* (sagas of the Icelandic bishops) or the various hagiographic accounts of the conversion of Norway and Iceland found in early *konungasǫgur*.

It is central to the Augustinian doctrine, however, that God is mightier than the devil. In spite of the devil's disruptive operations, history proceeds according to God's plan; He has foreseen everything that will happen and has predetermined the general course of events. Although His plan may never become fully known to man, it is partly revealed in prophecies and miracles. Certain historical characters and events, as well as many natural phenomena, are also edifying *exempla*. By studying the world around him, man becomes aware of such *exempla*, and he further increases his wisdom by studying the Bible, the lives of the saints, and even secular historiography. Like a patient schoolmaster, God has repeated the same patterns in history over and over again: their instructive value cannot be lost on the attentive student.

Even though God has made provisions for the future of this world, He also, by His grace, has granted man the freedom to choose between good and evil, i.e., to let man's actions be determined by his virtue or by his vice. Confronted with this choice, man seeks support in the Christian precepts and *exempla*.

28. On Augustinian interpretation of history in the Middle Ages, see, for example, E. Bernheim, *Mittelalterliche Zeitanschauungen in ihrem Einfluss auf Politik und Geschichtsschreibung* (Tübingen, 1918).

The doctrine of free will certainly may appear to contradict the doctrines of providence and predestination, and medieval theologians were, in fact, bothered by this problem. They generally solved the conflict by assuming that God could predict a person's life (providence) and also determine its general course (predestination) without "determining" individual moral decisions. God would, for example, determine what kind of character a person would have, how long his life would last, and what kind of worldly success or misfortune he would have. Within these limits, the person could still choose between good and evil actions. Thus Alexander was destined to become a great conqueror—but he was free to play this role well or badly. And although Placidus was fated for much suffering, it was by his own free will that he endured this suffering like a saint.

The Icelanders and Norwegians of the thirteenth century learned this general theology (which I have paraphrased and simplified) from theological tracts such as Gregory's *Dialogues*, *Elucidarius*, or *Konungs skuggsjá*. They also learned from the concrete applications of Augustinian thought found in chronicles, sainsts lives, and even in some *riddarasǫgur*.

It was natural that this theological interpretation of history and human conduct would blend with the native Icelandic ideas of fate (*auðna*) and luck or fortune (*gæfa*, *gipta*, *hamingja*). The traditional fatalism implied in pagan myths and heroic legends could easily be adjusted to suit the Christian ideas of predestination and providence. Man's luck could be identified with God's grace. The pagan belief in fetches (*fylgjur*) and other supernatural creatures which watched over a man's destiny could be transformed, without much difficulty, into the Christian belief in divine protection. There is no doubt that such transformations occurred at an early stage in the tradition, so early that it is often quite difficult to disentangle the genuine pagan and Norse ideas from their Christian counterparts.[29]

Some scholars have solved this problem by simply ignoring the existence of Augustinian Christian thought in thirteenth century Iceland. By so doing, they have been able to regard all "fatalistic" elements in the sagas (ominous dreams, prophecies, etc.) as pagan and Germanic, undiluted by Christian influence. In understandable reaction against such oversimplification, other scholars have recently attempted to show that the metaphysical machinery of the sagas, including fate and luck, is derived from Christian sources.

29. Good modern surveys of the discussion about this problem may be found in Gerd Wolfgang Weber's *Studien zum Schicksalsbegriff der altenglischen und altnordischen Literatur* (diss., Frankfurt a.M., 1969) and in Lennart Ejerfeldt's "Helighet, 'karisma' och kungadöme i forngermansk religion," *Kungl. Humanistiska Vetenskapssamfundets i Uppsala Årbok* (1969-1970), 112-175 (also published as *Skrifter utgivna av religionshistoriska institutionen i Uppsala*, 7).

Walter Baetke may be regarded as the main spokesman for this modern tendency to seek Christian origins of concepts in sagas that at first appear to be pagan. In a highly stimulating and provocative study on "Christian Elements in the Saga Religion,"[30] he showed that the terms *auðna, gipta, gæfa,* and *hamingja* do not appear in the sense of "fate" or "fortune" in early pagan texts like the Edda but seem to have Christian connotations in the texts where they are first attested. The case of *gæfa-gipta-hamingja* is particularly interesting and has been further explored by Baetke's followers.[31] The etymology of *hamingja* indicates that the word originally meant some kind of spirit similar to the fetch or *fylgja. Gæfa* and *gipta,* on the other hand, are both derived from a Germanic root meaning "gift, present"; they correspond to Gothic *gibu* and Anglo-Saxon *giefu,* both of which are used to translate Latin *gratia, donum,* or *munus* in the sense of (divine) grace. This Christian concept may also have influenced the use of *hamingja* in the sense of "luck," for such usage is first attested in clerical sagas dealing with Christian kings blessed by God's grace. The impersonal hamingja, "luck," which we find in the classical family sagas, may then be a further development of this concept.

Baetke and his followers may be right or wrong about the original meaning and development of the words used for "fate" and "fortune" in the sagas, but it is still obvious that the classical sagawriters saw a difference between words such as *auðna, gæfa, gipta,* and *hamingja,* which are used in non-Christian contexts, and, on the other hand, words such as *fyrirætlan, miskunn,* or *líkn,* which are exclusively Christian and are used to express the theological concepts of predestination and divine grace. The former group of words is much more common in the family sagas, the latter group of words is much more common in saints' lives and homilies. To put it differently: *auðna, gæfa,* etc. belong to the native "language of tradition" while *fyrirætlan, líkn,* etc. belong to "clerical style."[32]

<hr />

30. "Christliches Lehngut in der Sagareligion," *Sitz. ber. d. sächs. Akad. d. Wiss. zu Leipzig, Philol-hist. Kl.,* 98:6 (Berlin, 1951); reprinted in *Kleine Schriften* (Weimar, 1973), 319-50.

31. See, in particular, Ejerfeldt, *op. cit.* Baetke was strongly criticized by P. Hallberg in "The concept of *gipta, gæfa, hamingja* in Old Norse Literature," a paper presented at the First International Saga Conference in Edinburgh, 1971. See also the discussion between Hallberg and Lönnroth in *Arkiv för nordisk filologi* (1966, 1968).

32. For statistics showing the frequency of *gæfa, gipta, hamingja* in various types of Norse texts, cf. P. Hallberg, *Arkiv för nordisk filologi* (1966), 271. The undeniable fact that these words are more frequent in sagas about pagan Icelanders than in translated saints' lives is used by Hallberg as evidence that the concept of "luck" in the sagas is of pre-Christian origin. This conclusion is not permissible, however, since the texts used by Hallberg were written several centuries after the introduction of Christianity, and the

But even though a word like *gæfa* or *gipta* was not specifically Christian, it was not specifically pagan or unchristian either, and it could, therefore, be used to express Christian ideas if the sagawriter wanted to do so without using theological terms, which would have sounded strange to the audience. As an example of such usage, we may take the passage in *Vatnsdœla saga* where Þorkell krafla is described as "a very lucky man" (*mikill giptumaðr*) who "had the right faith and loved his God and prepared for his death in the most Christian manner" (chapter 47). The meaning is evidently that God has bestowed His grace on Þorkell, even though the author uses his native saga idiom and not the language of theologians to express it. No paganism whatsoever is implied in calling Þorkell a *giptumaðr*.

In other sagas, a belief in fortune sometimes appears to be associated with pagan worship and ritual, for example in *Heimskringla*, where we are told that King Dómaldi was sacrificed by his people as a means to obtain good crops and that Earl Hákon sacrificed his own son in order to be victorious against his enemies.[33] But sagawriters disapprove strongly of such barbaric actions, which probably did not occur as often as Christians in the twelfth and thirteenth centuries imagined. It is interesting that the writers rarely use the words *gæfa*, *gipta*, or *hamingja* when dealing with such pagan motifs. These words evidently had such positive connotations for Christians in the Sturlung Age that they could hardly describe something to be condemned. In most cases, *gæfa/gipta/hamingja* are used to express a "neutral" concept of luck or fortune which would appear acceptable to both Christians and non-Christians.

Occasionally, it is possible to detect certain elements of "pagan" superstition even in the most Christian sagawriter's treatment of *gæfa/gipta/hamingja*. This is particularly true of certain stories about fetches being "sent out" as manifestations of a person's soul to ensure his success or failure in dealing with others. Apparently, this old folk belief was never condemned

---

"pagan" connotation of luck in certain sagas may be a result of late development in the Christian era; cf. Lönnroth, *Arkiv för nordisk filologi* (1968), 242-243; L. Ejerfeldt, *op. cit.*, 156. While justly criticizing Hallberg's argument, Ejerfeldt unfortunately misrepresents my own views on this problem by claiming that Hallberg's statistical material nevertheless provides "ett argument mot Lönnroths framställning av språkbruket i sagorna" (*loc. cit.*). As far as I can see, my earlier statements about "luck" in the sagas are quite compatible with Hallberg's statistics and also with Baetke's and Ejerfeldt's theories about the origin of the concept; cf. Lönnroth (1963-64), 29-31. Yet I now prefer to leave the question of origin open, especially since this question (as Ejerfeldt points out) has very little bearing upon the problem of luck in thirteenth-century texts such as *Njála*.

33. *Ynglinga saga*, ch. 15; *Oláfs saga Tryggvasonar* (*Heimskr.*), ch. 337. Cf. F. Ström, "Kung Domalde i Svitjod och 'kungalyckan,'" *Saga och Sed*, 34 (1967-68), 52-66; Ejerfeldt, *op. cit.*, 158.

as unchristian, and thus it has managed to survive in Iceland until comparatively recent times.[34] Oddr's hagiographic biography of Olaf Tryggvason provides an unusually interesting example of how this superstition could be "Christianized" and yet reveal something of its pagan origin. The soothsayers of Garðaríki are reported to have spotted the presence of King Olaf's *hamingjur* (here equivalent to *fylgjur*, "fetches"), and from this they concluded that some great man must have arrived in their country.[35] It is also made clear that King Olaf's *gipta*, luck, was somehow operated by this fetches (this association between luck and fetches explains why the word *hamingja* could be used for both).[36] Nevertheless, Oddr makes it clear that King Olaf's luck was *ultimately* dependent on God's grace and his divine calling as King of Norway and "Apostle of the North."[37] God thus rules the fetches who rule the fortune of Olaf. A native folk belief has been integrated into the author's Christian world picture.

The situation is similar in *Njála*. In his treatment of *auðna*, fate, and *gæfa*, fortune—which are of major importance for the understanding of our saga—the author makes use of folk beliefs that are probably pagan or pre-Christian in origin, for example, the belief in fetches. His characters often speak about forces of destiny in non-Christian terms. Yet he manages to integrate non-Christian terms and motifs into an Augustinian world picture, so that what the saga calls fate is *actually* dependent on God's plan, and what the saga calls fortune is *actually* dependent on God's grace.

The Augustinian Pattern in Njála

It is particularly in the Conversion and Clontarf episodes (chapters 100-105, 154-157) that we find miracles and religious observations which indicate that God is steering the course of events while the devil is desperately trying to take over the wheel. Pagan sorcerers and berserks attempt to stop the Christian missionary, Þangbrandr, with their black magic, but he defeats them by the sacred power of his cross. The conversion itself has been foreshadowed in prophecies; as one of the characters puts it, it has been "ordained" (*ætlat fyrir*; cf. *fyrirætlan*, the Icelandic word for theological predestination).[38] Directly after it, God opens the eyes of a blind

---

34. See, for example, D. Strömbäck, *Sejd* (1935), 152-159.

35. Oddr Snorrason, *Saga Oláfs Tryggvasonar*, ed. Finnur Jónsson, 26-27.

36. Cf. Lönnroth (1963-64), 30-31. The hypothesis there presented (about influence from Latin *genius*) should be rejected.

37. See, for example, Oddr, pp. 1, 185, 241-43.

38. Cf. Gestr Oddleifsson's words in ch. 103: "ef þat er ætlat fyrir, at trúa þessi skuli við gangask, þá mun á alþingi við gangask." On the theological meaning, see A. Salvesen, *Studies in the vocabulary of the Old Norse Elucidarium* (Bergen, 1968), 39.

man so that he can strike down an enemy. At the Battle of Clontarf, people see visions of Hell and valkyries weaving the web of destiny of the warriors, but God manifests His power by letting the saintly King Brian win and work miracles as he gains the crown of martyrdom; the outcome of this battle has also been ordained. The battle as a whole serves as an *exemplum* for all who survive it and moves pagan warriors to become Christians.

The Augustinian perspective is found in other episodes as well. Less obtrusively, God is present in the action of *Njála* long before the conversion. The first time is probably in chapter 62, where Gunnarr, dreaming that he is fighting unprotected against a pack of wolfs, says, "and I did not know what protected me" (*ok þóttumsk ek þá eigi vita hvat mér hlífði*).[39] In chapter 81, his brother, Kolskeggr, dreams that a man, radiant with light, says, "Arise and follow me !" (*Statt þú upp ok far með mér.*) The man in the dream also promises him a wife and calls him to be his knight. The dream is interpreted as meaning that Kolskeggr will "go south" and become a "knight of God." Kolskeggr is soon converted to the new faith in Denmark, and he later becomes head of the Varangian guard in Constantinople, protecting the Christian emperor.

After the Conversion episode, the references to God's regiment increase. When Valgarðr the Grey destroys crosses and other sacred symbols, he immediately becomes sick and dies (chapter 107). When Hǫskuldr is murdered by the sons of Njáll (chapter 111), he asks God to help him and forgive them for their sin. But his widow, Hildigunnr, also invokes God's name when she tries to make Flosi avenge the murder (chapter 116). The "bad luck" (*ógæfa*) which then befalls the sons of Njáll (chapters 117-123) and prevents them from reaching an honorable settlement must be interpreted as God's punishment. Njáll before the Burning assures his family that "God is full of mercy and will not let us burn both in this world and the next" (chapter 129). This prediction is affirmed in chapter 132, where the dead bodies are found to be miraculously preserved, an indication that the souls have been saved (cf. above, p. 122). The Burning must then be interpreted as an atonement for the sin of killing Hǫskuldr. In accordance with this idea of atonement, Flosi and Kári cannot reach a final reconciliation until they make a pilgrimage to Rome and are absolved from sin by the Pope (chapters 158-159).[40]

---

39. One may conceivably interpret this statement as meaning that Gunnarr is protected by his *gæfa* or his *fylgja*, but, even so, the tone is Christian enough to suggest that the fatal powers are somehow operated by an Unknown God (cf. below, pp. 137-141).

40. My interpretation coincides, on the whole, with that of Sveinsson (1943), Maxwell (1957), Fox (1963), and Allen (1971).

There can be no doubt, therefore, that fate in *Njála* is Christian rather than pagan. Although fate sometimes appears to rule all the action, it conforms to Christian doctrine by allowing some room for man's free choice (*sjálfræði*). To a greater extent than other sagas, *Njála* makes use of prophecies and predictions which may be called "conditional," since their fulfillment is dependent on individual actions and decisions. Njáll predicts that Gunnarr will fall if he slays two men within the same line or if he violates a settlement arranged by good men. If he stays away from these two dangers, however, he will live to be an old man (chapter 55). Later on, he also predicts that Gunnarr will be much honored and have a long life if he accepts exile from Iceland for three years. If he does not accept, he will be killed (chapter 74). Before the conversion of Iceland, he predicts that whoever accepts the new faith will be fortunate (chapter 100); the implication is certainly that whoever does not accept it will not be fortunate—and this is exactly what happens. Before the Battle of Clontarf, a prophecy is made that King Brian will fall but be victorious if the battle is fought on Good Friday; if it is fought before that time, however, all his opponents will fall (chapter 157). At least some of these conditional predictions clearly imply the existence of a "free" but limited choice between alternatives provided by a Supreme Being.

The Ógæfa

As Sveinsson has pointed out,[41] *ógæfa* in *Njála* is presented as a kind of contagious moral disease, spreading from individual to individual throughout the saga. Although the transference of bad luck may be a traditional saga motif, it is used with unusual consistency in *Njála* and with much stronger moral overtones than in other family sagas. The *ógæfa* is, in fact, one of the major themes controlling the entire work. We first meet it in Hallgerðr's "thief's eyes" and in the curse which Queen Gunnhildr puts on Hrútr. From Hallgerðr the disease spreads to her three husbands and from Queen Gunnhildr to Hrútr and Unnr. From Unnr it spreads to her second husband, Valgarðr, and to her son, Morðr. From Morðr it spreads to Gunnarr's other enemies and later to the sons of Njáll. From Víga-Hrappr, a suddenly appearing *ógæfumaðr*, it spreads to Þráinn, who has already been infected by Hallgerðr. Christian men of good will such as Njáll, Hǫskuldr, Síðu-Hallr, and Flosi try to stop the disease. But it is only by atoning for past sins and by accepting peaceful settlements that the *ógæfa* can finally be defeated.

The *ógæfa* may be identified with the seeds of conflict that form part of the traditional Feud Pattern: impetuous behavior by *hávaðamenn*, the spirit

41. Sveinsson (1943), 160; trans. (1971), 192.

of revenge which prompts a Prima Donna to goad her men, and so on. But to the author of *Njála*, the *ógæfa* is more than that; it is sometimes a result of demonic influence, sometimes an instrument of divine retribution. If affects not only a man's success in this world but also the moral condition of his soul.

The demonic forces that steer man's fortune are most clearly shown to the reader in the Clontarf episode. Bróðir, the evil apostate, a medieval Antichrist figure dressed up as a traditional Norse berserk, is attacked in his sleep by ravens with iron claws. This miracle is interpreted by his wiser and more noble companion, Óspakr, to mean that the enemies of the saintly King Brian will fall in the battle and go to Hell: "the ravens that attacked you are the devils in whom you have believed and who will drag you to the torments of Hell" (chapter 156). The miracle prompts Óspakr to become a Christian and join King Brian's forces. He survives the battle, but Bróðir is horribly killed, as are several of his companions. One of them, Hrafn the Red, is chased into a river, where he sees into Hell, and it appears to him that the devils are trying to drag him down. But he saves himself by exclaiming: "Your dog, Saint Peter, has run twice to Rome and will run a third time with your permission." Then the devils set him free and he crosses the river (chapter 157).

The author of *Njála* saved such hagiographic effects for his very last chapters, but the same view of human destiny is implied in the story of Skarpheðinn's *ógæfa* after the killing of Hǫskuldr. The first seeds of his tragic downfall have been planted very early in the saga: he has been presented as a hero of the Grettir type, i.e., as a basically noble but impetuous troublemaker. He gains honor and success as long as he follows Njáll's advice, but he is bound to fall when he comes under the evil influence of Mǫrðr, who is himself an agent of demonic conspiracies. This fact is made clear in chapter 107, where Valgarðr the Grey returns to Iceland after the conversion, destroys Mǫrðr's crosses and other Christian symbols, and orders him to stir up dissent between Hǫskuldr and the sons of Njáll so that the saintly Hǫskuldr will be killed.

In the following chapter, Mǫrðr carries out this plan by slowly corrupting the minds of Skarpheðinn and his brothers; he pretends to be their friend, tells them that Hǫskuldr is plotting against their lives, and finally convinces them that they must murder Hǫskuldr in order to save themselves. He also attempts to goad Hǫskuldr against the sons of Njáll by the same method, but Hǫskuldr refuses. Finally, Skarpheðinn murders Hǫskuldr in a scene which makes the victim appear as a martyr. After this deed, Skarpheðinn is unable to gain support at the Allthing because his *ógæfa* manifests itself in his very appearance. No one wants to have any dealings with him because they are afraid that this would affect their own fortunes. Skarp-heðinn's actions become increasingly desperate until the Burning, when he suddenly decides to "accept his fate" and burn to death. When his body is found, it is partly burned and marked with crosses, indicating that he has made the necessary atonement for his crime. Like Hrafn the Red, he has escaped the devils.

The Author's Use of pagan Agents of Fate

There are, however, many scenes in *Njála* where the fortunes of men appear to be manipulated by forces that are pagan rather than Christian. As an example, we may take chapter 69, where Gunnarr is miraculously saved from an ambush. As his enemies are about to attack him, "drowsiness came to them, and they could do nothing but sleep" (*kom at þeim svefnþungi, ok máttu þeir ekki annat en sofa*). That night, Njáll, staying nearby at a farm, is unable to sleep: "I see many savage fetches (*fylgjur grimmligar*) of Gunnarr's enemies, and yet it is strange, for they are howling furiously but are going without guidance." A few moments later, a shepherd reports that he has found twenty-four fully armed men sleeping in the brushwood. A warning is sent to Gunnarr, and his enemies have to give up their plan as soon as they wake up.

The same motif recurs in chapters 145-146, where the sons of Sigfúss are beset by a drowsiness that enables Kári to overcome them as they are sleeping. In this case also, the sudden sleep is an instrument of fate or fortune, and although no fetches are mentioned, we may conclude that they are somehow involved. Earlier in the saga (chapter 12), the evil pagan magician Svanr manages to save Hallgerðr's henchman, Þjóstólfr, from his persecutor, Ósvífr, by conjuring up a fog after having sensed the presence of Ósvífr's approaching fetches. "Svanr spoke up and he was yawning much: 'Now Ósvífr's fetches are attacking'". The scene is reminiscent of the previously mentioned scene in Oddr's biography of Olaf Tryggvason, where the sooth-sayers of Russia spot the presence of the king's *hamingjur*.

The fetches are, as we have already indicated, manifestations of a person's soul or *mana*. There was evidently a folk belief that they could operate on their own while their "owner" was sleeping. They also acted as guardian spirits ensuring their owner prosperity and luck. Normally, they were in-visible, but they could be spotted by persons with "second sight"; Svanr's "yawning" indicates that he has this ability, for in order to see another man's fetch, one would have to be drowsy or sleeping oneself[42] (presumably in order to let one's own soul "travel" away from the body). In the sagas, fetches are

---

42. See, for example, Strömbäck, *Sejd* (1935), 152 ff.

seen particularly in connection with battles and often in the form of a wild beast (wolf, bear, etc.); sometimes they are seen as beautiful women, but this form probably represents a late development of the original pagan belief, a development influenced by the valkyrie motif.[43] A valkyrie also appears as a sort of guardian spirit and agent of fate at the battlefield, although she is not a manifestation of a person's soul but rather a servant of Odin in his capacity as god of War. In *Njála*, we find both valkyries and fetches in animal form, and many readers have found their presence inconsistent with the author's Christian faith.

But it would be wrong to think of the author as somehow torn between a pagan and a Christian interpretation of history. Fetches and valkyries belonged to the "lower" pagan mythology which survived the conversion and could be accepted by Christians as traditional elements of the saga world. As we have already seen in the case of Oddr's biography of Olaf Tryggvason, they could furthermore be interpreted as agents of God or the devil. The author of *Njála* appears to have made this interpretation as he worked the old pagan motifs into his Augustinian world picture.

For what is it that makes the enemies of Gunnarr and Kári fall asleep against their will? It surely cannot be their own fetches, who are simply manifestations of themselves and are furthermore described by Njáll as "going without guidance" (*ráðlausliga*). It appears more likely that Gunnarr's and Kári's own luck is working against their adversaries, for at one point Njáll tells Kári: "It will be difficult for them to go against your luck" (*Erfitt mun þeim veita at ganga í móti giptu þinni*; chapter 111). But this luck may in its turn be thought of as a manifestation of God's grace.

This interpretation is strengthened by several incidents in the saga. When Síðu-Hallr is converted to the Christian faith by Þangbrandr, he is promised that Saint Michael, "who measures everything that you do, good and evil," will become his *fylgju engill*, "fetch angel." Such a creature is otherwise unknown in saga literature. The author of *Njála* evidently made him up by combining the traditional Norse fetch motif with the Christian idea of guardian angels. In this case, he probably sought inspiration from an older Christian legend about the fetches of Síðu-Hallr's family.[44] He appears to have integrated the native belief in fetches into a theological framework.

43. Cf. Folke Ström, *Diser, nornor, valkyrior: Fruktbarhetskult och sakralt kungadöme i Norden* (Göteborg, 1954), 96-98.

44. Cf. Strömbäck, *Tidrande och diserna* (Lund, 1949); it is possible to translate *fylgjuengill* simply as "guardian angel" if *fylgja* is interpreted as synonymous with *fylgð*, "following," but the fetch motif is so prominent in *Njála* and the athor so explicitly refers to the legend about Síðu-Hallr's fetches (chapter 96) that "fetch angel" seems to be the best translation.

In the Clontarf episode, there is a vision of valkyries weaving the fates of the warriors with the intention of letting pagan Norsemen win their battle against King Brian (cf. p. 166). Yet the pagans are defeated because God is on King Brian's side; clearly, the pagan agents of fate are subordinated to God's plan. A combination of this sort is by no means unusual in the clerical literature of the Middle Ages. We find it, for example, in *Alexandreis* (and in *Alexanders saga*), where the three Fates and various other deities from Greek mythology appear within a universe ultimately ruled by God.[45]

A comparison between the story of Svanr and the story of Gunnarr's sleeping enemies can show us more clearly how the author's mind worked. Both stories are based on the same folk motif: a person's miraculous escape from the hostile fetches of his enemy. The hostile fetches appear to be good powers in the first case and evil powers in the second case. The man who defeats them is in one case an evil sorcerer destined for Hell (Svanr), and in the other case a saintly prophet destined for Heaven (Njáll).

Svanr is presented from the start (chapter 10) as "skilled in witchcraft" (*fjǫlkunnigr mjǫk*) and "unpleasant to deal with" (*ódæll ok illr viðreignar*). These two characteristics, closely associated in all sagas, express the medieval condemnation of pagan sorcery. In Oddr's biography of Olaf Tryggvason and in the Conversion and Clontarf episodes of *Njála*, such sorcerers are agents of the devil working against God's regiment. Svanr's evil character is further emphasized through his association with Hallgerðr and Þjóstólfr after the murder of Hallgerðr's first husband, Þorvaldr Ósvífsson. Svanr even praises Þjóstólfr for the murder and does everything in his power to protect him from the law. But old Ósvífr, father of the murdered man, has a sudden inspiration which enables him to "see" that Hallgerðr has sent Þjóstólfr under Svanr's protection. A search party is set up, and it is at this point that Svanr, yawning, feels the presence of Ósvífr's fetches. He conjures up the fog in which Ósvífr loses his way—this is one of the most powerful and demonic scenes in the saga—and the murderer escapes.

The reader is hardly surprised to learn, a few chapters later, that Svanr disappeared by going into the mountain Kaldbakshorn, "and there he was well received" (*ok var honom þar vel fagnat*). Although "going into the mountain" is an old folk motif, found in earlier sagas and not necessarily associated with evil sorcerers,[46] the author of *Njála* is evidently using this motif here to make Svanr's demonic character obvious to a Christian audience. Similarly, he later uses the motif of Njáll's burning to emphasize Njáll's saint-like character (cf. above, p. 96).

---

45. Cf. Lönnroth (1970), 23.
46. Cf. Sveinsson, *Njála* (1954), 46, note 5.

In the analogous story about Gunnarr and his enemies, the mysterious slumber fills the same function as the fog conjured up by Svanr. The slumber enables Njáll to save Gunnarr just as the fog enables Svanr to save Þjóstólfr. But Njáll has not *caused* the slumber; he merely uses his second sight to "see" the fetches after Gunnarr's enemies have already fallen asleep. This distinction is extremely important, for while sorcery is always condemnable to a medieval Christian, prophetic talents are not. Unlike Svanr, Njáll is a good man, "prescient, sound in advice and benevolent" (chapter 20). When he spots the "savage fetches" of Gunnarr's enemies, he is fulfilling his usual role as the hero's great protector and counseler. Gunnarr's enemies (unlike Þjóstólfr's persecutors) are evil men out to attack a noble and innocent victim as a result of a truly vile conspiracy (thought up by Mǫrðr; cf. chapter 67). It is quite clear that they deserve to be stopped. For these reasons, their slumber cannot be caused by Njáll's sorcery (which would have been evil) but must appear as a sudden miracle.

The motif of the miraculous escape is used again in chapter 88, where Þráinn helps Hrappr escape Earl Hákon. In this case, the persecutor is a man with a just cause who uses his second sight to find a "victim" who is evil and an *ógæfumaðr* (cf. Ósvífr and Þjóstólfr). But the helper, Þráinn, is neither an evil sorcerer nor a saintly prophet; he is a tragic hero whose tragedy consists in not being able to resist Hrappr's bad influence (cf. Mǫrðr and Skarpheðinn). The persecutor, Earl Hákon, is not foiled by magic fog or sudden drowsiness but by "mental fog" which makes his second sight impotent when he is near Hrappr and Þráinn. After being forced to give up his chase, the earl makes the following curious reflection, which is of great help in the understanding of "fatal forces" in *Njála*: "This was not caused by my lack of foresight but by that alliance between them which is pulling them both to their death" (*Eigi berr hér til óvizka mín, heldr þat samband þeira, er þeim dregr báðum til bana.*)

What the earl is talking about is evidently, as Sveinsson has pointed out,[47] the destructive power of the *ógæfa*: by taking a doomed *ógæfumaðr* under his protection, Þráinn has doomed himself, and the audience understands that he will soon die because of his decision to help Hrappr. But Earl Hákon's comment implies more than that: his impotence is also caused by the *ógæfa*, just as Ósvífr's impotence was caused by Svanr's magic fog. Since Earl Hákon is himself pictured as a heathen, it may appear most natural to interpret the implied philosophy in non-Christian terms. We could, for example, say that the Norwegian ruler's *mana* has been defeated by the more powerful and destructive *mana* exerted by Hrappr and Þráinn in conjunction.

47. Sveinsson (1943), 162; trans. (1971), 194.

Yet we cannot disregard the author's clerical mind, which reveals itself in the very subtlety of Earl Hákon's remark. Pagan characters simply do not talk like this in genuine oral tales. They may do so, however, in works inspired by medieval theology. For in Christian terms, which would, of course, not be used by a character like Earl Hákon, Hrappr's *ógæfa* emanates from the devil, with God's permission. It is a demonic force which may, temporarily, bring success against an enemy, but in the long run it always leads to disaster. Þráinn can choose to accept or to reject this demonic force when it presents itself to him in Hrappr's seductive shape. By accepting it, he strengthens Hrappr and makes Earl Hákon impotent. But very soon both he and Hrappr will be rightly punished according to God's plan.

One may, of course, read too much Christian theology into the fatal mechanisms of *Njála*, and we may perhaps have done so in our interpretation of Hrappr's *ógæfa*. It is quite possible that the author incorporated a good deal of pagan folklore concerning fate and *ógæfa* without integrating it with his own Christian faith. Such combinations are quite common in other sagas. We have seen that inconsistencies are part of the author's method, that he used many traditional elements which could not easily be reconciled with each other (above, p. 55).

There is, nevertheless, some truth in Bååth's statement that "the author has had such a command over his material that he wrote down his first line having the last line within his vision." The author of *Njála* may not have noticed various inconsistencies in his presentation of characters and events. But he did have a master plan for his saga, and this master plan is closely tied to his Christian faith. He certainly had no intention of contradicting himself in matters of theology, and he certainly did not make any conscious efforts to promote a non-Christian theology. As readers we must, therefore, interpret his story in light of the Christian doctrine of his time. It is only when such interpretation fails that we must look elsewhere for an explanation.

Why did he then choose pagans as spokesmen for his Christian ideas throughout the first half of his saga? And how could the pagan era seem at all attractive to him? In order to understand this, we have to penetrate more deeply the clerical thinking of thirteenth century Iceland. Our next subject will be the Christian Doctrine of Natural Law and Natural Religion.

4. THE NOBLE HEATHEN

The Doctrine of Natural Religion

Although Icelanders in the thirteenth century were Christians, they revered the pagan era as a kind of Golden Age. Their country had been settled in that era, and the first settlers were held up as models for their descendents. The native laws and important political institutions such as the Allthing were regarded as a legacy from these pagan ancestors. The pagan religion itself survived in myths and folktales, which formed part of the literary tradition, and the poetic language of the skalds presupposed knowledge of the pagan gods.

Even a clerical mind was compelled to accept much of the pagan heritage in order not to become alienated from the native culture. This acceptance had to be reconciled, in some way or other, with Christian doctrine. The solution for Icelandic clerics had already been suggested by Saint Paul and the early Fathers of the Church, and it had been further developed by medieval clerics on the Continent in their defense of the pagan culture inherited from the Greeks and the Romans. We may label this solution "The Concept of the Noble Heathen" or, in more theological terms, "The Doctrine of Natural Law and Natural Religion."[48]

According to Saint Paul, the Gentiles were originally in contact with God, but they turned away from Him. They could, however, still feel His presence, in spite of their heresies and false doctrines:

Because that which may be known of God is manifest in them; for God hath shewed it unto them. For the invisible things of him from the creation of the world are clearly seen, being understood by the things that are made, even his eternal power and Godhead; so that they are without excuse: Because that, when they knew God, they glorified him not as God, neither were thankful; but became vain in their imaginations, and their foolish heart was darkened. Professing themselves to be wise, they became fools, and changed the glory of the uncorruptible God into an image made like to corruptible man, and to birds, and fourfooted beasts, and creeping things.
(Rom. I, 19-23)

The Gentiles thus were guilty of sin in worshipping pagan gods; they should have known better. This, however, means that they *could* do the right thing if they wanted to. And some of them did, according to Saint Paul, for he praises "the Gentiles which have not the law" but still "having not the law, are a law unto themselves: which shew the work of the law written in their hearts" (Rom. II, 14-15). Such noble but untutored Gentiles could easily be identified with the worshippers of an "Unknown God" encountered by Saint Paul in Athens (Acts, XVII, 22-34). Although these worshippers were not Christian and thus did not "know" God, they were sufficiently

48. Cf. Lönnroth, "The Noble Heathen: A Theme in the Sagas," *Scandinavian Studies*, 41 (1969), 1-29.

aware of His existence to erect an altar in His honor, even though most Athenians worshipped pagan idols.[49]

In the Middle Ages, positive as well as negative attitudes to the pagans were generally derived from Saint Paul. The idea that the Gentiles had turned away from God was usually associated with the idea that pagan religions were inspired by the devil or by evil demons posturing as gods. Such ideas are prominently displayed in Oddr's biography of Olaf Tryggvason and in many Norse saints' lives. According to the Euhemeristic doctrine, on the other hand, the pagan gods were human beings whose worldly exploits had become so glorified that they had finally received apotheosis. This more sophisticated interpretation was applied to Norse paganism by such learned antiquarians as Snorri Sturluson and Saxo Grammaticus, but their ideas are still quite compatible with those of Saint Paul.[50]

The same authors who chided the pagans for their wicked idolatry would, however, praise them insofar as they believed in an "Unknown God" or acted nobly according to the divine precepts "written in their hearts." Examples of this can be found both in the sagas and in many other medieval narratives. We should thus not regard Natural Religion, Euhemerism, and the idea of demonic inspiration as mutually exclusive doctrines. Instead, they complement each other in the medieval view of pagan culture.

The doctrine of Natural Religion was applied to Norse paganism in several Icelandic works from the thirteenth century, most clearly in Snorri Sturluson's Preface to the *Prose Edda*. According to Snorri, the pagan Norsemen had turned away from God, but from their observations of nature, they understood "that there might be some governor of the stars of heaven" (*stjórnari himintunglanna*), although they did not know "where his kingdom was." This dimly perceived Supreme Being, clearly a variant of Saint Paul's "Unknown God," is, further on in the *Prose Edda*, identified with Odin. Or, to put it more exactly: Snorri implies that the pagan ancestors mistakenly identifed the unknown heavenly ruler with Odin, although the ruler was in actual fact (naturally) the Christian God, while Odin was a clever sorcerer who had fooled his fellow men into believing that he had divine powers. Though this interpretation it becomes possible to excuse the pagan worshippers of Odin, at least to some extent.

A similar theme is found in many saga episodes involving noble heathens. In *Vatnsdœla saga*, all the best members of the Vatnsdala family believe in

---

49. The story of the "Unknown God" is found in a Norse manuscript from about 1200; cf. *Postola sögur*, ed. C. R. Unger, 221.

50. Cf. R. Schomerus, *Die Religion der Nordgermanen im Spiegel christlicher Darstellung* (Leipzig, 1936); W. Baetke, *Die Götterlehre der Snorra-Edda* (Berlin, 1950); Lönnroth (1969), 4-6.

"Him who created the sun and all the world," although they cannot tell who this god is. Þorsteinn Ingimundsson talks about this creator when he convinces his younger and more impetuous brother not to seek immediate revenge after the slaying of their father: "I don't expect to find Hrolleifr at home, and we shall have to overcome him by cunning rather than by force. But we may console ourselves that there is a big difference between Father and Hrolleifr, and that Father will be rewarded by him who created the sun and the whole world, whoever he may be; but I know that somebody did" (chapter 23).

Later on in the same saga, Þorsteinn saves another young brother from his violent berserk fits by invoking "him who created the sun." He also makes a promise to bring up a child that has been set out to die, according to pagan custom, "so that He who created Man may later convert him [i.e., the child] to His faith, for I suspect that this has been ordained for him" (chapter 37). At the end of the saga, this prediction comes true when the child saved by Þorsteinn, Þorkell krafla, has become a grown man and is converted by a German missionary, Bishop Friðrekr. Þorkell is at first reluctant to have any other faith than that of his ancestors, i.e., the faith in "Him who created the sun and rules everything." The missionary then explains to him that this is the very faith that he is preaching, but with one important difference: "He who created the sun" should be understood as the trinity of Father, Son, and Holy Ghost (chapter 46). Upon this piece of theological exegesis Þorkell somewhat begrudgingly lets himself be baptized, and he dies a pious Christian.

The technique used by Bishop Friðrekr is the one used by Saint Paul when he assures the Athenians that he has come to preach about their "Unknown God." The distinction between Þorkell's faith and that of Bishop Friðrekr is explained in the Preface to the Prose Edda as a distinction between "wisdom of the earth" and "understanding of the spirit." Þorkell here represents the rationalism of the noble heathen while the missionary represents Christian faith aided by revelation.

In the Norse saints' lives and translated riddarasǫgur we find many such noble heathens. One of them is Placidus (before his conversion). Another is Alexander, in the beginning of Alexanders saga, before he has become corrupted by his desire for new conquests. As a young man he has been tutored by Aristotle, considered the greatest of the pagan philosophers. The saga describes in detail how Aristotle teaches Alexander to be wise and virtuous, to stay away from Bacchus and Venus and other pagan gods, to be moderate in his demands, respectful of the law, generous to others, etc. Later in the saga, the patriarch of Jerusalem appears in a dream to Alexander and admonishes him not to harm God's temple or its servants—and Alexander follows this admonition. Although the events in the saga take place long before the birth of Christ, the arrival of the Messiah is prefigured on a monument which Alexander orders made to honor one of his dead enemies. An astrologer in his army speaks aboutt he "Divine government which rules the heavenly bodies," forcing them to "move as the Creator of all things has decided." Clearly, this is another version of "Him who created the sun," Snorri's *stjórnari himintunglanna*, or Saint Paul's Unknown God.

While idolatry is always considered evil in such Christian texts, pagan fatalism is not. Noble heathens such as Alexander trust the wisdom of astrologers and recognize the power of the three Fates and the goddess Fortuna, pictured as the most fickle of all deities. In *Alexandreis* and *Alexanders saga*, these pagan rulers of human destiny appear as if the author, Gautier de Châtillon, actually believed in their existence. Of course, he did not; he merely used a traditional mythological apparatus. This apparatus was legitimized by being subordinated to the Unknown Ruler, just as the mythology of Norse poetry was legitimized in the Prose Edda.[51]

In many native Norse sagas, the noble heathen believes "in his own strength and power" (*á mátt sinn ok megin*). This "faith" is usually interpreted as a genuine folk belief from the pagan era.[52] Even so, a belief of this kind would be quite suitable for a noble heathen in a saga composed by a Christian author, for to believe in one's own power would certainly seem preferable to idolatry, and it would also provide an effective introduction to stories about dramatic conversions, when the hero at last realizes that there *is* a god worthy of his adoration, i.e., a god more powerful than the hero himself.

There is sometimes an interesting contrast between noble heathens and ignoble Christians. This contrast may also be traced back to Saint Paul, who praises the noble Gentiles at the expense of orthodox Jews who follow the law of Moses but refuse to accept Christ as the Messiah and who reject the non-Jews from their temples of worship. In Pseudo-Turpin's *Historia Karoli Magni et Rotholandi*, the pagan King Agolandus almost accepts the Christian faith but changes his mind when he sees how poor people are mistreated by Charlemagne's Christian soldiers. In the long *Óláfs saga Tryggva-*

---

51. On the mythology of *Alexanders saga*, see Lönnroth (1970); H. Christensen, *Das Alexanderlied Walters von Châtillon* (Halle, 1905); C. Giordano, *Alexandreis: Poema di Gautier da Châtillon* (Naples, 1917). On the goddess Fortuna, see H. R. Patch, *The Goddess Fortuna in Medieval Literature* (Cambridge, Mass., 1927). On the survival of the pagan gods in Christian writings of the Middle Ages, see F. von Bezold, *Das Fortleben der antiken Götter im mittelalterlichen Humanismus* (Bonn and Leipzig, 1922); J. Seznec, *La survivance des dieux antiques* (London, 1940).

52. Cf. F. Ström, "Den egna kraftens män," *Göteborgs Högskolas Årsskrift*, 54 (1948).

sonar found in *Flateyjarbók*, such a contrast is made in a speech by King Olaf, who compares two of his predecessors on the Norwegian throne: Harald Fairhair, a heathen, and Hákon Aðalsteinsfóstri, a Christian who was compelled by his subjects to become an apostate. Hákon is pictured as a most contemptible sinner for giving in to pagan pressure, while Harald is pictured as a noble heathen. believing in the Unknown God:

> King Harald was a heathen and did not know God, and [yet] he had those men killed whom he knew to be most prominent in witchcraft and the service of the Devil. It also appears from his words that he expected some protection from Him who created him (*at hann hafi vænt sér nokkurs traasts af þeim, er hann hefir skapat*) although he did not know for certain who this God is; and there is then a great difference between the man who did not take the right faith but yet turned his soul towards God by his own good nature (*með góðri náttúru*) and the man who had been baptized but rejected his Creator and His commands.[53]

Noble heathens and natural religion in Njála

The same contrast is carried out in straight narrative and without the clerical rhetoric in the Clontarf episode of *Njála*, where we are told of the two vikings Óspakr and Bróðir (chapters 155-157). Óspakr is a heathen but also "the wisest of men." Bróðir, on the other hand, "had been a Christian and a Deacon, but he had rejected his own faith and become an Apostate (*guðníðingr*) and sacrificed to heathen gnomes and was very skilled in witchcraft" (chapter 155). After a series of foreboding miracles, Óspakr understands that Bróðir will go to Hell and that he himself should accept the Christian faith and join the Christian forces of King Brian (chapter 156). The thoroughly evil Bróðir, however, sticks with the pagan forces against King Brian and is killed in the Battle of Clontarf, while Óspakr survives and reaps the fruits of victory with the Christians. Óspakr has wisely turned to God *með góðri náttúru*, "by his own good nature," i.e., in accordance with the divine precepts "written in his heart."

We find a similar pattern in the main structure of the saga. Its first half is dominated by noble heathens (Gunnarr, Kolskeggr, and Njáll), who do not worship pagan idols but believe in fate and are dimly aware of a divine presence. Hence Gunnarr's report about a dream in which he was fighting, and "it appeared to me that I did not know what protected me" (chapter 62). The implication is clearer in Kolskeggr's dream about the man "radiant with light" who asks him to follow him (chapter 81). And Njáll himself knows even before the arrival of the missionary, Þangbrandr, that the new faith will be beneficial. After he has expressed this conviction (chapter 100),

---

53. *Flateyjarbók*, ed. S. Nordal et al. (1944), I, 357-358.

he is reported to *þylja*, i.e., to "mumble" or "chant," all by himself—evidently an indication that he is somehow in contact with the supernatural, possibly speaking to an "Unknown God." Njáll and Gunnarr also show Christian charity long before the official conversion of Iceland, for example by helping their neighbors during a famine (chapter 47) and by being reluctant to take revenge. Gunnarr demonstrates his "good nature," "the law written in his heart," when he makes the famous pronouncement: "I do not know if I am less brave than other men because I am less eager to kill" (chapter 54).

In the second half of *Njála* all the characters have become Christians, and their conversion has brought a sense of increased responsibility to the scene of action. This is clearly expressed at the burning of Bergþórshváll (chapter 128), when Flosi decides to set fire to the house, "although this will be a matter of grave responsibility before God *since we are Christians ourselves*" (cf. above, p. 116). The implication is that a pagan could have been excused for such a deed, but a Christian will have to atone for it before he can be saved. This is also what happens at the end of *Njála*, when both Flosi and Kári make a pilgrimage to Rome and are absolved from sin by the Pope. The responsibility of the ignoble Christian is also implied in several other scenes: for example, at Skarpheðinn's murder of Hǫskuldr; or when Mǫrðr, having recently been baptized, allows his father to destroy the Christian symbols, thus making himself into a *guðníðingr* like Bróðir or Hákon Aðalsteinsfóstri.

Within the first and "pagan" half of the saga, the noble heathens are contrasted to evil heathen sorcerers such as Gunnhildr and Svanr and to foolish idolators such as Dala-Guðbrandr, the Norwegian farmer visited by Hrappr in chapters 87 and 88. The figure of Dala-Guðbrandr was a traditional one, first appearing in the early sagas about Olaf the Saint, where he is one of the saint's adversaries and an object of his missionary zeal. Guðbrandr is in charge of a pagan temple which Olaf destroys, an act showing that the pagan gods are impotent—a hagiographic motif which can be traced from the Old Testament to the Latin Life of Saint Martin of Tours and to various other medieval legends about missionaries.[54] In *Njála* Guðbrandr is a comic character, fooled and tricked by the mischievous Hrappr. Guðbrandr's pagan credulity is highlighted when he finds his temple burned and the idols standing outside, bereft of their precious golden ornaments (chapter 88). He draws the pious conclusion that the idols are powerful enough to walk out of a burning temple on their own, but Earl Hákon, a somewhat less credulous pagan, knows better: somebody (i.e., Hrappr) must have carried the idols out and robbed them before burning the temple. The scene il-

54. Cf. Lönnroth (1963), 70-71.

lustrates Saint Paul on the foolishness of pagan idolators: "Professing themselves to be wise, they became fools, and changed the glory of the uncorrubtible God into an image." Unlike Njáll or Gunnarr, Guðbrandr neither rejects the idols nor senses the presence of the Creator.

When, at the beginning of the second, "Christian" half of *Njála*, all Icelanders are converted, the most decisive role is played by Þorgeirr Ljósvetningagoði, a noble heathen who must decide whether the Allthing should have pagan or Christian law (chapter 105). The story is told in several sources older than *Njála*: Þorgeirr lies silent under a cloak for a whole day; he then proclaims that "This shall be the beginning of our law that all men shall be Christian in this country and believe in one god; father, son, and holy ghost. And they shall abolish all idolatry (*skurðgoðavilla*), cease exposing children, and stop eating horse-meat." Since Þorgeirr was previously a heathen, this speech must be a divine inspiration, received while Þorgeirr was lying silent under the cloak. This fits the doctrines of Natural Religion and Divine Revelation. Since Þorgeirr mentions not only "one god" (i.e., "He who created the sun") but also the trinity of Father, Son, and Holy Ghost, we may conclude that his shamanistic stay under the cloak has made him pass from the stage of natural reason or "wisdom of the earth" to the higher stage of mystical insight or "understanding of the spirit." In the version told in *Flateyjarbók*, we learn that "divine generosity so increased his [i.e., Þorgeirr's] eloquence, that all people at the Thing, both pagans and Christians, immediately agreed."[55]

Christian Attitudes to Pagan Law

Þorgeirr's proclamation may be interpreted as a compromise between Christian and pagan interests, but *Njála* makes it clear that only the pagans (not the Christians) had reasons to feel cheated. In fact, the proclamation conforms to Saint Paul's judgment concerning newly converted pagans:

My judgment therefore is that we should impose no irksome restrictions on those of the gentiles who are turning to God, but instruct them by letter to abstain from things polluted by contact with idols, from fornication, from anything that has been strangled, and from blood. (Acts, XV, 19-20)[56]

The laws followed by the characters of *Njála* after their conversion thus remain the same as before, but with Christian modifications. A Christian could respect these pagan era laws by believing that they were derived from Natural Law and thus from God's precepts. This is implied in a story told in *Konungs Skuggsjá* about a heathen king of Temere: when he does not

---

55. *Flateyjarbók*, 496.
56. An early Norse version of this passage is found in *Postola sögur*, ed. Unger, 76.

abide by the (pagan) laws of his own country, God punishes him by destroying his royal hall. This punishment would have been indefensible unless the pagan laws too emanated from God.

In the Swedish *Law of Uppland*, written about the same time as *Njála*, the laws are said to be derived from the pagan era: their "author" is "Viger the Wise, a heathen living in heathen times." The work also states that Christians have excluded some unacceptable pagen statutes and added new ones on the Church and true faith. The whole text has been authorized by Birger Magnusson, "by God's grace King of the Swedes and the Goths," who now sends it to his people just as God Himself sent the first law to his people through Moses.[57]

A similar attitude to pagan law appears in *Njála*. The Christian author of the saga has a tremendous respect for the old legal statutes which date from the pre-Christian period. He quotes them incessantly and pays close attention to legal procedure. Njáll himself is a lawyer and so are other noble heathens among the main characters. One of the narrative's most important "messages" is Njáll's famous dictum: "Our land shall be built with law and not laid waste with lawlessness." The same thought is expressed in Þorgeirr Ljósvetningagoði's proclamation of the new Christian statutes at the All-thing: "It seems to me that an impossible situation arises if we do not all have one and the same law. If the laws are divided, the peace will be divided, and we cannot tolerate that." Peace is, therefore, accomplished by a Christian modification of pagan law corresponding to the presumed modification of the pagan *Law of Uppland*.

Right after this event in *Njála*, a miraculous incident shows that the Christian God is the source of justice and the protector of Icelandic law, including the old pagan system of revenge. Ámundi, the blind and illegitimate son of Hǫskuldr Njálsson, demands compensation from his father's slayer, Lýtingr, who refuses because he has already paid compensation to Njáll and his sons. Lýtingr's refusal was reasonable from the standpoint of pagan Norse law. Nevertheless, Ámundi regards his right to receive compensation as guaranteed by God: "I cannot understand . . . that this is justice before God (*at þat muni rétt fyrir guði*), when you have struck so close to my heart. And I can tell you this, that if I could see with both my eyes, then I would have either money or revenge; and may God decide between us!" As soon as he has uttered these words, his eyes are suddenly opened and he is able to put an axe in Lýtingr's head, exclaiming: "Praise be to God, my lord! Now

<hr>

57. "Upplandslagen," *Svenska landskapslagar tolkade och förklarade av Å. Holmbäck och E. Wessén*, Vol. I (Stockholm, 1933), 5-7.

I see what he wants." When Lýtingr is dead, Ámundi's eyes are closed again forever (chapter 106).

The passage is often regarded as a curiously inconsistent mixture of pagan and Christian ideas.[58] But actually it reveals the author's subtle theological and legalistic mind. The phrase *rétt fyrir guði* refers to the Natural Law implanted by God in the human heart. This is evident from chapter 3 of *Járnsíða* (*Norges Gamle Love*, I, 260), which stipulates how a legal case should be settled at the Allthing when the written laws contain no clear provisions about the matter: in such a case, one should accept the verdict "which members of the Legislature unanimously decide upon as being the most just before God" (*er lǫgréttumenn verða á eitt sáttir ok þeim þykkir réttast fyrir guði*). In the case of Ámundi, the laws of the Independence era did not give him any automatic right to receive compensation since he was an illegitimate son of Hǫskuldr Njálsson. Yet, in the author's opinion, Natural Law gives him such a right, and when Lýtingr refuses to recognize this, he justly becomes— through God's intervention—the victim of Ámundi's revenge. The incident serves as an *exemplum* emphasizing the need to adjust existing law to God's will.

Literary critics often mistakenly assume that blood revenge was one of the Norse pagan customs that the Church condemned most categorically. In fact, the Icelandic and Norwegian church had to adjust to the realities of the Old Norse clan system, and the principle of revenge was inherent in that system. As long as no effective central authority existed, even the priests would have to admit that revenge was at times the only way to achieve justice. The old ethics of revenge could also be legitimized by the Augustinian doctrine of the Rightful War (*Bellum iustum*) and by the numerous examples of honorable deeds of revenge found in the Old Testament. During the thirteenth century, churchmen cooperated with the kings of Norway in trying to modify the laws that permitted revenge, to replace individual acts of retribution by official punishment, but this was a slow and laborious process, uncompleted when *Njála* was written.[59] Meanwhile, clerics were eager to specify when a Christian should condemn revenge and when he should accept it. The following quotations from *Konungs skuggsjá* represent an educated and enlightened view contemporary with *Njála*:

58. See, for example, Theodore Andersson's review of Allen's *Fire and Iron* in *JEGP*, 71 (1972), 104.

59. See, in particular, A. O. Johnsen, *Fra Ættesamfunn til Statssamfunn* (Olso, 1948) and O. Fenger, *Fejde og Mandebod* (Copenhagen, 1971). On the compatibility of Christianity and the "Ethics of Revenge," cf. Denton Fox (1963), 309 and Dorothy Whitelock, *The Audience of Beowulf* (Oxford, 1951), 13-19.

Keep your temper calm though not to the point of suffering abuse or bringing upon yourself the reproach of cowardice. Though necessity may force you into strife, be not in a hurry to take revenge; first, make sure that your effort will succeed and strike where it ought. Never display a heated temper when you see that you are likely to fail, but be sure to maintain your honor at some later time, unless your opponent should offer a satisfactory atonement . . . .

When you hear things in the speech of other men which offend you much, be sure to investigate with reasonable care whether the tales be true or false; but if they prove to be true and it is proper for you to seek revenge (*kemr til þín hefndir fyrir at vinna*), take it with reason and moderation and not in malevolent passion (*með hófi ok sannsýni, en eigi með illgjarnligri ákefð*).[60]

This is exactly the standpoint of noble men in *Njála* (Christians as well as pagans), and we may assume that the author of *Njála* himself held similar views, although he may have wished for a society in which revenge would be unnecessary. Shortly before the writing of the saga, the King of Norway introduced a law in Iceland, the previously mentioned *Járnsíða* ("Ironside"), which gave the king and his representatives more judicial power against the old clans and abolished many aspects of the traditional revenge system. The following quotation from its introduction may give some indication of the new spirit:

May it be known to all men that a barbaric custom has prevailed in our countries for a long time: when a man has been killed, his kinsmen want to remove the best man in the (killer's) family, even though he is ignorant and innocent of the slaying. And they do not want to avenge themselves on the real killer, even when they have an opportunity to do so, and the culprit thus profits by his own wickedness and lack of fortune (*oc nytr hinn vande maðr sua illzku sinnar oc ugiptu*). But the innocent man must pay for his wisdom and good character, and thus many a man has suffered great losses in his family, and the King has been deprived of his best subjects.[61]

The author of *Njála* is aware of such ill effects, as we can see in chapter 54, where Gunnarr seeks revenge on his malevolent enemy Otkell but is compelled by the circumstances to fight against Otkell's nobler brother, Hallbjǫrn. "Do not attack me," says Gunnarr, "for you are the last person I would like to harm, but I will not save anybody if I have to defend myself." But Hallbjǫrn is bound by the clan ethics not to retreat: "You are seeking to kill my brother, and it is then a shame to sit by idly." As a result of this heroic attitude, Hallbjǫrn is killed.

---

60. *Konungs skuggsjá*, ed. L. Holm-Olsen, 6, 66; trans. by L. M. Larson.

61. *Norges Gamle Love*, I, 266. The importance of this passage for the understanding of the concept of revenge in sagas has been stressed by D. Erlingsson, "Etiken i Hrafnkels saga Freysgoða," *Scripta Islandica*, 21 (1970), 38.

In like manner, Flosi wants to spare Njáll's life at the burning of Berg-þórshváll; he respects him and does not consider him responsible for the deeds of his sons. Throughout his revenge, Flosi takes care not to act rashly, "in malevolent passion," but with regard for justice and his own *ábyrgð fyrir guði*, "responsibility before God." Yet neither he nor Njáll rejects the ethics of revenge. In fact, Njáll refuses to let Flosi save him from the flames "because I am an old man, unable to avenge my sons, and I do not want to live with shame." In spite of such "pagan" statements, he seems almost a Christian saint in these last scenes, which indicates that the author of the saga considered revenge to be quite compatible with his faith.

Although the author of *Njála* was influenced by *Járnsíða* in his attitude to legal problems,[62] he must have grown up when the older law of the Icelandic Independence era, *Grágás* ("Grey goose"), was still in operation. This explains his ability to quote long sections from the *Grágás* text, and it also explains why he sometimes is guilty of confusing the old law with the new law (cf. the Appendix). The fact that the author had lived through a period of radical legislative reform can explain his ambivalence about pagan revenge ethics and the general legal system of his ancestors.

Grágás condoned revenge and other private settlements of legal disputes much more than *Járnsíða* did. As a matter of fact, the older law was largely concerned with rules for such private settlements and for arbitration at the Allthing in cases where two feuding clans could not reach agreement. Although *Járnsíða* did not outlaw all forms of private settlement and retribution, it did severely restrict the old freedom of the Icelandic clans to "take the law in their own hands" by making the king and his lawmen the final judges in all disputes, by limiting the collective responsibility of the clan and by replacing compensation with public punishment in cases of manslaughter. The author of *Njála* probably believed that the new system was in better accord with Christian doctrine than the old one; but he was obviously fond of *Grágás* and the pagan society out of which it had developed, and he wanted to find Christian excuses for this lost world.

Thus, he not only quotes incessantly from the old law, he also shows that the people who respected these statutes were either pious Christians or noble heathens, acting in the spirit of the new law by taking revenge only when they were prompted by justice, atoning for their sins like any good Catholic, sometimes even abstaining from seeking legal compensation when higher interests were at stake. This abstention is exemplified by Síðu-Hallr's speech after the battle at the Allthing (chapter 145), when he attempts a peaceful settlement by refusing to demand fines for the slaying of his own

---

62. See, in particular, Lehmann-Carolsfeld (1883).

son. The author adds that "everybody praised his goodness much," and the audience is probably to understand that Hallr acted so nobly because he was guided by his *fylgju engill*, Saint Michael, the great guardian of legal justice in medieval tradition.

In spite of his admiration for the old legal system, the author of *Njála* also knows, more than any earlier sagawriter, that the system led to disasters, which could be mitigated only by Christian charity and reconciliation, prompted by God. This is what happens in the second half of the saga and especially in the last chapter, when Flosi and Kári, both recently returned from their pilgrimage, embrace each other and declare an end to all feuds. The *ógæfa* has finally been defeated, and the noble heathens have become true Christians.

The Bible as a Structural Analogue

Considering the clerical mind of the author, it is not farfetched to compare the bipartite structure of *Njála* to that of the Bible, "Gunnarr's saga" as the Old Testament and "Njáll's saga" as the New Testament. In the first part, "Gunnarr's saga," people live under the old pagan law, corresponding to the Law of Moses, defended by noble heathen leaders (Njáll, Gunnarr). These noble heathens are dimly aware of God, and they expect the arrival of a new and better faith, which will both improve their law and society (cf. the waiting for the Messiah in the Old Testament) and increase their moral responsibility. The second part, "Njáll's saga," begins with the introduction of this new order, which is severely challenged when a Messiah figure, Hǫskuldr Þráinsson, is martyred. His death leads to catastrophic events which increase the guilt of the newly converted Christians and test their legal system until a sort of Armageddon is reached in the Battle of Clontarf. After this final cataclysm, the surviving heroes, Flosi and Kári, build the new Jerusalem—and the saga ends in peace and reconciliation.[63]

It would be foolish to claim that such parallels between *Njála* and the Bible were intended by the author—in fact, they probably were not. But it can be said that his clerical mind so shaped his understanding of history that a biblical pattern was placed over the inherited native legends. The

63. Cf. Allen (1971), 204. Allen has also pointed out that "at a very great distance, the curve of the saga [i.e., *Njála*] resembles that of the mythic poem, *Vǫluspá*, where the world of gods and men falls apart into the blaze and extinction of *ragnarǫk* only to reemerge into a new light" (*Fire and Iron*, 1971, p. 131). But he is also well aware of the fact that this same "curve" is found in the Bible—cf. his "Scheme: Parallel Evolution of Myths," *op. cit.*, 56. It seems to me, however, that the structural similarity between *Njála* and the Bible is greater than the structural similarity between *Njála* and *Vǫluspá*, even though the latter parallel is also worth noting.

traditional figures of Gunnarr and Njáll were given new roles as noble heathens in the medieval Christian world picture and in the author's justification of the legal system and social customs of his country.

The Coexistence of "Pagan" and "Christian"

Our interpretation differs from customary views about the relationship between Christian and pagan ideas in the sagas. Customary views see an irreconcilable gap between pagan and Christian; sagawriters must choose one or the other, unless they want hopeless inconsistencies and contradictions. Fatalism cannot coexist with Christian belief in divine providence. The pagan ethics of revenge cannot coexist with the Christian principle of charity. Admiration of pagan vikings cannot coexist with the medieval ideals of humility and asceticism. Pagan law cannot coexist with Christian law. When such coexistence is nevertheless attested, it is often explained as a result of multiple authorship or of insoluble conflicts in the author's mind.

Such interpretations are usually built on mistaken notions about medieval Christianity, which is often pictured as intolerant of all life save that of the saintly hermit or mendicant, opposed to all violence, hostile towards all forms of pagan culture, and so on. One thus makes a rule of the extreme cases and cites only those Christian authors who have most strongly condemned the pagan Norsemen. At the same time, the dubious testimony of such Christians is used to argue that Norse paganism was more barbaric, blood-thirsty, and hostile to Christian ideas than it really was. It is obvious that Christian Icelanders in the thirteenth century felt they had much in common with their pagan ancestors, and for this reason they were eager to find Christian excuses, even for aspects of pagan culture which did differ from their own. Medieval theology provided an arsenal of such excuses.

One may thus speak of a certain conflict, or ambivalence, in the Christian author's attitude to the past, for he was able to accept the pagan tradition only by making certain adjustments. This is certainly true of the author of *Njála*. But it would be nonsensical to imagine in him a fierce and conscious struggle between "paganism" and "Christianity." He would have abhorred the idea that *heiðinn siðr* could constitute even a temptation to his own mind. We may assume that he regarded himself simply as a Christian in the mainstream of theological tradition.

5. GUNNARR—NJÁLL—ALEXANDER

Gunnarr's Return: An Example of "Christian Reinterpretation"

In the most celebrated scene in *Njála*, Gunnarr decides to return to Hlíðarendi after having been condemned to exile. All critics agree that this scene is of major importance, bus its interpretations have varied considerably. Was Gunnarr's decision preordained and hence insecapable? Was it prompted by his romantic love for Iceland, his passion for Hallgerðr, his economic interests as a farmer, his unwillingness to let his enemies win, or his fears that exile would lead to some kind of diaster? And what is the narrator's moral attitude to his hero at this point in the narrative? All of these questions have been discussed.[64]

We shall here attempt to illuminate this scene by analyzing its traditional components and by comparing it to similar scenes in other sagas, "native" as well as "foreign." The text, we shall find, provides an excellent example of how the narrative "language of tradition" was reshaped by the author's "clerical mind."

The context is as follows. In the previous chapter (74), Gunnarr and Kolskeggr have agreed to a settlement which appears to put an end to their feud with Þorgeirr Starkaðarson (cf. above, p. 27). It has been agreed that both of them shall leave Iceland for three years, and Njáll has predicted that Gunnarr will return from his exile with much honor and become an old man, greatly respected; if he breaks the agreement and stays at home, however, he will be killed, "and that will be bad news for your friends" (ok er þat illt at vita þeim, er vinir þínir eru). Gunnarr has also declared to Njáll that he has no intention of breaking the settlement, and his mother, Rannveig, has expressed her satisfaction with this outcome.

The first narrative segment of chapter 75 describes how Þráinn Sigfússon, Gunnarr, and the sons of Njáll prepare to leave Iceland on three different ships. The stock motif here is the "preparation for útanferð," and it later turns out to be continued in the "travel episodes" or ferðarsǫgur of Þráinn and the sons of Njáll, eventually leading to their feud and Þráinn's death (chapters 82-92). So far, however, Gunnarr's preparations are described in much less detail than are the preparations of Þráinn and the sons of Njáll— a good example of the author's retarding technique to heighten the audience's suspense.

Next follows a brief "presentation segment," which informs us that Gunnar's two sons are now grown men: "Grani had much of the same character as his mother, but Hǫgni was a good man." The placement of this segment may appear strange since Grani and Hǫgni do not participate in the action until much later (chapter 78); we are evidently dealing with another re-

---

64. For interpretations of this scene, see especially Kinck (1916); Sigurður Guðmundsson (1918), 232-33; Sveinsson (1933), 209 f.; R. Pipping, "Ett dubbeltydigt omen," Budkavlen, XV (1936), 80-82; H. Lie, Studier i Heimskringlas stil (1937), 14-15; Sveinsson, Njála (1954), pp. XXXIV-XXXVII; Lönnroth (1970); Allen (1971), 147-52; Andersson, "The Displacement of the Heroic Ideal in the Family Sagas," Speculum, XLV (1970), 586-87.

tarding device, which serves to emphasize again the moral distinction between Gunnarr and Hallgerðr. Throughout these two introductory segments, the author appears to anticipate later events, and he can assume that his audience already knows of the tragedy he is about to present: the story of Gunnarr's fall.

Finally, he arrives at the main event of the chapter, conveyed in a narrative segment so much "expanded" and full of detailed "staging" that it is difficult to know if it should be regarded as one scene or as a unified sequence of successive scenes. In our presentation below, we have chosen the latter alternative:

Gunnarr sent his own and Kolskeggr's goods down to the ship. When everything was on board, and the ship almost ready to sail, Gunnarr rode to Bergþórshváll and other places to thank all those people who had given him support.

Early next morning he made ready to ride to the ship, and told all his people that he was going abroad forever. Everyone was dismayed at the news, but hoped that some day he would return. When he was ready to leave, he embraced them all, and the whole household came out to see him off. With a thrust of his halberd, he vaulted into the saddle, and rode away with Kolskeggr.

They were riding down towards Markarfljót when Gunnarr's horse stumbled, and he fell from the saddle. His glance was drawn upwards to the slopes (*Honum varð litit upp til hlíðarinnar*) and the farm at Hlíðarendi, and he said: "How lovely the slopes are, more lovely than they have ever seemed to me before, pale cornfields and new-mown hay. I am riding back home, and I will not go away" (*Fǫgr er hlíðin, svá at mér hefir hon aldri jafnfǫgr sýnzk, bleikir akrar ok slegin tún, ok mun ek ríða heim aptr ok fara hvergi.*). Kolskeggr said, "Do not make your enemies happy by breaking the settlement, something that no one would ever expect of you. For you can be quite sure that all of Njáll's predictions will come true." "I am not going away," said Gunnarr. "And I wish you would stay, too." "Never," said Kolskeggr. "I am not going to dishonor my pledge over this nor any other matter I am trusted in (*Hvárki skal ek á þessu niðask ok engu ǫðru, því er mér er til trúat*). This is the one and only thing that can separate us. Tell my kinsmen and my mother that I never mean to see Iceland again; for I shall hear of your death, brother, and there will then be nothing to draw me home." With that they separated. Gunnarr rode home to Hlíðarendi, but Kolskeggr carried on to the ship and sailed abroad.

Hallgerðr was delighted at Gunnarr's return, but his mother had little to say. Gunnarr stayed at home that autumn and winter, and did not have many men with him.

To appreciate the author's originality in staging this incident, we shall compare it to a more conventional treatment.[65] In *Grœnlendinga saga*, one of the "Vinland sagas," Leifr Eiríksson prepares an expedition from

---

65. Cf. Sven B. F. Jansson, *Sagorna om Vinland* (1944), 130.

Greenland to Vinland and tries to persuade his father, Eiríkr the Red, to come with him. But the old man is reluctant to go:

Leifr said that he [i.e., Eirikr] was probably still endowed with the most luck in their family. Eiríkr let Leifr decide; he rode away when they were ready for it, and there was only a short distance to the ship. The horse, on which Eiríkr was riding, stumbled, and he fell to the ground and injured his foot. Then Eiríkr said, "It does not seem to be ordained for me to find more countries than the one in which we are now living; we shall not proceed further together" (*"Ekki mun mér ætlat at finna lǫnd fleiri en þetta, er nú byggju ver: munu vér nú ekki lengr fara allir samt"*). Eiríkr went back to Brattahlíð [his home], but Leifr carried on to the ship with his companions.
                                        (*Grœnlendinga saga*, chapter 3)

The situation is almost identical in these two quotations, even though the presentation is more "normal" and less "expanded" in *Grœnlendinga saga*: two members of the same family prepare to leave their home and sail to foreign countries; they ride to their ship; suddenly, a horse stumbles; one of the two men falls to the ground; as a result, he decides to return home; but the other one carries on to the ship and sails away. In both cases, the dramatic "turning point" is emphasized through a brief declaration from the main protagonist after his fall from the horse, and there appears to be an element of fatalism in both declarations. Nevertheless, Gunnarr and Eiríkr the Red have different motivations in their decisions to return.

Eiríkr the Red is an old man, and he clearly interprets his fall from the horse as an omen that his luck has run out, so that it would be unwise to venture an expedition to Vinland. This version of the stumbling motif is evidently a very old one: *Grœnlendinga saga* appears to have been written in the early thirteenth century, and there are several parallels to this particular story in early *konungasǫgur* and in various other sources. A fall such as Eiríkr's was generally considered to indicate bad luck. In pagan times it was believed to be caused by the *dísir*, female agents of fate similar to the norns and valkyries.[66] King Haraldr Harðráði, for example, was said to have fallen from his horse on his way to conquer England, and soon afterwards he was defeated and killed in the Battle of Stamford Bridge.[67] The stumbling of the horse, then, is a stock motif, traditionally associated with the concepts of luck and fate.

In *Njála*, however, this motif has been given an entirely new twist. Gunnarr in no way regards his fall from the horse as an omen, and there is no reason

---

66. Cf. Strömbäck (1949), 25-31.
67. *Haralds saga Harðráða* (*Heimskr.*, III), ch. 90. The episode has been commented on by Pipping (1936), 81-82, and by Strömbäck (1949), 50.

why he should be *afraid* of going abroad—on the contrary, he risks his life by staying. It is the beautiful landscape, not the fall, that prompts him to turn back. There is no precedent for this motivation in earlier Icelandic saga tradition. His lyrical description of the beautiful slopes is, in fact, quite alien to conventional saga style and reminiscent of translated romances (*riddara sǫgur*).

There exists a very close foreign analogue: *Alexanders saga*, where Alexander is also at a crossroad in life and is prompted by a beautiful landscape to choose a fatal course.[68] Alexander has just left his home in Greece to fight King Darius, who is threatening his country by trying to incorporate most of the civilized world in the Persian empire. Before leaving, Alexander listens to a speech by his tutor, Aristotle, about his duties and responsibilities as a prince: he should respect law and order, he should not become too proud and ambitious, he should not fall for the temptations of this earth, etc. If he follows this advice, his "name will be famous as long as the world lasts." While sailing to Asia, Alexander is so eager to fight Darius that he never once looks back at his home, even though he has left his mother and his sister behind. After landing on the new continent, he climbs a mountain and looks out over the country:

Þar mátti hann alla vega sjá frá sér *fagra vǫllu, bleika akra*, stóra skóga, blómgaða víngarða, sterkar borgir. Ok er konungr sá yfir þessa fegrð alla, þá mælir hann svá til vildarliðs síns: "Þetta riki, er nu lít ek yfir, ætla ek mér sjálfum. En Grikkland, fǫðurleifð mína, vil ek nú gefa yðr upp," segir hann til hǫfðingianna. Ok svá treystiz hann nú sinni gæfu at honom þykkir sem þetta liggi laust fyrir. (*Alexanders saga*, chapter 1)

(There he could see in all directions *lovely meadows, pale cornfields*, large forests, blooming vinyards and strong cities. And when the king looked over all this beauty, he said to his attending officers: "This country, which I am now looking over, shall be all mine. But Greece, which my father has left me, I shall now give up to you." And he is now so confident about his own fortune, that he thinks he can easily carry out this plan.)[69]

---

68. Cf. Sveinsson, *Njála* (1954), p. XXXVI; Lönnroth (1970), *passim*.

69. The Icelandic text represents a rather free rendering of the following passage from *Alexandreis*, vv. 446-455:

> Hinc ubi vernantes cereali gramine campos,
> Tot nemorum saltus, tot prata virentibus herbis
> Lascivere videt, tot cinctas moenibus urbes,
> Tot Bacchi frutices, tot nuptas vitibus ulmos:
> Iam satis est, inquit, socii; mihi sufficit una
> Haec regio, Europam vobis patriamque relinquo.
> Sic ait, et patrium ducibus subdividit orbem,
> Nam timor ille ducum—tanta est fiducia fati—

Here Alexander is about to forget his tutor's good advice and become far too ambitious. A bit later, Alexander declares that he intends to conquer the world even if it means losing his soul: "If I have to choose, I would rather miss Heaven than Fame!"[70] And although Alexander becomes a great and famous conqueror, his greed has become so excessive that the eternal powers strike him down. He suddenly suffers an ignoble death, losing everything he has gained, including any hope of compensation in the next world.

Einar Ólafur Sveinsson has pointed out that the striking phrase "pale cornfields" (bleikir akrar) is not found in any sagas except Njála and Alexanders saga, and this strongly suggests that the author of Njála was influenced by the story of Alexander in presenting Gunnarr's fatal return.[71] More than this verbal echo connects the two scenes. It is true that Alexander decides to give up his home, while Gunnarr decides never to give it up; and that Alexander never looks back, while Gunnarr does look back. Yet both their choices represent a clear violation of the advice given to them by their respective Wise Counselors (Aristotle and Njáll). Both heroes seem motivated by excessive pride and by a foolish desire for what they should not desire. Both of them trust their own fortune too much for their own good.

The seduction theme

To a clerical mind in the Middle Ages, the beautiful landscapes seen by Gunnarr and Alexander must have represented a dangerous worldly temptation, snares of the devil. Such an interpretation is clearly intended in Alexanders saga, and it also fits well in Njála. Kolskeggr's strong condemnation of Gunnarr's decision to turn back must represent the author's own view;

Regnorum quaecumque iacent sub cardine quadro
Iam sibi parta putat.

It is worth observing that the phrase "bleikir akrar" has no exact equivalent in the Latin original although it is evidently meant to translate "vernantes cereali gramine campos." It is therefore conceivable, after all, that the Icelandic translator took the phrase "bleikir akrar" from his native "language of tradition," perhaps even from an oral tale about Gunnarr's return to Hlíðarendi. But the absence of such descriptive phrases in earlier sagas speaks against this interpretation. It appears more likely that the translator himself invented the phrase in a successful attempt to make the poetic language fo Gautier more succinct and effective. There are many other examples of such inventive condensations in Brandr Jónsson's rendering of Gautier's style; cf. Finnur Jónsson's preface to his edition of Alexanders saga, XV.

70. "Ef ek skyldi annars hvárs, þá vildi ek himinríkis heldr missa en frægðarinnar" (Lat. "Elysiisque velim hanc solam præponere campis"); Alexanders saga, ed. Finnur Jónsson, 16; Alexandreis, v. 502.

71. Sveinsson, Njála (1954), p. XXXVI; cf. above, note 69.

why else would he have emphasized it so? From the beginning, Kolskeggr has been a good and trustworthy person, and his words at this occasion are completely consistent with his character: "I am not going to dishonor my pledge over this nor any other matter I am trusted in."[72] There is no reason to believe that this comment belonged to the traditional saga motif of the "hero who turned back" (note that Leifr Eiríksson appears to silently accept his father's return in the passage from *Grœnlendinga saga*!); the author of *Njála* probably introduced it on his own initiative. And Hallgerðr is the only character in the saga who is said to have approved of Gunnarr's decision. We know, of course, that Hallgerðr constantly brings destruction and misfortune on Gunnarr.

The attraction Gunnarr feels for the "pale cornfields" appears to be similar to his attraction for Hallgerðr. When he first met her at the Allthing (chapter 33), he was strongly warned against her by Njáll and even by her own relatives. She had destroyed two husbands, and Njáll predicted that a marriage with her would bring more disaster. But Gunnarr was bewitched by her beauty and by the heroic challenge that she offered:

One day, as he was walking from the Law Rock, Gunnarr went down past the Mosfell booth. There he saw some well-dressed women coming towards him; the one in the lead was the best dressed of all. As they met, this woman at once greeted Gunnarr. He made a friendly reply, and asked her who she was. She said that her name was Hallgerðr and that she was the daughter of Hǫskuldr Dala-Kollsson. She spoke to him boldly and asked him to tell her about his travels. Gunnarr replied that he would not deny her that. So they sat down and talked. Hallgerðr was wearing a red richly-decorated tunic under a scarlet cloak trimmed all the way down with lace. Her beautiful thick hair flowed down over her bosom. Gunnarr was dressed in the robes that King Haraldr Gormsson had given him, with the gold bracelet from Earl Hákon on his arm. They talked aloud for a long time, until finally he asked if she were unmarried. "Yes," she replied, "and there is little risk of anyone changing that." "Do you think no one is good enough for you?" he asked. "Not at all," said Hallgerðr. "But I may be a little particular about husbands." "How would you answer if I asked for your hand?" "That thought has not entered your mind," she replied. "But it has," said Gunnarr. "If you have any wish to do that," said Hallgerðr, "then speak to my father." With that they ended their conversation.

What the author skillfully conveys in this scene is the gradual seduction of a great hero who is flawed by vanity and ambition. Notice how Hallgerðr teases him into desiring her by suggesting that very few men would *dare* to ask for her hand! Notice also how the description of her appearance emphasizes her beauty at the exact moment that they are talking about

72. Cf. Andersson (1970), 586-587.

his famous travels! Before this moment, he has managed to gain honor by following Njáll's good advice, and it had been explicitly pointed out in the previous chapter that he and Kolskeggr returned from their travels "without having become more conceited" (*ok hafði ekki vaxit dramb þeira,* 32). We are now witnessing his first moral fall. The second and more serious one occurs as he catches sight of the "pale cornfields" in chapter 75. The same fatal psychological mechanism is at work in both cases.[73]

The theme of seduction is Christian rather than Norse or Germanic. We find it several times in *Alexanders saga* as well as in other translated sagas from the thirteenth century. Chivalric knights are bound to lose their wits and forget their pledges when they look into the eyes of a beautiful temptress. Aristotle warned Alexander against the powers of Venus, but the whole Greek army was defeated by these powers when it reached the sinful city of Babylon and its many beautiful women.[74] At one point in the story, "Master Galenus" makes the following sad reflection:

Oh, fickle is the Fortune of this world (*Ho! Ho! Blekkilig er þessa heims hamingja*) and it is often made manifest what she may accomplish! King Cyrus was in his days the most powerful and victorious ruler. His fame had travelled all over the world, and wherever he had been, all the people had been forced to obey him. And yet, mighty and powerful as he was, he was defeated by one woman!

The conclusion that "Master Galenus" draws is that "mortal men should not brag of the power and the wealth allotted to them," for God may take such things away at any moment.[75]

The same Christian moral could easily be drawn from the story of Gunnarr and Hallgerðr in *Njála.* It is also possible to apply the same medieval theory about the human passions which "Master Galenus" presents as follows:

The body of man is lured by desire for worldly things (*verðr svikinn af tilfýsi stundlegra luta*) as it is pursuing the unstable happiness of this earth, and it [i.e. the body] tempts the soul to go along in such a way that the soul forgets God and does not remember in whose image it is created or where it is destined to go when it must part from the body, and from this such foolishness arises in man, that he cannot see what true happiness is

---

73. Cf. Lönnroth (1970), 20-21; Allen (1971), 147-152. Quite independent of each other, Allen and I noted the similarity between these two scenes and drew roughly the same conclusion from the parallel. The only important difference between our interpretations is that Allen sees the parallel between Hallgerðr's beauty and the beauty of Hlíðarendi in "archetypal" terms, while I try to explain it as a result of the author's "clerical mind"; cf. my review of Allen's book in *Speculum,* XLVIII (1973), 333-34.

74. Cf. *Alexanders saga,* ed. Finnur Jónsson, 7, 84-85.

75. *Alexanders saga,* 37.

and desires many times what even Nature denies him, saves himself from nothing that is bad and ceases to care about law and justice.[76]

If our interpretation is correct, this is what eventually happens to Gunnarr, just as it happens to Alexander. In both cases, the seduction is closely associated with the high status and worldly ambition of a great legendary hero. The royal gifts that Gunnarr is wearing at his first meeting with Hallgerðr emphasize both his status, which makes him desirable to her, and his pride, which prompts him to take up her challenge, foolishly disregarding all dangers. Before his "second fall," in chapter 75, his pride and his status are emphasized again in the description of his departure from Hlíðarendi: he is surrounded by a large household; all the people are sad to see him leave; he declares that he will never come back; he vaults into the saddle with a thrust of his halberd. Such extravagant behavior indicates that he is a very proud man who may again do something foolish if he encounters the kind of seductive challenge Hallgerðr presented in chapter 33. And that, of course, is exactly what happens: suddenly the horse stumbles, Gunnarr's glance is drawn back to the beautiful slopes with their deceptive promise of continued prosperity and happiness, and his soul cannot resist the temptation. He "ceases to care about law and justice."

The Author's Judgment of Gunnarr

It is a mistake to interpret Gunnarr's return to Hlíðarendi as prompted by a noble nationalism, as many critics have tried to do.[77] The beauty of nature was never associated with such nationalism before the nineteenth century; it is doubtful that the author of Njála can be called a "nationalist" in any sense of the word. Kolskeggr clearly has the author's sympathies when he says that he never intends to see Iceland again (because he knows that Gunnarr is going to die as a result of his foolish decision to stay). And the last thing we learn about Kolskeggr (in chapter 81) is that he becomes a Christian guardsman at the court of the Byzantine emperor, after receiving his calling from Heaven.[78] This calling is another indication that it was Kolskeggr, not Gunnarr, who did the right thing as they stood beneath the beautiful slopes of Hlíðarendi. For the clerical mind of our author is truly cosmopolitan: not only does he regard Constantinople as the proper last station for Kolskeggr, but he sends Flosi and Kári to Rome for absolu-

---

76. *Alexanders saga*, 110.

77. See in particular Sveinsson (1933), 212-213.

78. Kolskeggr's dream is paralleled in *Alexanders saga* by Alexander's dream about the patriarch in Jerusalem; cf. *Njála*, chapter 81; *Alexanders saga*, pp. 17-18. This is another case of possible literary influence.

tion, and he sides with the Irish Christians against the Norse vikings in the Clontarf episode.

When Gunnarr talks about "new-mown hay" (*slegin tún*), he may, as some critics have observed, be talking like an Icelandic farmer eager to return to his work.[79] Such an interpretation is compatible with our basic thesis that Gunnarr is not nobly motivated when he returns. But it would be a mistake to stress the agricultural matter. In fact, the heroes of *Njála* are rarely shown as normal farmers. It is typical that both Gunnarr and Hǫskuldr sow their land while dressed in beautiful silk cloaks and equipped with weapons; they seem more like chivalric knights taking a stroll over their property than like typical Icelandic farmers struggling to get a decent harvest out of their barren soil.[80] Whatever else may be said about the author and his heroes, they are *not* practical men.

Gunnarr is beset by a romantic but dangerous passion which is appropriate to a hero near final collapse. There is a strong element of fate in this passion, indicated by such lines as "his glance was drawn upwards to the slopes" (*Honum varð litit upp til hlíðarinnar*), and especially by the motif of the stumbling horse.[81] Kolskeggr's reaction and the author's attitude to *sjálfræði* (cf. above, pp. 128-130) indicate that Gunnarr *should* have been able to control his passion and resist the temptation exerted by the beautiful slopes (*and*, one might add, by his beautiful wife). The psychological notion underlying this scene (and the scene with Hallgerðr in chapter 33) is thus the same as the one we analyzed in connection with Flosi and Þórhallr Ásgrímsson: the struggle between passion and will. It is here uncertain whether we should interpret the struggle in terms of native folklore or in terms of learned Christian speculation about the "nature of man." What is certain, however, is that the author of *Njála* shows a more subtle interest in the psychology of his characters than most earlier sagawriters, who were usually satisfied with the presentation of a stock scene such as the one in *Grænlendinga saga* where Eiríkr returns to Brattahlíð.

Gunnarr's behavior in chapter 75 may be compared to that of Flosi later in the saga. For the Burning of Njáll, Flosi must make exactly the same atonement as the one previously demanded of Gunnarr: three years of exile. But, in contrast to Gunnarr, Flosi is eager to do what is asked, and he encourages his men to do the same thing: "It is not yet proper for us to live in peace. For we must prepare ourselves to leave the country and pay the

---

79. The "agricultural aspect" is stressed by Hans Kinck (1916) and criticized by Sveinsson (1933), 211.

80. Chapters 53, 111.

81. "Fate" is stressed particularly by Bååth (1885), 127.

compensation and keep our settlement as best we can" (*Eigi mun oss enn duga kyrru fyrir at halda. Munu vér hljóta at hugsa um utanferðir várar ok féggjǫld ok efna sættir vár sem drengiligast*; chapter 149). Nor does he complain when Kári kills some of his followers for their participation in the burning. "He never said a bad word about Kári" (chapter 158). And when he has finally made his atonement and been absolved from sin, Flosi returns to Iceland and embraces his old enemy. Clearly, this is the author's idea of how Gunnarr *should* have acted.

Several times after Gunnarr's return to Hlíðarendi, the author seems to stress his hero's arrogance and pride. At the end of chapter 75, we learn that "it is said that Gunnarr rode to all gatherings and Thing meetings and his enemies never dared to attack him. So it continued for a while, that he went about as if he had not been declared guilty of anything" (*Fór svá fram nǫkkura hríð, at hann fór sem ósekr maðr*). When he is finally attacked in his home, he fights so well that his enemies are ready to give up, but he then provokes them by using one of their arrows, even though he was warned against this action by his wise mother (chapter 77). After his death, his ghost appears and recites a skaldic stanza, in which it is said that he preferred to die in battle rather than yield to the demands of his enemies (ch. 78).

Since the stanza is probably older than the saga,[82] and the arrow incident is referred to in an earlier saga, *Eyrbyggja*,[83] Gunnarr's arrogance was probably stressed in the oral traditions about his fall. But the author of *Njála* has elaborated this theme by combining it with the landscape motif from *Alexanders saga*. Quite possibly, *Alexanders saga* provided him not only with this particular motif but also with the entire structural framework he used to transform the various oral tales about Gunnarr into one consecutive "Gunnarr's Saga." For the basic pattern is, as we have seen, the same: a young hero gains honor as long as he follows the advice of his Wise Counselor (Njáll, Aristotle), but he is beset by misfortune when he forgets the advice in his desire for the alluring beauties of this world.

It may be objected that such a pattern is too common and general to be borrowed, specifically, from *Alexanders saga*. In the heroic lays of the Edda, for example, Sigurðr Fafnisbani plays a role similar to that of Gunnarr; Odin often appears in the role of Wise Counselor; and Brynhildr is the destructive beauty who brings about the hero's fall (cf. above, p. 63, concerning traditional roles and stock characters in the sagas). But the treatment of this pattern in *Njála* is closer to *Alexanders saga* than to the Volsung legend or other traditional Norse tales: it is more Christian and didactic, more con-

---

82. Cf. Sigurður Guðmundsson (1918), 231-232; Sveinsson (1933), 209-210.
83. Cf. Sveinsson (1933), 124-125; 213-214.

cerned with psychological problems. Njáll is not *merely* shrewd and equipped with second sight like Odin, but is also a "noble heathen" teaching Christian morals in much the same way Aristotle did. Gunnarr is not *merely* a "Siegfried type" but, like Alexander, is a chivalric hero with romantic passions which must be tempered by asceticism in order to merit our approval. Hallgerðr is not *merely* a vengeful Norse "Prima Donna" but, like some of the women encountered by Alexander, is a seductive temptress, once even characterized as a *púta*, "whore."[84] Hlíðarendi is not *merely* the traditional home of an Icelandic hero; its pale cornfields represent vanity and temptation, as did the Asian landscape to Alexander. And, as we have seen, in both sagas a man's fortune is dependent on his morals and the fate of the world is dependent on God's will.

There are no indications that Njáll and Gunnarr were associated with each other in the oral traditions that formed the basis of *Njála*. Hence the author may well have been inspired by *Alexanders saga* to combine the various tales into one narrative tracing Gunnarr's ascendence to fame and consecutive downfall, a narrative built of traditional Norse saga elements but expressive of Christian ideas which "Master Galterus" conveyed much more directly (and less skillfully!) in his story of Alexander and Aristotle. But speculation about sources must always be uncertain. What is certain is that the structure of "Gunnarr's Saga" would have been quite different had it not been shaped by the author's "clerical mind." Perhaps the story of Gunnarr's return to Hlíðarendi would have been more similar to the story of Eiríkr the Red in *Grœnlendinga saga*; it would, at any rate, have been more conventional. The combination of old building blocks and new patterns makes chapter 75 of *Njála* one of the most original and memorable chapters in saga literature.

6. SOME CONCLUDING REMARKS ABOUT SAGA STYLE

In his extremely influential book *Mimesis*, Erich Auerbach distinguished "two basic modes of imitation": "foreground style" and "background style." One is called typical of Homer and the classical pagan world picture in general; the other is called typical of the Bible and expressive of the Judeo-Christian interpretation of the world and human history. Auerbach describes the difference between the two styles as follows:

> On the one hand externalized, uniformly illuminated phenomena, at a definite time and in a definite place, connected together without lacunae in a perpetual foreground; thoughts and feeling completely expressed; events

84. Chapter 91. Cf. above, p. 116.

taking place in leisurely fashion and with very little of suspense. On the other hand, the externalization of only so much of the phenomena as is necessary for the purpose of the narrative, all else left in obscurity; the decisive points of the narrative alone are emphasized, what lies between is nonexistent; time and place are undefined and call for interpretation; thoughts and feelings remain unexpressed, are only suggested by the silence and the fragmentary speeches; the whole, permeated with the most un-relieved suspense and directed toward a single goal (and to that extent far more of a unity), remains mysterious and "fraught with background."[85]

Auerbach's attempt to relate literary style and world picture is extremely interesting and worth discussing also in connection with the sagas, which he excluded from his very extensive study of "the representation of reality in Western literature." Yet one wonders if his categories and generalisations are as applicable as his followers believe.

As Richard Allen has argued very convincingly, the sagas exhibit features of both "foreground style" and "background style." For, on one hand, they concentrate on "objective" phenomena, "at a definite time and in a definite place." But, on the other hand, they externalize "only so much of the phenomena as is necessary for the purpose of the narrative," "the decisive points alone are emphasized," much "thought and feeling remain unexpressed," and very often "the whole" appears to be "directed towards a single goal" and full of mysterious "background."[86]

Allen calls this hybrid form a result of Christian influence on the pagan Germanic saga tradition. Yet he is unable to find in the saga any strong *stylistic* influence from medieval Christian literature. He thus has to refer to the general "Christian sensibility" of the sagawriters. But he also comes up with this solution: "It is tempting to suggest a parallel evolution of Judeo-Christian creation and hero myth with Germanic creation and Germanic heroic myths in order to explain why many of Auerbach's remarks on Christian literature seem applicable to sagas."[87] He follows up this idea by noting a series of parallels between the Christian world picture and that of pagan Icelanders (The Last Judgment corresponds to *Ragnarǫk*, Christ corresponds to Balder, etc.).[88]

Individually, each of Allen's observations is excellent. But he fails to combine them in a convincing theory about the development of saga style

85. *Mimesis: The Representation of Reality in Western Literature*, trans. Willard Trask (1953: paperback reprint, Princeton, 1968), 11-12.
86. Allen (1971), 39. An earlier attempt to apply Auerbach's theories on *Njála* was made by Fox (1963), 291-292.
87. Allen (1971), 46.
88. Allen (1971), 56.

because he is far too dependent on Auerbach's theories and not sufficiently familiar with clerical writings in Old Norse. In fact, it follows from our own analysis of "saga style" and "clerical style" that Auerbach's categories are untenable.

For the clerical style of a work like *Alexanders saga* is clearly much more of a "foreground style" than the style of any native family saga. It is *here*, in clerical writings, that we find "externalized, uniformly illuminated phenomena . . . connected together without lacunae in a perpetual foreground; thoughts and feelings completely expressed; events taking place in leisurely fashion and with very little of suspense." But it is also here that we find the most obvious concern for divine providence. Most family sagas contain little of this; *Njála* is a clear exception.

The native saga style evidently was formed in oral tradition by storytellers whose "Christian sensibility" was rather limited; it is, at any rate, not much reflected in their traditional narrative grammar. Their feud stories did not promote any kind of theology—either Christian or pagan. Neither Christ nor Balder, neither the Last Judgment nor *Ragnarǫk*, can be called important ingredients even in the "background" of these stories. Fate and fortune were more important, but it is only in a few family sagas, usually the ones most obviously influenced by Christian ideas, that these concepts are as strong as the concept of providence in the Bible.

The traditional Icelandic feud saga is concerned with action, and that is the main reason why it shares some characteristics of "background style" ("the decisive points of the narrative alone are emphasized," "thoughts and feelings remain unexpressed," etc.). Another reason is that the Norsemen were taught to hide their thoughts and emotions much more than either the Greeks of Homer's time or the Jews of ancient Palestine; their heroic ideal was the strong silent man, and this ideal is reflected in their way of telling a story (cf. above, p. 84).

The author of *Njála* tried, however, to use the saga style, with only a few "clerical" modifications, to convey a Christian world picture. He was, of course, not the first to try this feat: the authors of *Laxdœla*, *Vatnsdœla*, and *Fóstbrœðra* tried to do the same thing, and so did the authors of early *konungasǫgur* and sagas of the Icelandic bishops. In a few cases, the ambition had been stated more explicitly. The author of *Hrafns saga Sveinbjarnar-sonar*, for example, makes the following pronouncement at the beginning of his narrative:

In these events we may see the patience which Almighty God has with us each day, and also the Free Will which he gives to each man (*sjálfræði þat er hann gefr hverjum manni*), so that each may do as he wants, either good or evil.   (*Biskupa Sögur*, I, 639)

But it was not easy to convey such theological messages in the native saga idiom. The author of *Hrafns saga* did not succeed very well, in spite of his good intentions. In some chapters of his saga, particularly at the very end, he did manage to introduce a Christian perspective through various dreams, visions, and miracles. In other sections, he merely follows the traditional Feud Pattern or Travel Pattern, apparently forgetting about "God's patience" and "Free Will."

Such inconsistency is even more typical of *Fóstbrœðra*, *Vatnsdœla*, and *Laxdœla*. To a certain extent, we also find it in *Njála*. Several times, our author's clerical mind rests while he is carried away by the traditional patterns of oral saga narrative. Yet he succeeds much better than any previous sagawriter in unifying these patterns until they become "directed toward a single goal," which may be called both Christian and didactic.

In his pioneering and unduly neglected book on saga structure, A. U. Bååth concluded that the best structures sagas are those dominated by the idea of Fate. From this standpoint, *Njála* seemed to him more advanced than any other family saga (cf. above, p. 9). Perhaps Bååth's thesis can be restated in the light of what we have said about the clerical interpretation of Fate: the best structured among the longer sagas are those which are dominated by the idea of Divine Providence but which use the native saga techniques and native metaphysical concepts such as *auðna*, Fate, and *gæfa*, Fortune, to convey their message.

It is clear, at any rate, that some of the most Christian sagas, e.g., *Njála* and *Laxdœla*, are among the best structured, that their episodes are subordinate to an overall plan. This is not so much a *literary* plan as a plan for human history: certain events foreshadow other events; the course of action itself appears to be directed toward a metaphysical or ethical goal (the introduction of a new and better faith; the replacement of the old revenge ethics by an ethics of love and peace). The characterization in such sagas also is unusually rich and subtle, for clerical minds have provided the stock characters of the traditional saga world with "inner" lives which often bring them into conflict with their roles as viking adventurers or heroic participants in family feuds. It was prescribed by native convention that Gunnarr and Flosi in *Njála* (or Kjartan and Bolli in *Laxdœla*) should commit a series of revenge acts against their enemies. But individual Christian sagawriters in the thirteenth century appear to have decided that their actors should suffer serious moral conflicts as they were committing these acts. It was prescribed by native convention that Gunnarr should return to Hlíðarendi rather than go abroad. Yet the psychology of his decision to return was established by clerical thinking, not by saga convention.

So Richard Allen is on the right track when he asserts that "certain features of saga style" resulted from "an interaction between the saga-man's evaluation of what events in Icelandic history were worth telling and his Christian awareness of the potential immense significance of each man and each man's deeds." But his analysis of this "interaction" is insufficient; it cannot be explained in terms of Auerbach's theories about Homeric "foreground style" and biblical "background style"; nor is it possible to arrive at an explanation that holds true for all sagas. The "interaction" affected saga style *per se* much less than it affected the overall composition of some of the best sagas, especially *Njála.*

V

The Social Context

1. INTRODUCTION

Njála was written at a time of radical change in Icelandic history. The country had just lost its political independence; the Norwegian king was about to deprive the native chieftains of power and replace them with his own appointees; the Allthing had been drastically reformed, and new laws had replaced those in effect since the time of Njáll and Gunnarr. The church, which had conformed to native tradition, was transformed into a copy of the Roman model. And the classical saga culture was rapidly deteriorating under the influence of foreign romance.

Critics who read *Njála* as an homage to a vanishing culture generally fail to realize, however, that the period preceding Iceland's loss of independence was so filled with internal strife that the Norwegian take-over must have been a blessing to much of the population. For several decades the country had been torn apart by feuds larger and more vicious than any described in our saga. The political power, which in Njáll's time had been divided between a large number of local chieftains and free farmers meeting at the Allthing each year, had gradually been usurped by a small number of wealthy chieftain families, each of which owned several chieftainships as personal property and who exploited both the church and the farmers in their efforts to defeat one another. The Allthing was largely corrupt, and its proceedings often bordered on open fights. The most powerful of the chieftains, with small armies of followers, had been waging war against each other and demanding loyalty from the farmers. As owners of church property these rulers could use the tithes and control the clergy with very little opposition from the bishops, generally selected from among their own. The chieftains sought to become retainers of the Norwegian king in order to receive sanction and support for their conquests.

It was because of such rivalry between the chieftains that the Norwegian king finally succeeded in taking over the country. He was aided by church leaders who wished to make the Icelandic church independent of secular influence and by various laymen who wished to protect themselves against further assaults. The decline of Icelandic shipping and the need to import grain and other necessities from abroad also made an alliance with Norway seem attractive. When Icelanders at the Allthing in 1262 swore allegiance to the Norwegian king, they evidently did so voluntarily in the hope that the allegiance would inaugurate peace and prosperity. And, their hopes were fulfilled, at least briefly. Iceland in the later thirteenth and early fourteenth centuries was indeed more peaceful and prosperous than in the Sturlung Age. The foreign exploitation and general decline of Iceland did not begin until later, and it could hardly have been foreseen when *Njála* was written.

These basic historical facts are necessary in order for us to place this saga in its social and political context. Modern Icelandic nationalism has tended to picture the Independence era as a golden age—of which *Njála* is the last and most glorious manifestation—before the country was polluted by foreign culture. Such a view is correct only in the sense that the native culture was a precondition for works such as *Njála*. When this culture died, the quality of saga writing declined, even though the production of saga manuscripts increased.

In this chapter we shall first consider the general conditions of saga production and saga entertainment in thirteenth century Iceland. We shall then try to define the milieu in which *Njála* was written and the influence this milieu had on the composition of the saga and the narrator's view of Icelandic history. After an attempt to determine the social roles of the author and his audience, we shall conclude our study with some thoughts about *Njála*'s place in the development of Norse sagawriting.

2. THE SOCIAL CONDITIONS OF SAGA PRODUCTION

Medieval books were usually written by clerics for other clerics or for the aristocracy; literacy was generally confined to the clergy, and manuscripts were so expensive to produce that only very wealthy individuals could afford to own them. For the same reasons, literary texts were normally meant to be recited or read aloud if they were intended for a large audience. These were the conditions in most of Europe, and it is unlikely that they were much different in Iceland.

Scholars of the "Icelandic School" have nevertheless tried to show that classical sagawriting was rooted in a nonclerical and nonaristocratic farm culture, where literacy was more widespread and manuscripts more available to the common man than in other European countries. Einar Ólafur Sveinsson has been one of the chief proponents of this view,[1] and it is therefore hardly surprising to find him arguing that the author of *Njála* was neither a priest nor a chieftain, although he admits the possibility that the author was a well-born layman with some clerical training.[2] As we shall see, Sveinsson is probably correct on this point, and he may also be correct to assume that Icelandic laymen were unusually literate for their time; but such a picture of saga production should not mislead us into believing that works such as *Njála* were either written or read by ordinary farmers.[3]

It is indeed true that Icelandic farmers in modern times have been remarkably literate compared to farmers in other countries. They had this reputation at least as early as the sixteenth century, and it may well be that they had earned it even earlier.[4] But since farmers in most other countries were almost completely illiterate until the nineteenth century, even a minimum of literary activity among Icelandic farmers would seem remarkable to outsiders. Therefore, any theory about literacy and literary activity at the time of classical sagawriting must be based exclusively on Icelandic evidence from the Middle Ages.

Members of the "Icelandic School" have built their case on the following evidence: (1) the large number of preserved vellum manuscripts from the thirteenth and fourteenth centuries;[5] (2) information in medieval documents about laymen sending and receiving letters or doing other things which

---

1. See, in particular, his *Sturlungaöld* (Reykjavík, 1940), available in an English translation by J. Hannesson, *The Age of the Sturlungs: Icelandic Civilization in the Thirteenth Century* (Ithaca, New York, 1953). Also: "Lestrarkunnátta Íslendinga í fornöld," *Skírnir* (1944), reprinted in Sveinsson's *Við uppspretturnar* (Reykjavík, 1956), 166-192.

2. *Njála* (1954), C-CV.

3. The following discussion summarizes and modifies some of the arguments presented by Lönnroth (1964), later criticized by Hallberg (1965), and again defended by Lönnroth (1967).

4. On testimonies about Icelandic literacy in the sixteenth century, see, in particular, Stefán Karlsson, "Bókagerð bænda," *Opuscula*, 4 (*Bibliotheca Arnamagnæana*, 30, 1970), 133-135. Karlsson's article does not pay sufficient attention to the fact that the testimonies appear to be dependent on each other and hence cannot be fully trusted. Cf. Lönnroth (1967), 183.

5. See, in particular, Sigurður Nordal, "Time and Vellum," *Annual Bulletin of the Modern Humanities Research Association*, 24 (1952), 15-18.

seem to presuppose a high level of literacy[6]; (3) the absence of saga manuscripts from medieval inventories of monastic libraries;[7] (4) indications that farming conditions in Iceland were such that farmers could make inexpensive vellum from their surplus of calfskin after the annual slaughter and find time to prepare saga manuscripts during the long winter months;[8] (5) Sveinsson's interpretation of political events in the Sturlung Age as a struggle between two conflicting cultures, one secular and nationalistic, the other representing the church and the Norwegian king and aspiring to overthrow Iceland's independence. Most sagas, according to Sveinsson, were written by people belonging to the first camp, while most "clerical" literature was written by those in the second camp.[9]

Since these views of the "Icelandic School" prevail in modern English handbooks dealing with the age of sagawriting,[10] it is important to present some opposing arguments:

1. The number of preserved vellum manuscripts is indeed rather large for such a small country. But the yearly production (including law-texts, homilies, etc.) could not have exceeded one full-sized manuscript per 5,000 inhabitants![11] Insofar as early owners of the manuscripts can be identified, they are members of the highest social strata or, in the case of homilies and saints' lives, wealthy ecclesiastic institutions (churches and monasteries).[12]

2. People mentioned in medieval Icelandic sources as sending or receiving letters also generally belong to the highest social strata (members of leading chieftain families, etc.), and they appear to have used clerical scribes for much if not all of the writing they needed. Practically all persons said to have personally *written* documents or literary works (rather than dictating or commissioning the writing) are clerics. The fact that the same scribal hands appear in several manuscripts from the same period also indicates that writing was a highly specialized art in Iceland throughout the Middle

6. Sveinsson, *Við uppspretturnar* (1956), 184-190; Stefán Karlsson, *Islandske original-diplomer indtil 1450* (Copenhagen, 1963), XXXVI-LXII; *Opuscula*, 4 (1970), 131-140.

7. Halldór Hermannsson, *Icelandic Manuscripts* (Ithaca, 1929), 29-37. Sveinsson refers to Hermannsson and accepts his conclusions in *Njála* (1954), CIII.

8. Nordal (1952), 20-26.

9. Sveinsson, *The Age of the Sturlungs* (1953), especially 116-117, 150-154. A similar view was earlier expressed by Hermannsson (1929), 29 and by Rudolf Meissner, *Die Strengleikar* (1902).

10. See for example Hallberg's *The Icelandic Saga* (1962), 24-34, 46-48.

11. Cf. Lönnroth (1964), 43-44.

12. Cf. Lönnroth (1964), 45-46. Valuable data on Icelandic book owners and book collections in the Middle Ages have been compiled by E. Olmer (1902) and T. J. Oleson (1957, 1959-1961).

Ages. Many scribes were undoubtedly professionals or semiprofessionals who accepted commissions from wealthy farmers as well as churches.[13]

3. Monastic inventories show only books that belonged to monasteries, and it would be unreasonable to expect them to contain anything but works of a "clerical" nature. These inventories cannot tell us whether monks or other clerics used to write sagas for wealthy laymen, but there are other indications that clerics did so, especially as private secretaries of prominent chieftains.[14]

4. Whatever the nature of Icelandic farming conditions and the theoretical possibilities for cheap manuscript production, contemporary documents (church inventories, testaments, etc.) show that manuscripts were frightfully expensive. An average saga manuscript must have been quite beyond the means of ordinary farmers, whatever their level of literacy.[15]

5. Sveinsson's view of the Sturlung Age as a struggle between a native-secular and a foreign-clerical culture is based on political developments as they appear from contemporary chronicles such as *Sturlunga saga*. In fact, there were many different feuds and conflicting camps during this troublesome period of Iceland's loss of independence: power struggles between chieftains; feuds between leaders and secular chieftains over jurisdiction of the churches; and continuous attempts by the Norwegian monarchy to gain influence at the expense of both church leaders and secular chieftains. None of these conflicts, however, implied a conflict between "saga culture" and "clerical culture"; there were clerics as well as farmers on both sides of the major struggles. No "nationalistic" front existed in Iceland before the nineteenth century, and there is no sign of any conscious attempts before then to proclaim the sagas as a patriotic alternative to foreign or "clerical" literature. On the contrary, there is much to suggest that the indigenous and the foreign genres could be appreciated by the same people.[16]

Nevertheless, it is possible to distinguish both a "clerical" and a "secular" literary milieu in thirteenth century Iceland. The clerical milieu is centered in the monasteries and the cathedrals, where undoubtedly most of the saints' lives were first written for the purpose of being read aloud on holidays. The secular milieu is centered in some of the largest farms owned by such leading chieftain families as the Sturlungs, who claimed to be the descendants of saga heroes and had sufficient power and wealth to immortalize the deeds of their ancestors in written form. Sagas such as *Njála* are likely to have

---

13. Lönnroth (1964), 52-75. For some examples of wealthy laymen writing saga manuscripts in the fifteenth century, cf. Karlsson (1970), 136-139.

14. Lönnroth (1964), 62-63.

15. Lönnroth (1964), 46-50. Data on book prices may be found in Oleson (1957, 1961).

16. Lönnroth (1964), 33-42.

originated in this secular milieu, even though occasionally they may have been written in a monastery for the benefit of a local benefactor.[17] A few lay members of the leading families (for example, Snorri Sturluson) must have been sufficiently educated to read, dictate, or even write sagas themselves, and many of them must have known old stories and poems as part of their cultural heritage. But most of the actual *writing* of a saga was probably done by clerics who were either members of the family or employed as secretaries, chaplains, etc.

There had to be many close contacts between the two literary milieus, for saints' lives and native sagas are sometimes found in the same manuscripts, and are often written by the same scribal hands in different manuscripts.[18] Even without specific examples of foreign literary influence, it is reasonable to suppose that the men who first wrote works like *Njála* or *Laxdœla* also at times translated romances and saints' lives, even though they did not produce everything for the same type of audience. Saints' lives are written to be read aloud in church or at more private gatherings of worship, while sagas and romances are primarily written for secular entertainment. But the same people may well have attended both types of gathering.

The fact that under these circumstances sagas have not incorporated more of foreign literary genres is a testimony to the strength of the native oral tradition. If the saga as narrative form had not existed before sagas were written in the thirteenth century (as members of the "Icelandic School" have argued), it would indeed be difficult to explain the originality of this literature without assuming that sagawriters were a completely different breed from the writers who simultaneously transcribed pious saints' lives and chivalric romances. Such a distinction between types of writers is hardly conceivable in the homogeneous culture of thirteenth-century Iceland.

As Hermann Pálsson has argued,[19] secular sagas (as well as romances) were probably meant to be read aloud at the larger farms. The institution of sagareading, during the thirteenth century, was evidently about to replace the older native tradition of *sagnaskemtan*, oral saga entertainment in which the performers had to rely on their memory and narrative skill. In *Þorgils saga ok Hafliða* (early thirteenth century) there is an often quoted

17. Concerning the role of Icelandic monasteries in the production of saga manuscripts for extramural consumption, see, for example, Ólafur Halldórsson, "Helgafells bækur fornar," *Studia Islandica*, 24 (1966) and Lönnroth, "Styrmir's Hand in the Obituary of Viðey?," *Mediaeval Scandinavia*, 1 (1968).

18. Lönnroth (1964), 65-75.

19. *Sagnaskemmtun Íslendinga* (Reykjavík, 1962).

description of such entertainment at a large wedding at the farm of Reykja-hólar in 1119:

And now there was much merriment and happiness, good entertainment and many kinds of games, dancing as well as wrestling and saga entertainment (*sagnaskemtan*). The feast went on for seven full days and nights (*sjau nætr fastar ok fullar*), because Saint Olaf's Feast was to be held there each summer, if grain could be bought, two meal-riddles, at the Þórsnes Thing, and many guild-brothers were there. Reykjahólar had such good land at this time that the fields were never barren. It was always customary to have new flour for the accommodation of the guests, and the feast was held on Saint Olaf's Day [July 29] each summer. People have told, although this is hardly a matter of importance, who provided the entertainment and how it was done (*Frá því er nǫkkut sagt, er þó er lítil tilkváma, hverir þar skemmtu eða hverju skemmt var*). Such tales were told which now many people object to and pretend not to have known, for many are ignorant about truth and believe in fiction while they cast doubt upon facts (*Þat er í frásǫgn haft, er nú mæla margir í móti ok látast eigi vitat hafa, því at margir ganga duldir ins sanna ok hyggja þat satt, er skrǫkvat er, en þat logit, sem satt er*). Hrólfr from Skálmarnes told the saga (*sagði sǫgu*) about Hrǫngviðr the Viking and Óláfr Liðsmanna King and how Þráinn the Berserk broke into the burial mound and about Hrómundr Gripsson—and several verses were included. This saga was used for King Sverrir's entertainment, and he said that such lying sagas were the most enjoyable (*En þessarri sǫgu var skemmt Sverri konungi, ok kallaði hann slíkar lygisǫgur skemmtiligstar*). And yet people know how to trace their ancestry back to Hrómundr Grípsson! Hrólfr himself had composed this saga (*Þessa sǫgu hafði Hrólfr sjálfr saman setta*). Ingimundr, the priest, told the saga of Ormr Barreyjarskáld including many verses and at the end of the saga, a good poem, by Ingimundr (*flokk góðan við enda sǫgunnar er Ingimundr hafði ortan*), and yet many wise men hold this saga to be true.[20]

Although this account portrays events more than 150 years before the writing of *Njála*, people in the thirteenth century probably enjoyed sagas in a similar social context. The entertainment is sponsored by a wealthy chieftain family, but it attracts farmers, clerics, and merchants (guild-brothers), who are present not only as wedding guests but also as traders and as worshippers of Saint Olaf. It was evidently convenient to schedule the entertainment for such large gatherings, which had to serve several social functions since people in the country could only come together a few times each year. (In the Faroes, Saint Olaf's feast is still the main annual event,

20. *Sturlunga saga*, I, ed. Jón Jóhannesson (Reykjavík, 1946), 27. Cf. Peter G. Foote, "Sagnaskemtan: Reykjahólar 1119," *Saga-Book of the Viking Society*, 14 (1955-56). Pálsson (1962) has concluded (pp. 52-53) that the sagas told at Reykjahólar were read aloud from manuscripts, but this interpretation has no basis in the text, and it is perfectly clear that written sagas did not exist as early as 1119.

to which people come from all the islands to the town of Tórshavn in order to trade, dance, sing, and celebrate!)

Of the two saga entertainers mentioned, Hrólfr is a prominent farmer and also an excellent lawyer, while Ingimundr is a wealthy priest belonging to the chieftain class; he, in fact, was host at this feast, according to the saga. Both men are evidently thought to have composed their sagas themselves. (However, the narrator emphasizes this mainly to show that the sagas were "lying tales," unlike more realistic sagas about historical characters, such as *Njála* or *Þorgils saga ok Hafliða.*) The saga composed by Hrólfr is later supposed to have been told at the Norwegian court, evidently by some other storyteller, since Hrólfr must have been dead when Sverrir became king around 1180. But the saga is also supposed to be still living in the oral tradition of thirteenth century Iceland, where the narrator of *Þorgils saga ok Hafliða* has evidently met some people naive enough to trace their ancestry back to the legendary hero of Hrólfr's "lying tale."

These points can shed light not only on the presentation and composition of oral sagas but also on how they were transmitted to later generations as part of a family tradition. They also travelled on merchant ships from Iceland to Norway with members of prominent families who gained favors from foreign princes through their talents as skalds and storytellers. At the Norwegian court, skaldic poetry and *sagnaskemtan* were monopolized by such visiting Icelanders from the end of the tenth to the middle of the thirteenth century, judging from accounts in the sagas themselves and in foregin sources.[21] When the travelers returned from Iceland, they brought new poems and stories, which could then in turn be treasured as part of a family tradition.

The change from storytelling to the reading of saga manuscripts was stimulated by the Norwegian court, where the kings in the thirteenth century, inspired by the chivalric fashions of continental courts, commissioned clerics to translate French romances for the enjoyment and education of courtiers. References to public reading as a form of entertainment are first found in such royally sponsored translations, e.g., this admonition from the Norse translator of *Elie de Saint-Gille* to his audience: "Now listen well, for a beautiful story (*fǫgr froeði*) is better than a full belly. You should drink while listening to a saga, but not gulp down too much. It is an honor to tell a story when the audience is listening, but the labor is in vain if they cease to pay attention."[22]

21. See, for example, Pálsson (1962), 166-176.
22. *Elis saga ok Rosamundu*, ed. E. Kölbing (Heilbronn, 1881), 33. Cf. Thorkil Damsgaard Olsen, "Den høviske litteratur" in H. Bekker-Nielsen *et al.*, *Norrøn Fortællekunst: Kapitler af den norsk-islandske middelalderlitteraturs historie* (Copenhagen, 1965), 92-117.

It is obvious, however, that only the wealthiest of Iceland's aristocracy could afford such noble entertainment if they had to pay for the performers' manuscripts. The less wealthy or less educated would have to be satisfied with the old and native form of *sagnaskemtan*, in which the performer simply told a traditional story from memory, perhaps with elements of oral improvisation. Significantly, one of the earliest mentions of saga *reading* in Iceland involves the wealthy Sturlung chieftain Þorgils skarði, a retainer of the Norwegian king. The night before his death, in 1258, he is said to have been asked whether he preferred dance or sagareading as entertainment for his people. When learning that a manuscript of *Tómass saga erkibyskups* (the Icelandic version of Saint Thomas Becket's biography) was available, Þorgils decided that this saga should be read because he loved Saint Thomas more than all other holy men.[23]

Another Sturlung leader and royal retainer, Sturla Þórðarson (the alleged author of *Íslendinga saga* and *Hákonar saga*), is said to have entertained King Magnus of Norway and his men at the drinking table with a saga about a troll woman, *Huldar saga*, which he evidently had in manuscript form. The king was so impressed by Sturla's literary talents that he commissioned him to compose the biography of his father, King Hákon.[24]

Although Sturla was an aristocratic layman (like his uncle, Snorri Sturluson), his brother Ólafr, poet and learned commentator of skaldic verse, was a *subdiaconus*, and his son Þórðr was the court chaplain of King Magnús. Furthermore, there is reason to suppose that both Sturla and Snorri dictated their works to clerical scribes, who also helped to collect and organize the saga material and perhaps composed some of the stories later attributed to their more well-known masters.[25]

23. *Sturlunga saga*, II, 218. The account is naturally untrustworthy insofar as it is told to certify Þorgils' pious state of mind before his death. One may conclude from the context (*sǫgur eða dans*) that a secular saga would have been considered more normal for this kind of entertainment. Pálsson (1962) has concluded that the saga read to Þorgils was offered to him by the farmer at Hrafnagils, where Þorgils was staying overnight with his followers. This conclusion is not warranted by the text, however, since the account does not preclude the possibility that Þorgils' followers had brought with them whatever manuscripts were considered necessary for their entertainment. When Þorgils' liege-lord, King Hákon, travelled in Scotland, manuscripts were evidently brought along with him for such entertainment. Cf. *Hákonar saga*, ed. Vigfússon (*Rolls Series*, 88:2, 1887), 353-354.

24. *Sturlunga saga*, II, 232-235. The wording of this testimony does not make absolutely clear whether Sturla is telling *Huldar saga* to the court or is reading it from a manuscript, but Pálsson (1962) is probably right in assuming (p. 52) that Sturla did use a manuscript, since he is asked before the entertainment to "bring with him the saga about the troll woman" (*hafa með sér trǫllkonusǫguna*).

25. Cf. Lönnroth (1964), 78-94, criticized by Hallberg (1965), 180-183, defended by Lönnroth (1967), 180, 185-187. See also Lönnroth (1968), 100.

These examples may help us to picture the milieu in which *Njála* was produced. It was aristocratic insofar as it was dominated by the leading chieftain families and influenced by the Norwegian court, where the reading of chivalric romance had recently been introduced as a more refined alternative to drinking, dancing, and games. Yet the Icelandic version of this milieu appears to have been more rustic and homespun than its Norwegian equivalent, and it includes clerics as well as prosperous farmers and their families. Although translated romance had given an impetus to the recording and reading of native sagas and also influenced their form, the atmosphere was still that of the old Icelandic *sagnaskemtan*, more concerned with heroic fights and troll women than with the courtly love of Tristan or Lancelot.[26]

Sagnaskemtan, during the thirteenth century, had become increasingly dependent not only on the use of manuscripts but also on the clergy for its execution and on the wealthiest chieftain families for its economic support. A previous chapter studied the "clerical" patterns in *Njála*. We shall now turn to the effects of aristocratic sponsorship.

3. NJÁLA AND THE SVÍNFELLING FAMILY

The evidence of placenames, genealogy, and topographical data in *Njála* suggests that its author had an intimate knowledge of southeastern Iceland but was less familiar with the southwestern part of the country, where Njáll and Gunnarr lived and where most of the action took place. The author no doubt knew his way around the southern East Fjords and the farm of Svínafell where Flosi lived, and he evidently expects his audience to know the geography and the local traditions of this area. He makes occasional errors, however, when the saga "moves west" to Hlíðarendi and Bergþórs-hváll.[27]

When *Njála* was written, during the last decades of the thirteenth century, southeastern Iceland, and indeed a good deal more, was dominated by one

26. The transformation of Norse romances in Iceland to suit the native taste for heroic sagas has been noted by many scholars, e.g., by Sveinsson, *The Age of the Sturlungs* (1953), 41-42, and Damsgaard Olsen (1965), 114.

27. Cf. Sveinsson, *Njála* (1954), LXXXIV-C (with numerous references to earlier discussions of the sagawriter's place of origin, topographical knowledge, and sense of directions). Unfortunately, this is an area where non-Icelandic scholars cannot contribute much to the discussion, but Sveinsson's arguments appear convincing, and his conclusions coincide, on the whole, with those of earlier saga scholars. One fact which appears significant is the sagawriter's tendency to explain the location of farms in Njáll's district (e.g., "Njáll bjó at Bergþórshváli *í Landeyjum*"), while presenting farms in Flosi's district as if no such explanation were necessary to his audience, e.g., "Flosi bjó at Svínafelli" (without further specification). Cf. Sveinsson, *op. cit.*, XCV.

very old and very powerful family, the Svínfellings. Their name came from Flosi's old farm and their most ancient chieftainship stemmed from Flosi himself. Svínafell was still one of their most important residences, but they had others, particularly in the East. In the Sturlung period they had acquired chieftainships in addition to Flosi's, and they had vastly expanded their territory, probably through the usual combination of feuds with other chieftain families, negotiations with the Norwegian king and with the farmers, successful marriage deals, exploitation of church revenue, and various other maneuvers. After the loss of Iceland's independence in the 1260s they had become even more powerful by serving the Norwegian king, who appointed some of their leading men to positions that enabled them to outrival most of their competitors. Their interests must have been served by the writing of a long saga in which their ancestor is a major hero and which contains genealogies emphasizing the importance of his heirs. Several scholars have therefore assumed that our author was associated with the Svínfellings.[28]

Nobody has explained, however, why a writer associated with the Svínfelling family would concentrate throughout most of the saga on Njáll and Gunnarr rather than on Flosi. Why, in fact, does he focus on Flosi's adversaries, Njáll and his sons, whose death at Bergþórshváll could not have added to the stature of the thirteenth century Svínfellings? The answer lies in the oral tradition enveloping the major saga heroes before the writing of *Njála*.

The memory of both Gunnarr and Njáll was revered in the tradition long before the author composed his saga. Gunnarr's image was that of a great fighter finally overcome by a superior force of enemies. Njáll's image was that of a wise and noble old lawyer burned in his home by a pack of ignoble scoundrels.[29] Flosi's image, on the other hand, was apparently a bad one. He was known as "Brennu-Flosi," the man who instigated and led the Burning of Njáll. He was known to have killed a certain Arnórr Qrnulfsson at the Skaftafell Thing in 997,[30] and killings at a Thing meeting were considered especially outrageous when committed by a chieftain, a

---

28. On the author of *Njála* and the Svínfellings, see Sveinsson, *Njála* (1954), CVII-CXII; Barði Guðmundsson, "Goðorð forn og ný," *Skírnir*, 111 (1937), 56-83; *Höfundur Njálu* (1958), 1-91. On the political activities of the Svínfellings and other chieftain families in the thirteenth century, see Jón Jóhannesson, *Íslendinga saga*, I-II (Reykjavik, 1956-58).

29. On early sources about Njáll and Gunnarr, see above, Chapter II. Gunnarr's image can be attested with more certainty than Njáll's from these early sources, but there can be no doubt that the Burning of Njáll was regarded as a crime and as a major tragedy (see, in particular, the skaldic verses quoted in *Njála*, chapters 125-135).

30. This killing is referred to in *Landnámabók*, *Droplaugarsona saga* and the Icelandic annals, cf. Sveinsson, *Njála* (1954), 291, note 1.

keeper of the peace. Also, he was reputed to have played a somewhat unhonorable role during the conversion of Iceland. According to *Kristni saga* and the long version of *Óláfs saga Tryggvasonar*—both based on clerical sources older than the writing of *Njála*—he had jeopardized Olaf Tryggvason's Christian mission in Iceland by sending word to the Allthing about the arrival of the King's emissaries, Gizurr and Hjalti, allowing the pagans to be up in arms when the Christians arrived to preach the new faith.[31] These actions may in fact represent Flosi's only claim to celebrity, for nothing else is known about him from any written sources before *Njála*.

Flosi's reputation must have been embarrassing to the thirteenth century Svínfellings. One of their leading members, Brandr Jónsson (the translator of *Alexanders saga*), was appointed Bishop of Hólar in 1263, and other members of the family contended for the highest secular positions in the country. Their greatest leader after Brandr's death, Þorvarðr Þórarinsson, was in 1273 appointed bailiff (*sýslumaðr*) in southwestern Iceland and lived not very far from Njáll's home—in fact, he lived at Keldur,[32] a farm inherited from his father-in-law and often mentioned in *Njála* as the home of Ingjaldr á Keldum, the man who deserts Flosi shortly before the Burning because he feels obligated to Njáll's family (chapter 124). It is reasonable to suppose that Þorvarðr had to contend with local traditions about Njáll in which his ancestor, Flosi, was pictured as a major villain.

Furthermore, the heirs of Njáll had married into the Svínfelling family. A brother of Bishop Brandr and uncle of Þorvarðr, the powerful chieftain Ormr at Svínafell (dead in 1241) was married to the daughter of Njáll í Skógum of the Skógverja family, which *Njála* (chapters 20 and 96) says is descended from Njáll's half-brother Holta-Þórir. As if this were not enough, a son of Njáll í Skógum, Skeggi, had married Solveig Jónsdóttir, who was the sister of Brandr and Ormr and the aunt of Þorvarðr.[33] The fact that the

31. *Óláfs saga Tryggvasonar en mesta*, ed. Ó. Halldórsson, II (1961), 188; *Kristni saga*, ed. B. Kahle (*Altnordische Saga-Bibliothek*, 11, 1905), 37. In both these sources as well as in *Heimskringla* and in Oddr's *Óláfs saga Tryggvasonar* we are also told that "Brennu-Flosi's" brother Kolbeinn was one of the pagan Icelanders detained by King Olaf in Norway as hostages until the Allthing accepted the new faith. This tradition, which is widespread and can be traced back before 1200, is completely neglected by *Njála*'s author, even though he does mention Kolbeinn several times (chapters 95, 116, 130) and also mentions King Olaf's detainment of Icelanders in Norway (chapter 104) in a manner suggesting that while he was quite well informed about Kolbeinn's legendary role as a hostage, he deliberately chose to ignore it.

32. Cf. Barði Guðmundsson (1958), 17; Sveinsson, *Njála* (1954), CIX-CX.

33. See Sveinsson, "Njála og Skógverjar," *Skírnir*, 111 (1937), 15-45. Sveinsson at this time argued that a descendent of Skeggi Njálsson had written *Njála*, e.g., Þorsteinn

extremely uncommon name Njáll was still used in the Skógverja family indicates that they were proud of their heritage from Burnt Njáll. Their double alliance with the heirs of Flosi is likely to have occasioned a good deal of speculation about the past by members of both families as well as by outsiders.

Our present text of *Njála* may to a large extent be regarded as the result of such speculations. It tells the story of Njáll in a way that is flattering to his heirs and presumably faithful to local tradition but is yet compatible with the ambition of the Svínfellings to be regarded as good Christians and as great and venerable protectors of law and order. The entire second part of our saga may, in fact, be described as an attempt to save Brennu-Flosi's reputation: it pictures him as a noble chieftain and a devout Christian who was driven against his will to burn Njáll in his home and who later regained his honor by making full atonement for his deed.

The author's attempt to improve Flosi's image can be seen, first of all, in the Conversion episode, where the story of Flosi's word-sending has been omitted; in most other respects the episode is based on the same legends as those in *Kristni saga* and *Óláfs saga Tryggvasonar*. In direct contrast to these sources, Flosi in *Njála* is described as one of the chieftains first converted by King Olaf's earliest missionary, and it is hinted that he and other men from the East Fjords, together with Njáll, were particularly eager to support the new faith at the Allthing.[34] To anybody familiar with the older and widespread accounts of the conversion of Iceland, this must have been a radical departure—so radical, in fact, that it could hardly have been accepted unless the author had skillfully integrated Flosi's new role as missionary hero with an otherwise completely traditional account (cf. the Appendix).

Further, Flosi's Christian spirit and his reluctance to take revenge on Njáll's family are emphasized throughout the story of the Burning, even though Flosi is indeed pictured as the leader of the Burners (evidently an

---

Skeggjason or Klœngr Skeggjason, both mentioned in *Svínfellinga saga* as followers of their cousin, the young chieftain Sæmundr Ormsson of Svínafell, killed in a famous feud in 1952. As Sveinsson points out, there are interesting parallels between the description of Sæmundr Ormsson in *Svínfellinga saga* and the description of Skarpheðinn in *Njála*. Yet in his introduction to *Njála* (1964), Sveinsson rejects Barði Guðmundsson's theory about the saga as a *roman à clef* and claims that he himself is unable to identify its author.

34. "Þaðan fóru þeir [i.e., Þangbrandr and Síðu-Hallr, who has just been converted by the missionary] til Svínafells, ok tók Flosi prímsigning, en hét at fylgja þeim á þingi" (chapter 101); "Veittu þeir Njáll ok Austfirðingar Þangbrandi" (chapter 102). Even if these chapters are based on a lost *Kristni þáttr*, as Sveinsson and other scholars have assumed (cf. the Appendix), it would certainly seem most reasonable to suppose that the author of *Njála* added these two sentences on his own, cf. Sveinsson, *Njála* (1954), XLIV.

accepted fact, not to be tampered with). Before the feud breaks out as a result of Hǫskuldr's death, Flosi tries to persuade Hǫskuldr to move to the East in order to avoid Skarpheðinn and his brother (chapter 109), and the sagawriter clearly implies that the whole tragedy could have been avoided if Hǫskuldr had taken this advice. Once Hǫskuldr has been killed, Flosi tries to make peace with Njáll's family, but he is always pushed to more violence by people or events outside his control: by Hildigunnr's taunts, Skarpheðinn's insults, the belligerence of his own followers, Njáll's refusal to leave the house at Bergþórshváll, and so on. The sagawriter seems to be doing everything he possibly can to excuse Flosi's deed.

When Hildigunnr scorns Flosi for being unwilling to take revenge for Hǫskuldr's death, she says: "Arnórr Ǫrnólfsson from Forsárskógar never did your father, Þórðr Freysgoði, as grave an injury as this, and yet your brothers Kolbeinn and Egill killed him at the Skaftafell Thing" (chapter 116). The sagawriter thus expects his audience to know the story of Arnórr Ǫrnólfsson's death; but, in contrast to earlier tradition, he does not attribute the killing to Flosi himself but to his brothers Kolbeinn and Egill, who must have been of less concern to the thirteenth century Svínfellings, since Kolbeinn and Egill had no legal authority as chieftains and left no heritage to later generations of the family. Compared to his two brothers, Flosi appears moderate and peace-loving, and it is obvious that the sagawriter wants his audience to side with Flosi against Hildigunnr when Flosi answers her taunts with: "Monster, you want us to take the course which will turn out worst for all of us. Cold are the counsels of women!"

The last chapters of Njála emphasize, as we have seen, Flosi's eagerness to atone for the Burning of Njáll. Unlike Gunnarr, he accepts his exile, tolerates the revenge taken on his followes, makes a pilgrimage to Rome, is absolved from sin by the Pope himself, and finally embraces his enemy. When he makes Kári his heir by letting him marry Hildigunnr, the audience is to understand that he has not only made full atonement for the Burning of Njáll but is actually worthy of being Njáll's follower and successor. The concluding list of descendents from Kári and Hildigunnr can thus symbolize the heritage from both Flosi and Njáll.

Flosi's character and actions can be understood if we assume that the saga was originally written to explain the Burning of Njáll from the standpoint of the Svínfelling family. The Burning is clearly the central event of the saga of Njáll and Flosi. Seen from any other standpoint than that of the Svínfellings—for example, from the standpoint of people living in the Bergþórshváll area—there is no reason to place such emphasis on Flosi's Christian spirit and final atonement. Nor would it be natural to conclude the saga with a list of Svínfellings, who could only by a stretch of literary imagination be considered Njáll's true heirs.[35]

Once the decision was made to "explain" the Burning of Njáll, however, it was natural to relate it to the other major tragedy known to have taken place in the same area: the Death of Gunnarr. As a result, "Gunnarr's saga" was combined with "Njáll's saga," even though Gunnarr was probably of little direct concern to the Svínfellings. Yet the author of *Njála* has managed to imply that even Gunnarr could be part of the glorious Svínfelling heritage. For, instead of following Gunnarr's descendents through later generations, the author first suggests (in chapters 82-92) that Gunnarr's kinsman, Þráinn Sigfússon, should be regarded as his true heir and successor in a heroic sense. He then shows how Þráinn's son and only heir, Hǫskuldr, acquired his authority as a chieftain through the combined efforts of Njáll and Flosi. This authority is then evidently inherited by Flosi, who passes it on to the later Svínfellings![36]

The author has also connected the Svínfelling heritage with another great legendary character from the saga age, Síðu-Hallr, one of the first Christian chieftains, a supporter of the Christian party at the Allthing in the year 1000, and the ancestor of several prominent bishops and chieftains in the twelfth and thirteenth centuries. Although he is mentioned in these capacities earlier than *Njála*,[37] the author of our saga is the first sagawriter to relate him to the Svínfellings and the only one to make him the father-in-

---

35. *Landnámabók* gives no evidence that Njáll had any direct descendents *or* that Kári was his son-in-law *or* that Kári married into Flosi's family. According to *Þorsteins saga Síðu-Hallssonar* (chapter 7), Kolbeinn Flosason (who in *Njála*, chapter 159, is said to be the grandson of Kári and Hildigunnr) is presented as a son of Flosi himself, and this is probably correct (cf. below, p. 186). The story that Njáll's only surviving heir married into the family of his enemy is thus not at all supported by the sources, nor is it in itself very plausible.

36. This conclusion was first drawn by Barði Guðmundsson (1937), 75-76. From the genealogies of *Sturlunga*, he further concluded that the *Hvítanessgoðorð*, once owned by Hǫskuldr, had passed from Flosi through several generations to his descendent Flosi Bjarnason, who had passed it on to his son-in-law, Filippus á Hvoli, who gave it up to the Norwegian king in 1250. Guðmundsson's calculations are somewhat uncertain, but we do not need to concern ourselves with the intricate problem of who in fact owned the *Hvítanessgoðorð* at the end of the Icelandic Independence era. When *Njála* was written, all the chieftainships had been transferred to the king, who in turn delegated his power to former chieftains such as Þorvarðr Þórarinsson. From the standpoint of Þorvarðr and other Svínfellings at this time, it would be of interest to emphasize that Hǫskuldr's chieftainship had once belonged to their family, regardless of whether or not they in fact owned it when the king officially took it over.

37. See, for example, *Kristni saga*, chapter 7, *Íslendingabók*, chapter 7, *Landnámabók*, ed. Jakob Benediktsson, II (1968), 310-11, 317-18.

law of Brennu-Flosi. It is thus obvious that even though the greatest heroes of *Njála* were in real life probably unrelated to the Svínfellings—at least if we may judge by sources such as *Landnámabók*—the composition serves the interests of that family to a remarkable degree.

In connection with the lawsuit against the Burners (chapter 141), the saga informs us that Flosi transferred his own chieftainship (the original *Svínfellinga goðorð*) to his brother Þorgeirr. It was from this brother that the Svínfellings of the thirteenth century were thought to be descended, and the information thus serves to explain how their branch of the family had acquired Flosi's chieftainship.[38] But their alleged heritage from Síðu-Hallr and Njáll may, as we shall see, have been of even greater importance to the thirteenth century Svínfellings since it bases their authority not only on their own local chieftainship in the Svínafell area but on a more grandiose legal tradition, one connected with the legislative policy after the loss of Iceland's independence and the decline of the old chieftainships.

Both Síðu-Hallr and Njáll are pictured in *Njála* as major authorities at the Allthing and as initiators of major legislative reforms. As the first Christian Law-speaker in Iceland, Hallr engineers the acceptance of Christian law (chapter 100). And he is the first chieftain to deny compensation for the death of a kinsman, thereby preparing for peace and reconciliation after the Battle of the Allthing (chapter 145). Njáll, although he is not a chieftain, introduces the plan for the Fifth Court and the "new" chieftainships designed to rectify injustices in the old legal system (chapter 97). In contrast to most of the other chieftains, who are often corrupt or at least selfish, these two men are noble, Christian, and unselfish lawmakers, concerned about the welfare of the whole community. Their counsels are always good, and when other people refuse to follow them, the results are usually disastrous.

It was to this kind of authority that Þorvarðr Þórarinsson, the last and most powerful of the Svínfelling chieftains, aspired during the last decades of the thirteenth century.[39] Like Njáll and Síðu-Hallr in the saga, Þorvarðr had engineered a major legislative reform by introducing *Járnsíða* at the Allthing in 1271. After a long series of feuds with other chieftains, controversies with the farmers, and conflicts with the Norwegian king, he finally became one of the two highest royal officials in Iceland. Since the old, inherited chieftainships had at this time been surrendered to the king, Þorvarðr's authority was based mainly on royal appointment, but it was

---

38. Cf. Guðmundsson (1937), 76. The genealogy of the thirteenth-century Svínfellings is presented in *Sturlunga*, I, 53-54.

39. Cf. Björn Þórðarson's biography, *Síðasti goðinn* (Reykjavík, 1950). My own principal guide on this subject, however, is Jón Jóhannesson (1956-58).

still essential that such royal appointees belong to the old chieftain families. A saga that traced his heritage to Njáll and Síðu-Hallr would serve his interests perfectly.

Parallels between Þorvarðr's life, as outlined in *Sturlunga saga*, and incidents in *Njála* convinced Barði Guðmundsson that the saga was written by Þorvarðr himself.[40] Although most of these parallels are too general to prove anything about authorship, there are now good reasons to look at Þorvarðr's kinship relations, career, and role in Icelandic history as we place the saga in its social and political context.

From the genealogies of *Njála* and *Sturlunga*,[41] Þorvarðr could claim a heritage from Njáll, Flosi, and Síðu-Hallr not only through his own family but also through that of his wife, Solveig Hálfdansdóttir, who had grown up at Keldur near Njáll's home. Solveig's family, the Oddaverjar, was descended from Kolbeinn Flosason the Law-speaker, mentioned in *Njála* as one of the most prominent of Kári's and Hildigunnr's descendents. The Oddaverjar were also, according to *Njála* (chapters 25, 26, 113), related to Úlfr aurgoði, Ásgrímr Elliða-Grímsson, and Guðmundr the Mighty, all prominent chieftains in the saga. Furthermore, Þorvarðr Þórarinsson's brother Oddr was married to another member of the Oddaverjar family, a descendent of Kolbeinn the Law-speaker on her mother's as well as on her father's side. It would be impossible to determine to what extent all these kinship relations were historically correct, but it is evident at the least that Þorvarðr had better reason to feel personally involved in the character of *Njála* than most of his contemporaries. Some of the most important relations are presented below in charts, with the names of persons known to have held chieftainships italicized. Þorvarðr's interest in claiming a heritage from such persons of course would be strong; but we do not know for certain which of them contributed to his legal inheritance of wealth and

---

40. See, in particular, Guðmundsson (1958), 19-91. I have found no reason to deal with most of these parallels since I agree, on the whole, with Sveinsson's judgment of Guðmundsson's arguments: "Í ritgerð Barða um staðþekkinguna er fjallað skipulega um einn þátt sögunnar frá upphafi til enda, en í öðrum greinum hans tekur hann til meðferðar einstaka atburði úr ævi Þorvarðar Þórarinssonar og leitar að spegilmyndum þeirra í Njálu. Hins vegar er hvergi að finna allsherjarröksemdir þess, að Þorvarður hafi skrifað söguna. Slíkur samanburður á einstökum atvikum í ævi hans og frásögnum Njálu hefði mikið gildi, ef vitað væri, að Þorvarður væri höfundur, en svo framarlega sem það er ekki vitað, gegnir nokkuð öðru máli .... Mundi ekki (Barði) ... geta fundið með sama hætti líkingu og tengsl með atvikum úr ævi ýmissa annara kunnra manna og sögunni?," *Njála* (1954), CVIII-CIX. A few of the parallels, however, are interesting, irrespective of whether or not Þorvarðr is the author of *Njála*.

41. See the convenient genealogical charts in *Njála* (1954), 481-88, and *Sturlunga*, II (1946), 328-62.

power. We do know; however, that at the time *Njála* was written (around 1280) Þorvarðr could claim an enormous inheritance—all of his most powerful kinsmen were dead, which left no one to compete with him.

CHART I. SVÍNFELLINGS AND SKÓGVERJAR

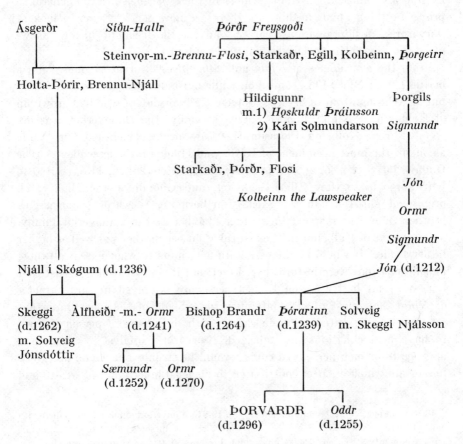

It had taken Þorvarðr much time and effort to reach his position. He was born around 1230 and as a young man had participated in the feuds of the Sturlung period. Many of his closest kinsmen—his brother, his cousins, and several others—had been killed in these feuds while trying to defend the power of the Svínfellings against other ambitious chieftain families. Þorvarðr had survived, however, and he had shown himself skillful and ruthless in forming the right alliance at the right time. For a while he had cooperated closely with Þorgils skarði, the powerful Sturlung leader and

CHART II. ODDAVERJAR AND THE DESCENDENTS OF KOLBEINN FLOSASON THE
LAWSPEAKER

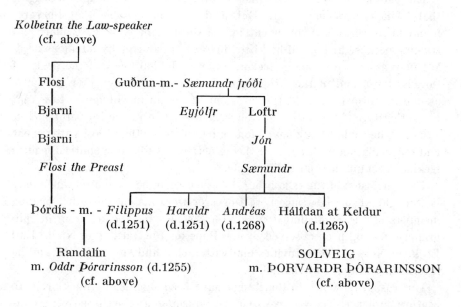

Kolbeinn the Law-speaker
(cf. above)

Flosi   Guðrún-m.- *Sæmundr fróði*

Bjarni   *Eyjólfr*   Loftr

Bjarni   *Jón*

Flosi the Preast   Sæmundr

Þórdís - m. - *Filippus*   *Haraldr*   *Andréas*   Hálfdan at Keldur
                (d.1251)   (d.1251)   (d.1268)   (d.1265)

        Randalín   SOLVEIG
    m. *Oddr Þórarinsson* (d.1255)   m. ÞORVARÐR ÞÓRARINSSON
            (cf. above)   (cf. above)

retainer of the Norwegian king, who had recently begun to take over Iceland.
In 1258, however, when Þorgils had by royal permission taken over some
land that Þorvarðr claimed, the young Svínfelling promptly attacked and
killed his former ally and another royal retainer, Bergr Ámundason; the
incident is pictured as a gruesome deed in *Sturlunga*, where the story of
Þorgils' *sagnaskemtan* (cf. above, p. 173) is used to emphasize the victim's
pious serenity before the sudden attack. The king was understandably
annoyed, but five years later (1263) Þorvarðr was apparently persuaded by
his uncle, Bishop Brandr Jónsson, to atone for the slaying of Þorgils and
to make peace with his enemy, just as their kinsman Brennu-Flosi was supposed to have done in the old days. Þorvarðr travelled to Norway, gave
up his chieftainship, and placed himself at the mercy of the king. He was
rewarded by himself becoming a royal retainer and one of the king's most
trusted servants in Iceland.

From that time until his death in 1297 Þorvarðr apparently represented
the king's interests with great success. In 1271 he introduced *Járnsíða* at
the Allthing and managed to get it accepted. He became the king's *sýslumaðr* at Keldur in 1273 and was later knighted. At the end of his life he
held the highest position in the country, that of *hirðstjóri*, "Governor of the

King's Court." Like Flosi after the Burning of Njáll, Þorvarðr had indeed climbed from disgrace to respectability![42]

The parallel between Flosi and Þorvarðr is not close enough to suggest that Njála is a *roman à clef*. But it does seem possible that Þorvarðr found his ancestor's involvement in the Burning of Njáll particularly intriguing because he himself had been involved in an equally infamous deed. We may assume that many Icelanders around 1280 knew of the death of Þorgils skarði and of Þorvarðr's subsequent rise to power. We may also assume resentment against Þorvarðr and a certain unwillingness to accept his authority. If the author of the saga wished to please Þorvarðr in this situation, he could hardly have found a better theme than Flosi's atonement and reconciliation with Kári—a theme perfectly suited for political leaders seeking redemption from their people.[43]

The conclusion of the saga brings together a number of motifs which may be thought of special concern to Þorvarðr Þórarinsson and other leading members of the Svínfelling family. Flosi comes to Norway from his pilgrimage, having been absolved by the Pope for the Burning of Njáll. Earl Eiríkr of Norway then provides him with a ship and "much flour," and he returns in triumph to Svínafell.

This casual reference to flour must have been significant to a thirteenth century audience. As we have seen, *sagnaskemtan* appears to have been arranged in connection with the trading of flour each summer at the Feast of Saint Olaf (cf. the quotation from *Þorgils saga ok Hafliða* above, p. 171). Furthermore, the Icelanders in 1262 had accepted the Norwegian king on the condition that he allow a sufficient number of ships to sail from Norway to Iceland with grain and other necessities the farmers could not produce on their barren land.[44] To present the Norwegian rulers as generous providers

42. On the biographical details, see, in particular, Jóhannesson (1956-58) and the primary sources there quoted or referred to, especially *Þorgils saga skarða* (*Sturlunga*, II, 104-226), *Svínfellinga saga* (*Sturlunga saga*, II, 87-103), *Árna saga biskups* (*Biskupa Sögur*, I, 689-786), *Hákonar saga Hákonarsonar*, and *Magnúss saga lagabætis*.

43. Strangely enough, Barði Guðmundsson does not pay much attention to Þorvarðr's famous attack on Þorgils skarði, even though he does find various other and much more private incidents in Þorvarðr's life reflected in *Njála*! The basic mistake Barði Guðmundsson makes is to be excessively concerned about Þorvarðr as a private individual instead of concentrating on his political role and public image, which are much more likely to have influenced the saga. This mistake may in turn be said to derive from the general tendency of the "Icelandic School" to see the sagas as expressions of individual authors rather than as attempts to accommodate a specific audience.

44. Cf. Jóhannesson, I (1956), 333-36, 349-54, 364. It should be noted that *Njála* appears to be more concerned about the import of flour (and about Norwegian protection of such import) than is any other saga. See, for example, chapter 6, where King Haraldr,

of such necessities must therefore have been a major concern for Þorvarðr Þórarinsson and other royal officials at this time. In addition, Earl Eiríkr's gift to Flosi emphasizes the fact that Flosi had now regained his status as a great chieftain and had made himself worthy of our respect.

The saga now turns to Kári, showing how he was driven by a snowstorm to Svínafell and received by Flosi with open arms. They are fully reconciled, and Hildigunnr is married to Kári, Njáll's only surviving heir (just as the heirs of Njáll í Skógum were married into the Svínfelling family two hundred years later!). We are then told that Kári and Hildigunnr "at first lived at Breiðár," a farm in the vicinity of Svínafell.

When presenting this marriage, the sagawriter specifically reminds his audience that Hildigunnr had previously been married to Hǫskuldr. This reminder[45] can only emphasize that the new marriage reestablishes the alliance between Njáll's family and Flosi's, an alliance broken through Hǫskuldr's death and the subsequent Burning of Njáll. The audience is to remember here that Flosi and Hildigunnr had advised Hǫskuldr to "move east" in order to be closer to Svínafell and to avoid conflicts with Mǫrðr and the sons of Njáll (cf. chapter 97 and, especially, chapter 109). Flosi had also suggested that his brother Þorgeirr should take over Hǫskuldr's farm, Ossabær, in the West—a move which, incidentally, would have placed Þorvarðr Þórarinsson's branch of the Svínfelling family in control of Hǫskuldr's "new" chieftainship! The audience has in fact been led to believe that the death of Hǫskuldr and the Burning of Njáll could have been avoided if Hǫskuldr had followed this advice. When Kári, in the last chapter of Njála, settles at Breiðár, he thus undoes the mistake made by his predecessor. The information that he "first" settled there implies, however, that he soon moved to some other place[46]—probably to Svínafell itself, vacated after Flosi's death a few years later. If that was what the sagawriter had in mind, it would not have been necessary to spell it out specifically to an audience familiar with local traditions at Svínafell.

This interpretation is further strengthened by the fact that the sagawriter moves directly from saying that Kári and Hildigunnr "first" settled at Breiðár to the famous account of Flosi's death. The account is one of the most

---

in spite of the fact that Norway is suffering from a famine, gives flour to Hrútr, who later passes it on to his brother Hǫskuldr; see also chapter 32 (Earl Hákon's gift of flour to Gunnarr).

45. "Gipti Flosi þá Kára Hildigunni, bróðurdóttur sína, er Hǫskuldr Hvítanessgoði hafði átta" (my italics). Sveinsson thinks this wording indicates that the author is using a written genealogical source, cf. Njála (1954), LII-LIII, but there is no reason to suppose that this source ever existed (cf. the Appendix).

46. Cf. Sveinsson, Njála (1954), 463, note 4.

poetic in the saga. As an old man, Flosi goes to Norway to collect timber for his farm at Svínafell. He starts his journey back too late in the autumn, and he is warned that his ship may not survive the wintry storms of the North Atlantic. Flosi answers that the ship is good enough for an old and death-marked man. "And he boarded the ship and went out to sea, and nothing has been heard about that ship since."

This final scene has been compared to the departure of Scyld Scefing in *Beowulf*,[47] and it does have a mythical aura possibly inherited from early Germanic legends. As told in *Njála*, however, the scene not only emphasizes Flosi's heroic serenity but also his ambition to build up Svínafell for later generations. Perhaps his use of Norwegian timber to strengthen the old headquarter of the Svínfellings had a symbolic significance for his descendents in the thirteenth century. In a figurative sense Þorvarðr Þórarinsson had tried to do the same thing, but with much greater success.

None of Flosi's children were mentioned earlier in the saga, and we are prompted by the context to conclude that Kári and Hildigunnr were his only heirs. The sagawriter now turns to them. First he lists the descendents of Kári and Helga Njálsdóttir: "Þorgerðr and Ragneiðr, Valgerðr and Þórðr, who was burned to death." This list emphasizes that the Burning of Njáll had left Kári without any male heirs. Next follows a list of Kári's and Hildigunnr's descendants: "Starkaðr and Þórðr and Flosi; the son of Flosi was Kolbeinn, who has been one of the most capable men in that family" (*Son Flosa var Kolbeinn, er ágætastr maðr hefir verit einn hverr í þeiri ætt*). In this case the male heirs are strongly emphasized, and the genealogy ends with Kolbeinn Flosason, the famous Law-speaker between 1066 and 1071, in fact the only early Svínfelling who appears with a first-rate, national reputation before *Njála* was written.[48] Although the thirteenth century Svínfellings did, as we have seen, derive their original chieftainship from Flosi's brother Þorgeirr rather than from Kolbeinn Flosason, their kinship with Kolbeinn was evidently more worthy of remembrance. As we have seen, Þorvarðr Þórarinsson had especially good reasons to remember Kolbeinn: he aspired to a similar national role and was related to Kolbeinn not

47. Allen (1971), 178-79.
48. Kolbeinn is mentioned in *Íslendingabók*, *Landnámabók*, *Sturlunga*, and other sources. In all these sources he is said to be either the son of Brennu-Flosi himself or the son of a certain Flosi Valla-Brandsson; cf. the literature referred to by Sveinsson in *Njála* (1954), 463-64, note 7. The X-branch of the *Njála* manuscripts also makes Kolbeinn the son of Brennu-Flosi, but the context clearly shows that the author wanted to present him as the grandson of Kári and Hildigunnr, possibly because Kolbeinn was thought to have inherited Hǫskuldr's chieftainship, cf. note 36, above.

only through his own family but also through that of his wife (cf. above, p. 176).

When the author of *Njála* characterized Kolbeinn as *"one of* the most capable" rather than *"the* most capable" of the Svínfellings, he probably expected his audience to have Þorvarðr, his uncle Brandr, and various other prominent members of the family in mind. The thirteenth century Svínfellings were in fact so well known to their contemporaries that no introduction was necessary. They appear in practically every source describing events in Iceland between 1250 and 1300. The sagawriter could also probably count on his audience to draw the genealogical lines from Kolbeinn Flosason to later generations since these lines appear to have been quite familiar to several other sagawriters. Perhaps that explains why the genealogy on the last page of *Njála* is suddenly cut short by the author's tantalizing remark: "And there I end *Brennu-Njáls saga*" (*Ok lýk ek þar Brennu-Njáls saga*).

One of the first scribes who transcribed the text, however, evidently felt a need to include more genealogical information. This scribe, who is responsible for the text of the so-called Y-branch of the *Njála* manuscripts, was particularly displeased with a passage in chapter 113 where the author of *Njála* had made a careless statement about the descendants of Guðmundr the Powerful: "All the greatest people in the country are descended from him: Oddaverjar, Sturlungar, Hvammverjar, Fljótamenn, Bishop Ketill, and many other outstanding men." After the word "Sturlungar," the Y-branch scribe added *"and Þorvarðr Þórarinsson."*[49] The addition is indicative of the milieu in which *Njála* was first written and transcribed, even though it cannot help us to identify the author or determine his exact relationship to the thirteenth century Svínfellings.

Some details in our interpretation of this relationship must necessarily be uncertain since we do not possess sufficient information about the individuals who formed part of *Njála's* original milieu. It is also important to point out that the genealogical and political implications of the saga constitute only a small part of its "meaning" as a whole—an undercurrent easily disregarded by modern readers, who can enjoy the story of Gunnarr and Njáll without caring at all about the heritage of the Svínfellings or the political ambitions of Þorvarðr Þórarinsson. Yet it is safe to conclude that the Svínfelling activities of the late thirteenth century have made an imprint not only on the genealogies but on the saga as a whole.

49. Cf. Sveinsson, *Njála* (1954), 285-86, note 12. Guðmundr the Powerful is treated with much more respect in *Njála* than in other sagas, where he often appears as a ridiculous and overbearing person. Did our author improve Guðmundr's image out of concern for his descendents?

4. THE FIFTH COURT AND THE LEGAL REFORM OF 1271

Þorvarðr Þórarinsson's most important political action in the king's service was the introduction of *Járnsíða* in 1271. Even though this new law did not officially invalidate the older statutes of *Grágás* (which continued to be respected for some time), the new statutes in practice made the old chief-tainships obsolete and led to the decline of the Allthing as a general assembly.

As we have indicated above (Chapter IV), the concepts of law in *Njála* are influenced by *Járnsíða*. Such influence does not by itself suggest that the author of *Njála* was trying to promote Þorvarðr's political cause; any sagawriter in the last decades of the thirteenth century would be likely to absorb legal concepts from *Járnsíða* and apply them unconsciously, even when describing the laws of an earlier period. Yet there are indications that the author, consciously or unconsciously, attempted to justify the reform of 1271 by showing that it was somehow heralded by such legal authorities of the saga age as Njáll himself. This is particularly apparent in the story of the Fifth Court (chapter 97), a story that grossly distorts the legal history of Iceland.[50] Before we examine this story, however, we must briefly explain how the Icelandic Allthing functioned before and after the introduction of *Járnsíða*.[51]

From its beginning, the Allthing had been divided into a legislative branch, the *Lǫgrétta*, and a judicial branch, originally consisting of the four Quarter Courts, to which the Fifth Court was later added. The *Lǫgrétta* consisted of the Law-speaker (*lǫgsǫgumaðr*), the 36 (later 39) chieftains (*goðar*), each with two assistants, plus, in later years, the bishops and a few others; by the last years of Icelandic independence, the body totaled 147 men. They were seated as follows on three long benches at the Allthing meetings: the chieftains and the Law-speaker (later also the bishops) sat on the middle bench, with the assistants behind and in front of their respective chieftains on the other two benches. The function of the *Lǫgrétta* was not only to make new laws but also to determine what the prevailing laws said in uncertain cases and to grant exemptions from the law when warranted. In addition,

50. Cf. K. Maurer, *Die Entstehung des Isländischen Staates* (München, 1852), 179-210; Lehmann-Carolsfeld (1883), 128-36; Jóhannesson, I (1956), 90-94; V. Finsen, *Om den oprindelige Ordning af nogle af den islandske Fristats Institutioner* (Copenhagen, 1888), 98 f.

51. For an excellent and much more detailed explanation, cf. Jón Jóhannesson, I (1956), 53-113; II (1958), 30-45. My own interpretation of the historical facts owes much to his work, but my judgment of the reform of 1271 is definitely more positive than his; Jóhannesson never departs from the traditional view (expressed in works such as Sveinssons' *Sturlungaöld*) that the government of the Independence era was far better for the country than the one imposed by the Norwegian king.

the *Lǫgrétta* could make various political decisions on behalf of the people. Only the chieftains had full voting rights; but the others participated in the discussions. The chieftains acquired their positions through inheritance or purchase. They could thus be, and often were, completely incompetent, corrupt, and ruthless (as evidenced by many sagas!).

The Quarter Courts consisted of farmers from each of the four Quarter Districts. They did not need qualifications as lawyers but were appointed by the chieftains of their home district for a specific session of the Allthing. Their role was simply to listen to the plaintiff and the defendant and then vote for either side. Verdicts had to be unanimous. The court may thus be said to have functioned more like a jury than like a modern court. All questions of legal interpretation had to be referred to the Law-speaker and the *Lǫgrétta*.

If a case could not be settled in the Quarter Courts, it was referred to the so-called Fifth Court, which also served as a court of first instance in cases of perjury and other crimes having to do with legal procedure. According to Ari's *Íslendingabók*, our most trustworthy source, the Fifth Court had been established in the early eleventh century at the instigation of Skapti Þóroddsson, who was then the Law-speaker of the *Lǫgrétta*.[52] *Grágás* stipulated that 48 judges should sit in this court, one from each of the 36 original chieftainships (or 9 from each Quarter District) plus 12 appointed by chieftains who held socalled "new" chieftainships, positions apparently established at about the same time to rectify injustices in the older system. In order to insure the impartiality of the Fifth Court, both the plaintiff and the defendant had the right and the duty to exclude six judges at the beginning of each litigation. Thus, "only" 36 judges participated in the actual verdict.[53]

The laws regulating the Fifth Court, the Quarter Courts, and the *Lǫgrétta* illustrate the delicate balance between regional interests on which the Icelandic state had been founded. This balance was destroyed, however, and the intention of the law-makers was corrupted when a small number of ruthless chieftains in the thirteenth century acquired all the chieftainships and were able to pack both the courts and the *Lǫgrétta* with their proxies. If it was difficult even in Njáll's time to win a lawsuit against a powerful and over-

---

52. *Íslendingabók*, chapter 8.

53. The *Grágás* stipulations on the Fifth Court are quoted by Sveinsson in *Njála* (1954), 244-246. Scholars have not been able to agree on why the "new" chieftainships were established and how they differed from the "old" chieftainships since the evidence of both *Grágás* and *Njála* differs on this point from the evidence of *Íslendingabók*. Cf. Barði Guðmundsson (1937); Sveinsson, *Njála* (1954), 234, note 2. It is clear, however, that the author of *Njála* thinks that the "new" chieftainships were created specifically for the Fifth Court, and most modern scholars have in fact agreed with him on this point.

bearing chieftain, it must have been much more difficult in the Sturlung Age. Whatever can be said about *Járnsíða*, it did attempt to abolish this kind of injustice by making leadership at the Allthing dependent on merit and royal appointment rather than on wealth and inheritance.

When *Járnsíða* was introduced in 1271, all the chieftainships ("old" as well as "new") had been given up to the king, who then delegated his power over them to representatives such as Þorvarðr Þórarinsson. The new law divided the country into twelve new judicial districts, *sýslur*, governed by appointed *sýslumenn*. The Quarter Courts and the Fifth Court were abolished. The *Lǫgrétta* was transformed from a legislature to a supreme court, combining some of the functions of the older *Lǫgrétta* with some of the functions of the Fifth Court. This new court contained only 36 judges (i.e., the same number as the original chieftains or the participants in each verdict of the Fifth Court) under the leadership of another royal official, the *Lǫgmaðr*, who was endowed with more power than the old *Lǫgsǫgumaðr*. The judges were appointed by the *Lǫgmaðr* and the *sýslumenn* from a body of 140 men from all the new districts on the basis of merit and experience; they served for life or for as long as they were able to attend the Allthing.[54]

The reform meant, on one hand, that the number of people attending the Allthing was greatly reduced and the real decision-making entrusted to a small number of appointed experts. Meetings of the Allthing would never again be the popular gatherings they had once been. On the other hand, the new system must have seemed to guarantee justice better than the old one, at least during the first years. The new *Lǫgrétta* was less likely to be corrupted and manipulated. Verdicts became less dependent on the power struggle between chieftains and on the support solicited from kinsmen and wealthy benefactors. The king's rule must have seemed preferable to that of most chieftains, and during the first decades he left most of the government in the hands of Icelanders. Farmers no longer had to make the costly and time-consuming journey to the Allthing merely to oblige some chieftain or to defend their interests against possible attacks from hostile neighbors. They probably valued their peace more than their formal right to participate in the government.[55]

---

54. Cf. Jóhannesson, II (1958), 37-38. *Járnsíða*, in its first paragraph, stipulates that the *sýslumaðr* shall swear, on the first day that he arrives at the Allthing, "at hann leggr þess hond a helga bok oc þui skytr hann til guðs at þa menn hever hann nefnda til alþingis at þui sinni er honom þotte vel falner til oc vænir til scila epter sinne samvitzko oc æigi gerðe hann fire annarra manna saker, oc sua skal æc iafnan gera meðan ek hǫfe þetta starf" (*Norges Gamle Love*, I, 259). *Grágás* contains no such provision to insure the appointment of competent and impartial judges, and it is apparent that the authors of *Járnsíða* felt that something had to be done to improve the situation.

55. The unwillingness of many farmers to attend the Allthing is evident both from the

If this view of the reform was not shared by all members of the old chieftain families (and it probalby was not), we may at least be certain that it was shared by Þorvarðr Þórarinsson. With this knowledge in mind we may now turn to chapter 97 of *Njála*.

There the establishment of the Fifth Court is pictured—contrary to all earlier evidence—as engineered by Njáll in order to insure his foster son Hǫskuldr's alliance with Flosi's family. Hǫskuldr must have a chieftainship to be accepted as Hildigunnr's suitor, but nobody is willing to sell him one, even though Hǫskuldr has all of the qualifications of an ideal leader: he is of good family, just, noble, and tutored in Icelandic law by Njáll himself, the greatest lawyer in Iceland. Njáll then clogs the legal machinery of the Allthing by giving people such advice that no verdicts can be reached in the Quarter Courts. As fighting is about to break out, Njáll proposes the establishment of the Fifth Court and the institution of new chieftainships as ways to solve the dilemma. When his proposal has been accepted by Skapti Þóroddsson and the *Lǫgrétta*, Njáll further suggests that one of the new chieftainships be given to Hǫskuldr. This move also succeeds, and Hǫskuldr can now marry Hildigunnr at Svínafell.

Some modern readers have condemned Njáll's manipulations,[56] but the medieval audience of *Njála* probably did not see it that way. To them Njáll's ends justified his means. They knew that their old legal system made peace and justice depend on skillful manipulation. They knew that their country needed an appeal court such as the Fifth Court. Furthermore, the association between Njáll/Hǫskuldr and the people of Svínafell is pictured in the saga as a guarantee of peace and social order, a muchneeded defense against corrupt chieftains such as Mǫrðr and Valgarðr. A conversation between these two arch-villains in chapter 107 also makes it abundantly clear that the Fifth Court and Hǫskuldr's new role as a chieftain led to their well-deserved downfall in the district.[57] Although they do manage revenge by engineering the death of Hǫskuldr and the Burning of Njáll, these tragic

---

stipulations of *Járnsíða* about fines for nonattendance and from some incidents reported in late thirteenth-century sources; cf. Jóhannesson, II (1958), 37.

56. "In der Einführung des Fünftengerichts liegt die Schuld des Helden und der Mordbrand ist die Sühne," Lehmann-Carolsfeld (1883), 131.

57. "Valgarðr inn grái kom út; hann var þá heiðinn.—Hann mælti til Marðar: 'Riðit hefi ek hér um byggðina viða, ok þykki mér eigi mega kenna, at in sama sé. Ek kom á Hvítanes, ok sá ek þar búðartoptir margar ok umbrot mikil. Ek kom á Þingskálaþing, ok sá ek ofan brotna búð vára alla, eða hví sæta firn slík?' Mǫrðr segir: 'Hér eru tekin upp ný goðorð ok fimmtardómslǫg, ok hafa menn sik sagt ór þingi frá mér ok í þing með Hǫskuldi.' Valgarðr mælti: 'Illa hefir þú launat mér goðorðit, er ek fekk þér í hendr, at fara svá ómannliga með. Vil ek nú, at þú launir þeim því, at þeim dragi ǫllum til bana.'" (chapter 107)

events cannot be seen as caused by Njáll's legal reform, for the sagawriter implies that everything would have turned out well if only Hǫskuldr had accepted Flosi's suggestion to "move east" and let Flosi's brother Þorgeirr take over his farm at Ossabær (cf. above, p. 185).

Njáll's program for the Fifth Court is outlined in his long speech to the *Lǫgrétta* in chapter 97. This speech, an extremely skillful but deceptive collage of quotations from *Grágás*, emphasizes the need for peace, the danger of corruption inherent in the legal system, and the desirability of strong judicial and legislative authority based on competence rather than inherited rights. Njáll first sternly rejects the suggestion that Allthing members settle their differences by force if they cannot be settled by the courts:

"That must never happen," said Njáll. "It would be quite wrong to have no law in this land. But you have good reasons for complaint, and your problems should be solved by us who know the law and are set to govern (*kemr þat til vár, er kunnum lǫgin ok þeim skulum stjórna*)—It seems to me that the situation is impossible if we raise actions in the Quarter Courts, and they become so involved that we cannot conclude the cases or make any progress. It then seems best that we institute a Fifth Court for cases that cannot be concluded in the Quarter Courts."—

"To this court shall come—all cases of irregular court procedure (*þingsafglǫpun*) if witnesses or members of the jury commit perjury; all cases which could not be solved by unanimous verdict in the Quarter Courts; these shall all be transferred to the Fifth Court. Further, cases of offering or accepting bribes in court actions or of harboring runaway slaves or debtors."

"In this court, only the strongest kind of oath shall be taken, and the probity of the man who swears the oath must be warranted by two others, who make themselves responsible for what the first person swears."

"This court shall favor those who plead their cause correctly against those who plead it incorrectly."

"The court procedure shall be the same as in the Quarter Court, except that the plaintiff shall exclude six judges and the defendant six more from the four dozen originally appointed. But if the defendant does not want to exercise this right, the plaintiff must exclude all twelve, and if he fails to do that, the case shall be dismissed, for three dozen judges shall make the verdict."

"We shall also make such provisions for the *Lǫgrétta*, that those sitting on the middle bench shall be the ones to make law and grant exemptions from it (*skulu réttir at ráða fyrir lofum ok lǫgum*), and for this office we shall choose (*velja*) the wisest and most honorable men (*er vitrastir eru ok bezt at sér*). That is where the Fifth Court shall also be. But if those who sit in the *Lǫgrétta* cannot agree on how to make law or grant exemptions from it, the issue shall be decided by a majority of the whole *Lǫgrétta*. But if somebody is prevented from entering the *Lǫgrétta* or finds himself coerced, he shall veto the proceedings (*verja lýriti*), so that it is heard in the *Lǫgrétta*, and he has then invalidated all the exemptions and legal provisions that were vetoed."

In spite of the fact that this speech is based on *Grágás*, its philosophy is more in the spirit of 1271 than of Njáll's time. First, the laws of the Independence era gave Njáll no authority to say that the problems "should be solved by us who know the law and are set to govern." As we have seen, legislation was at this time the prerogative of the chieftains, who acquired their position by inheritance or purchase, and Njáll is not a chieftain, even though he is the greatest lawyer in Iceland.

Second, legislators in Njáll's time would never have accepted the idea that those who sat on the "middle bench" in the *Lǫgrétta* should be *chosen* from among the "wisest and most honorable men" since that would have meant giving up their inherited (or purchased) privileges as chieftains! Again, Njáll's words reflect the thinking of a much later era. Although his speech does not make clear who should choose the legislators on the "middle bench" (the chieftains? the legal experts? the Allthing community at large?), he appears to be in agreement with *Járnsíða*, which stipulated that the members of the new *Lǫgrétta* should be chosen by royal officials on the basis of merits and be limited to the same number (36) as the chieftains originally seated on the "middle bench."[58]

Third, Njáll's speech blurs the distinction between Fifth Court and *Lǫgrétta*, two entirely different institutions. There would have been no reason to discuss the function of the *Lǫgrétta* in a story about the establishment of the Fifth Court unless the author of *Njála* had seen both institutions as predecessors of the new *Lǫgrétta* of 1271. By juxtaposing quotations from completely different sections of *Grágás*, the author thus creates the impression that Njáll is somehow heralding *Járnsíða's* much later merging of judicial and legislative Allthing functions.

Later in the saga (chapter 144), the author shows the Fifth Court in action when Njáll's kinsmen try to bring their lawsuit against the Burners.[59]

---

58. According to Sveinsson, *Njála* (1954), 245 (note 3), the sagawriter's thinking is influenced by the fact that many seats on the mid-bench of the Lǫgrétta at the end of the Independence era had to be filled out with proxies selected by the chieftains; the chieftains themselves usually owned more than one chieftainship and were too few to fill out the whole bench. It seems unlikely, however, that the selection of such proxies would be considered a selection of the "wisest and most honorable men." Njáll's words are much more likely to reflect conditions prevailing after 1271.

59. The fact that Njáll's speech in chapter 97 serves as a preparation for the event pictured in chapter 144 was first convincingly demonstrated by Lehmann-Carolsfeld (1883), 128-136. Yet, their overall interpretation of the Fifth Court story is very unconvincing because they fail to relate the story to the saga as a whole. If the sagawriter had wanted to show that the Fifth Court was a major mistake for which Njáll had to suffer (cf. note 56, above), there would have been no reason to picture the supporters of the new

At the instigation of Þórhallr Ásgrímsson, Mǫrðr sues Flosi for procedural irregularity (*þingsafglǫpun*) and for bribing Eyjólfr Bǫlverksson, just as Eyjólfr and Flosi are about to sue Mǫrðr for another procedural irregularity. By neglecting to exclude judges from the Fifth Court, however, Mǫrðr loses the case against the Burners, and the Battle of the Allthing breaks out since there is no way left to settle the matter in court.

This episode does not show that the establishment of the Fifth Court was a mistake—as some critics have thought[60]—but it does show that the court could not stop the violence and manipulations of certain Allthing members. Again, the author's attitude, which at first appears to jar with his favorable presentation of the Fifth Court in chapter 97, is understandable if we assume that he regarded this court as an important but not sufficiently strong innovation—a "right step" in the direction of the *Lǫgrétta* of 1271. Such an interpretation is supported by the fact that the most famous of all statements about law in *Njála*—"Our land must be built with law or laid waste with lawlessness"—appears to have been borrowed from the section in *Járnsíða* that outlines the rules for this new *Lǫgrétta*.[61] Again and again the author of *Njála* provides his audience with narrative illustrations of this celebrated quotation, whose truth must have been felt by many Icelanders after the feuds and lawlessness of the Sturlung period.

5. THE AUTHOR AND HIS AUDIENCE

It is extremely uncertain whether or not *Njála* was ever intended to express the author's *personal* opinions. As we have seen, he probably was commissioned to write the saga. No sagawriter would have undertaken such a work merely as a means of self-expression—unless he were enormously wealthy. At any rate, the text shows our author's ambitions to accomodate a specific type of audience more than any traits of his own personality.

He evidently wrote the saga in a milieu dominated by the Svínfellings shortly after the introduction of *Járnsíða*. His perspective on early Icelandic history is that of a native and somewhat rustic aristocracy with a heroic legacy from the early days of the Independence era. Yet, at the time of writing, his main allegiance was not with the old chieftains but with the new order represented by officials such as Þorvarðr Þórarinsson and committed to the ideals of peace and strong central government.

---

court as noble men and its adversaries as villains, and we would at least have expected Njáll to show some remorse for his "mistake" at a later stage in the narrative.

60. Cf. notes 56 and 59, above.

61. *Norges Gamle Love*, I, 260; cf. Sveinsson, *Njála* (1954), LXXVIII f.

Although the saga promotes aristocratic interests, its audience was probably not exclusively aristocratic. Reasonably well-born farmers without chieftainships are often favorably contrasted to cowardly, corrupt, and overbearing chieftains. *Njála* also presents humble farmers in a flattering light, especially when they show loyalty to more aristocratic heroes. The author's ambition to both court the low-born farmer and stress his duties to social superiors can be seen clearly in the story of Kári's friendship with Bjǫrn í Mǫrk (chapters 148-52). Kári, a noble man of good family, is pictured like a chivalric hero of the *riddarasǫgur*. Bjǫrn is a farmer of undistinguished lineage, descended from a man who had been the slave of Njáll's mother. He becomes Kári's liege man and comrade-in-arms after the Burning of Njáll, but at first he appears to be a laughable, cowardly braggart. His wife, who comes from a more noble family and had to marry him for money, scorns him openly in Kári's presence. At last, however, Bjǫrn gains the affection of both his wife and Kári by proving himself a brave and loyal warrior in confrontations with the Burners. In spite of the author's rather patronizing attitude towards Bjǫrn, the story can be read as a political *exemplum* for Icelandic plebeians striving for social acceptance. Other such *exempla* can be found within *Njála*.[62]

The presentation of social distinctions in *Njála* is easy to explain if we assume that the saga was written for a "mixed" audience, such as the one assembled at the *sagnaskemtan* of Reykjahólar. Let us suppose that Þorvarðr Þórarinsson, or one of his wealthier kinsmen, wished to provide his guests, kinsmen, and presumptive local supporters among the farmers with saga entertainment. *Njála* would be ideal for such an occasion, especially since each saga episode is very suitable for one night's reading. To read the entire saga in this manner would probably take about two weeks, but social gatherings in Iceland tended to last quite a while, for people had to travel long distances to meet and hence did not want to return home immediately once their errand had been accomplished.

A setting of this sort is perhaps suggested also by some of the scenes in the saga itself, where such social gatherings are described in detail. Consider, for example, the brief but meticulous description of Gunnarr's and Hallgerðr's wedding (chapter 34), specifying where each of more than twenty wedding

---

62. See, for example, the chapters about Atli and Þórðr leysingjason (38-42), Njáll's noble servants who sacrifice their lives for their master. At one point Atli refers to Njáll as his *lánar-drottinn* (chapter 38), liege-lord, a term associated with the old Germanic *comitatus* but also with the chivalric feudal relations between king and vassal prevailing in thirteenth century Norway.

guests are seated.[63] Such a description would be of particular interest to an audience with intimate knowledge of the social significance of each character's place at the table. The description is in fact meaningless to anybody not aware of the social distinctions upheld at feasts sponsored by the leading families of Iceland. One must imagine being present at such a feast as the saga is being read aloud to those who are themselves concerned about their placement at the table and whose position and heritage stems from legendary characters who once attended Gunnarr's wedding.

The atmosphere of the *sagnaskemtan* is most clearly present in chapter 22, where Njáll outlines to Gunnarr the conversation that will take place between him and Hrútr when Gunnarr arrives at Hrútsstaðir in his disguise as Kaupa-Heðinn, the travelling merchant:

"You will be given a place on the lower bench, facing Hrútr's high seat. You will greet him, and he will then give you a friendly greeting in return and ask if you are a northerner. You reply that you are from Eyjafjǫrðr. He will then ask you whether there are a lot of good men up there; to which you reply, 'A lot of perverts, that's about all' (*Œrinn hafa þeir klækiskap*). 'Do you know Reykjadalr at all?' he will ask. 'I know the whole of Iceland,' you reply. 'Are there any great champions in Reykjardalr?' he will ask. 'Nothing but thieves and scoundrels,' you reply. Hrútr will laugh, and think this excellent entertainment. You will go on to discuss the men of the East Fjords, and you must find something abusive to say about all of them, too. In this way your talk will lead on to the men of Rangárvellir, and at that point you must remark that there has been a lack of men of any note there since Mǫrðr Fiddle died. Hrútr will ask you what makes you think that no one can fill his place, and you must reply that Mǫrðr was so clever and so experienced a lawyer that his chieftainship was quite faultless."

63. "Gunnarr hafði marga fyrirboðsmenn, ok skipaði hann svá sínum mǫnnum: Hann sat á miðjan bekk, en innar frá Þráinn Sigfússon, þá Úlfr aurgoði, þá Valgarðr inn grái, þá Mǫrðr ok Rúnólfr, þá Sigfússynir; Lambi sat innstr. It næsta Gunnari utar frá sat Njáll, þá Skarpheðinn, þá Helgi, þá Grímr, þá Hǫskuldr, þá Hafr inn spaki, þá Ingjaldr frá Keldum, þá synir Þóris austan ór Holti. Þórir vildi sitja yztr virðingamanna, því at þá þótti hverjum gott þar sem sat. Hǫskuldr sat á miðjan bekk, en synir hans innar frá honum: Hrútr sat utar frá Hǫskuldi. En þá er eigi frá sagt, hverjum ǫðrum var skipat. Brúðr sat á miðjum palli, en til annarrar handar henni sat Þorgerðr, dóttir hennar, en til annarrar handar Þórhalla, dóttir Ásgríms Elliða-Grímssonar." It should be noted that, among these people, Hafr inn spaki has not even been introduced and his identity is unknown; Úlfr aurgoði and Holta-Þórir have only briefly been mentioned in the context of genealogical namelists (chapters 20, 25), and most of the others play very subordinate roles in *Njála*. Úlfr was, however, an ancestor of the Oddaverjar, and Holta-Þórir was an ancestor of the Skógverjar, and their placement at the table is therefore of interest to the audience. The author's reference to oral tradition ("En þá er eigi frá sagt," etc.) suggests that people had been discussing the seating arrangements at this wedding in order to establish the status of various local families during the saga age.

Through this dialogue a modern reader glimpses *Njála*'s original audience. It is an audience familiar with the custom of chieftains and wealthy farmers to encourage storytelling as they entertained guests from the high seat of their hall or *skáli*. It is an audience thoroughly familiar with gossip and oral traditions from various parts of the country and expecting more of the same when seated in such a hall, listening to the talk of some visiting stranger. Jokes at the expense of people from other regions in Iceland must have been quite popular. In this case the entertainment appears to be a variant of the so-called *mannjafnaðr*, or "comparison of men," mentioned in numerous other sagas, often in connection with drinking bouts at large parties.[64] In the most orthodox type of *mannjafnaðr* two men will compare their achievements in the form of short and grossly insulting ditties, recited as a kind of toast. But there are many variants of this entertainment, e.g., the kind exemplified by Skarpheðinn's exchange of insults with various chieftains at the Allthing shortly before the Burning (chapters 119-20).

It is obvious that the author of *Njála* expects his audience to have a thorough knowledge of legends and traditions especially from the south (Árnessýsla, Rangárvallasýsla, Skaftafellssýsla). Hildigunnr's allusion to the killing of Arnórr Qrnólfsson (above, p. 175) may serve as one example. Consider also the following quotations, all practically meaningless to the modern reader: "The sons of Síðu-Hallr were Þorsteinn, Egill, Þorvarðr, Ljótr, and Þiðrandi, the one who is said to have been killed by the *dísir*" (chapter 96; only Þorsteinn and Ljótr are mentioned later in the saga, and the reference to Þiðrandi's death is never explained)[65]; "You call yourself Skapti Þóroddsson, but before you called yourself Burstakoll, when you had killed Ketill ór Eldu" (one of Skarpheðinn's insults in chapter 119; the identity of Ketill ór Eldu and the significance of the name Burstakoll are never clearly revealed)[66]; "You would be better employed fetching back your sister

64. Cf. J. de Vries, *Altergermanische Religionsgeschichte*, I, 2nd edition (Berlin, 1956), 504-05; W. Gehl, *Ruhm und Ehre bei den Nordgermanen* (Berlin, 1937), 110-16.

65. Cf. Strömbäck, *Tidrande och diserna* (Lund, 1949), 13-17; Sveinsson, *Njála* (1954), XLIII. Both Strömbäck and Sveinsson assume that the author of *Njála* had read the *Þiðranda þáttr* found in fourteenth century manuscripts of *Óláfs saga Tryggvasonar*, a story believed to emanate from the Conversion episode of Gunnlaugr Leifsson's lost Latin biography of Olaf Tryggvason. But is it likely that the author of *Njála* would have referred to Þiðrandi's death in this manner unless the story had also circulated in oral tradition? He could not very well have expected his audience to be familiar with Gunnlaugr Leifsson's Latin work.

66. Cf. Sveinsson, *Njála* (1954), 299, note 1. This story about Skapti Þóroddsson is evidently dependent on oral traditions in Southwest Iceland. The reference in *Njála* suggests a skipper's yarn circulating around the important landing place at Eyrar, since Skarpheðinn also mentions a certain "Þórólfr Loptsson á Eyrum," who is supposed to

Svanlaug, whom Eydís Iron-Sword and Anvil-Head kidnapped from your home" (another one of Skarpheðinn's puzzling insults in chapter 119; neither the story nor the characters are known from any other source).[67]

Adherents of the "book-prose" theory often explain such allusions by referring to lost written sources. The explanation is not convincing (cf. the Appendix, p. 237). Even in cases where the saga alludes to a story which *can* be found in a still extant source (as in the case of Þiðrandi's death, which is described in *Flateyjarbók*), the author of *Njála* cannot have expected his audience to know the story from manuscripts; such a level of literacy was not present in thirteenth-century Iceland. He *must* be referring to oral traditions familiar to his audience, although some of these traditions may have been derived from a written source.

Most likely, several of the main episodes of the saga were also familiar to his audience from oral traditions, although the author often gives the oral tales a new twist. His new evaluation of Flosi's role and his reinterpretation of Gunnarr's return to Hlíðarendi are only the most obvious examples.[68] Furthermore, allusions are made to events the author expects his audience to know *in detail* long before they are officially introduced. Chapter 96 provides a good example: "Síðu-Hallr had a brother called Þorsteinn Broad-Paunch; he was the father of Kolr, whom Kári will kill in Wales." The mention of Kolr is pointless unless the audience knows: a) that Kolr is one of the Burners of Njáll, b) that Kári is the great hero who avenged the Burning, and c) that Kolr was killed by Kári in Wales as told in chapter 158 of *Njála*. But in chapter 96 none of these basic facts has yet been pre-

---

have smuggled Skapti "out" (i.e., into the country) in some flour sacks after the killing of Ketill at Elda in Norway. The author of *Njála* is obviously quite familiar with the landing place at Eyrar, and he also expects his audience to be familiar with it; cf. below, p. 000; *Njála* (1954), pp. 225, 269, 437, 439.

67. Cf. Sveinsson, *Njála* (1954), 301, note 2. Unlike the previous tales, this one would seem to emanate from northern Iceland, for the person advised to fetch back his sister is Hafr inn auðgi, a chieftain from the Skagafjǫrðr district (also mentioned in *Þorvalds þáttr víðfǫrla*, chapter 6). Svanlaug's kidnappers may, however, have been southerners, in which case the story would have been known in the South. One reason to suspect this is the author's general tendency to explain traditions in the North as if the audience could *not* be expected to know these traditions; see, for example, the references to Guðmundr the Powerful and Þorkell hákr in the same chapter (p. 302).

68. Other examples are: (1) his reinterpretation of Hǫskuldr Dala-Kollsson's and his half-brother Hrútr's relationship after Hrútr's return from Norway (chapter 6; cf. *Laxdœla saga*, chapter 19), (2) his new version of the story about Þorkell hákr's slander of Guðmundr the Powerful (chapters 119-20; cf. *Ljósvetninga saga*, chapters 5-8), (3) his new version of the story about Síðu-Hallr's conversion, in which Saint Michael becomes Hallr's "fylgju engill" (chapter 100; cf. *Kristni saga*, chapter 7). A detailed analysis of these variants would, however, go beyond the scope of this book.

sented. Kolr has not even been introduced; Kári has only recently become acquainted with the sons of Njáll, and the Burning of Njáll is still far away. Surely the author under these circumstances would not have mentioned Kolr's death in Wales unless he felt certain that the audience already knew what he planned to tell them later.[69]

For the audience, the enjoyment must to a large extent have consisted in recognizing well-known tales presented in a new shape and in a new context. As they listened to the story, they would hear echoes from other stories and anticipate further developments in a way that modern readers can never do. Consciously or unconsciously, they would also probably draw parallels to their own time and compare the saga heroes to their contemporary descendents. Consider the following brief and straightforward exchange between Morðr and Gizurr the White as Gunnarr is attacked in chapter 77:

Morðr said, "Let us burn him to death inside the house."
"Never," said Gizurr, "even though I knew that my own life depended on it."

This exchange does not advance the story of Gunnarr's last moments, for Gunnarr is never burned to death. Nor was the burning motif part of the tradition about Gunnarr's death before *Njála*. The dialogue between Morðr and Gizurr may thus have been introduced by the author as an aleboration of the original tradition. The function of this intermezzo is to make the audience compare the Death of Gunnarr to the Burning of Njáll, an event presented only much later in the saga. Modern readers, however, do not understand that this is an intentional allusion to the Burning until they have read chapter 128, where Njáll and Skarpheðinn discuss whether or not their enemies will burn them if they decide to go into the houses at Berg-þórshváll. Njáll claims that they will be able to defend themselves inside the houses just as well as Gunnarr did before his death. Skarpheðinn answers that Gunnarr's enemies were "chieftains of such noble mind" that they would not burn him in his house, but Flosi and his men cannot be so trusted. This prediction, of course, turns out to be correct, and, as a result of their activities, the Burners acquire a heavier burden of guilt than Gunnarr's slayers.

The original audience of *Njála* could be expected to recognize the allusion to the Burning of Njáll in the dialogue of chapter 77 even the first time they heard the saga read. They would also know well that Gizurr the White was a revered founding father of the Icelandic church, even though *Njála* does not present him in that role until several chapters later (chapters 104-105). Furthermore, they would immediately recognize Morðr's advice as that of an evil Loki figure trying to corrupt honorable chieftains. Finally,

69. Cf. the Appendix, below, p. 222.

they could perhaps be expected to know that Gizurr the White's descendent and namesake, Gizurr Þorvaldsson, had been the most powerful man in Iceland in the 1260s, having narrowly escaped the famous Burning of Flugumýrr in 1253, an event involving members of the Svínfelling family.[70] All this knowledge, which must have been easily available to all Icelanders around 1280, adds to the exchange between Mǫrðr and Gizurr, emphasizes the contrast between the two characters, and makes clear the meaning of the chapter, even to people who heard it out of context or had never heard Njála's version of the Burning or the conversion of Iceland (or, for that matter, Sturlunga's version of the Burning at Flugumýrr).

The passage quoted from chapter 77 does not necessarily contain everything I have just read into it. My point is that the original audience could make such an interpretation and could encourage the author to insert subtle allusions without fear of being misunderstood. It is true that his composition, delived orally, did not allow "close reading" by sophisticated literary experts. Still, in dealing with native saga tradition and genealogy, he could scarcely appear too esoteric for his public.

Giving full expression to his "clerical mind" when addressing such an audience, however, was more difficult. This is probably the main reason why his literary education is only sporadically revealed and why his Christian themes, though extremely important in the overall structure, are hidden under thick layers of traditional saga motifs.

Let us now draw some tentative conclusions about the author and his social status. His clerical mind and his occasional use of Latin phraseology certainly suggest that he had some clerical schooling, but nothing proves that his principal occupation was that of a priest or a monk. His extensive knowledge of secular Icelandic law and genealogy, his familiarity with the setting and proceedings of the Allthing, and his evident ambition to promote the interests of the Svínfellings suggest instead that he lived in a secular environment, perhaps as secretary to Þorvarðr Þórarinsson or as one of the officials appointed after the introduction of Járnsíða. There are some indications that he dictated at least some of the Allthing speeches to a scribe,[71]

---

70. Cf. Sturlunga saga, I, pp. 484-494; Barði Guðmundsson (1958), 225-234. There is no reason to suppose that Guðmundsson is right in assuming that the author of Njála in describing the Burning of Njáll "actually" meant to describe the Flugumýrarbrenna. But he is probably right in assuming that memories of the Flugumýrarbrenna influenced audience reactions to stories such as the one about Njáll's burning.

71. Cf. the Appendix, below, p. 248. Dictation could also explain the occurrence in the saga of certain parenthetic remarks which are highly unusual in written composition but quite common in oral presentation, e.g., the just quoted reference to Kolr "er Kári vegr í Bretlandi" (chapter 96; note the present tense !). One particularly revealing example

and this also suggests a man of some authority. He may have been a member of the Svínfelling family (or the Skógverja family), but this is something we will never know.

His detailed knowledge of Iceland shows that he had travelled extensively outside of his home area, particularly along the routes leading to the Allthing. He had certainly seen the beautiful slopes at Hlíðarendi (which are clearly perceived by any passing traveller), even though his memory of this district appears to have been somewhat imperfect at the time of writing. He must have visited the West Fjord district, where most of the action in the Prologue takes place, and the East Fjord district, where Flosi solicits support in chapter 134. In fact, he moves with greater ease than almost any other sagawriter from one district to another, and although some of his information about remote areas could well have been based on hearsay, it appears unlikely that his conception of distances and directions could have been as clear as it is without considerable personal experience.[72] Perhaps such extensive knowledge would be collected by an administrative official or by the secretary of such an official. He would have travelled on horseback, which explains his frequent and knowledgeable references to horses and horsemanship.[73]

His descriptions of sea voyages and military campaigns, on the other hand, are far too stereotyped and traditional to indicate personal experience in these areas. Yet his surprisingly detailed knowledge of obscure placenames and local traditions in the Scottish viking colonies (Orkney, Shetland, The Hebrides, Caithness) suggests that he had travelled in this part of the world or had talked extensively to people who had travelled there.[74] Some of the

---

is found in chapter 122, where Flosi announces his arbitrators to the Allthing: "Flosi mælti 'Nú mun ek nefna mína gerðarmenn. Nefni ek fyrstan Hall ok Qzur frá Breiðá, Surt Ásbjarnarson ór Kirkjuboe, Mórðólf Ketilsson,'—*hann bjó þá í Ásum*—'Hafr ok Runólf ór Dal, ok mun einmælt, at þessir sé bezt til fallnir af ǫllum mínum mǫnnum!'" (my italics). The narrator thus quite suddenly interrupts Flosi's announcement to make one of his own about Móðólfr Ketilsson—whom he had previously failed to introduce, but whom, he now realizes, his audience should know something about! As a matter of fact, Móðólfr had been mentioned in passing once before, in chapter 115, but his identity and domicile had never been clarified, unlike the other characters enumerated by Flosi. A slip of this kind certainly appears to be a slip of the tongue rather than of the pen. Note also the author's repeated references to his own narration as an *oral* activity: "Nú er þar *til máls* at taka," "Nú skal *nefna* sonu Njáls," etc. Concerning dictation of sagas, see also Lönnroth (1964), 18, 59-60, 78-96.

72. This subject has been very well explored by Sveinsson, *Njála* (1954), LXXXIV-C.

73. See, for example, *Njála*, chapters 53 (Otkell's ride), 59 (the *hestavíg*), 124-26 (Flosi's ride from Svínafell to Bergþórshváll).

74. See, in particular, chapters 85-86, 89 (the sons of Njáll raid in Scotland), 153-54, 158-59 (Flosi's and Kári's travels). The Clontarf episode may in this context be disregarded

same obscure placenames appear also in accounts of King Hákon Hákonar-
son's military campaign in Scotland during the 1260s, a campaign which
probably engaged some of the leading Icelandic families.[75] It is therefore
tempting to speculate that the author—or some prominent members of
his audience—took part in this campaign. The traditions about the Battle
of Clontarf also evidently emanate from the Orkney-Caithness area, not
from Ireland (a country the author clearly did not know much about).
It is quite possible, however, that these traditions had existed in Iceland
long before they were incorporated in *Njála*, for some of the same legends
appear also in *Orkneyinga saga*, written around 1200.[76] As Sveinsson has
shown, such traditions may have been cultivated within the Oddaverja
family because of their close kinship with the Earls of Orkney.[77]

The author does not give as much detailed information about other foreign
countries, and his information is sometimes unreliable. In chapter 88,
for example, he seems to imply, incorrectly, that only a short distance lies
between Guðbrandsdalir and Hlaðir in Norway. From such apparent errors
Sveinsson concluded that the author had never been in Norway,[78] but
this is unwarranted. He could very well have been there without acquiring
detailed topographical knowledge, or, if he did acquire such knowledge,
he may have felt no need to incorporate it in his saga. In fact, he does
mention places along the sea routes of the North Atlantic and the Baltic:
Stokkssund in Sweden; Rafala and Eysýsla in Estonia; Limgarðssíða,
Konungahella, Túnsberg, and Agðanes in Norway; Heiðabær in Denmark;
Dover, Berwick, and Anglesey in England, and so on. He is also aware of

---

since Sveinsson thinks it is derived from a separate written source (cf. the Appendix
below, pp. 226-236). Among the most obscure placenames are the following: *Þrasvik*
(modern Freswick, a small village south of Duncansby Head on the eastern coast of Caithness), *Straumey* (modern Stroma, a small island in the Pentland Firth), *Mýræfi* (mod.
Moray, Irish *Muirebe*), *Dungalsbær* (mod. Duncansby), *Friðarey* (Fair Island, between
Orkney and Shetland), *Saltíri* (Mull of Kintyre, from Irish *Sáltíre*, a promontory extend-
ing into the North Channel, south of Argyll), *Kola* (Coll, a small island in the Hebrides).
Most of these names have been commented on by A. B. Taylor in *Proceedings of the Society of Antiquaries of Scotland*, 71 (1936-37).

75. Cf. Sturla Þórðarson's *Hákonar saga*, chapters 314-330. It is interesting to note
that Bishop Brandr Jónsson, according to Sturla's account, was staying with King Hákon
in Norway while this Scottish campaign was being prepared in the winter of 1262-63.
When Brandr returned to Iceland, he must have brought news about the war to the other
Svínfellings, and he may in fact have travelled home by way of Orkney on one of the king's
ships.

76. Cf. Finnbogi Guðmundsson's preface to *Orkneyinga saga* (*Íslenzk Fornrit*, 34, 1965).

77. Sveinsson, *Sagnaritun Oddaverja* (*Studia Islandica*, I, Reykjavik, 1937).

78. Sveinsson, *Njála* (1954), XCIV-XCV, CX.

the major pilgrim routes to Rome (chapters 158-59) and of the old trade route from Denmark to Constantinople by way of the Russian rivers (chapter 81). Surely his world is not limited to his own corner of Iceland!

On the other hand, nothing prompts us to believe that he had travelled extensively or studied abroad. All of his knowledge *could* have been acquired in Iceland, though hardly in an average farmhouse. His travels were probably not undertaken as a tradesman, for his attitude toward merchants is contemptuous.[79] He is more likely to have travelled as an official for the King or for the Archbishop of Niðaróss; such travels had become common in his time.[80]

Whatever clerical education he received most likely came from the monastery of Þykkvabær, which was both the center of learning in Southeast Iceland and the intellectual Mecca of the entire country in the 1250s and 1260s. The most learned of Svínfellings, Brandr Jónsson, supervised the school there before he became the Bishop of Hólar in 1263. Most of the leading Icelandic clerics at the end of the thirteenth century are known to have been Brandr's students,[81] and it is likely that all of them became familiar with his *Alexanders saga* and with his family traditions. One of these students was Árni Þorláksson, later Bishop of Skálholt and known to have been brought up at Svínafell. Árni helped Þorvarðr Þórarinsson and the king to prepare the way for *Járnsíða*. His later activities as a staunch advocate of canon law, however, brought him into serious conflict with most secular officials, including Þorvarðr Þórarinsson.[82] Hence it is not very likely that Árni wrote *Njála*. It is nevertheless tempting to search for the real author within Árni's circle of childhood friends and fellow students. But we shall not fall for this temptation; a lack of detailed information allows no positive identification.

There is no reason to make further guesses about the author's personality. If his soul were torn by conflict, as some critcs have suggested, he did not show it. The conflicts he expresses are those inherent in the tradition of oral *sagnaskemtan*, in the audience for which he wrote, and in the social class whose interests he served.

79. Cf. *Njála*, chapters 22 (Kaupa-Heðinn), 83 (the sons of Njáll and the cowardly merchants in Scotland).

80. On such travels between Iceland and Norway, see, in particular, Jóhannesson, II (1958).

81. *Biskupa Sögur*, I, 681; cf. Jóhannesson, II (1958), 91-92.

82. Cf. Jóhannesson, II (1958), 93-109.

6. NJÁLA AND THE DEVELOPMENT OF SAGAWRITING

Scholars of all persuasions have seen *Njála* as the grand culmination of a long evolutionary process. Free-prose theorists have argued that the evolution occurred primarily in the oral tradition. Book-prose theorists have tried to show that the evolution should instead be regarded as a development of saga*writing* in the thirteenth century. If the former view is correct, the early stages of the development cannot now be reconstructed, and the latter stages can only be dimly perceived in the saga manuscripts. If, on the other hand, the latter view is correct, the chronology of sagawriting should guide us in reconstructing the various stages of the evolution.

Sigurður Nordal has made a systematic attempt to reconstruct such stages from the book-prose stand.[83] His theory of evolution, which has become extremely influential, begins with two different "literary schools" in twelfth century Iceland: the dry, factual historiography of Ari the wise, and the clerical *konungasǫgur* written in the monastery of Þingeyrar. According to Nordal, the classical saga form developed around 1220 from the combination of the "scholarship" (*vísindi*) of Ari and the "art" (*list*) of the Þingeyrar school. To a considerable extent, Nordal makes Snorri Sturluson personally responsible for this synthesis, which he believes led to a "purer," more objective prose, a conscious avoidance of both clerical style and popular folklore, and a more rationalistic approach to history. Later sagawriters then followed Snorri's example and refined his techniques until the end of the thirteenth century, when *vísindi* and *list* again part company—historiography is taken over by the Icelandic annals, while saga entertainment again incorporates popular folklore and foreign literary patterns, this time primarily borrowed from French romance.

Nordal divides the *Íslendingasǫgur* into five chronological groups, each representing a new stage in the development. The first stage (1200-1230) is influenced by the Þingeyrar school; sagas in this group (e.g., *Fóstbrœðra saga* and *Hallfreðar saga*) deal largely with skalds and other Icelanders associated with the Norwegian court. *Egils saga* is supposed to be the first "classical" saga from this period, probably written by Snorri himself.

The second group (1230-1280) contains most of the classical "family" sagas, including *Laxdœla saga*, *Eyrbyggja saga*, *Gísla saga*, *Víga-Glúms saga*, and the two Vinland sagas (*Eiríks saga rauða* and *Grœnlendinga saga*). These are all supposedly built on genuine folk tradition, but the individual

---

83. "Sagalitteraturen," *Nordisk Kultur*, 8 B (Uppsala, 1953), 180-269. Nordal's basic theory about the synthesis of *vísindi* and *list* was first presented in his introduction to *Egils saga* (*Íslenzk Fornrit*, 2, 1933), LXIII-LXX.

sagawriters have rationalized the supernatural and fantastic elements. They have composed according to their own literary tastes, influenced mostly by the rationalism of Snorri and other writers of his generation.

The third group (1280-1300) is dominated by *Gunnlaugs saga*, *Hrafnkels saga*, and *Njála*, all of which are said to be composed as historical novels rather than historiography; "scholarship" (*vísindi*) is now on its way out of the saga, leaving "art" (*list*) as the primary object of the composition. Of the writers in this group, the author of *Njála*, is "the Shakespeare of saga literature, a freebooter who takes his material from everywhere, uses the earlier saga-literature as it suits him best, great in his virtues and his vices, his strength and weaknesses . . . bordering on decadence but, in spite of all this, one of the greatest of all times as a stylist, narrator and psychologist. He is for his time a learned man . . . . He has used more literary sources than any other writer of *Íslendingasǫgur*."[84]

Like Sveinsson, Nordal thus sees the author of *Njála* as a sort of superhuman Renaissance man—yet inaugurating "decadence" rather than revitalization. After this characterization "one could expect," as Nordal points out, "that the *Íslendingasǫgur* would continue as free fiction but in a less realistic manner, more strongly influenced by the . . . *oldtidssagaer*," i.e., by the *fornaldarsǫgur* and *riddarasǫgur* written at the end of the thirteenth century. Yet Nordal has to admit that many of the sagas in his fourth group (beginning of the fourteenth century) contain "clear signs of genuine, popular, historical tradition, separating them from sagas in the fifth group and even making them closer to the second than to the third group."[85] The fifth and last group (fourteenth century), however, completes his schema reasonably well by containing several sagas apparently written as almost pure fiction.

Nordal's theory of evolution is both attractive and ingenious. It places most of the extant saga texts in a neat system which seems logical and compatible with accepted chronology. The evolutionary process is outlined without reference to large unknown factors such as oral sagas. The theory also appears to explain the wide variations between sagas, variations which would seem to speak against the free-prose assumption that one is dealing with a fairly uniform and homogeneous oral genre, developed before sagas were written down.

Nevertheless, several objections can be raised against this theory. To begin with the chronological objections, *Njála* is in fact one of the few sagas that can be dated with any precision. The dating of most other sagas is so uncertain that we cannot know clearly whether *any Íslendingasaga* was

---

84. Nordal (1953), 259-60.
85. Nordal (1953), 261-62.

written before 1230 or whether *any* of the texts in Nordal's Group 1 is earlier than the texts in his Group 2. Nordal's own chronology is partly based on theories of literary borrowings which have not been fully accepted.[86] It is also partly based on his own assumptions about evolutionary stages, so that his argument sometimes tends to be circular.[87]

Even if all his datings are correct, however, the difference between his five stages is hardly more remarkable than the variation between sagas *within* each age group. From the standpoint of theme and structure, *Hallfreðar saga* (Group 1) has more in common with *Gunnlaugs saga* (Group 3) than it has with *Heiðarvíga saga* (also Group 1). From the same standpoint, *Njála* (Group 3) has more in common with *Laxdœla saga* (Group 2) or even with Oddr's *Óláfs saga Tryggvasonar* (a *konungasaga* from the "Þingeyrar school") than it has with either *Hrafnkels saga* or *Bandamanna saga* (both Group 3). As Nordal himself makes clear, most sagas in Group 4 also resemble *Njála* less than they resemble sagas in Group 2, and the same may in fact be said about some of the sagas in Group 5. When a few comparisons of this sort have been made, the value of Nordal's evolutionary scheme is reduced, although it may still be useful for showing the development of historical *vísindi* in relation to fiction within classical sagawriting.

The problem is that this is the *only* development that Nordal is really concerned about. He never attempts to classify sagas on the basis of formal properties such as structure or narrative technique. His own classification system—*Íslendingasaga, konungasaga, fornaldarsaga,* etc,—is quite useful for distinguishing subject areas within saga literature, but it is not very useful for distinguishing narrative forms or genres in a literary sense. From this standpoint the distinction between *vísindi* and *list* is not very helpful either since it separates texts that are formally identical and brings together texts that are formally very different merely on the basis of the sagawriter's respect for historical truth.

None of Nordal's classifications (*vísindi, list, Íslendingasaga,* etc.) were used by the sagawriters themselves. To them a saga was just a saga, although

---

86. See in particular Andersson (1964), 95-108; Jónas Kristjánsson (1972), 144-223.

87. Note, for example, his motivation for assigning *Heiðarvíga saga* to Group 1: "Dens stil og fremstillingsmaade er i mange henseender saa ujævn, ubehjælpsom og sær, at man har følt, at den traditionelle sagastil her endnu ikke var udviklet og fastslaaet" (Nordal, 1953, 236). This argument has been flatly and, I think, justly rejected by Ole Widding in *Norrøn Fortællekunst* (1965), 83: "Det er dog alt sammen ganske svævende, og det sproglige støttepunkt for, at sagaen er gammel, må blankt forkastes, og en datering alene ud fra ubehjælpsomhed med hensyn til stilen kan vel aldrig være bindende." Nordal's theory about the development of *vísindi* and *list* in sagawriting before Snorri has also been criticized on chronological grounds by Bjarni Guðnason, *Um Skjöldungasögu* (Reykjavík, 1963), 269-78.

some of them would occasionally use a term like *ævisaga* to designate a secular saga with biographical content or *dæmisaga* (Latin *exemplum*) to designate a short saga with a "moral" attached to it.[88] As we have seen in Chapter III, however, they had a strong awareness of genre in the sense that they believed particular themes and motifs required a particular type of narrative treatment: the Feud Pattern had its particular set of rules as had the Travel Pattern, the Introduction of New Characters, and so on.[89]

Nordal's discussion of literary development gives us no reason to suppose that these narrative rules were invented by sagawriters in the thirteenth century. In fact, most elements of *Njála*'s "language of tradition" can be attested in the earliest written sagas. Snorri and his contemporaries may well have refined the techniques and temporarily purged them from clerical influence. They may also have consciously avoided certain folklore motifs involving supernatural forces. Even so, their contribution to classical saga form was, at the most, a reform, not a revolution.

The greatest weakness of Nordal's theory is its failure to define the social context in which sagawriters worked. From his survey of literary causes and effects one would think that sagawriting existed in a social vacuum, that written sagas were influenced only by other written sagas. Nordal often refers to tradition ("folk tradition," "folklore," "historical tradition," etc.) as a source of sagawriting, but only as a sort of shapeless raw material sought out by the sagawriter; he does not seem to think about it as oral *literature*. Nor does he attempt to analyze the audience or to explain how the sagawriter would gain access to either his oral or his written sources in the milieu in which he lived. As a result, he fails to see that not even the author of *Njála*, perhaps the most original and "literary" of all sagawriters, is a "free-booter," using sources as they suit him best, but a writer deeply committed to the traditions and narrative forms known to his audience through generations of oral *sagnaskemtan*.

---

88. On the generic concepts used by the sagawriters, cf. Lönnroth (1964), 9-32. Most of these concepts are clearly of foreign origin, and their value for the understanding of the native saga genres is therefore limited; cf. Joseph Harris (1972), 1-27. Even the imported generic concepts (*ævisaga, dæmisaga,* etc.) may, however, help us to understand the principles that guided sagawriters in their overall composition when the native "language of tradition" did not give them any clear rules. *Egils saga* and most of the *konungasǫgur* are thus composed as *ævisǫgur*, while some of the digressive *Íslendinga þættir* inserted in *Morkinskinna* and *Flateyjarbók* are meant to function as edifying *dæmisǫgur*. Cf. Lönnroth, "The Concept of Genre in Saga Literature," a paper presented at the meeting of the Society for the Advancement of Scandinavian Studies in Minneapolis, 1973.

89. This kind of generic "awareness," which is not necessarily manifested in any consistent generic terminology, has been particularly emphasized by Harris (1972) and also by Clover (1972 and 1974).

We have argued that the author's originality should not be sought in any one story that he told, nor in his narrative grammar, style, or action patterns but rather in the way he combined all the traditional elements in his overall structure. It is in such structural combinations and in the use of foreign literary patterns that sagawriters generally differ most markedly from each other. Such difference between two contemporary sagawriters is often greater than the difference between writers of different periods because the narrative elements themselves appear to have changed very little. This is why it is impossible to establish a reliable chronology based on saga types or to perceive *major* evolutionary trends in thirteenth century sagawriting.

Yet it is possible to classify sagas into certain genres and "schools of composition," some of which started later than others and prevailed in particular milieus for a limited period of time. One such early "school" is the one Nordal associates with the monastery of Þingeyrar around 1200. Writers of this school subordinated the traditional saga elements to overall structures borrowed from Latin hagiography: the life of a saintly king or bishop was told from beginning to end, and the narrator emphasized prophecies about his greatness, his good deeds and virtues, his sufferings and martyrdom, and the miracles that occurred after his death. Within this broad hagiographic frame the sagawriter incorporated, rather loosely and without much concern for narrative order, a series of traditional saga *þættir*: feuds, viking exploits, and anecdotes about both skalds and other Icelandic heroes. Oddr's *Óláfs saga Tryggvasonar*, in which the Battle of Svolder serves both as heroic saga climax and as hagiographic *passio* at the end, may serve as a good example of this genre, which apparantly went out of fashion in the thirteenth century but returned with increased vigor after 1300.[90]

Another school or genre manifested in writing around 1220, used the biography (*ævisaga*) of a skald as a basic narrative frame, filling it with travel episodes and feuds. *Kormaks saga*, *Hallfreðar saga*, and *Fóstbrœðra saga* all belong to this type, apparently popular throughout the century. This genre, evidently of native origin, may well have been taken over from the oral tradition without much adaptation, for the skald sagas are often sufficiently uncomplicated in structure to be easily remembered and sufficiently short to be told in one sitting of *sagnaskemtan*. Late variants of this type (e.g., *Gunnlaugs saga*) show influence from translated romance.[91]

90. Clover (1972 and 1974) is so far the only scholar who has made a detailed and convincing study of the relationship between hagiographic structure and indigenous narrative building blocks in such early sagas (the text she uses as example is the *Legendary Saga of Olaf the Saint*).

91. Bjarni Einarsson (1962) made an attempt to derive this whole saga type from French romance and Provençal Troubadour tradition. Theodore Andersson defended the notion

A third type, the "family saga" proper, tells the history of one family from the first *landnámsmenn* through several generations, with emphasis on heroes in the later tenth or early eleventh centuries. This may well be a literary elaboration of the "skald saga" inspired by *Egils saga*, which starts with Egil's grandfather Kveldúlfr's settlement in Iceland around 890 and ends with Egill's death around 990. While *Egils saga* contains more "Travel *pættir*" than domestic "Feud *pættir*," the Feud Pattern dominates most of the later family sagas, which also become increasingly concerned with genealogy and local traditions.

The family type appears to be the most popular saga type from about 1230 to 1350, evidently because its composition promoted wealthy families and powerful local interests. Once the genre had been established, it did not change much; from a strictly literary standpoint there is no great difference between *Reykdœla saga* (Nordal's Group 2) and *Kjalnesinga saga* (Nordal's Group 5), although the former may be based on more genuine oral tradition. In the longer of these sagas, e.g., *Vatnsdœla saga* or *Eyrbyggja saga*, the structure is very loose: a series of episodes constitutes a rough family chronicle, with some dramatic highlights from the lives of particularly important characters.

In a few family sagas before *Njála*, however, notably in *Laxdœla* saga, we find a tendency to connect the story through anticipations, various causal links between the episodes, and also through an overriding theme: the introduction of Christianity in Iceland. These compositional devices were probably derived from works such as Snorri's *Óláfs saga Tryggvasonar* and *Óláfs saga helga*, which, in their turn, were inspired by early "clerical" works such as Oddr's *Óláfs saga*.[92]

This is the literary tradition the author of *Njála* follows. More radically than any previous writer of long sagas, however, he tries to tie *everything* together in his "network of events." Unlike the author of *Laxdœla*, he does not tell any stories about *landnámsmenn* merely to tell who the ancestors

---

of the "skald saga" as an indigenous Icelandic form in "Skalds and Troubadours," *Mediæval Scandinavia*, 2 (1969), 7-41. Bjarni Einarsson answered Andersson's criticism in "The Lovesick Skald: A reply to Theodore M. Andersson," *Mediæval Scandinavia*, 4 (1971), 21-41.

92. Snorri's role as an innovator of saga *composition* has not yet been sufficiently investigated. In his own pioneering studies of Snorri as a sagawriter, Nordal emphasized other aspects of his work (style, attitude to history, sources, etc.). A new approach was inaugurated by Clover (1972 and 1974), who shows how the *Heimskringla* version of the Battle of Stiklastaðir has been composed through a skillful rearrangement of narrative segments from earlier versions. See also Halvdan Lie, *Studier i Heimskringlas stil* (Oslo, 1937).

of his main heroes were. He starts directly with Hallgerðr's thief's eyes
and with Hrútr's marriage. Such a beginning was inconceivable in the earliest of the written sagas. Hence, *Njála* is indeed a product of *literary* development, of saga*writing*.

There are several other details in the composition which indicate that
Njála was written later than most classical sagas: the skillful and consistent
use of chapter divisions; the masterful integration of miracles and other
Christian motifs in the Feud Pattern; the expansion of presentation segments
by the inclusion of romance material; the superior handling of staging and
scene-shifting techniques, especially in episodes such as the Burning of Njáll
and the Death of Gunnarr. None of this could have been achieved in the
first half of the thirteenth century, when sagawriters had not learned to
combine the elements of oral saga tradition into large literary compositions.
In these early days, the writers would solve the problem of large-scale
composition either by imposing a hagiographic pattern, which was detrimen-
tal to saga style (example: Oddr's *Óláfs saga*), or by simply juxtaposing a
series of *þættir* in the manner probably most natural to the oral storyteller
(example: *Eyrbyggja*). *Heimskringla* was one of the first works in which a
more sophisticated literary saga structure was achieved on a large scale,[93]
but not even Snorri knew as well as the author of *Njála* how to integrate a
mass of native and foreign elements into one large and harmonious pattern.
This knowledge cannot be the result of oral tradition only; it presupposes
a development of the saga as literary art.

On the other hand, *Njála* was written at a time when the oral tradition
had not yet begun to dry up. Without this still-living oral tradition, the
author could never have told his story with such a mastery of narrative
technique on the segment and *þáttr* level. About a hundred years later, sagawriters would often have excellent notions about overall structure, but
they simply did not know how to build a dramatic scene or present a conflict
because they had lost touch with the oral tradition and with the saga as
spoken art. This change is evident in many ways when late fourteenth century sagas are compared to the classical saga literature of the thirteenth
century. The later sagawriters were much more dependent upon written
sources and foreign literary models. When they used an earlier text, they
tended to copy it word for word instead of retelling it in their own idiom.[94]

93. Clover (1974), 80, emphasizes the role of Snorri and his somewhat older contemporary, Styrmir Kárason, in developing "the larger possibilities of paratactic construction."
94. The trend towards more faithful copying may be appreciated if early manuscript
versions of *Óláfs saga Tryggvasonar* are compared with late fourteenth and fifteenth century versions. The early versions differ so much from each other that it is often impossible
to see that they are ultimately derived from the same exemplar. The later versions, how-

When they presented an old legend previously unrecorded, they elaborated its basic plot with "literary" reflections and descriptions instead of letting it unfold freely in a sequence of dramatic scenes.[95] And they no longer took for granted that their audience was familiar with a wealth of orally transmitted legends and genealogies, as the audience of *Njála* had been.

The decline of oral tradition shortly after the writing of *Njála* is evident also from the fact that the later history of leading Icelandic families is extremely difficult to follow, even though these families evidently remained active in politics and in literature. In the later Middle Ages, members of the old chieftain families may still have been interested in their family heritage, but they evidently did not memorize long lists of their ancestors or tell long stories about them as a form of regular entertainment. The production of saga manuscripts increased in the fourteenth and fifteenth centuries, but these manuscripts tell us practically nothing about the generations after Þorvarðr Þórarinsson and his contemporaries. Genealogies were still written down, but they were copies from earlier manuscripts and tend to stop with people who lived around 1300.

What is the explanation for this major change in the literary history of Iceland? Scholars have assumed that the change was somehow affected by Iceland's loss of independence, by the translation of French romance, by the writing of *fornaldarsǫgur*, and by various other factors. But it is difficult to understand how any of these factors, alone or in combination, could have led to such a drastic change, especially when *Njála* and other classical sagas continued to be transcribed and to be popular in each new generation.

The answer to the problem should be sought, I think, in the transformation of *sagnaskemtan* that took place in the thirteenth century. When sagas were read aloud from manuscripts instead of being told directly to an audience, the storyteller's art must have declined. The preservation of old family legends must gradually have become less dependent on memory than on written texts. During the transition period, when manuscripts were still very scarce, there remained people who knew how to tell a good story, using memory and oral improvisation alone, some of whom learned to transform their art into literary compositions. As literacy and the number of manuscripts increased, however, saga entertainment did not require such talent and memory. Anyone who could read could now serve as performer, and

---

ever, are basically identical. It may also be noted that the *Njála* manuscripts contain much fewer variant readings than some of the earlier sagas such as *Egils saga*.

95. For examples of the later saga style, see *Hrólfs saga kraka*, *Gautreks saga*, or one of the other late *fornaldarsǫgur*. See also Å. Lagerholm, *Drei Lygisǫgur* (Halle, 1927) and M. Schlauch, *Romance in Iceland* (London, 1934).

the texts would not have to come from native tradition but could be adapted from French romance or any other literature the sponsors of *sagnaskemtan* could acquire.

An analogous development took place in other cultures where oral epic traditions gave way to written literature. The effect of written texts on the oral "singer of tales" has been described by Albert Lord:

When [a singer] thinks of the written songs as fixed and tries to learn them word for word, the power of the fixed text and of the technique of memorizing will stunt his ability to compose orally. But this process is not a transition from an oral to a literary technique of composition. It is a transition from oral composition to simple performance of a fixed text, from composition to reproduction. This is one of the most common ways in which an oral tradition may die; not when writing is introduced, but when published song texts are spread among singers."[96]

To a very great extent Lord's description is applicable to saga tradition. Unlike the epic songs of Yugoslavia, the sagas were not, as far as we know, *memorized* word for word from written texts before a performance, but the public reading of a fixed saga text would have the same paralyzing effect on oral tradition as did the memorizing of written song texts. As long as the transition from oral to written culture had not yet been completed, a few individual writers, such as the author of *Njála*, would be able to combine the native art of storytelling with foreign literary models into new saga structures surpassing anything that had been created before. But their very success as writers killed the tradition by making their texts canonical to later generations of Icelanders participating in *sagnaskemtan*. Who could possibly improve on *Heimskringla*'s version of the Battle of Svolder or *Njála*'s version of the Burning of Njáll? Instead of presenting their own versions of these celebrated events, people would admiringly listen to a faithful rendition of the established written texts, copied over and over again in the centuries that followed. Later writers would not even try to compete. Instead they would turn to subjects unexplored by the classical sagawriters, subjects more difficult to treat because less firmly rooted in the oral tradition.

The written sagas did not, of course, completely destroy oral tradition in Iceland. In fact, much of this tradition has lingered on until the present day in the form of *rímur*, folktales, ballads, and even sagas, especially *fornaldarsǫgur*. But as literacy and the production of manuscripts increased, the purely oral saga entertainment ceased to be the concern of the native aristocracy, i.e., families such as the Svínfellings or the Sturlungs. These families could now rely exclusively on written literature for their entertain-

---

96. Lord, *The Singer of Tales* (1960), 129-30.

ment. It was they who had kept up the oral tradition of family sagas and kings' sagas, and it is therefore natural that this part of the tradition died out first. The less aristocratic traditions cultivated by common farmers and farm hands lived much longer, but they were not recorded in writing until comparatively recent times, unless they found sponsors among the wealthier and more educated members of society. All texts preserved in medieval Icelandic manuscripts, we can assume, emanated from the *sagnaskemtan* of the upper classes. It is the deterioration of oral tradition within *this* milieu that explains the decline of sagawriting.

If our explanation is correct, the death of the classical sagas was thus at least partly a result of sagawriting itself. *Njála*, possibly the last of the great sagas, was truly a "novel to end all novels." For centuries to come, nothing could measure up to it; it had exhausted the power that kept its genre alive. It found no match until a different milieu and a completely different narrative idiom produced the modern novel.

The decline of oral tradition within the chieftain families is not, however, the result of sagawriting alone. The reform of governmental and judicial practices brought about by *Járnsíða* (and later by its successor, *Jónsbók*) must also have played a decisive role—it made justice dependent on the authority of written lawtexts. In the days of *Grágás*, chieftains would not have been able to function unless they had been trained from childhood to memorize legal formulas and precedent cases, with which they could control the Allthing proceedings and assert their interests against other chieftains. As we have seen, every legal case was handled as a case of civil litigation, in which neither plaintiff nor defendant could base his arguments on written documents but had to rely on oral tradition merely in order to find out what the law said. No wonder, then, that legal knowledge was often as jealously guarded as a family secret or that genealogies—on which inheritance claims could be based—were carefully memorized.[97] No wonder, either, that the memory of past lawsuits at the Allthing were preserved through several generations within families. The preservation of oral traditions was simply a matter of selfpreservation for the chieftain class, but only as long as written records and lawbooks did not exist. The various redactions of *Landnámabók* made it unnecessary to memorize long lists of ancestors. The systematic learning of oral tradition about legal cases was made superfluous by *Járnsíða* and especially by *Jónsbók*, manuscripts of which were spread to most members of the Allthing during the fourteenth, fifteenth, and sixteenth centuries.

The narrative idiom of oral sagas, once enabling the performer at a *sagnaskemtan* to *selja saman sǫgur* without any help of manuscripts, gradually

97. On the function of legal sources and genealogies, see also the Appendix, 236-248.

sank into oblivion for the same reason that the memorized legal formulas and genealogies were forgotten when they no longer had to be used in order to win a case at the Allthing. As a result of this process, not only the literature but the whole "world" of Icelandic aristocrats changed, for their mode of perception had largely been determined by the action patterns, stock scenes, stock characters, genealogies, and formulas of traditional sagas (just as their concept of law and order had been formed by the formulas and conventions of traditional Allthing meetings).

In *Sturlunga saga*, thirteenth century events are still perceived and depicted according to the old narrative and social conventions, ultimately derived from the Viking Age: men such as Snorri Sturluson or Þorvarðr Þórarinsson move over the pages in structural patterns originally established for earlier saga heroes like Gunnarr and Njáll. In the later *biskupa sǫgur*, annals, and other historical writings of the fourteenth and fifteenth centuries, however, the descendents of these heroes enter a completely different world, much more obviously dependent on foreign and clerical models. It is often impossible to say whether it is the literary conventions or the society itself that has changed the most. Life imitates art as much as art imitates life.

Njála transcends both the old and the new world by combining them in a symbiosis which was possible only within a short period of time and in a particular aristocratic milieu, where the transition from one culture to another was probably felt more strongly than in any other segment of Icelandic society during the thirteenth century.

Appendix
The Problem of Written Sources

1. *KRISTNI ÞÁTTR

It is generally recognized that the Conversion episode in *Njála* contains numerous parallels with other Icelandic accounts of the conversion, especially those preserved in Ari fróði's *Íslendingabók*, the so-called *Kristni saga*, and the so-called *Óláfs saga Tryggvasonar hin mesta*. It is also generally recognized that none of these accounts could have been the direct source of *Njála*. The conclusion scholars have drawn from these two undeniable facts is that the author of *Njála* used a lost source related to the preserved texts. This source is *Kristni þáttr*, supposedly derived from *Íslendingabók* and possibly from a Latin biography of King Olaf Tryggvason which is now also lost but is believed to be an ancestor of both *Kristni saga* and of *Óláfs saga Tryggvasonar hin mesta*.[1]

What is the basis of this theory? Actually, all the accounts of the conversion are rather different, not only in language and style but also in terms of the facts and opinions they present. Although there is a general similarity among the basic facts, there are only a few direct verbal parallels. Any theory about a *manuscript* relationship between the texts must rest on these parallels alone, for the more general similarities could easily be explained by assuming that the authors used the same oral traditions.

Among the verbal parallels, we may on the whole disregard the skaldic verses since these were memorized and transmitted orally without the aid of manuscripts. Thus the occurrence of the same verses in different manu-

---

1. Cf. Sveinsson (1933), 44-49, 67-76; *Njála* (1954), pp. XLIII-XLV.

scripts cannot prove that the manuscripts are related, unless they contain the same scribal errors or other signs of manuscript kinship, and such is *not* the case. Although several verses in the Conversion episode in *Njála* are also quoted in other texts, the versions in *Njála* contain many peculiarities of their own, a fact which suggests that the author recorded the verses independently from oral tradition.

As an example we shall take a famous insulting stanza which one of the Christian Icelanders, Hjalti Skeggjason, is said to have composed against the pagan gods after his conversion. In *Njála* the first lines run:

"Spari ek eigi goð geyja.   ("I don't hesitate to scorn the gods.
Grey þykki mér Freyja."   I think Freyja is a bitch.")

But in all other sources, these lines run as follows:

"*Vil ek* eigi goð geyja.   ("*I don't want* to scorn the gods.
Grey þykki mér Freyja."   I think Freyja is a bitch.")
                                                       (my italics)

In view of such variants, which are typical of oral tradition, we have no right to assume that the author of *Njála* copied his verses from an earlier manuscript. A verse of this sort may well have circulated in somewhat different forms in the oral tradition without any help of manuscripts. On the whole, the variant forms in the *Njála* verses suggest that they may well have been recorded independently from oral tradition.[2]

We must therefore turn to the verbal parallels in the prose. The only ones accepted by Einar Ólafur Sveinsson as conclusive evidence of written influence are those which exist between *Njála* and *Íslendingabók*. The relevant passages are quoted below with the closest parallels italicized:

---

2. The following variant forms may be used to support this view; cf. Konráð Gíslason, "Bemærkninger til kvadene i Njála" in *Njála*, II (1889), 481-519. Numbers refer to stanzas and lines in *Njála* (1954):

6^5 *síðan*. Other versions: *sínu* (or: *sonar*).
7^2 *endils ok boð*. Other versions: *einhendis boð*.
7^5 *at gnýskúta Geitis*. Other versions: *at gnyfeta Geitis* (or: *at geirhriðar gæðir*).
8^1 *Getka ek sumz*. Other versions: *Tekka ek sunds*.
8^2 *sann élboði*. Other versions: *sannreynir boð*.
8^5 *þó at ráfáka rækim*. Other versions: *erat ráfáka rækis*.
11^1 *þunnis*. Other versions: *þvinnils*.
11^3 *búss*. Other versions: *borð* (or: *blakk*).

Occasionally, Einar Ólafur Sveinsson has "corrected" the *Njála* version of the verses by introducing variants from the other texts. In order to see all the differences between the versions, it is necessary to consult Konráð Gíslason, *op. cit.*, which contains all variants in their manuscript forms.

Óláfr rex Tryggvasonr, Óláfssonar, Haraldssonar ens hárfagra kom kristni í Norveg ok á Island. Hann sendi hingat til lands prest þann, es hét Þangbrandr ok hér kenndi mǫnnum kristni ok skírði þá alla, es við trú tóku. En Hallr á Síðu Þorsteinssonr lét skírask snimhendis ok Hjalti Skeggjasonr ýr Þjórsárdali ok Gizurr enn hvíti Teitsson, Ketilbjarnarsonar frá Mosfelli, ok margir hǫfðingjar aðrir; en þeir váru þó fleiri, es í gegn mæltu ok neittu. En þá es hann hafði hér verit einn vetr eða tvá, þá fór hann á braut ok hafði vegit hér tvá menn eða þrjá, þá es hann hǫfðu nítt. En hann sagði konunginum Óláfi, es hann kom austr, allt þat es hér hafði yfir hann gingit, ok lét ørvænt, at hér mundi kristni enn takask. En hann *varð við þat reiðr mjǫk ok ætlaði at láta meiða eða drepa ossa landa fyrir*, þá es þar váru austr. En þat sumar et sama kvómu útan heðan þeir Gizurr ok Hjalti ok *þágu þá undan* við konunginn ok hétu hónum umbsýslu sinni til á nýjaleik, at hér yrði enn við kristninni tekit, ok létu sér eigi annars ván en þar mundi hlýða. En et næsta sumar eptir fóru þeir austan ok prestr sá es Þormóðr hét, ok kvómu þá i Vestmannaeyjar, *es tíu vikur váru af sumri*, ok hafði allt farizk vel at. Svá kvað Teitr þann segja, es sjalfr vas þar. Þá vas þat mælt et næsta sumar áðr í lǫgum, at menn skyldi svá koma til alþingis, es tíu vikur væri af sumri, en þangat til kvómu viku fyrr. En þeir fóru þegar inn til meginlands ok síðan til alþingis ok gátu at Hjalta, at hann vas eptir í Laugardali með tolfta mann, af því at hann hafði áðr *sekr orðit* fjǫrbaugsmaðr et næsta sumar á alþingi *of goðgá*. En þat vas til þess haft, at hann *kvað* at lǫgbergi *kviðling þenna:*
Vil ek eigi goð geyja,
grey þykki mér Freyja.

Þat spurðisk . . . , at siðaskipti varð í Nóregi, ok hǫfðu þeir kastat inum forna átrúnaði, en konungr hafði kristnat Vestrlǫnd . . . (255) Þangbrandr var sendr út hingat af Óláfi konungi Tryggvasyni at boða trú . . .(256) Tók Hallr þá skírn ok ǫll hjú hans. Um várit eptir fór Þangbrandr at boða trú ok Hallr með honum . . . (257-58)

. . . fór Þangbrandr utan . . . (269) Þangbrandr sagði Óláfi konungi frá meingerðum Íslendinga við sik . . . (269)

Þá *varð Óláfr konungr svá reiðr* at hann lét taka alla íslenzka menn ok setja í myrkvastofu ok *ætlaði þá til dráps*. Þá gengu þeir Gizurr hvíti at ok Hjalti ok buðu at leggja sik í veð fyrir þessa menn ok fara út til Íslands at boða trú; konungr tók þessu vel, ok *þágu þeir alla þá undan*. Þá bjoggu þeir Gizurr ok Hjalti skip sitt til Íslands ok urðu snemmbúnir; þeir tóku land á Eyrum, *er tíu vikur váru af sumri*. Fengu þeir sér þá þegar hesta, en menn til at ryðja skip. Ríða þeir þá þrír tigir manna til þings ok gerðu þá orð kristnum mǫnnum, at við búnir skyldi vera. (269-70)

Hjalti var eptir at Reyðarmúla, því at hann hafði spurt, at hann var *sekr orðinn um goðgá.* (270)

Hjalti Skeggjason *kvað kviðling þenna:*
Spari ek eigi goð geyja!
Grey þykki mér Freyja;
æ mun annat tveggja

En þeir Gizurr fóru, unz þeir kvómu
í stað þann í hjá Ǫlfossvatni, es kal-
laðr es *Vellankatla*, ok gørðu orð
þaðan til þings, at á mót þeim skyldi
koma allir fulltingsmenn þeira, af því
at þeir hǫfðu spurt, at andskotar
þeira vildi verja þeim vígi þingvǫl-
linn. En fyrr en þeir fœri þaðan, þá
kom þar ríðandi Hjalti ok þeir es
eptir váru með hónum. *En síðan riðu
þeir á þingit*, ok kvómu áðr á mót
þeim frændr þeira ok vinir sem þeir
hǫfðu æst. En enir heiðnu menn
hurfu saman með alvæpni, ok *hafði
svá nær, at þeir myndi berjask*, at
(eigi) of sá á miðli. En annan dag
eptir gingu þeir Gizurr ok Hjalti til
lǫgbergs ok báru þar up erendi sín.
En svá es sagt, at þat bæri frá, hvé
vel þeir mæltu. En þat gørðisk af
því, at þar *nefndi annarr maðr at
ǫðrum vátta, ok sǫgðusk hvárir ýr
lǫgum við aðra*, enir kristnu menn ok
enir heiðnu, ok gingu síðan frá lǫgbergi. Þá báðu enir kristnu menn
Hall á Síðu, at hann skyldi lǫg þeira
upp segja, þau es kristninni skyldi
fylgja. En hann leystisk því undan
við þá, at hann keypti at Þorgeiri
lǫgsǫgumanni, at hann skyldi upp
segja, *en hann vas enn þá heiðinn*. En
síðan es menn kvómu í búðir, þá
lagðisk hann niðr Þorgeirr ok breiddi
feld sinn á sik ok hvíldi þann dag
allan ok nóttina eptir ok kvað ekki
orð. En of morguninn eptir settisk
hann upp ok gørði orð, at menn skyldi
ganga til lǫgbergis. En þá hóf hann
tǫlu sína upp, es menn kvómu þar,
ok sagði, at hónum *þótti þá komit
hag manna í ónýtt efni, ef menn skyldi
eigi hafa allir lǫg ein* á landi hér, ok
talði fyrir mǫnnum á marga vega, at
þat skyldi eigi láta verða, ok sagði,
at þat mundi at því ósætti verða, es
vísa ván vas, at þær barsmíðir gørðisk
á miðli manna, es landit eyddisk af.
Hann sagði frá því, at konungar ýr
Norvegi ok ýr Danmǫrku hǫfðu haft

Óðinn grey eða Freyja. (264)
En þá er þeir kómu í *Vellandkǫtlu*
ofan frá Gjábakka, þá kom Hjalti
þar eptir þeim ok kvazk eigi vilja
sýna þat heiðnum mǫnnum, at hann
hræddisk þá. (270)

Riðu þá kristnir menn margir í móti
þeim, *ok riðu þeir með fylkingu mikil-
li á þing*. Heiðnir menn hǫfðu ok
fylkt fyrir, *ok var þá svá nær, at allr
þingheimr mundi berjask*, en þat varð
þó eigi. (270) Kristnir menn tjǫldudu
búðir sínar, ok váru þeir Gizurr ok
Hjalti í Mosfellingabúð. Um daginn
eptir gengu hvárirtveggju til lǫgbergs,
*ok nefndu hvárir vátta, kristnir menn
ok heiðnir, ok sǫgðusk hvárir ór lǫgum
annarra*, ok varð þá svá mikit óhljóð
at lǫgbergi, at engi nam annars máls.
Síðan gengu menn í braut, ok þótti
ǫllum horfa til inna mestu óefna.
Kristnir menn tóku sér till lǫgsǫgu-
manns Hall af Síðu, en Hallr fór at
finna Þorgeir goða frá Ljósavatni ok
gaf honum til þrjár merkr silfrs, at
hann segði upp lǫgin, en þat var þó
ábyrgðarráð, *því at hann var heiðinn*.
Þorgeirr lá svá dag allan, at hann
breiddi feld á hǫfuð sér, ok mælti
engi maðr við hann. En annan dag
gengu menn til lǫgbergs; þá beiddi
Þorgeirr sér hljóðs ok mælti:

"Svá *lízk mér sem málum várum sé
komit í ónýtt efni, ef eigi hafa ein lǫg
allir.*

ófrið ok orrostur á miðli sín langa tíð, til þess unz landsmenn gørðu frið á miðli þeira, þótt þeir vildi eigi. En þat ráð gørðisk svá, at af stundu sendusk þeir gersemar á miðli, enda helt friðr sá, meðan þeir lifðu. "En nú þykkir mér þat ráð," kvað hann, "at vér látim ok eigi þá ráða, es mest vilja í gegn gangask, ok miðlum svá mál á miðli þeira, at hvárirtveggju hafi nakkvat síns máls, ok hǫfum allir ein lǫg ok einn sið. Þat mon verða satt, *es vér slítum í sundr lǫgin, at vér monum slíta ok friðinn.*" En hann lauk svá máli sínu, at hvárirtveggju *játtu því, at allir skyldi ein lǫg hafa, þau sem hann réði upp at segja.* Þá vas þat mælt í lǫgum, at allir menn skyldi kristnir vesa ok skírn taka, þeir es áðr váru óskírðir á landi hér; en of barnaútburð skyldu standa en fornu lǫg ok of hrossakjǫtsát. Skyldu menn blóta á laun, ef vildu, en varða fjǫrbaugsgarðr, ef váttum of kvæmi við. En síðarr fám vetrum *vas sú heiðni af numin sem ǫnnur.* (*Íslendingabók*, ed. Jakob Benediktsson, 1968, chapter 7, pp. 14-17)

en ef sundr skipt er lǫgunum, þá mun ok sundr skipt friðinum, ok mun eigi við þat mega búa. Nú vil ek þess spyrja heiðna menn ok kristna, hvárt þeir vilja hafa lǫg þau, er ek segi upp." *Því játuðu allir.* Hann kvazk vilja hafa svardaga af þeim ok festu at halda. Þeir játuðu því, ok tók hann af þeim festu. "Þat er upphaf laga várra," sagði hann, "at menn skulu allir vera kristnir hér á landi ok trúa á einn guð, fǫður ok son ok anda helgan, en láta af allri skurðgoðavillu, bera eigi út bǫrn ok eta eigi hrossaslátr; skal fjǫrbaugssǫk á vera, ef víst verðr, en ef leynilega er með farit, þá skal vera vítislaust." *En þessi heiðni var ǫll af numin fám vetrum síðar.* (271-72) (*Njála*, 1954, chapters 100-105)

The factual differences between these two accounts are comparatively slight, the most important one being that exposure of children and the eating of horse-meat were prohibited at the conversion according to *Njála*, whereas *Íslendingabók* claims that these pagan customs were allowed for some years afterwards. On the whole, however, the texts agree remarkably well, even in details, so that we must assume that there is some kinship between them.

On the other hand, there are only a few really striking verbal parallels, the most important ones being the following:

1. the statement that Gizurr and Hjalti landed in Iceland *er tíu vikur váru af sumri.*

2. the phrase used to describe the split between the Christians and the Pagans at the Allthing: *sǫgðusk hvárir úr lǫgum annarra (við aðra).*

3. Some of the expressions used in Þorgeirr's speech at the Allthing: *komit í ónýtt efni, ein lǫg allir,* and, most particularly, the proverbial saying

concerning the relationship between law-breaking and peace-breaking, although this saying is given in slightly divergent forms: *slíta sundr lǫgin* vs. *skipta sundr lǫgunum.*

The occurrence of these phrases in both accounts cannot be coincidental, but it does not necessarily indicate a manuscript kinship. We are dealing here with expressions that could easily have been preserved in oral transmission. The conversion of Iceland was, after all, considered to be one of the most important events in the history of the country. Stories about the major Allthing meeting and about Þorgeirr's speech were probably told over and over again during the twelfth and thirteenth centuries, constantly circulated by the priests and carefully remembered by the faithful. Under such circumstances, it would not be very surprising to find two writers giving closely similar versions of the event on the basis of oral tradition alone.

Such an explanation of the relationship between the two texts actually is much simpler than the current one; it accounts for the differences as well as the similarities without having to make complicated assumptions about lost manuscript versions, editorial changes, and so forth. There are other possible explanations: the author of *Njála* may, for example, have heard or read *Íslendingabók*, or a similar source, and remembered phrases from it as he was writing his own account of the conversion. But the parallels from *Íslendingabók* do not permit the conclusion that our author was working with a lost *Kristni þáttr*, or any other manuscript, before his eyes.

Arguments derived from the parallels with other accounts, such as *Kristni saga* and *Óláfs saga Tryggvasonar*, must be even more inconclusive, for these texts are generally admitted to be much less similar to *Njála*. The case for a lost written *Kristni þáttr* would thus have to rest on the intrinsic evidence of *Njála* itself.

According to Einar Ólafur Sveinsson, the Conversion episode is written in a style different from the rest of *Njála*. It is "dryer" and more concise; it does not dwell as much on dramatic incidents and characterization; it is also more Christian and "clerical" in its outlook. "It is a clerical chronicle, not a 'drama' such as *Njála*" (*hann er klerklegt sagnfræðirit, ekki 'sjónleikur' eins og Njála*).[3]

Although this comparison may seem to contain an element of truth, there are several other passages in *Njála* that are just as "dry" and just as "clerical," even though they are generally recognized as composed by the author himself. The story about the Battle at the Allthing, for example, is full of dry enumerations, and the same is true of several introductory genealogies, legalistic accounts of lawsuits, and so on. And, as Einar Ólafur Sveinsson

3. Sveinsson (1933), 68.

himself has pointed out, religious rhetoric also occurs elsewhere, notably near the end of the saga and in the story of Njáll's death. It would be natural for the author to sound more religious than usual when speaking of the conversion of his country. And the "dryness," as we have already seen, can be explained by assuming that the author felt a responsibility to provide historical information for his audience, even when there were no artistic reasons for it. The "dryness" may indicate that he is doing just as much as can be expected from him and no more.

In a few instances, the Conversion episode provides information provided elsewhere in the saga, so that the reader is introduced twice to the same facts: the seaport Gautavík, for example, is presented as if the reader had never heard of it, although it was mentioned several chapters earlier.[4] Such minor irregularities have been used as evidence that the author of *Njála* transcribed his source for the conversion without thinking of fitting it properly into his own account. But there are numerous examples of the same thing in other sections of *Njála*: characters are, in fact, often introduced several times.[5] The simplest explanations are that the author slipped unconsciously or that he wanted to make it easier for his audience by reminding them of matters already mentioned. The usefulness of such reminders should be obvious to any reader of the saga.

One single expression has been used by Einar Ólafur Sveinsson as *linguistic* evidence that the Conversion episode was written by someone other than the author of *Njála*. This is the phrase *þar sem heitir*, used once in reference to Gautavík, where the Christian missionaries are said to have landed: *þetta it sama haust kom skip út austr í Fjǫrðum í Berufirði, þar sem heitir Gautavík*. The phrase is thought to be characteristic of "clerical" style. Sveinsson cites a few parallels from other texts: *vatn þat er Lagarfljót heitir*; *fjalli því, er Gerpir heitir*, and so on.[6]

Quite apart from the fact that *one* such expression does not constitute very strong evidence, the examples are not analogous. In the Conversion episode, the phrase *þar sem heitir* is not merely introductory; it specifies previously given information about the locality. The author is, in other words, not just saying that the ship landed at a place called Gautavík but *in that part of Berufjord* which is called Gautavík. How could he have expressed this thought in a more natural way? As Sveinsson himself observed

4. Cf. Sveinsson, *Njála* (1954), 256 (note 1).

5. See, for example, the introductions of Runólfr Úlfsson (chapters 34 and 52), Mǫrðr Valgarðsson (chapters 25 and 46), Þórhallr Ásgrímsson (chapters 26-27, 109).

6. Sveinsson (1933), 69-70.

after the writing of his dissertation,[7] there is a close parallel in chapter 10 of *Njála*, a chapter obviously not derived from a lost *Kristni þáttr: hann bjó í Bjarnarfirði á bæ þeim, er heitir á Svanshóli* (32), i.e., "he lived in Bjarnarfjord, *on that farm which* is called Svanshóll." Therefore the phrase *þar sem heitir* cannot be regarded as indicative of "clerical language," much less of a lost *Kristni þáttr*.

In chapter 101 (a part of the Conversion episode), the author refers to a certain Glúmr, "who went to the burning with Flosi" (*er fór til brennu med Flosa*, 258). This phrase is also regarded by Sveinsson as derived from the lost *Kristni þáttr* because it does not seem to fit into the immediate context but anticipates later events in a way which, according to Sveinsson, is abnormal in *Njála*.[8] But, as Maxwell has pointed out,[9] there is a close parallel in chapter 96, in which we hear of a Kolr Þorsteinsson, "whom Kári will kill in Wales" (*er Kári vegr í Bretlandi*, 251). As we have seen, anticipation of this sort is rather typical of the saga (cf. above, p. 199), and the very phrase about Glúmr "who went to the burning with Flosi" was used by Bååth as evidence that the Conversion episode was indeed an integral part of *Njála*.[10]

In chapter 104 (another part of the Conversion episode), we are told that the chieftains Gizurr and Hjalti travelled from Norway to Iceland and landed "at Eyrar" (*á Eyrum*, 269). According to Brenner and Einar Ólafur Sveinsson, the phrase *á Eyrum* is a mistranscription of *á Eyjum*, i.e., "at Vestmannaeyjar," where Ari says that they landed (cf. the quotation from *Íslendingabók* above, p. 217). The lost *Kristni þáttr* is supposed to have contained the correct form.[11] Maxwell, however, rightly observed that "it would seem strange to maroon them on Vestmannaeyjar when nothing is said of their doings there, and there was no reason to land them east of Eyrar if the trouble with Rúnólf Úlfsson's thingmen was not to be mentioned."[12] It might be added that Eyrar is mentioned as an important landing place in other parts of the saga, and there is even one parallel close enough to suggest that it was indeed written and composed by the same man who wrote about Gizurr's and Hjalti's arrival:

7. Cf. *Njála* (1954), p. XLIV (note 1).

8. "Eflaust er þessi setning teking af vangá eftir hinni gömlu heimild, en ekki fer vel á henni í Njálu, og ekki er þar vant að segja um ókomna atburði á þennan hátt," Sveinsson, *Njála* (1954), XLV.

9. Maxwell (1957), 35, note 7.

10. "Ett bevis på, att afdelningen *i detalj* står i samband med det följande," Bååth (1885), 146 (note).

11. Cf. Brenner (1878), 113-114; Sveinsson (1933), 70; Sveinsson, *Njála* (1954), 269, note 6.

12. Maxwell (1957), *loc. cit.*

Þá *bjoggu* þeir Gizurr ok Hjalti skip sitt *til Íslands* ok urðu *snemmbúnir*; þeir tóku land *á Eyrum*

(269)

Þat sumar *bjoggusk* þeir Kári ok Njálssynir *til Íslands*. Ok þá er þeir váru *albúnir*, gengu þeir á fund jarls ... Láta þeir nú í haf, þeir hafa útivistir skammar, ok gaf þeim vel byri, ok kómu *við Eyrar*.

(225)

Other parallels show that Gizurr and Hjalti are simply following the conventional pattern for travelers set down by the author of *Njála*.[13]

It may seem surprising that the arguments so far examined constitute all the major evidence in favor of a lost *Kristni þáttr*. The fact that this evidence is negligible does not, of course, exclude the remote possibility that such a source did exist. But the similarities between the Conversion episode and other sections of *Njála* suggest that all were written and composed by the same man.

Although Einar Ólafur Sveinsson tends to dismiss such similarities as insignificant,[14] he himself has admitted that the author of the saga has put his own stamp on the Conversion episode, at least in passages where the main characters are mentioned, since he tends to regard such passages as additions to the material borrowed from the lost *Kristni þáttr*.[15] If we look a little closer, however, the Conversion episode can be shown to contain many formulas, phrases, and narrative patterns that are also found in other parts of *Njála*. (In the examples below, page references to the Conversion episode are introduced by a capital C; page references to parallels from other sections of the saga are introduced by a capital P.)

Þangbrandr's journey around Iceland to gain support for the Christian faith (chapters 100-103) follows the same pattern as Flosi's journey to gain support for the Burners after the death of Njáll (chapter 134; cf. above p. 50). In both cases the visitor is preparing for a confrontation with his adversaries at the Allthing. Each stage in his journey is meticulously reported in the same stereotyped fashion: *Þaðan fóru þeir til* (placename). *Þar bjó* (name, often followed by a genealogy; see especially C:258f., P:349f.). The result of the mission is briefly indicated through an ap-

---

13. Examples: "Þeir Kári létu út hálfum mánaði síðar *af Eyrum*" (439), "Þráinn Sigfússon *bjó þá skip sitt til Íslands* ok var þá mjǫk *albúinn*" (214), "Um sumarit eptir *bjósk* Kári *til Íslands* . . . þeir *urðu heldr síðbúnir*; sigldu i haf. Þeir hǫfðu langa útivist, en um síðir *tóku þeir* Ingólfshǫfða" (462). My italics indicate phrases which are similar in form, content, and context to expressions in the sentence about Gizurr and Hjalti quoted above; see also Chapter V, note 66.

14. "En þetta eru ekki nema smámunir, og ef spurt er, hve vandlega *Krþ sé fylgt i sögunni, þá hlýtur svarið að verða: allvandlega," (1933), 68.

15. Cf. Sveinsson (1933), *loc. cit.*; Sveinsson (1954), p. XLIV.

propriate formula: *Þeir hǫfðu þar góðar viðtǫkur; hann tók við trú, hét at fylgja þeim á þingi*, etc. In some cases, however, when the visit is especially important, the conversation is quoted in full, and the formal promise of support is specifically emphasized: *"Því mun ek heita,"* segir Þangbrandr (C:257), *"Þetta er vel mælt,"* segir Gestr, *"ok mun ek þessu játa"* (C:268). *Því mun ek heita þér"* (P:350) *"mun ek gera þér um vinveitt ok ríða til þings ok veita þér sem ek munda bróður mínum"* (P:352). The visitor's gratitude at the generosity of his host is reported in the same conventional way: *Þangbrandr þakkaði honum* (C:257); *Flosi þakkaði honum* (P:350, 3 times; 353). At the parting, the host gives presents to his guests, a ceremony also described with conventional formulas: *gaf Gestr Þangbrandi góðar gjafir* (C:269),[16] *gaf Njáll honum góðar gjafir* (C:269); *Þorkell gaf Flosa góðar gjafir* (P:353), *Hólmsteinn gaf Flosa góðar gjafir* (P:353), *Hallr gaf honum góðar gjafir* (P:353).

The Thing meeting which concludes the Conversion episode (chapter 105) follows the pattern of other major Thing meetings in *Njála*. Just before the meeting, we are introduced to an important chieftain, Þorgeirr, who will be the decisive figure in the upcoming dispute (cf. the introduction of Eyjólfr Bǫlverksson, P:363; of Síðu-Hallr, P:239; of Snorri goði, P:286). We then hear about the arrival of the feuding parties at the Allthing, where they put up their booths—an act reported with the oft-repeated formula *tjǫlduðu búðir sínar* (C:271; cf. P:141, 297, 359). On the following day, the parties walk to the "hill of law" (*Lǫgberg*) and "name their witnesses"—another stereotyped action in stereotyped phrases: *Um dagin eptir gengu hvárirtveggju til lǫgbergs, ok nefndu hvárir vátta* (C:271; cf., for example, *Ein hvern dag, er menn gengu til lǫgbergs nefndi Mǫrðr sér vátta*, P:27; *Nú ganga menn til lǫgbergs .... nefndu sér vátta*, P:142-43; *Þat var einn dag, er menn gengu til lǫgbergs .... Mǫrðr nefndi sér vátta*, P:374). When the two parties cannot settle their dispute, the whole case is entrusted to Þorgeirr, who then makes his impressive speech. Although this speech in *Njála* has much in common with the one in *Íslendingabók* (cf. above, p. 218-219), it is in part even closer to certain speeches by Njáll, delivered in similar situations at other Thing meetings in our saga:

---

16. *Reykjabók* seems to have the variant *gjafar* for *gjafir* at this point, a reading which Sveinsson accepts as the main text and notes as an example of differences between the Conversion episode and the rest of the saga (1954, note 2). But *Möðruvallabók*, the second main manuscript, has *gjafir*. It seems to me impossible to decide whether the author of *Njála* himself used *gjafir* or *gjafar*, since variants of this sort are easily interchangeable in the manuscripts. They certainly do not provide any evidence in favor of a lost *Kristni þáttr*.

Þá beiddi Þorgeirr sér hljóðs ok mælti: "Svá lízk mér sem málum várum
sé komit í ónýtt efni"
(C:271)

Hann (Njáll) mælti: "Svá sýnisk mér
sem þetta mál sé komit í ónýtt efni"
(P:309)
Þá mælti Njáll: ". . . mér þykkir sem
málum várum sé komit í ónýtt efni"
(P:242)

We may continue in this way to point out verbal parallels between the
Conversion episode and the rest of *Njála*. Some of them are listed below:

1) "Ok ætla ek ekki," segir hann,
"at vera ginningarfífl hans"
(C:263-64)

"ok mun ek ekki vera eggjunarfífl
þitt" (P:91)
"engi maðr þarf sér þat at ætla at
hafa hann at ginnungarfífli" (P:367)

The words *ginningarfífl* and *eggjunarfífl* seem to be very rare in Old
Norse literature and can thus be said to be characteristic of *Njála*.

2) hann komsk í skotfæri við hann
(C:260)

"munt þú komask í skotfæri við
Þorgeir" (P:177)

The expression *komask í skotfæri* also seems to be fairly uncommon.

3) Guðleifr var vígamaðr mikill ok
manna rǫskvastr ok harðgǫrr í ǫllu
(C:256)

Ragi var vígamaðr mikill (P:41)
Manna kurteisastr var hann, harðgǫrr
í ǫllu (P:53) Þórhallr var rǫskr maðr
ok harðgǫrr í ǫllu (P:279)

There are common clichés in the traditional "presentation segments" of
the sagas, but that they are employed in the Conversion episode speaks
against Einar Ólafur Sveinsson's contention about its "clerical" style.

4) ok var þá svá nær, at allr þingheimr mundi berjask, en þat varð þó
eigi (ekki). (C:270)

ok ætluðu allir, at þeir myndi tala
um mál sín, en þat varð ekki (eigi).
(P:27)

In this case, the two passages are strikingly similar, more in their narrative
technique then in the wording *per se*. Andreas Heusler observed this parallel years ago and found it indicative of the author's style.[17]

If we had to assume that the Conversion episode was transcribed from a
lost written source, we could presumably explain such parallels by the further
assumption that the author of *Njála* had been influenced by the style and
language of his source. Or we could assume that the author of *Njála* and
the author of the lost source belonged to the same literary tradition, the
same area in Iceland, or something along these lines. But nothing prompts
us to make any such assumption. The Conversion episode appears to be
an integral part of the saga as a whole, whether it is analyzed from a literary,

17. Cf. Heusler (1914), 229 (note); Sveinsson (1933), 68.

ideological, or linguistic point of view. The simplest and by far the most satisfactory explanation of this fact is that the author of *Njála* composed the episode entirely on his own.

2. *BRJÁNS SAGA

Let us now turn to the Clontarf episode and its presumed dependency on a lost *Brjáns saga*. No such source is mentioned in *Njála* itself, but there may be an obscure reference to it in *Þorsteins saga Síðu-Hallssonar*, which describes the Battle of Clontarf in a way reminiscent of our saga. The hero of *Þorsteins saga*, Þorsteinn Síðu-Hallsson (who appears in *Njála*), has offered his services to Earl Sigurðr of Orkney. In this context, the following passage occurs:

Jarl þakkaði honum orð sín. Þeir fóru síðan til Írlands ok borðusk við Brján konung, ok urðu þar morg tíðendi senn, *sem segir í sogu hans*.[18]
(The Earl thanked him for his words. Then they went to Ireland and fought against King Brján, and there many remarkable things happened afterwards, *as it is said in his saga*.)

It is difficult to ascertain the precise meaning of the phrase *sem segir í sogu hans*. It may seem natural to interpret it as a reference to a written *Brjáns saga*, but it may also refer to an oral tale about this king. As Jón Jóhannesson has pointed out,[19] the words may also refer to a saga about Earl Sigurðr, who appears in the preceding sentence; this saga may of course also have been either written or oral. There is finally a possibility that the author is thinking of the story about King Brjánn and Earl Sigurðr which has been preserved in *Njála* itself, i.e., the Clontarf episode.[20] This last possibility must be seriously considered in view of the fact that there is an explicit reference to *Njála* only a few sentences earlier in *Þorsteins saga*:

Þetta haust kom Brennu-Flosi til Orkneyja ok hans menn, ok fóru skipti þeira Sigurðar jarls *sem segir í Njáls sogu*.[21]

(This fall Brennu-Flosi and his men came to Orkney, and they had such dealings with Earl Sigurðr *as it is said in Njáls saga*.)

---

18. *Austfirðinga sogur*, ed. Jón Jóhannesson (*Íslenzk Fornrit*, 11, 1950), 301 (my italics).
19. Jón Jóhannesson (1950), pp. CI-CVIII.
20. This was suggested as early as 1900 by Finnur Jónsson (*Litt.-hist.*, II, 762). Later, however, he became convinced by Bugge's arguments (Bugge, 1901, 52 f.) that the words probably referred to a lost *Brjáns saga*, even though he did not consider his old theory obsolete, cf. Finnur Jónsson (1904), 160: ". . . skönt jeg ikke betragter min tidligere mening som modbevist, at Þorst. s. beror på Njála, men da i en ældre skikkelse."
21. *Austfirðinga sogur*, 300 (my italics).

Although Carolsfeld and Jón Jóhannesson believed this sentence to be interpolated, the manuscripts do not provide any evidence of such interpolation, and the passage has therefore been accepted as genuine by most scholars, including Finnur Jónsson and Einar Ólafur Sveinsson.[22] The date of *Þorsteins saga* is uncertain (its manuscripts date from the seventeenth century) but it seems evident that it was written when *Njála* was already well known among Icelanders. We thus have to assume that the author of *Þorsteins saga* knew both Earl Sigurðr and King Brjánn from our still extant Clontarf episode. It would then seem completely unnecessary for him to refer to still another source—and a very obscure one at that—for additional information about their famous battle. A second reference to Njála would be quite enough. The phrase *sem segir í sǫgu hans* may, in fact, be interpreted as such a reference, viz., "as it is said in the story about him told in *Njáls saga.*" But I will readily admit that there are alternatives to this comparatively simple solution.

It is obvious that the ambiguous reference to *sǫgu hans* cannot in itself constitute strong evidence that a written *Brjáns saga* ever existed. We must examine the textual relationship between *Þorsteins saga* and *Njála*, both of which are assumed to have derived at least certain parts of their account independently from this lost source.[23] I quote the relevant passages on which this assumption is based:

Þorsteins saga:

Þar fellu þrír merkismenn jarls, ok þá *bað jarl Þorstein bera merkit.* Þorsteinn svarar: *"Ber sjálfr krák þinn, jarl!"* Þá mælti einn maðr: "Vel gerðir þú, Þorsteinn, því at af því hefi ek misst þrjá sonu mína." *Jarl tók merkit af stǫnginni ok lét koma milli klæða sér* ok barðisk alldjarfliga. Litlu síðar heyrðu þeir mælt í loptinu: "Ef Sigurðr jarl vill sigr hafa, þá sœki hann á Dumazbakka með lið sitt." Þorsteinn fylgdi jafnan jarli, ok svá var þá. Þar fell jarl í þeiri atlǫgu, ok dreifðusk þá víða liðsmenn. Ok í þessu drap Bróðir Brján konung. Óspakr, bróðir hans, tók hann, ok *hleypðu út þǫrmunum ok leiddu hann of eik eina.* Þá urðu mǫrg tíðendi senn

Njála:

Sigurðr jarl bað Þorstein Hallsson bera merkit. Þorsteinn ætlaði upp at taka merkit. Þá mælti Ámundi hvíti: "Þú skalt eigi bera merkit," segir hann, "því at allir eru drepnir, þeir er bera." "Hrafn inn rauði," sagði jarl, "ber þú merkit!" Hrafn svaraði: *"Ber þú sjálfr fjanda þinn."* Jarl segir: "Þat mun vera makligast, at allt fari saman, karl ok kýll." *Tók hann síðan merkit af stǫnginni ok kom í millum klæða sinna.* Litlu síðar var veginn Ámundi hvíti. Þá var ok jarl skotinn spjóti í gegnum. Óspakr hafði gengit of allan fylkingararminn; var hann orðinn sárr mjǫk, en látit sonu Brjáns báða áðr. Sigtryggr konungr flýði fyrir honum.

22. Cf. Lehmann-Carolsfeld (1883), 164-65; Jón Jóhannesson (1950), pp. CI-CII; Finnur Jónsson (1904), 158-60; Sveinsson (1933), 77.

23. See especially Bugge (1901), 52 f.; Sveinsson (1933), 77 f.; Goedheer (1938), 87 f.

í mannalátum. Þorsteinn ok þeir nǫkkurir saman námu stað við skóginn. Þá mælti einn maðr: "Hví flýr þú eigi, Þorsteinn?" Hann svarar: "Því at ek tek eigi heim í kveld, þó at ek flýja." Þorsteini váru grið gefin, ok fór hann aptr til Orkneyja ok þaðan til Nóregs ok kom til hirðar Magnúss konungs Óláfssonar.[24]

Brast þá flótti í ǫllu liðinu. Þorsteinn Hallsson nam staðar, þá er aðrir flýðu, ok batt skóþveng sinn. Þá spurði Kerþjálfaðr, hví hann rynni eigi. "Því," sagði Þorsteinn, "at ek tek eigi heim í kveld, þar sem ek á heima út á Íslandi." Kerþjálfaðr gaf honum grið. (451-52)
. . . var þá Bróðir hǫndum tekinn. Úlfr hræða reist á honum kviðinn ok leiddi hann um eik ok rakti svá ór honum þarmana; dó hann eigi fyrr en allir váru ór honum raktir. (453)

The two versions have some fairly striking parallels (italicized above), but the differences between them are even more striking. The events are not told in the same order, and the details are the same only to a limited extent. Words ascribed to Þorsteinn in Þorsteins saga are ascribed to Hrafn the Red in Njála. The gruesome killing of Bróðir is attributed to Óspakr in Þorsteins saga but to Úlfr hræða in Njála. Furthermore, each of the sagas contains material which the other does not have: for example, the strange prophecy about "Dumazbakki" in Þorsteins saga, and the information concerning Ámundi, Hrafn, Óspakr, Sigtryggr, and Kerþjálfaðr in Njála. Not even the italicized passages have exact equivalents in the other text; there are little variations in wording at almost every point (krák þinn vs. fjanda þinn, Jarl tók merkit vs. Tók hann síðan merkit, milli klæða sér vs. í millum klæða sinna, etc.).

Whereas the similarities have been used as evidence of a close textual kinship, some of the differences have been used to show that the account in Þorsteins saga cannot be derived from Njála alone but must be derived independently from *Brjáns saga; certain differences have also been explained as a result of conscious adaptation of this lost source by the author of Þorsteins saga, the author of Njála, or by both of them.[25]

This whole argument (which is further complicated by the fact that the author of Þorsteins saga also knew Njála) falls entirely to pieces, however, as soon as we admit the possibility that texts may be related in ways other than by means of copying from one manuscript to another. In the case of the Conversion episode, we could find at least some parallels with other texts, enough to make the theory of written sources fairly plausible. In this case, the versions are so dissimilar that the most natural way to explain their few similarities would be to assume that they had both independently made

24. Austfirðinga sǫgur, 301-02.
25. See especially Sveinsson (1933), 78-86; Jón Jóhannesson (1950), pp. CI-CVIII.

use of oral tradition—if it were not for the fact that the author of *Þorsteins saga* explicitly refers to *Njála*! Under these circumstances, we must consider the possibility that the version in *Þorsteins saga* may depend on a vague and confused memory of our still extant Clontarf episode, which may have been transmitted by means of several oral intermediaries and may even have acquired some new details during the process.

A theory of this kind would explain most of the similarities as well as the differences between the two texts. While the Clontarf episode in *Njála* is long and elaborate, the corresponding section in *Þorsteins saga* is brief and unprecise; most of its details also appear in *Njála*, but in a less vague and generalised form. Where *Njála* speaks of Ámundi hvíti and Kerþjálfaðr, for example, *Þorsteins saga* speaks of "a man" in general; where *Njála* speaks of two men, Óspakr and Úlfr hræða, *Þorsteins saga* speaks only of one, Óspakr, but features him in the role which *Njála* reserves for the other one—and so on. This is exactly the kind of simplification that so easily results from lapses of memory and unconscious adaptation when a story is transmitted without any help of writing material.[26] If, on the other hand, we try to explain all the differences as a result of *conscious* adaptation during the written transmission, we are immediately confronted with problems in finding tenable motivations for these changes. Why would anybody want to change all these apparently irrelevant little details? Why would anybody strive to make all these needless little variants in facts and wording and in the order of events? These are questions that have never been answered by the proponents of the theory about **Brjáns saga*.

The only detail in the Clontarf version of *Þorsteins saga* which could not possibly have been derived from our still extant *Njála* version is the curious incident involving *Dumazbakki* (cf. above, p. 227). According to Sophus Bugge, the name *Dumazbakki* comes from an Irish word meaning "grave-hill," and its spelling in Icelandic may indicate that it was taken over from an Irish-Norwegian source written in the neighborhood of Dublin in the eleventh century.[27] Few if any scholars have been convinced by this argument, but they have nevertheless felt that the story of *Dumazbakki* forms part of an old tradition, dating from the time of the battle and transmitted to *Þorsteins saga* by way of *Brjáns saga*.[28]

It is indeed likely that the story was old and traditional, but there is no reason to believe that it was ever written in its present form before the

26. For general studies of the transformational laws of oral tradition, see, for example, Alan Dundes (ed.) *The Study of Folklore* (Englewood Cliffs, N. J., 1965), 243 ff.

27. Bugge (1901), 60-64.

28. Cf. Goedheer, 1938, 95 (note); J. Ryans, "The Battle of Clontarf," *Journal of the Royal Society of Antiquaries of Ireland* (1938), 35 f.; Jón Jóhannesson (1950), p. CIII.

writing of *Þorsteins saga*. Bugge's argument about the spelling is unconvincing, and his theory about the Irish-Norwegian eleventh century source is somewhat surprising in view of the fact that no such sources are known to have existed at any time; in Norway and Iceland sagas were not written until the end of the twelfth century.[29] *If* the sagas preserve any genuine Irish-Norwegian traditions from the eleventh century, they must consequently have been transmitted orally, probably by way of Orkney, where people in the twelfth and thirteenth centuries still seem to have remembered Earl Sigurðr and his fight against the Irish.

As Bugge himself has pointed out,[30] there is an obvious parallel to the *Dumazbakki* incident in *Njála*, where Earl Sigurðr is seen riding into a hill right after his death in the battle. This looks like another version of the same oral tale. If this is so, it is unlikely that *both* versions were directly transcribed from a lost *Brjáns saga*. It seems more likely that the author of *Þorsteins saga* derived the *Dumazbakki* detail from an oral tradition which he used to complement the information received from *Njála*. There is also the possibility, however, that this detail was included in an earlier version of *Njála* itself. The critics have noted that our present *Njála* text in the Clontarf episode seems abbreviated, so that certain details—including the one about Earl Sigurðr riding into a hill—have become almost completely incomprehensible. According to Einar Ólafur Sveinsson, the abbreviations were made in the text of *Brjáns saga* by the author of *Njála*.[31] But it is also possible, and perhaps more likely, that they were made by a scribe at an early stage in the transmission of *Njála* itself. As a matter of fact, there are other indications that the last chapters of *Njála*—not just the Clontarf episode—may have been somewhat (although not very radically) abbreviated.[32]

---

29. Cf. Finnur Jónsson (1904), 165.

30. Bugge (1901), 63.

31. Sveinsson (1933), 80-81.

32. The following example of abbreviation (or omission) is particularly interesting and revealing, although it has never been observed by editors of *Njála*: "Þeir urðu heldr síðbúnir; sigldu í haf. Þeir hǫfðu langa útivist, en um síðir tóku þeir Ingólfshǫfða ok brutu þar skipit allt í spán, en þó varð mannbjǫrg. Kafahríð var á" (chapter 159, the section on Kári's shipwreck near Svínafell). The last sentence of this quotation is taken from the text of *Gráskinna* (G); *Möðruvallabók* (M) at this point has the variant reading: "Hríðin var in sama," while manuscripts of the X branch all have the variant "Þá gerði (ok) á hríð veðrs (mikla)"; cf. Sveinsson, *Njála* (1954), p. 462, note 3. Of these variant readings the one from M is the most perplexing since no snowstorm had previously been mentioned in the text. Yet M represents the author's original manuscript better than G or X. For the snowstorm must originally have been introduced *before* Kári reaches Ingólfshǫfði; it is this storm which causes the shipwreck. At a very early stage in the manu-

Whatever the origin of the mysterious *Dumazbakki* episode, it cannot be used as proof that there was ever a written *Brjáns saga*. Nor can the abbreviations in *Njála* be used as such proof. (It should be noted here that the obscure references to otherwise unknown people and events in the Clontarf episode does not necessarily indicate that a longer text has been adapted or abbreviated since we cannot know what kind of knowledge the author of *Njála* presupposed among his audience; cf. above, p. 198). Generally speaking, the traditional methods of textual criticism and *Quellenkritik* do not provide us with any evidence at all.

We must now deal with the arguments based on general differences between the Clontarf episode and the rest of *Njála*. According to Einar Ólafur Sveinsson,[33] there are many such differences: the style of the episode is less realistic and "objective," its characterization more abstract and schematic, its Christian didacticism more obvious, etc. Even though these differences have been somewhat exaggerated, it is quite possible to agree that they exist while still not accepting them as evidence that the author of *Njála* used a *Brjáns saga*. Some differences may be due to the nature of the theme, which in turn is dependent on the oral traditions on which this episode is based; other differences may be explained by the author's desire to dramatize the conflict between Christianity and paganism in one final climactic confrontation (cf. above, p. 148).

A closer comparison between the Clontarf episode and other sections of the saga will reveal parallels of style and narrative technique *when the same motif is treated*. (Page references to the Clontarf episode are introduced by "Cl."; the references to parallel sections are introduced by "P.") To me these parallels appear more significant than the general differences noted by Einar Ólafur Sveinsson. For we may well imagine an author changing his style as he moves on to a new theme, especially when the theme is unusual or even unique (as the Battle of Clontarf undoubtedly was). But we may expect him to maintain a certain uniformity in his treatment of the same incidental

---

script transmission some scribe must have omitted the presentation of the snowstorm, and thus the author's later observation that "the snowstorm continued as before" ("Hríðin var in sama") became so puzzling to the X-scribe and the G-scribe that both of them, independently of each other, changed the sentence completely so that it would not seem to refer to something that had never been mentioned earlier. The same early scribe who "lost" the first reference to the snowstorm may also have "lost" various other important pieces of information in his impatience to get to the end of *Njála*. This may explain such puzzles as the observation later in the same chapter that Kári "first" settled at Breiðár (cf. above, p. 185) or the mysterious reference to an otherwise unknown "Hárekr" in chapter 157.

33. Sveinsson (1933), 82-83.

motifs, especially those that are very common (e.g., presentation of characters, descriptions of fights, Thing meetings, etc.).

In the beginning of the episode (chapters 154-155) we are thus told about a feast arranged in Orkney by Earl Sigurðr. The description of this feast parallels the description of Gunnar's wedding in chapter 34. We are first introduced to the people who were invited, and this gives the narrator an opportunity to present a great deal of genealogical information which will be needed as background material later (cf. P:87-88, Cl:440-442). Next follows a detailed description of the seating arrangements, starting with the man who sat on the high seat in the middle and enumerating the guests on each side of him, first those sitting *innar frá* and then those sitting *utar frá*:

Svá var skipat, at konungr sat í miðju hásæti, en til sinnar handar honum hvárr jarlanna. Sátu menn þeira Sigtryggs ok Gilla innar frá, en utar frá Sigurði jarli sat Flosi ok Þorsteinn Hallsson.

(Cl:442)[34]

(Gunnarr) sat á miðjan bekk, en innar frá Þráinn Sigfússon, þá Úlfr aurgoði, þá Valgarðr inn grái, þá Morðr ok Runólfr, þá Sigfússynir; Lambi sat innstr. It næsta Gunnari utar frá sat Njáll, þá Skarpheðinn, þá Helgi, þá Grímr, þá Hoskuldr, þá Hafr inn spaki, þá Ingjaldr frá Keldum, þá synir Þóris austan ór Holti.

(P.:88-89)

In both cases, the description of the seating arrangements is immediately followed by a dramatic confrontation at the table (between Kári and Gunnarr Lambason in the Clontarf episode, between Þráinn Sigfússon and his wife in chapter 34).

The presentation of King Brjánn and his sons in the Clontarf episode parallels the presentation of Njáll and his sons in earlier chapters (cf. above, p. 32). Brjánn and Njáll are both ideal judges, mild and forgiving but very just. It is said about Brjánn that he *gaf upp útlogum sínum þrysvar ina somu sok; en ef þeir misgerðu optar, þá lét hann dæma þá at logum* (Cl:442). Njáll seems to have had the same principles, if we may judge from a passage in chapter 124, right before the Burning, where one of the prospective Burners, Ingjaldr, is reproached by his sister for turning against a man who had three times saved him from outlawry: "*Allmikill níðingr ertú,* "*segir*

---

34. According to Sveinsson (1933), 78 (cf. Lehmann-Carolsfeld, 1883, 141; Finnur Jónsson, 1904, 160), this particular passage and some other paragraphs which follow it were indeed written by the author of *Njála*, even though the beginning of the story of Earl Sigurðr's party is supposed to have been copied word for word from *Brjáns saga*! It would seem logical, however, to suppose that whoever wrote about the *invitations* to the party also wrote about the *seating arrangements*. This is clearly a case where the analytical methods of philology and *Quellenkritik* have led to results that seem absurd from the standpoint of structural analysis.

hon, "þar sem Njáll hefir þik þrysvar leyst ór skógi" (P:319). It should be noted that the term *þrysvar* occurs only here and in one other place, also in the Clontarf episode (*Úlfr hræða . . . lagði til hans þrysvar sinnum*, Cl:450). In *Heimskringla* and *Egils saga*—the only two long comparable texts for which a reliable concordance exists[35]—the word does not appear at all.

It is also said about Brjánn that he loved his foster son, Kerþjálfaðr, more than his own sons (*unni meira en sínum sonum*, Cl:441). In an earlier chapter (122), right after the murder of Hǫskuldr, Njáll himself declares that he loved *his* foster son more than his own sons (*ek unna meira Hǫskuldi en sonum mínum*, P:309). Both these foster sons are sons of former enemies of their foster fathers, and they have been adopted as a sign of peace and reconciliation.

In the Clontarf episode, the two vikings, Bróðir and Óspakr, are presented in a way that closely resembles earlier presentation of such vikings. We first hear about them in a conversation between King Sigtryggr and his mother, Kormlǫð. The mother informs her son that two vikings have arrived and are now lying with their ships off the Isle of Man: "*Víkingar tveir liggja úti fyrir utan Mǫn ok hafa þrjá tigi skipa ok svá harðfengir, at ekki stendr við. Heitir annarr Óspakr, en annarr Bróðir*" (Cl:445).

This situation is paralleled by two similar situations in the episode about Gunnarr's travels abroad and fights against various vikings. We have already quoted both these passages in our analysis of the Travel Pattern (above, p. 73), so we do not need to quote them again in order to document their similarity to the Óspakr/Bróðir incident.

It is obvious that the same stereotyped pattern of narration is followed in all three treatments of the viking motif. One may perhaps argue that this motif is so common that one may expect to find the same clichés and formulas even in sagas that are completely unrelated. Nevertheless, the vikings of the Clontarf episode conform remarkably well to the specific narrative conventions of *Njála*, which prescribe that such villainous characters should be introduced dramatically in a concrete situation where they appear as a threat to the landlubbers (cf. also the presentation of Hrappr, chapter 87, and Hallgerðr, chapter 1).

Bróðir, the more evil of the two vikings in the Clontarf episode, is said to be *bæði mikill ok sterkr ok hafði hár svá mikit at hann vafði (drap) undir undir belti sér* (Cl:446). About the equally evil Hallgerðr it is said as early

---

35. I have made use (both here and elsewhere) of Einar Haugen's *Norwegian Word Studies*, Volume 2: *The Vocabularies of the Old Norse Sagas and of Henrik Wergeland*, a mimeographed concordance distributed by the University of Wisconsin Press (Madïson, Wisconsin, 1942)

as in chapter 1 that she was *mikil vexti ok hárit svá fagrt sem silki ok svá mikit, at þat tók ofan á belti* (P:6). The identical combination of inner and outer characteristics—evil mind, large size, long hair, measured in relation to the belt—indicates that we may have encountered a cliché. Although such clichés are fairly common in the literary portraits, which tend to be among the most formulaic passages in the sagas, this particular one seems to be a specialty of *Njála*.

Kormlǫð, the other major villain of the Clontarf episode, is also described in terms reminiscent of earlier passages in *Njála*. The narrator says about this evil queen, who could well have been a twin sister of Hallgerðr, that *hon var allra kvenna fegrst ok bezt orðin um allt þat, er henni var ósjálfrátt, en þat er mál manna, et henni hafi allt verit illa gefit, þat er henni var sjálfrátt* (C1:440). The use of the word *sjálfrátt* (*ósjálfrátt*) is what strikes the reader as most original in this presentation. *Sjálfræði* is a theological term expressing the idea of free will.[36] Neither this word nor any of its derivatives occurs in *Heimskringla* or in *Egils saga*, but it does occur in similar contexts elsewhere in *Njála*, e.g., in Unnr's words about her husband, Hrútr, in chapter 7: *"Gott má ek frá honum segja þat allt, er honum er sjálfrátt"* (P:24). Thus, in this case as well, we can see that characterization in the Clontarf episode tends to follow the same pattern as in the rest of the saga.

The Clontarf battle itself contains some interesting parallels with other major fights in *Njála*, although Einar Ólafur Sveinsson has pointed out that the description is less concrete than usual, with fewer details about specific wounds and weapons[37]—a fact which may be due to the author's wish to be brief. A recurrent formula states that somebody advanced (or attacked) with such vigor (*gekk svá fast fram, lagði til hans svá fast*, etc.) that the enemy fell or retreated (*at hann felldi alla, at þeir urðu at hlífa sér*, etc.). This particular formula recurs with the same stereotyped intensity in the description of the Battle at the Allthing in chapter 145. Sometimes we find almost identical phrases, e.g.,:

Úlfr hræða *sneri* þá *í móti* honum ok *lagði til hans* þrysvar sinnum *svá fast, at* Bróðir *fell fyrir* í hvert sinn ok við sjálft, at hann *mundi eigi á fœtr komask*, en þegar er hann gat upp staðit, *flýði hann undan* ok í skóginn. (C1:450)

Nú *sneri* Þorgeirr *í móti* Leiðólfi sterka . . . (P:418) Þorgeirr *lagði til hans svá fast* með annarri hendi, *at* Hallbjǫrn *fell fyrir* ok komsk nauðuliga *á fœtr* ok sneri þegar undan. (P:403)

---

36. Cf. Salvesen (1968), 45; above p. 130.

37. "Lýsingar á vopnaskiptum eru ónákvæmar, og stingur það alveg í stuf við Njálu," Sveinsson (1933), 83.

The anecdote about Þorsteinn Síðu-Hallsson's escape from the battle contains a few details which are absent from the version presented in *Þorsteins saga Síðu-Hallssonar* (cf. above, p. 228) but have interesting parallels in other sections of *Njála*.[38] He is said to have halted in order to tie up his shoe-thong (*nam staðar, þá er aðrir flýðu, ok batt skópveng sinn*; Cl:452). The same thing is said to have happened to Skarpheðinn during his battle against Þráinn in chapter 92 (*Þat varð Skarpheðni, þá er þeir hljópu ofan með fljótinu, at stǫkk í sundr skópvengr hans ok dvalðisk hann eptir*; P:233). It also happened to the slave Melkólfr right after his theft at Kirkjubœr in chapter 48 (*Hann ferr upp með Rangá; þá slitnar skópvengr hans*; P:123). The motif seems to be peculiar to *Njála*, and the word *skópvengr* appears to be highly infrequent in other sagas—it does not, for example, appear anywhere in *Heimskringla* or in *Egils saga*.

The miracles and other supernatural events are generally thought of as making the Clontarf episode especially "different" and incompatible with the rest of *Njála*. In this case, too, however, it is possible to indicate parallels. Earl Gilli's dream right after the battle, for example, can be compared to Flosi's dream after the Burning of Njáll (chapter 133). In both cases, the dreamer sees a giant—who calls himself Herfiðr in Gilli's dream but Járngrímr in Flosi's—and asks him for news. The giant answers in the form of a stanza. The same narrative formulas are used in these two anecdotes, even though the one in the Clontarf episode is much briefer and more concentrated and told in the third person (whereas the other one is told in the first person by the dreamer, i.e., Flosi):

Gilla jarl í Suðreyjum dreymði, at maðr kom at honum ok nefndisk Herfiðr ok kvazk vera kominn af Írlandi. Jarl þóttisk spyrja tíðenda. Hann kvað þetta: "Var ek þar, er bragnar bǫrðusk." etc.

(Cl:459)

"*Mik dreymði þat,*" segir Flosi, "*at ek þóttumsk vera at Lómagnúpi ok ganga út ok sjá upp til gnúpsins. Ok opnaðisk hann, ok gekk maðr út . . . gekk hann at mér*; ek *spurða hann tíðenda*. Hann kvezk segja mundu tíðendin. Ok spurða ek hann at nafni; *hann nefndisk Járngrímr*.
Ek spurða, hvert hann skyldi fara; *hann kvezk fara skyldu* til alþingis . . . Síðan *kvað hann þetta*: "Hǫggorma mun hefjask . . ." etc.

(P:346-48)

The parallels cited above (some others could have been included) do not necessarily exclude the possibility that a written *Brjáns saga* was used by the author of *Njála* when writing the Clontarf episode. It is entirely con-

---

38. Cf. Kersbergen (1927), 76-77; Goedheer (1938), 96 (note).

ceivable that some of the parallels are coincidental or that they result from the general uniformity of saga style; some of them may also have come about because the author of *Njála* made changes in his source, or because he was influenced by it when writing his own saga (the last two explanations have been used by previous scholars when confronted with some of the most obvious parallels). But in view of the facts a) that the Clontarf episode is an integral part of *Njála*, and b) that there are very slight documentary reasons to believe that a written *Brjáns saga* existed, it is better to assume that the whole episode was composed by the author of *Njála*, who created it out of his own memory and his own imagination.

He may have read something in a manuscript about the Battle of Clontarf. Or he may have based his story on oral tales alone. In either case, he probably felt that he had to respect older traditions about this famous battle. But assuming this, and regardless of his sources, he made the story into his own by integrating it thoroughly into his main narrative.

3. GENEALOGIES

There are several long genealogical sections in *Njála* which merely provide pedigrees for the major characters. The style and general content of these sections might suggest that they were taken over from earlier sources, such as *Landnámabók*. Yet it has been conclusively demonstrated that the source was *not* any of the extant *Landnáma* versions, from which the pedigrees in *Njála* differ in many important respects. Carolsfeld and Lehmann, who share the main responsibility for this demonstration, did not commit themselves to any further theories about the matter, but Guðbrandur Vigfússon and Sigurður Nordal assumed that the author of the saga made excerpts from a lost written genealogical source, and Einar Ólafur Sveinsson later tried to prove their assumption. According to Sveinsson, the pedigrees in this lost source(which he calls *Æ) were compiled in Southeastern Iceland in the twelfth century.[39]

It may be assumed that the pedigrees were older than the saga, and it is indeed very likely that the author became familiar with them in Southeastern Iceland, since that is evidently where he lived. But do we have to assume that the written twelfth century source (*Æ) ever existed?

Most of Sveinsson's arguments are based on the nonfunctional nature of the *Njála* pedigrees and on their use of material that is irrelevant, superfluous, or inconsistent with the rest of the saga. As I shall try to show, however, these arguments are based on false premises.

39. Sveinsson (1933), 39-44, 86-100; Sveinsson (1954), pp. XLIX-LIV.

If the pedigrees contain material that seems unnecessary to us, there are several possible explanations for this fact. It is possible that the material was taken over mechanically from an older manuscript *Æ without any attempt to reconcile it to its new context. But it is also possible—and indeed more likely—that the pedigrees represent the author's own learning, which he could not always use in the story but which he had reason to expect that his audience would appreciate. He may also have drawn some of his genealogical information from oral "sources" that he consulted as he was writing this story. Finally, he may have used a combination of oral and written sources, more or less well remembered and never fully integrated into one written text until *Njála* was written.[40]

We must always remember that genealogical knowledge—*ættvisi* and *mannfrœði*—was a very important part of the oral heritage. It is said about Bishop Þorlákr, for example, that he gained such knowledge as a child from his mother, whenever he was not reading or writing or saying his prayers.[41] We may assume that pedigrees were often memorized, and we may further assume that the audience of *Njála* would be quite familiar with a fairly large number of the men and women that were enumerated in its introductions. This is indeed the most pausible reason why so much genealogical material is included and why there are so many casual references to traditions outside the saga itself: *Móðir Þóris var Ingunn. dóttir Helga ins magra, er nam Eyjafjǫrd* (237-38); *Synir Halls á Síðu váru þeir Þorsteinn ok Egill, Þorvarðr ok Ljótr ok Þiðrandi, þann er sagt er, at dísir vægi* (239); *Eiriks sonar ǫrðigskeggja, er felldi Grjótgarð í Sóknardal í Nóregi* (300).[42] It seems unlikely that such sentences would be included unless the author could take a good deal of knowledge for granted, and if that was so, he may not necessarily have needed a written source to compile his material.

As we have seen (Chapter V), the genealogies sometimes contain references to incidents later on in the saga: ... *hét móðir hans Bjartey ok var systir Þorvalds ins veila, er veginn var við Hestlæk í Grímsnesi* (191; cf. the death of Þorvaldr in chapter 102); *son hans var Kolr, er Kári vegr í Bretlandi* (239). We have also studied such references in connection with the Conversion epi-

40. Cf Andersson (1964), 83-95.

41. *Biskupa sögur*, I (1858), 91. For general discussion of *ættvisi* in the oral tradition, see for example Guðni Jónsson, "Genealogier," *KLNM*, V (1960), 247-249 (with references to earlier studies).

42. Most of these references are conveniently collected by Guðbrandur Vigfússon in *Origines*, I (1905), 237 f., and by Sveinsson (1933), 41-43, 89-92, 94 f; see above, p. 197.

sode (above, p. 000). According to Sveinsson, they indicate that the author transcribed these sentences from a written source.[43]

As we have already seen, however, this kind of evidence is very inconclusive. It would, as a matter of fact, be far more reasonable to argue that such references were made by the author himself to prepare his audience for later episodes, the contents of which were already known to many of his readers or listeners through oral tradition. By a similar line of reasoning, references in the saga to genealogical facts which were already mentioned in an earlier chapter should not be interpreted as unnecessary repetition caused by thoughtless excerption from a written source but rather as a reminder from the author to his audience (e.g., the reference in chapter 159 to Hildigunnr, *er Hǫskuldr Hvítanessgoði hafði átta*).[44] Sveinsson has attempted to show[45] that the genealogies sometimes contain information that is slightly inconsistent with the rest of the saga. A man who generally appears under the name of *Þorgeirr Skorargeirr*, for example, is presented as just *Skorargeirr* in some pedigrees. But these names seem easily interchangeable, since one is merely an abbreviated form of the other. The longer form does appear also in the genealogies of some manuscript versions, and there is nothing to prevent the assumption that this form in all cases actually represents the original reading, which may later have been corrupted (by haplography or by conscious abbreviation) in some manuscripts. An intepretation along these lines is possible also in the case of the variant forms *Skógar* and *Forsárskogar*, each of which is used once in the saga to refer to the same place in southern Iceland, a fact which makes Sveinsson draw the unwarranted conclusion that one of these forms was taken over from **Æ*. In this case it is also possible that the author of *Njála* knew both names without being aware of the fact that they refer to the same place, for the longer form appears only in conjunction with a personal name (*Arnórr Ǫrnólfsson ór Forsárskógum*), which may well have been a part of his memorized genealogical knowledge.

What is noteworthy is not such minor inconsistencies, which actually amount to nothing, but the fact that the genealogical information provided in *Njála* on the whole is extremely consistent and bears witness to the sagawriter's profound knowledge of his subject. As Sveinsson himself has pointed out,[46] information presented in the introductory pedigrees is often referred

---

43. "Er það á móti venju fornsagnanna að drepa með þessu móti á atvik, sem síðar er sagt frá, en skiljanleg vangá, ef skrifað var eftir ritaðri heimild," Sveinsson (1954), p. LII.

44. Cf. Sveinsson (1954), *loc. cit.*, and above, p. 185.

45. Sveinsson (1933), 96; *Njála* (1954), p. L, note 1.

46. Sveinsson (1933), 94-95, cf. 41-43.

to later in the dialogues of the saga. In the presentation of Ásgrímr Elliða-Grímsson and his pedigree (chapter 26), for example, there is a reference to the tradition that Ásgrímr had killed his foster brother, Gaukr Trandilsson. Several hundred pages later we find another reference to this tragic slaying in a heated exchange of insults between Ásgrímr and Skapti Þóroddsson at the Allthing. In other dialogues, we hear Hallgerðr praising her grandmother for being a descendent of Sigurðr Fáfnisbani (chapter 14; cf. her pedigree in chapter 1), Bjarni Brodd-Helgason flattering Eyjólfr for having Ragnarr loðbrók as his ancestor (chapter 138; cf. pedigrees at the beginning of the same chapter and in chapter 114), and Skamkell comparing Otkell to his grandfather Hallkell (chapter 49), a man whose heroic exploits have been referred to in the pedigree of chapter 47.

According to Sveinsson, such references in the dialogues were constructed by the author of Njála on the basis of the information he had gathered from his written genealogical source, *Æ. But are we then to assume that the author of Njála, while constructing his dialogues, made an effort to look up relevant pedigrees in his source merely to find suitable conversational topics for his characters? This seems highly unlikely.[47] Deriving the genealogical information in the dialogues from the written pedigrees alone would in fact imply a considerable amount of detective work. In order to figure out, for example, that Eyjólfr was indeed a descendent of Ragnarr loðbrók, it would first be necessary to note in the pedigree of chapter 138 that his great-great-grandfather was Óleifr feilan; second, it would be necessary to remember from the pedigree of Snorri goði in chapter 114 that Óleifr feilan's great-grandfather was Ingjaldr Helgason, whose mother was descended from Ragnar loðbrók. No Icelandic sagawriter would go through such a process just to drop a name in a dialogue.

When the author of Njála does use a name in this casual manner, we can be certain that he is either a very skillful fraud or—more likely—that he is a very learned man who knows exactly what he is talking about, without having to consult any written sources. This man evidently also expects his audience to be able to follow him into the more advanced exercises of genealogical computation and combination. Like other learned men, he may well have expected too much from his audience; but there can hardly be any doubt that he himself could trace pedigrees in his head without much effort. It is not impossible to assume that he, like Bishop Þorlákr, had spent

47. The absurdity of this sort of reasoning is very aptly summarized by Theodore Andersson: "Bookprose supposes that a thirteenth-century Icelander could write a saga about people of whom he knew so little that he was, in a manner of speaking, forced to look them up in a dictionary," Andersson (1964), 89.

considerable time at his mother's knees learning *ættvísi* and *mannfrœði* until he had become thoroughly familiar with all the leading chieftain families in Iceland. Thus he may not have needed an *Æ* or a *Landnáma* or any other written source as he was writing *Njála*, except perhaps now and then to check some particular detail.

Theodore Andersson, whose criticism of Sveinsson and the book-prose school in general is very similar to my own with regard to written genealogical sources, still admits that the use of such sources in this case "may be granted on the common-sense basis that the author of *Njáls saga* could not have had six hundred names from the Saga Age in his head."[48] I am not certain, however, that such memorization is unfeasible, or even unlikely. As a matter of fact, there are almost as many names in the works of Theodore Andersson, and I suspect he has most of these names in his head, even though he may have to look them up now and again to check, for example, the spelling. It is true that he has learned the names primarily from written sources—the same may in fact be true of *Njála*'s author—but he did not necessarily have to make excerpts from these works whenever he wanted to use the names in writing.

In some of the *Njála* manuscripts Sveinsson has found certain archaic name-forms within the genealogies, name-forms he finds it "most natural to explain by the assumption that they have come from an old written source (or sources)."[49] For example, Hildigunnr is referred to as "Hildiguðr" (an obsolete variant of the same name) the first time she appears in *Reykjabók*; Hǫskuldr is occasionally called "Hǫskollr" in *Reykjabók* and *Gráskinna*, and so on. But as Sveinsson himself seems to admit,[50] some of these archaic forms are also found in parts of *Njála* other than the genealogies. At the time *Njála* was written, they may still have been considered acceptable variants by conservative writers. Thus the linguistic evidence by no means forces any written sources upon us, and especially not *one* specific source, i.e., the source that Sveinsson calls *Æ*.

I shall nevertheless willingly admit that the author of *Njála* probably consulted written sources now and then while working on his genealogies, and the archaic name-forms may well be a result of this consultation. We just do not know enough to be certain. Considering the meager evidence,

---

48. Andersson (1964), 90.

49. "Virðist mér eðlilegast að skýra það svo, að það sé komið úr gamalli ritaðri heimild (eða heimildum)," Sveinsson, *Njála* (1954), p. L.

50. "Ég nefni nú nokkur dæmi gamalla nafnmynda. sem ég hef rekizt á, *án þess að fara út í, hvort hvert dæmi sé úr ættartöluheimild þeirri, sem eg geri ráð fyrir,*" Sveinsson (1954), p. L, note 1 (my italics).

we should probably let Sveinsson's presupposed source *Æ go the same way as *Brjáns saga, *Kristni þáttr and *Gunnars saga.

4. THE JUDICIAL SOURCES

It is generally recognized that the judicial sections of Njála are unlike those of any other saga. Not only are they much longer, but they also reveal a passion for legalistic details and judicial theory which must be attributed mainly to the author himself and not to the oral narratives used by him. The laws and the legal formulas quoted, as well as the court procedures described, are largely those of the thirteenth century, even though they have been projected back into Njáll's time and possibly blended with legal traditions from earlier periods.[51] As a consequence, the saga is extremely unreliable as a source of information about the earliest, pre-Christian laws. This was convincingly demonstrated by Lehmann and Carolsfeld,[52] and it is now accepted by most scholars, even though Vilhjálmur Finsen[53] and Finnur Jónsson[54] both made energetic attempts to defend the historicity of the saga from this particular point of view.[55] As a matter of fact, even these two scholars had to admit that the saga contains quite a few judicial anachronisms and other mistakes in its accounts of legal procedures, although they tended to blame such mistakes on late redactors and on scribes tampering with the genuine traditions.

But the problem of historicity is one thing, and the problem of written sources is quite another. Lehmann-Carolsfeld did in fact try to prove that the author of Njála transcribed long sections mechanically from thirteenth-century law scrolls. They pictured the author as a rather amateurish, although enthusiastic, jurist who had not quite digested what he had read in sources such as Grágás, and who consequently made continual blunders when writing about matters of law. Later scholars have found this criticism too harsh and based on a rigid and pedantic concept of legal knowledge. Vilhjálmur Finsen, the most outstanding expert of his time on early Icelandic law, managed to refute several of their arguments on that point by showing that many of the legal provisions in Njála make good sense and

---

51. A particularly well-balanced and concise statement on this topic may be found in Heusler's Strafrecht (1911), 13 f.

52. Lehmann-Carolsfeld (1883), 11-138.

53. Om den oprindelige Ordning af nogle af den islandske Fristats Institutioner (Copenhagen, 1888), 100 f.

54. Finnur Jónsson (1904), 97-154.

55. Cf. the later contributions by Lehmann in Tidsskrift for Retsvidenskab (1905), 183 f. and particularly by Sveinsson (1933), 155-69, 305-11, (1954), pp. LIV-LVI.

may well have been valid, even though they cannot now be perfectly reconciled with the wording in any of the preserved *Grágás* manuscripts.[56]

It must be remembered that there was no canonical written text of the Icelandic laws during the Independence era. The laws were primarily preserved through memorization and oral transmission; hence it was only natural that different individuals had different ideas about the exact wording and content of the laws. This is the reason why the Law-speaker's role was so important; it was his function to serve as the highest authority on what the law actually said when there were divergent opinions about it. From the twelfth century on, the laws were also recorded in manuscripts, but these were evidently intended as aids for the memory rather than as substitutes for the Law-speaker's judicial authority. In any case, the extant redactions of *Grágás* differ considerably from each other and seem to represent independent private collections. The very fact that *Njála* differs so much from any of these redactions was used by both Finsen and Finnur Jónsson as evidence that the author of the saga did *not* use any written laws but drew his knowledge entirely from oral tradition.[57]

If we accept this theory, the author's occasional mistakes and inconsistencies may be explained as the result of faulty memorization, or as misunderstandings of memorized legal provisions that had become obsolete at the time when the saga was written. The puzzling mixture of early Icelandic and late Norwegian law may in fact seem quite natural if we assume that the blending occurred in the head of an author who had memorized a considerable amount of older Icelandic laws during the early part of his career and who was trying to recall them at a much later time when they had already been substituted (officially and also in his own mind) by a foreign judicial system and several new provisions. It is to be expected that even the best of jurists would slip under such circumstances, especially if he did *not* have access to lawscrolls from the earlier period.

Einar Ólafur Sveinsson has accepted some of Vilhjámur Finsen's and Finnur Jónsson's objections against Lehmann-Carolsfeld, but he nevertheless defends the main contention of his German precursors that the author of *Njála* incorporated transcripts from lawscrolls in his text, even though he admits that the text of these scrolls must have differed considerably from any extant law manuscript.[58] As in the case of *Brjáns saga, *Kristni þáttr, and *Æ, he thus resorts to theories about a *lost* source. One of his main arguments (adapted from Lehmann-Carolsfeld) is that the legal formulas

---

56. Finsen (1888), 102-05.
57. Finsen, *loc. cit.*; Finnur Jónsson (1904), 154.
58. Sveinsson (1933), 159 f.

used in the saga have some rather close verbal parallels in the *Grágás* redactions.[59] Another, and perhaps stronger, argument (also adapted from the Germans) is that some of these formulas do not seem to fit any specific situation as described in the saga, but are rather to be seen as thoughtless echoes of the purely hypothetical world presented in a lawbook. At some occasions, for example, a courtsuit is said to have been brought *í Austfirðingadóm yfir hǫfdi Jóni* ("in the East Fjord court in the presence of Jón")[60]; the name "Jón" corresponds to the English "John Doe"; it does not refer to any of the known people in the saga but seems to have been taken over mechanically from a legal source. Within the same formula, there are also references to a "mortal body wound, brain wound, or marrow wound" (*holundar sár eða heilundar eða mergundar*[61]), even though only one of these alternatives would seem to apply in the specific situation in which the formula is used; also in this case, it would seem natural to explain the superfluous phrases as a result of thoughtless copying.

There is, however, another explanation. When describing certain court scenes in *Njála*—and especially the important one in which the Burners of Njáll are prosecuted—the author obviously felt a very strong urge to enlighten his audience on the subject of proper procedures and formulas to be used in a case of this sort. He may well have acquired this knowledge from his legal training, but he almost certainly did not have all the historical information necessary to present an accurate account of the individual case in all its details. In order to give a complete picture of the procedures he would thus either have to invent a large number of details—names of witnesses and judges, various specific circumstances, etc.—or present an abstract "model case" in which much of the specific information is left open. As a matter of fact, he may very well have tried to follow both courses of action at the same time. The narrative laws of the saga would prompt him to include names and other details, even when he did not know them from the oral tradition. Pedagogical considerations would, on the other hand, prompt him to convey his judicial knowledge in such a way that it could be applied by his audience to other similar cases.

The use of phrases such as *yfir hǫfdi Jóni* and *holundar sár eða heilundar eða mergundar* may be interpreted as consistent with both of these basic desires. Even though "Jón" may be translated as "John Doe," it may also be interpreted as the real name of the *reifingarmaðr* in the case, i.e., the man whose function it was to sum it up before the court.[62] In the story

59. *Op. cit.*, 161-68.
60. Chapter 142; cf. Sveinsson (1933), 163 f.
61. Cf. Sveinsson (1933), 161.
62. Cf. Finnur Jónsson (1904), 145 f.

about the prosecution of the Burners, the author makes clear references to this *reifingarmaðr* in a way indicating that he is to be identified with the Jón previously mentioned in the prosecutor's formula of declaration (*lýsing*) against the defendents.[63] In the parallel formula of declaration presented in *Grágás*, there is no mention of a Jón but instead of "N. N.,"[64] which is a much more abstract designation for an unknown person—a designation not to be found anywhere in our saga. Even though the name Jón was not introduced in Iceland until after the conversion, the use of it in the prosecution scenes of *Njála* is well within the confines of saga realism.[65] Regardless of whether or not the author had got the name from law-scrolls, there is thus no compelling reason to interpret it as merely a result of thoughtless transcription.

The same holds true of the formulaic references to *holundar sár eða heilundar eða mergundar*, which the author may in part have included in the prosecutor's declarations in order to teach his audience the proper terms for the three kinds of fatal wounds that constituted evidence of slaying in an Icelandic court. But whatever pedagogical reasons for their inclusion, the repeated reference to them makes perfect sense in the narrative context since it may be assumed that the prosecutor does not know for certain which kind of wounds applied in the particular case (the beheading of Helgi Njálsson) and hence does not want to commit himself to any particular alternative. In another court scene of *Njála*, the author proves himself to be well aware of the fact that one of the three alternatives was enough, since he lets the prosecutor use the same formula but with reference to *holundar sár* only[66]—apparently because in this case (the slaying of Þorgeirr Otkelsson) the exact nature of the deadly wound was better known to the prosecutor (Gizurr hvíti). If the author had copied the declaration formula from a manuscript without any real understanding of what he was doing, we would at least have expected him to copy it in the same form both times.

The extent to which the author of *Njála* has "internalized" his legal knowledge may on the whole be determined by comparing his handling of the same formulas in different contexts. As a matter of fact, he seems to handle them rather freely and intelligently, with numerous small variations, largely dependent on the circumstances of the case but without any very strict consistency in phrasing and word order. Could there be any more

63. *Þá stóð sá upp, er sǫk hafði yfir hǫfði verit fram sǫgð, ok reifði málit* (chapter 144).
64. Cf. *Njála* (1954), 381, note 1.
65. "Selve navnet Jón kendes fra Island ved 1100 og blev stadig mere almindeligt," Finnur Jónsson (1904), 145-46; cf. Lind, *Norsk-isländska dopnamn* (Uppsala, 1905-15), 647-49.
66. *Njála* (1954), 178.

convincing evidence that he did *not* just copy the formulas from a manuscript?

Let us, for example, take a close look at the declaration (*lýsing*) formula already referred to above in connection with homicide cases. The first time it is used it has the following form:

"Ek lýsi lǫgmætu frumhlaupi á hǫnd Gunnari Hámundarsyni um þat, er hann hljóp lǫgmætu frumhlaupi til Þorgeirs Otkelssonar ok særði hann holundarsári því, er at ben gerðisk, en Þorgeirr fekk bana af. Tel ek hann eiga at verða um sǫk þá sekjan skógarmann, óœlan, óferjanda, óráðanda ǫllum bjargráðum. Tel ek sekt fé hans, hálft mér, en hálft fjórðungsmǫnnum þeim, er sektarfé eigu at taka at lǫgum. Lýsi ek til fjórðungsdóms þess, er sǫkin á í at koma at lǫgum, lýsi ek lǫglýsing i heyranda hljóði at lǫgbergi, lýsi ek nú til sóknar ok til sektar fullrar á hǫnd Gunnari Hámundarsyni"   (178)

This is the *frumhlaup* version of the formula, i.e., the version used to declare the violent assault (which was distinguished from the actual wounding that resulted from the assault) at the very beginning of Allthing proceedings against an accused killer. We find it again in Mǫrðr's first declaration against Flosi after the burning of Njáll and his sons:

"Nefni ek í þat vætti," segir hann, "at ek lýsi lǫgmætu frumhlaupi á hǫnd Flosa Þórðarsyni, er hann hljóp til Helga Njálssonar (*Möðruvallabók* adds: á þeim vættvangi, er Flosi Þórðarson hljóp til Helga Njálssonar) ok veitti honum holundar sár eða heilundar eða mergundar (*var.* holundarsár eða mergundar), þat er at ben gerðisk, en Helgi fekk bana af. Tel ek hann (*var.* þik) eiga at verða un sǫk þá sekjan skógarmann, óalanda, óferjanda, óráðanda ǫllum bjargráðum; tel ek sekt fé hans (*var.* þitt) allt, hálft mér, en hálft fjórðungsmǫnnum þeim, er sektarfé eigu at taka eptir hann at lǫgum. Lýsi ek vigsǫk þessi til fjórðungsdóms þess, er sǫkin á í at koma at lǫgum; lýsi ek lǫglýsing; lýsi ek í heyranda hljóði at lǫgbergi; lýsi ek nú til sóknar (*var.* til sóknar í sumar) ok til sektar fullrar á hǫnd Flosa Þórðarsyni. Lýsi ek handseldri sǫk Þorgeirs Þórissonar."   (374-75)

Although the wording is almost identical in these two passages, there are several small differences that deserve attention: *særði sári* vs. *veitti sár*, *óœlan* vs. *óalanda*, *er hann hljóp lǫgmætu frumhlaupi* vs. *er hann hljóp*, *fé hans* vs. *fé hans allt*, *taka* vs. *taka eptir hann*, *lýsi ek lǫglýsing í heyranda hljóði* vs. the more prolix *lýsi ek lǫglýsing, lýsi ek í heyranda hljóði*. There are also some additional phrases at the beginning and the end of the second version, which on the whole seem more expanded and loquacious. Some of the variants could conceivably have been caused by faulty or careless transcription in the course of manuscript transmission, but the only variants that clearly seem to belong to this category are those which have been included within parenthesis in the quotation above. Generally speaking, the wealth of manuscripts makes it possible to say with some confidence that the text in the editions at these points must be close to the author's own text. If he copied the formula both times out of a law manuscript, he must have been clever enough to cover up his plagiarism by making little changes here and there each time so that it would seem as if he were using his own words.

The *frumhlaup* declaration is followed by the declaration of *áverk*, in which the *results* of the assault are emphasized rather than the action itself. The formula in this case, according to *Njála*, is a mere variation of the *frumhlaup* formula: a few phrases have changed place in such a way that the wounding (*áverk*) is now mentioned before the assault itself. In the lawsuit against Gunnarr in chapter 73, this second formula is not quoted in full but is summarized in indirect speech:

I annat sinn nefndi Gizurr sér vátta ok lýsti sǫk á hǫnd Gunnari Hámundarsyni um þat, er hann særði Þorgeir Otkelsson holundarsári því, er at ben gerðisk, en Þorgeirr fekk bana af á þeim vættvangi, er Gunnarr hljóp til Þorgeirs lǫgmætu frumhlaupi áðr. Síðan lýsti hann þessi lýsing sem inni fyrri.   (179)

In the lawsuit against the Burners in chapter 141, however, the *áverk* formula is given in full. Its beginning corresponds to the wording in chapter 73, except that it is now presented in direct speech, the names are different, and the expression *særði . . . holundarsári því, er* has been replaced by the more elaborated phrase *særði . . . holundar sári eða heilundar eða mergundar* (var. *holundar sári eða mergundar*), *því sári, er . . .* (375). The rest of the formula corresponds to the *frumhlaup* formula of the same chapter, except that it is now addressed directly to the defendent, according to all manuscripts (*Tel ek þik, Flosi, eiga at verða*). In the following chapter (142), both the *frumhlaup* and the *áverk* formulas are repeated in the past tense, as Mǫrðr names witnesses to his previous *lýsing: Þórodd nefnda ek í vætti, annan Þorbjǫrn nefnda ek í vætti, at ek lýsta lǫgmætu frumhlaupi* (or: *at ek lýsta sǫk á hǫnd Flosa þórðarsyni um þat er hann særði*), etc. Apart from the shift from the present to the past tense, there are also some other minor variations at the end of these versions: the expanded phrase *særði . . . holundar sári eða heilundar eða mergundar, því sári er* is contracted into *særði . . . holundar sári eða mergundar því er* (380; cf. *Njála*, 1875, 767, line 62), and *til sóknar ok til sektar fullrar* is expanded in all manuscripts into *til soknar í sumar ok til sektar fullrar.* Furthermore, some new phrases are added at the end—these are the ones that contain the much discussed *yfir hǫfði Jóni.*

Immediately afterwards, the formula is varied again as the witnesses testify to the previous declarations by Mǫrðr. All verbs are now transposed into third person singular, past tense (*Mǫrðr nefndi okkr í þat vætti, at hann lýsti lǫgmætu frumhlaupi*, etc.). Instead of the phrase *særði . . . holundar sári*, we find the equivalent *veitti holundar sár.* And similar variations occur again as the formula is used by *kviðinn* and other functionaries in the long and exceedingly formalistic procedure of the suit (cf. 356-358, 382, 390). Sometimes the word order is slightly altered, sometimes the tense is changed; sometimes a phrase is expanded, contracted, or omitted altogether; sometimes several new sentences are added; at other times, only part of the formula is used. These variations constitute what may be regarded as conclusive proof that the author of *Njála* knew his formula by heart and also knew how to vary it for different occasions, but without necessarily paying too much attention to such—in oral tradition—insignificant details as minor variations of wording and wordorder, as long as this variation did not affect the legal substance of what was said.

As Lehmann pointed out, the *lýsing* formula of *Njála*—in all its variations—significantly differs from the corresponding formula in the extant *Grágás* text.[67] In particular, there is one very important omission which might conceivably be explained by assuming that the author skipped a line in his legal source or possibly that he used a faulty law manuscript.[68] But, as Finnur Jónsson has pointed out, it is much more likely that the omission is a result of faulty memory. On the whole, one cannot but agree with Jónsson's somewhat irritated dictum: "at afskrive en tekst nogenlunde rigtig måtte vi dog kunne forudsætte, at sagaforf. havde været i stand til, især da der ikke for ham var nogen grund til at foretage nogen ændring."[69]

It is worth observing that the author of *Njála* repeatedly stresses the ability of individual characters to pronounce the legal formulas well and clearly at the Allthing: *mæltu allir, at honum mæltisk vel* (179); *Mǫrðr var allra manna snjallmæltastr. Gizurr mælti þá, at hann skyldi lýsa vígsǫkunum, ok bað hann mæla svá hátt, at vel mætti heyra* (374); *At lǫgbergi var mikill rómr at því gǫrr, at Mǫrðr hefði mælt vel ok skǫruliga* (375); *var þat mál manna, at honum mæltisk furðuliga vel* (376); *mæltisk þeim ǫllum vel* (376). This kind of praise would seem out of order if it referred *only* to the ability of speaking loudly and with a pleasant voice. On the other hand, it is hardly a question of "eloquence" in our sense, since the phrases used are all traditional and formulaic without any element of personal innovation. What the Allthing community, as well as the author, seems to admire above all is the ability to pronounce the formulas correctly from memory, without any fumbling or hesitation. The importance of this skill is further emphasized in the speeches themselves when the speakers refer to possible mistakes in their own wording of the formulas—for example, when Mǫrðr says:

67. Lehman-Carolsfeld (1883), 82-85.
68. This is the sentence *Tel ek mér rétt ór fé hans eða þeim manni, er aðili er sakarinnar, átta lǫgaura ins fimmta tigar*; Cf. Sveinsson, *Njála* (1954), 178, note 5.
69. Finnur Jónsson (1904), 133.

Nefni ek í þat vætti, at ek tek miskviðu alla ór máli mínu, hvárt sem mér verðr ofmælt eða vanmælt. Vil ek eiga rétting allra orða minna, unz ek kem máli mínu til réttra laga (379). It is thus evident that the author of *Njála* is very much concerned about the importance of not just knowing the laws but knowing the formulas so well *by heart* that no mistake in pronouncing them can occur, thereby denying the opponent the chance of wrecking the case. Is it then not reasonable to assume that he himself had at least *some* of this ability?

If he had himself been so ignorant that he had to look up the formulas in a law book every time he used them, there would have been no temptation for him to repeat these formulas over and over again, even when their exact wording is strictly irrelevant to his story. This temptation would be strong, however, if he did indeed know the formulas so well that he could rattle them off without any effort whatsoever, especially if he dictated his text to a scribe and hence did not have to be concerned with the dreary business of writing everything down himself. If this was his situation, it is easy to understand that he decided to give his audience a very thorough lesson in legal procedure, partly at the expense of narrative structure. As every professor should know, nothing breeds unnecessary lecturing as much as a good opportunity to unburden oneself of esoteric learning.

Our conclusion about the author's use of written sources must be the same in this caze as in the previous ones: we cannot exclude the possibility that he did consult written law manuscripts, but there is nothing that prompts us to insist, that he did so.

5. OTHER SOURCES

After the previous considerations, it should not be necessary to go into the problem of other possible written sources, such as *Laxdœla*. If it cannot be proved that the author of *Njála* used either a **Brjáns saga*, a **Kristni saga*, written genealogies, or law scrolls, it cannot be proved that he used any of the other written sources that have been proposed. It should be enough to refer the reader to Theodore Andersson's excellent discussion of these matters in *The Problem of Icelandic Saga Origins*, chapter 5. Yet it may be necessary again to emphasize that the author of *Njála* probably had read extensively and that he evidently knew very well the stories told in *Laxdœla* and many other sagas (cf. above, pp. 40, 123). But, unfortunately, he has left us very few clues as to which particular texts he had at his disposal while he was composing his own saga. Whatever he read at that time seems to have been digested and transformed beyond certain recognition. And the saga that he made was essentially his own from the first chapter to the last.

Bibliography

Aðalbjarnarson, Bjarni. See *Heimskringla*.

Adamus Bremensis. *Gesta Hammaburgensis ecclesiae pontificum.* Ed. B. Schmeidler. Hannover and Leipzig, 1917.

Alexanders saga: Islandsk Oversættelse ved Brandr Jónsson. Ed. Finnur Jónsson. Copenhagen, 1925.

—. See Gautier de Châtillon.

Alfræði Íslenzk. 3 vols. Ed. N. Beckman and K. Kålund. Samfund til udgivelse af gammel nordisk litteratur. Copenhagen, 1908-18.

Allen, Richard F. *Fire and Iron: Critical Approaches to Njáls saga.* Pittsburgh: University of Pittsburgh Press, 1971.

Andersson, Theodore M. *The Icelandic Family Saga: An Analytic Reading.* Cambridge, Mass.: Harvard University Press, 1967.

—. "The Displacement of the Heroic Ideal in the Family Sagas." *Speculum,* 45 (1970), 575-93.

—. *The Problem of Icelandic Saga Origins: A Historical Survey.* Yale Germanic Studies, vol. 1. New Haven, 1964.

—. "Skalds and Troubadours." *Mediaeval Scandinavia,* 2 (1969), 7-41.

—. Rev. of *Fire and Iron,* by R. F. Allen. *Journal of English and Germanic Philology,* 71 (1972), 100-04.

Arngrímur Jónsson. *Arngrimi Jonae opera latine conscripta.* Ed. Jakob Benediktsson. Bibliotheca Arnamagnæana, 9-12. 4 vols. Copenhagen, 1950-57.

Auerbach, Erich. *Mimesis: The Representation of Reality in Western Literature.* Trans. by Willard R. Trask. Princeton: Princeton University Press, 1953 (rpt., 1968).

Austfirðinga sǫgur. Ed. Jón Jóhannesson. Íslenzk Fornrit, 11. Reykjavík: Hið íslenzka fornritafélag, 1955.

Bååth, A. U. *Studier öfver kompositionen i några isländska ättesagor.* Lund, 1885.

Baden, Torkel. *Nials Saga, den bedste af alle Sagaer.* Copenhagen, 1821.

Baetke, Walter. *Christliches Lehngut in der Sagareligion.* Berichte über die Verhandlungen der Sächsischen Akademie der Wissenschaften zu Leipzig. Phil.-hist. Klasse, 98:6. Berlin, 1951.

—. *Die Götterlehre der Snorra-Edda.* Berichte über die Verhandlungen der Sächsischen Akademie der Wissenschaften zu Leipzig. Phil.-hist. Klasse, 97:3. Berlin, 1950.

—. *Kleine Schriften.* Weimar: Hermann Böhlaus Nachfolger, 1973.

Bayerschmidt, Carl F. See *Njál's saga.*

Bekker-Nielsen, Hans, Thorkil Damsgaard Olsen, and Ole Widding. *Norrøn Fortællekunst: Kapitler af den norsk-islandske middelalderlitteraturs historie.* Copenhagen: Akademisk Forlag, 1965.

Benediktsson, Jakob. See Arngrímur Jónsson and *Íslendingabók.*

Benoît de Sainte Maure. *Le Roman de Troie.* Ed. Léopold Constans. 6 vols. Paris, 1904-12.

Benson, Larry D. "The Pagan Coloring of Beowulf." *Old English Poetry: Fifteen Essays,* ed. Robert P. Creed. Providence, R. I., 1967, 193-213.

Berges, W. *Die Fürstenspiegel des hohen und späten Mittelalters.* Berlin and Leipzig, 1938.

Bernheim, Ernst. *Mittelalterliche Zeitanschauungen in ihrem Einfluss auf Politik und Geschichtsschreibung.* Tübingen, 1918.

Bertelsen, Henrik. See *Þiðriks saga.*

Bezold, F. von. *Das Fortleben der antiken Götter im mittelalterlichen Humanismus.* Bonn and Leipzig, 1922.

Biskupa sögur. Ed. Jón Sigurðsson and Guðbrandur Vigfússon. 2 vols. Copenhagen, 1858-78.

Bjarnarson, Þorvaldur. "Rök um aldur Njálu." *Skírnir,* 96 (1922), 147-53.

—. See *Leifar.*

Blanck, Anton. *Den nordiska renässansen i sjuttonhundratalets litteratur.* Stockholm, 1911.

Bloomfield, Morton W. "Patristics and Old English Literature: Notes on Some Poems." *Comparative Literature,* 14 (1962); rpt. in *An Anthology of Beowulf Criticism,* ed. by L. E. Nicholson. Notre Dame: University of Notre Dame Press, 1963, 367-72.

Bolton, W. F. "The *Njála* Narrator and the Picture Plane." *Scandinavian Studies,* 44 (1972), 186-209.

Booth, Wayne C. *The Rhetoric of Fiction.* Chicago and London: The University of Chicago Press, 1961.

Borgfirðinga sǫgur. Ed. Sigurður Nordal and Guðni Jónsson. Íslenzk Fornrit, 3. Reykjavik: Hið íslenzka fornritafélag, 1938.

Bredsdorff, Thomas. *Kaos og kærlighed: En studie i islændingesagaers livsbillede.* Copenhagen: Gyldendals Uglebøger, 1971.

Brenner, Oscar. *Über die Kristni-Saga.* Munich, 1878.

Brennu-Njáls saga. Ed. Einar Ól. Sveinsson. Íslenzk Fornrit, 12. Reykjavik: Hið islenzka fornritafélag, 1954.

Brennu-Njáls saga. Ed. Finnur Jónsson. Altnordische Saga-Bibliothek, 13. Halle, 1908.

"Brudstykker af den islandske *Elucidarius.*" Ed. Konráð Gíslason. *Annaler for Nordisk Oldkyndighed og Historie* (1858).

Bugge, Sophus. *Norsk sagafortælling og sagaskrivning i Irland.* Kristiania, 1901-08.

Christensen, H. *Das Alexanderlied Walters von Châtillon.* Halle, 1905.

Clover, Carol. *"Óláfs saga helga, Runzivals þáttr,* and *Njáls saga*: A Structural Comparison." Diss. Berkeley 1972.

—. "Scene in Saga Composition." *Arkiv för nordisk filologi,* 89 (1974), 57-83.

Constans, Léopold. See Benoît de Sainte Maure.

Curschmann, Michael. "Oral Poetry in Mediaeval English, French, and German Literature: Some Notes on Recent Research." *Speculum,* 42 (1967), 36-52.

Curtius, Ernst Robert. *Europäische Literatur und lateinisches Mittelalter.* 7th edition. Bern, 1969.

Dares Phrygius. *De excidio Troiae historia.* Ed. Ferdinand Meister. Leipzig 1873.

Davidson, J. A. "The Homeric Question." *A Companion to Homer,* ed. by A. Wace and F. Stubbings. London and New York, 1962.

Donahue, Charles. "Beowulf and Christian Tradition: A Reconstruction from a Celtic Stance." *Traditio,* 21 (1965), 55-116.

—. *"Beowulf,* Ireland and the Natural Good." *Traditio,* 7 (1949-51), 263-77.

Drei Lygisǫgur. Ed. Åke Lagerholm. Altnordische Saga-Bibliothek, 17. Halle, 1927.

Dundes, Alan, ed. *The Study of Folklore.* Englewood Cliffs, N. J.: Prentice Hall, 1965.

Egils saga Skalla-Grímssonar. Ed. Sigurður Nordal. Íslenzk Fornrit, 2. Reykjavik: Hið íslenzka fornritafélag, 1933.

Egilsson, Sveinbjörn. See *Lexicon Poeticum.*

Einarsson, Bjarmi. "The Lovesick Skald: A Reply to Theodore M. Andersson." *Mediaeval Scandinavia,* 4 (1971), 21-41.

—. *Skáldasögur: Um uppruna og eðli ástaskáldasagnanna fornu.* Reykjavik: Bókaútgáfa Menningarsjóðs, 1961.

Einarsson, Stefán, *A History of Icelandic Literature.* New York, 1957.

Ejerfeldt, Lennart. "Helighet, 'karisma' och kungadöme i forngermansk religion." *Kungliga Humanistiska Vetenkapssamfundets i Uppsala årsbok* (1969-70), 112-175. Also published as *Skrifter utgivna av religionshistoriska institutionen i Uppsala,* 7.

Eldjárn, Kristian. See *Sturlunga saga.*

Elis saga ok Rósamundu. Ed. Eugen Kölbing. Heilbronn, 1881.

Elucidarius. See "Brudstykker."

Erlingsson, Davið. "Etiken i Hrafnkels saga Freysgoða." *Scripta Islandica,* 21 (1970), 3-41.

Eyfirðinga sǫgur. Ed. Jónas Kristjánsson. Islenzk Fornrit, 9. Reykjavik: Hið íslenzka fornritafélag, 1956.

Eyrbyggja saga. Ed. Einar Ól. Sveinsson and Matthías Þórðarson. Íslenzk Fornrit, 4. Reykjavik: Hið íslenzka fornritafélag, 1935.

Fenger, Ole. *Fejde og Mandebod.* Diss. Copenhagen, 1971.

Finnbogason, Magnús. See *Sturlunga saga.*

Finsen, Vilhjálmur. *Om den oprindelige Ordning af nogle af den islandske Fristats Institutioner.* Copenhagen, 1888.

—. See *Grágás*.

Fischer, Frank. *Die Lehnwörter des Altwestnordischen*. Palaestra, 85. Berlin, 1909.

Flateyjarbók. Ed. Sigurður Nordal. 4 vols. Akranes, 1944-45.

Foote, Peter. *The Pseudo-Turpin Chronicle in Iceland*. London Medieval Studies, 4. London, 1959.

—. "Sagnaskemtan: Reykjahólar 1119." *Saga-Book of the Viking Society*, 14 (1955-56), 226-39.

Fox, Denton. "*Njáls Saga* and the Western Literary Tradition." *Comparative Literature*, 15 (1963), 289-310.

Frye, Northrop. *Anatomy of Criticism: Four Essays*. Princeton; Princeton University Press, 1957. Rpt. New York: Atheneum, 1965.

Gautier de Châtillon. *Alexandreis*. Ed. J. P. Migne. *Patrologia Latina*, 209 (1855), 463-512.

—. See *Alexanders saga*.

Gehl, Walter. *Der germanische Schicksalsglaube*. Berlin, 1939.

—. *Ruhm und Ehre bei den Nordgermanen*. Berlin, 1937.

Gering. Hugo. "Altnordische Sprichwörter und sprichwörtliche Redensarten." *Arkiv för nordisk filologi*, 32 (1915-16), 1-31.

Gillet. See Gregory.

Giordano, C. *Alexandreis: Poema di Gautier da Châtillon*. Naples, 1917.

Gíslason, Konráð. See "Brudstykker" and *Njála* (1875).

Goedecke, A. *Die Darstellung der Gemütsbewegungen in der isländischen Familiensaga*. Hamburg, 1933.

Goedheer, A. J. *Irish and Norse Traditions About the Battle of Clontarf*. Diss. Utrecht, 1938. Haarlem: H. D. Tjeenk Willink & Zoon N.V., 1938.

Goetz, Wilhelm. *Die Nialssaga ein Epos und das germanische Heidenthum in seinem Ausklängen im Norden*. Berlin, 1885.

Grágás. Islændernes Lovbog i Fristatstiden, udgivet efter Det Kongelige Bibliotheks Haandskrift. Ed. and Danish trans. by Vilhjálmur Finsen. 4 vols. Copenhagen, 1852-70.

Greenway, John L. "The Wisdom of Njál: The Representation of Reality in the Family Sagas." *Mosaic*, 4, No. 2 (1970), 15-26.

Gregory the Great, Saint. *Morales sur Job: Livres 1 et 2*. Ed. Gillet and Gaudemaris. Sources chrétiennes, 32. Paris, 1952.

Grønbech, Vilhelm. *The Culture of the Teutons*. Translated by W. Worster. 2 vols. London and Copenhagen, 1931.

—. *Vor Folkeæt i Oldtiden*. 2nd revised edition. 2 vols. Copenhagen: Gyldendal, 1955.

Guðmundsson, Barði. "Goðorð forn og ný." *Skírnir*, 111 (1937), 56-83.

—. *Höfundur Njálu. Safn ritgerða*. Ed. Skúli Þórðarson and Stefán Pjetursson. Reykjavik: Bókaútgáfa Menningarsjóðs, 1958.

Guðmundsson, Finnbogi. See *Orkneyinga saga*.

Guðmundsson, Sigurður. "Gunnar á Hlíðarenda." *Skírnir*, 92 (1918), 63-88, 221-51.

Guðnason, Bjarni. "Njáls saga." *Kulturhistorisk Leksikon for Nordisk Middelalder*, 12 (1967), 318-22.

—. *Um Skjöldungasögu*. Diss. Háskóli Íslands, 1962. Reykjavik: Bókaútgáfa Menningarsjóðs, 1963.

Haeckel, Margaret. *Die Darstellung und Funktion des Traumes in der isländischen Familiensaga.* Hamburg, 1934.

Hakonar Saga, and a Fragment of Magnus Saga, with Appendices. Ed. Gudbrand Vigfusson. Rolls Series, 88:2. London, 1887.

Hallberg, Peter. *The Icelandic Saga.* Trans. by Paul Schach. Lincoln: University of Nebraska Press, 1962.

—. "Medeltidslatin och sagaprosa." Några kommentarer till Lars Lönnroths studier i den isländska sagalitteraturen." *Arkiv för nordisk filologi,* 81 (1966), 258-76.

—. "Några anteckningar om replik och dialog i Njáls saga." *Festschrift Walter Baetke,* ed. K. Rudolph, R. Heller, and E. Walter (Weimar, 1966), 130-50.

—. "Nyare studier i den isländska sagan." *Edda,* 53 (1953), 219-47.

—. "Om teser och 'översättningsgrodor'." *Arkiv för nordisk filologi,* 83 (1968), 250-55.

—. "Slutreplik till en respondent." *Samlaren,* 88 (1967), 190-97.

—. Rev of *European Sources of Icelandic Saga-Writing,* by Lars Lönnroth. *Samlaren,* 86 (1965), 157-84.

Halldórsson, Jóhannes. See *Kjalnesinga saga.*

Halldórsson, Ólafur. *Helgafellsbækur fornar.* Studia Islandica, 24. Reykjavik, 1966.

—. See *Óláfs saga Tryggvasonar.*

Harris, Joseph C. "Genre and Narrative Structure in Some *Íslendinga þættir.*" *Scandinavian Studies,* 44 (1972), 1-27.

Hauch, Carsten. "Indledning til Forelæsninger over Njalssaga og flere med den beslægtede Sagaer." In *Afhandlinger og æsthetiske Betragtninger* (Copenhagen, 1855), 411-67.

Haugen, Einar. *Norwegian Word Studies. II. The Vocabularies of the Old Norse Sagas and of Henrik Wergeland.* Madison, Wisconsin, 1942.

Hauksbók udg. efter de Arnamagnæanske Handskrifter No. 371, 544 og 675,4°. Ed. Eiríkur Jónsson and Finnur Jónsson. Copenhagen, 1892-96.

Heilagra Manna Sögur. Fortællinger og Legender om hellige Mænd og Kvinder. Ed. C. R. Unger. Christiania, 1877.

Heimskringla. Ed. Bjarni Aðalbjarnarson. 3 vols. Íslenzk Fornrit, 26-28. Reykjavik: Hið íslenzka fornritafélag, 1951.

Heinzel, Richard. *Beschreibung der isländischen Saga.* Wien, 1880.

Helgason, Jón. "Gauks saga Trandilssonar." *Heidersskrift til Gustav Indrebo.* Oslo, 1939.

——. See *Njáls saga.*

Heller, Rolf. *Die literarische Darstellung der Frau in der Isländersagas.* Halle, 1958.

Hermannsson, Halldór. *Icelandic Manuscripts.* Islandica, 19. Ithaca, N.Y., 1929.

Heusler, Andreas. *Die Altgermanische Dichtung.* 2nd ed. Potsdam, 1945.

—. "Die Anfänge der Isländischen Saga." *Abhandlungen der K. Preuss. Akad. d. Wiss., Phil.-Hist. Classe* (1913), 1-87.

— (trans.). *Die Geschichte vom weisen Njál.* Thule, 4. Jena, 1914.

—. *Das Strafrecht der Isländersagas.* Leipzig, 1911.

Historia Karoli Magni et Rotholandi. Ed. C. Meredith-Jones. Paris, 1936.

Historia Niali et Filiorum. Trans. Jón Johnsonius. Copenhagen, 1809.

Hollander, Lee M. See *Njál's Saga.*

Holm-Olsen, L. See Sveinsson and *Konungs skuggsjá.*

Holmbäck, Å. See *Svenska Landskapslagar.*

Hruby, A. *Zur Technik der Isländischen Saga: Die Kategorien ihrer Personen-characteristik.* Wien, 1929.

Ingarden, Roman. *Das literarische Kunstwerk.* 3rd ed. Tübingen, 1965.

Islandske originaldiplomer indtil 1450. Ed. Stefán Karlsson. Editiones Arnamagnæanæ, Series A, vol. 7. Copenhagen, 1963.

Íslendingabók, Lándnámabók. Ed. Jakob Benediktsson. 2 vols. Íslenzk Fornrit, 1. Reykjavik: Hið íslenzka fornritafélag, 1968.

Jansson, Sven B. F. *Sagorna om Vinland. I. Handskrifterna till Erik den Rödes saga.* Stockholm and Lund, 1945.

Johannessen, Matthías. *Njála í íslenzkum skáldskap.* Reykjavik, 1958.

Jóhannesson, Jón. *Gerðir Landnámabókar.* Reykjavik, 1941.

—. *Íslendinga saga.* 2 vols. Reykjavik: Almenna Bókafélagið, 1956-58.

—. See *Austfirðinga sǫgur* and *Sturlunga saga.*

Johnsen, Arne Odd. *Fra ættesamfunn til statssamfunn.* Oslo, 1948.

Johnsen, O. A. See *Óláfs saga helga.*

Jónsson, Arngrímur. See Arngrímur.

Jónsson, Finnur. "Oldislandske Ordsprog og Talemåder." *Arkiv für nordisk filologi,* 30 (1913-14), 61-111, 170-217.

—. *Den oldnorske og oldislandske Litteraturs Historie.*
1st ed. 3 vols. Copenhagen, 1894-1902.
2nd ed. 3 vols. Copenhagen, 1920-24.

—. "Om Njála." *Aarbøger for Nordisk Oldkyndighed og Historie,* 19:2 (1904), 89-166.

—. See *Alexanders saga, Brennu-Njáls saga, Hauksbók, Óláfs saga Tryggvasonar, Lexicon Poeticum,* and *Prose Edda.*

Jónsson, Guðni. "Genealogier." *Kulturhistorisk Leksikon for Nordisk Middelalder,* 5 (1960), 247-49.

—. See *Borgfirðinga sǫgur, Vestfirðinga sǫgur.*

Kålund, Kristian. See *Alfrœði,* Magnússon.

Karlamagnús saga ok kappa hans. Ed. C. R. Unger. Christiania, 1860.

Karlsson, Stefán. "Ritun Reykjafjarðarbókar. Excursus: Bókagerð bænda." *Opuscula,* IV. Bibliotheca Arnamagnæana, 30. Copenhagen: Munksgaard, 1970, 131-40.

—. See *Islandske originaldiplomer.*

Kelchner, Georgia D. *Dreams in Old Norse Literature and their Affinities in Folklore.* Cambridge, 1935.

Ker, W. P. *Epic and Romance: Essays on Medieval Literature.* 2nd ed., 1908; rpt. New York: Dover, 1957.

Kersbergen, Anna Cornelia. *Litteraire Motieven in de Njála.* Rotterdam, 1927.

Keyser, R. See *Norges Gamle Love.*

Kinck, Hans E. "Et par ting om ættesagaer: Skikkelser den ikke forstod." *Til Gerhard Gran 9 des. 1916;* rpt. in *Mange slags kunst.* Kristiania: Aschehoug, 1921, 3-58; *Sagaenes ånd og skikkelser.* Oslo: Aschehoug, 1951, 9-46.

King's Mirror. See *Konungs skuggsjá.*

Kjalnesinga saga. Ed. Jóhannes Halldórsson. Íslenzk Fornrit, 14. Reykjavik: Hið íslenska fornritafélag, 1959.

Kölbing, Eugen. See *Elis saga.*

Konungs skuggsjá. Ed. Ludvig Holm-Olsen. Oslo, 1945.

——. *The King's Mirror.* Trans. L. M. Larson. New York, 1917.

Kristjánsson, Jónas. "*Íslendingadrápa* and Oral Tradition." A paper delivered at the Second International Saga Conference in Reykjavik, 1973.

Kristjánsson, Jónas. *Um Fóstbræðrasögu.* Diss. Háskóli Íslands. Reykjavik: Stofnun Árna Magnússonar, 1972.

Kristni saga. Þáttr Þorvalds ens víðfǫrla. Þáttr Ísleifs biskups Gizurarsonar. Hungrvaka. Ed. B. Kahle. Altnordische Saga-Bibliothek, 11. Halle, 1905.

Lagerholm, Åke. See *Drei Lygisǫgur.*

Landnámabók. See *Islendingabók.*

Laxdœla saga. Ed. Einar Ól. Sveinsson. Islenzk Fornrit, 5. Reykjavik: Hið íslenzka fornrítafélag, 1934.

Lefèvre, Yves. *L'Elucidarium et les Lucidaires: Contribution, par l'histoire d'un texte, à l'histoire des croyances religieuses en France au moyen âge.* Paris, 1954.

Lehmann, Karl, and von Carolsfeld, Hans Schnorr. *Die Njálssage insbesondere in ihren juristischen Bestandtheilen: Ein kritischer Beitrag zur altnordischen Rechts- und Literaturgeschichte.* Berlin, 1883.

Lehmann, Karl. "Jurisprudensen i Njála." *Tidsskrift for Retsvidenskab,* 18 (1905), 183-99.

Leifar fornra kristinna frœða íslenzkra. Ed. Þorvaldur Bjarnarson. Copenhagen, 1878.

Lexicon poeticum antiquæ linguæ septentrionalis. By Sveinbjörn Egilsson and Finnur Jónsson. 2nd ed., 1931; rpt. Copenhagen, 1966.

Lie, Hallvard. *Studier i Heimskringlas stil: Dialogene og talene.* Oslo, 1937.

Liestøl, Knut. *The Origin of the Icelandic Family Sagas.* Trans. by A. G. Jayne. Oslo, 1930.

Lind, E. H. *Norsk-isländska dopnamn och fingerade namn från medeltiden.* Uppsala, 1905-15.

Ljósvetninga saga. Ed. Björn Sigfússon. Islenzk Fornrit, 10. Reykjavik: Hið íslenzka fornritafélag, 1940.

Lönnroth, Lars. *European Sources of Icelandic Saga-Writing: An Essay Based on Previous Studies.* Diss. Stockholm, 1965.

——. "Filologi och ordräkning." *Arkiv för nordisk filologi,* 83 (1968), 241-49.

——. "Hetjurnar líta bleika akra. Athuganir á Njáls sögu og Alexanders sögu." *Skírnir,* 144 (1970), 12-30.

——. "*Hjálmar's Death-Song* and the Delivery of Eddic Poetry." *Speculum,* 46 (1971), 1-20.

——. "Kroppen som själens spegel-ett motiv i de isländska sagorna." *Lychnos,* 1963-64, 24-61.

——. "Det litterära porträttet i latinsk historiografi och isländsk sagaskrivning. En komparativ studie." *Acta Philologica Scandinavica,* 27 (1965), 68-117.

——. "The Noble Heathen: A Theme in the Sagas." *Scandinavian Studies,* 41 (1969), 1-29.

—. "Rhetorical Persuasion in the Sagas." *Scandinavian Studies,* 42 (1970), 157-89.

—. "Structural Divisions in the *Njála* Manuscripts." *Arkiv för nordisk filologi,* 90 (1975) 49-79.

—. "Studier i Olaf Tryggvasons saga." *Samlaren,* 84 (1963), 54-94.

—. "Styrmir's Hand in the Obituary of Viðey?" *Mediaeval Scandinavia,* 1 (1968), 85-100.

—. "Svar till min fakultetsopponent." *Samlaren,* 88 (1967), 178-90.

—. "Tesen om de två kulturerna. Kritiska studier i den isländska saga-skrivningens sociala förutsättningar." *Scripta Islandica,* 15 (1964), 1-97.

—. Rev. of *Fire and Iron,* by R. F. Allen. *Speculum,* 48 (1973), 330-34.

—. Rev. of *The Icelandic Family Saga,* by T. M. Andersson. *Speculum,* 43 (1968), 115-19.

—. Rev. of *Einarsbók: Afmæliskveðja til Einars Ól. Sveinssonar,* ed. B. Guðnason and J. Kristjánsson. *Mediaeval Scandinavia,* 4 (1971), 175-81.

—. Rev. of *Njáls saga: A Literary Masterpiece,* by E. Ó. Sveinsson. *Scandinavica,* 11 (1972), 48-49.

Lord, Albert B. *The Singer of Tales.* Cambridge, Mass: Harvard University Press, 1960; rpt. New York: Atheneum, 1965.

Magnússon, Árni. *Brevveksling med Torfaeus.* Ed. Kristian Kålund. Copenhagen, 1916.

Magnússon, Magnús. See *Njál's Saga.*

Manuscripta Islandica, see *Njáls saga.*

Maurer, Konrad von. *Die Bekehrung des Norwegischen Stammes zum Christen-thume.* 2 vols. Munich, 1855.

—. *Die Entstehung der isländischen Staates.* Munich, 1852.

Maxwell, I. R. "Pattern in *Njáls saga.*" *Saga-Book of the Viking Society,* 15 (1957-61), 17-47.

Meissner, Rudolf. *Die Strengleikar. Ein Beitrag zur Geschichte der altnordische Prosa-Literatur.* Halle, 1902.

Meletinsky, E. M. See Propp.

Meredith-Jones, C. See *Historia Karoli Magni.*

Migne, J. P. See Gautier de Châtillon.

Mjöberg, Jöran. *Drömmen om sagatiden.* 2 vols. Stockholm: 1967-68.

Möðruvallabók (Codex Möðruvallensis). Facsimile edition with an introduction by Einar Ól. Sveinsson. Corpus Codicum Islandicorum Medii Aevi, 5. Copenhagen, 1933.

Monumenta Historica Norvegiae. Latinske kildeskrifter til Norges historie i middelalderen. Ed. Gustav Storm. Kristiania, 1880.

Müller, Peter Erasmus. *Sagabibliothek.* 3 vols. Copenhagen, 1817-20.

Munch, P. A. See *Norges Gamle Love.*

Mundt, Marina. "Observations on the Influence of *Þiðriks saga* on Icelandic Saga-Writing." A paper delivered at the First International Saga Conference in Edinburgh, 1971.

Myres, Sir John. *Homer and his Critics.* London, 1958

Nagler, Michael N. "Towards a generative view of the oral formula." *Transactions and Proceedings of the American Philological Association,* 98 (1967).

Njála (1908, 1954). See *Brennu-Njáls saga.*

Njála, udgivet efter gamle Handskrifter. Ed. Konráð Gíslason *et al.* Vol. I (Text), 1875. Vol. II (Commentary), 1879-96. Copenhagen: Den Gyldendalske Boghandel.

Njáls saga: The Arnamagnæan Manuscript 468, 4ᵗᵒ (Reykjabók). Facsimile edition with an introduction by Jón Helgason. Manuscripta Islandica, 6. Copenhagen, 1962.

—. *Sagan af Niáli Þórgeirssyni ok sonvm hans.* Ed. O. Olavius. Copenhagen, 1772.

Njál's Saga. Trans. Magnús Magnússon and Hermann Pálsson. Penguin Classics. Middlesex and Baltimore, 1960.

Njál's Saga. Trans. Carl F. Bayerschmidt and Lee M. Hollander. New York: New York University Press, for The American-Scandinavian Foundation, 1955.

Nordal, Sigurður. "Sagalitteraturen." *Nordisk Kultur,* 8 B. Uppsala, 1953, 180-273.

—. "Time and Vellum." *Annual Bulletin of the Modern Humanities Research Association,* 24 (1952).

—. See *Borgfirðinga sogur, Egils saga, Flateyjarbók.*

Norges Gamle Love indtil 1387. Ed. R. Keyser and P. A. Munch. 1st vol. Christiania, 1846.

Nygaard, M. "Den lærde stil i den norrøne prose." *Sproglig-historiske studier tilegnede C. R. Unger.* Kristiania, 1897.

—. *Norrøn Syntax.* Kristiania, 1905.

Oddr Snorrason. See *Óláfs saga Tryggvasonar.*

Óláfs saga helga. Den store saga om Olav den hellige. Ed. Oscar Albert Johnsen and Jón Helgason. 2 vols. Oslo, 1941.

Óláfs saga Tryggvasonar en mesta. Ed. Ólafur Halldórsson. 2 vols. Editiones Arnamagnæanæ, Series A, 1-2. Copenhagen, 1958-61.

Óláfs saga Tryggvasonar, by Oddr Snorrason. Ed. Finnur Jónsson. Copenhagen, 1932.

Olavius, Olavus. See *Njáls saga.*

Oleson, Tryggvi J. "Book Collections of Icelandic Churches in the Fifteenth Century." *Nordisk Tidskrift för Bok- och Biblioteksväsen,* 47 (1960), 90-103.

—. "Book Collections of Icelandic Churches in the Fourteenth Century." *NTBB,* 46 (1959), 111-23.

—. "Book Collections of Mediaeval Icelandic Churches." *Speculum,* 32 (1957), 502-10.

—. "Book Donors in Mediaeval Iceland, 1-2." *NTBB,* 44 (1957), 88-94; *NTBB,* 48 (1961), 10-22.

Olmer, E. *Boksamlingar på Island 1179-1490.* Göteborgs Högskolas Årsskrift, 8 (1902).

Olsen, Thorkil Damsgaard. See Bekker-Nielsen, Hans.

Orkneyinga saga. Ed. Finnbogi Guðmundsson. Islenzk Fornrit, 34. Reykjavik: Hið íslenzka fornritafélag, 1965.

Page, R. I. Rev. of *Fire and Iron,* by R. F. Allen. *Scandinavica,* 11 (1972), 149-151.

Pálsson, Heimir. "Rittengsl Laxdælu og Njála." *Mímir,* 6 (1967), 5-16.

Pálsson, Hermann. *Art and Ethics in Hrafnkel's Saga.* Copenhagen: Munksgaard, 1971.

—. *Sagnaskemmtun Íslendinga.* Reykjavik: Mál og menning, 1962.

—. *Siðfræði Hrafnkels sögu.* Reykjavik, 1966.

—. See *Njal's Saga.*

Patch, H. R. *The Goddess Fortuna in Mediaeval Literature.* Cambridge, Mass., 1927.

Petersen, N. M. *Bidrag til den oldnordiske Litteraturs Historie.* Copenhagen, 1866.

Pipping, R. "Ett dubbeltydigt omen." *Budkavlen,* 15 (1936), 80-82.

Postola Sögur. Legendariske fortællinger om Apostlernes liv. Ed. C. R. Unger. Kristiania, 1874.

Propp, Vladimir, *Morphology of the Folktale.* Translated by Laurence Scott. Revised by Louis Wagner. 2nd ed. Austin and London, 1968.

—. *Morfologiya skazki.* 2nd ed. with an essay by E. M. Meletinsky. Moscow, 1969.

The Prose Edda by Snorri Sturluson. Trans. Arthur G. Brodeur. New York, 1916.

—. *Edda Snorra Sturlusonar udg. efter håndskrifterne.* Ed. Finnur Jónsson. Copenhagen, 1931.

Die Religion in Geschichte und Gegenwart. 3rd ed. Tübingen, 1957-65.

Reykjabók. See *Njáls saga.*

Ryan, John. "The Battle of Clontarf." *Journal of the Royal Society of Antiquaries of Ireland,* 67 (1938), 1-50.

Salvesen, Astrid. *Studies in the Vovabulary of the Old Norse Elucidarium.* Bergen: Universitetsforlaget, 1968.

Saxon, Anne Martha. "Unity and Narrative Technique in the *Brennu-Njáls saga.*" Diss. Berkeley 1964.

Schach, Paul. "The Anticipatory Literary Setting in the Old Icelandic Sagas." *Scandinavian Studies,* 27 (1955), 1-13.

—. Rev. of *Fire and Iron,* by R. F. Allen. *Scandinavian Studies,* 44 (1972), 555-566.

—. See Hallberg, Peter and Sveinsson, Einar Ól.

Schlauch, Margaret. *Romance in Iceland.* New York, 1934.

Schomerus, R. *Die Religion der Nordgermanen im Spiegel christlicher Darstellung.* Leipzig, 1936.

Seznec, Jean. *La survivance des dieux antiques.* Studies of the Warburg Institute, 11. London, 1953.

Sigfússon, Björn. See *Ljósvetninga saga.*

Sigurðsson, Jón. See *Biskupa sögur.*

Snorri Sturluson. See *Heimskirngla, Prose Edda.*

Ström, Folke. *Diser, nornor, valkyrjor. Fruktbarhetskult och sakralt kungadöme i Norden.* Kungl. Vitterhets Historie och Antikvitets akademiens handlingar, filologisk-filosofiska serien, 1. Stockholm, 1954.

—. *Den egna kraftens män. En studie i forntida irreligiositet.* Göteborgs Högskolas Årsskrift, 54 (1948).

—. "Kung Domalde i Svitjod och 'kungalyckan.'" *Saga och Sed,* 34 (1967-68), 52-66.

Strömbäck, Dag. "Some Remarks on Learned and Novelistic Elements in the Icelandic Sagas." *Nordica et Anglica: Studies in Honor of Stefán Einarsson.* The Hague, Mouton, 1968, 140-47.

—. *Sejd. Textstudier i religionshistoria.* Nordiska texter och undersökningar, 5. Diss. Uppsala, 1935.

—. *Tidrande och diserna. Ett filologiskt-folkloristiskt utkast.* Lund, 1949.

Sturla Þórðarson. See *Hákonar saga, Sturlunga saga.*

Sturlunga saga. Ed. Jón Jóhannesson, Magnús Finnbogason and Kristján Eldjárn. 2 vols. Reykjavík, 1946.

Sturlunga Saga, including the Íslendinga Saga of Lawman Sturla Thordarson and other works. Ed. Guðbrandur Vigfússon. 2 vols. Oxford, 1878.

Suhm, P. A. *Critisk Historie af Danmark, udi den hedenske Tid fra Odin til Gorm den gamle.* Vol. 4. Copenhagen, 1781.

Sveinsson, Einar Ól. *Á Njálsbúð. Bók um mikið listaverk.* Reykjavík, 1943.

—. *The Age of the Sturlungs: Icelandic Civilization in the Thirteenth Century.* Trans. Jóhann S. Hannesson. Islandica, 36. Ithaca, 1953.

—. "Lestrarkunnátta Íslendinga í fornöld." *Skírnir,* 118 (1944), 173-97; rpt. *Við uppspretturnar. Greinasafn.* Reykjavik: Helgafell, 1956, 166-92.

—. "Njála og Skógverjar." *Skírnir,* 111 (1937), 15-45.

—. *Njáls Saga: A Literary Masterpiece.* Ed. and trans. Paul Schach. Lincoln: University of Nebraska Press, 1971.

—. *Njåls saga: Kunstverket.* Trans. Ludvig Holm-Olsen. Bergen and Oslo: Universitetsforlaget, 1959.

—. *Sagnaritun Oddaverja. Nokkrar athuganir.* Studia Islandica, 1. Reykjavik, 1937.

—. *Studies in the Manuscript Tradition of Njáls saga.* Reykjavik, 1953.

—. *Sturlungaöld.* Reykjavik, 1940.

—. *Um Njálu.* Diss. Háskóli Íslands. Reykjavik, 1933.

—. See *Brennu-Njáls saga, Eyrbyggja saga, Laxdœla saga, Möðruvallabók, Vatnsdœla saga.*

Svenska landskapslagar tolkade och förklarade, by Å. Holmbäck and E. Wessén. Vol. 1. Stockholm, 1933.

Taylor, A. B. "Karl Hundason, 'King of Scots.'" *Proceedings of the Society of Antiquaries of Scotland,* 71 (1936-37), 334-42.

Thesaurus Linguae Latinae, editus auctoritate et consilio Academiarum quinque germanicarum. Leipzig, 1900-.

Þiðriks saga af Bern. Ed. Henrik Bertelsen. Samfund til udgivelse af gammel nordisk litteratur, 34. 2 vols. Copenhagen, 1905-11.

Þórðarson, Matthías. See *Eyrbyggja saga*

Þórólfsson, Björn. See *Vestfirðinga sǫgur.*

van den Toorn, M. C. *Ethics and Moral in Icelandic Saga Literature.* Assen, 1955.

—. "Zur Struktur der Saga." *Arkiv för nordisk filologi,* 73 (1958), 140-68.

Torfæus, Thormodus. *Series regum Daniae.* Copenhagen, 1705.

Turville-Petre, Joan. *The Story of Rauð and his Sons.* Viking Society, Payne Memorial Series, 2. London, 1947.

Tveitane, Mattias. *Den lærde stil. Oversætterprosa i den norrøne versjonen av Vitæ Patrum.* Diss. Bergen, 1968.

—. "Europeisk påvirkning på den norrøne sagalitteraturen. Noen synspunkter." Edda, 69, No. 2 (1969), 73-95.

Unger, C. R. See *Heilagra Manna Sögur, Karlamagnús saga, Postola Sögur.*

Vatnsdœla saga. Ed. Einar Ól. Sveinsson. Íslenzk Fornrit, 8. Reykjavik: Hið íslenzka fornritafélag, 1939.

Vestfirðinga sǫgur. Ed. Björn K. Þórólfsson and Guðni Jónsson. Íslenzk Fornrit, 6. Reykjavik: Hið íslenzka fornritafélag, 1943.

Vigfússon, Guðbrandur. "Um tímatal í Íslendinga sögum i fornöld." *Safn til sögu Íslands*, 1. Copenhagen, 1856, 185-502.

—. See *Biskupa sögur, Hákonar Saga, Sturlunga Saga.*

de Vries, Jan. *Altgermanische Religionsgeschichte.* 2nd ed. 2 vols. Grundriss der germanischen Philologie, 12. Berlin: Walter de Gruyter, 1956-57.

—. *Altnordische Literaturgeschichte.* 2nd ed. 2 vols. Grundriss der germanischen Philologie, 15-16. Berlin: Walter de Gruyter, 1964-67.

Weber, Gerd Wolfgang. *Studien zum Schicksalsbegriff der altenglischen und altnordischen Literatur.* Diss. Frankfurt am Main, 1969.

Whitelock, Dorothy. *The Audience of Beowulf.* Oxford, 1951.

Widding, Ole. See Bekker-Nielsen, Hans.

Wolf, Alois. *Gestaltungskerne und Gestaltungsweisen in der altgermanischen Heldendichtung.* Munich, 1965.

Worster, W. See Grønbech.

Index of Subjects

Action patterns, 53, 54, 55, 68-82; of feuds, 69-71, 76-82; of travels, 71-75, 81-82

Ættvísi, 237, 240. *See also* Genealogies

Ævisaga, defined, 207, 208

Agents of Fate, 90, 152; pagan, 132-136; role of in sagas, 60, 61, 65

Alliteration, 47, 84, 98, 119

Allthing, 19, 30, 31, 45, 88, 113, 137; corruption of, 165; decisions of, 60; decline of, 188; functions and branches of, 57, 188-194; Gunnarr convicted at, 27; killings at, 175; legislative reforms of, 180, 183; narrative patterns for meetings of, 224-225; and natural law, 145; pagan vs. Christian law at, 29, 143, 144, 219; as powerless, 59; role of memory at, 213, 214, 247-248. *See also* Battle of the Allthing

Angel. *See* "Fetch Angel"

Arbitrator, 65, 66

Armor, description of, 116-117

Assault vs. wounding, 245-246

Assonance, 84, 119

Atonement, 142; and concept of bad luck, 130; of Flosi and Gunnarr, 158-159

Audience: rhetorical manipulation of, 82-101; in social context, 21-22, 194-203

Auðna. *See* Fate

Augustinian theology, 122; in Iceland, 123-128; in *Njála*, 128-136 *passim*; and the Rightful War, 145

Author: as a chieftain, 17; as a lawyer, 7; as a layman, 17, 167; as Sæmundr the Wise, 4; attitudes of on pagan and Christian law, 144, 145, 147-149; as characterized by Nordal, 205; Christian philosophy of, 102; Christian world picture of, 162-164; clerical education of, 167, 200, 203; clerical style and mind of, 113-116, 148-149, 157, 160, 162-164, 200; as commissioned, 194; consistency of, 32; and the Conversion episode, 221-223; as distinct from the narrator, 84; and genealogies, 239-240; imagination and originality of, 37-38, 42, 208; judicial knowledge of, 243-245; probable travels of, 201-203; role

Index of Proper Names

Index prepared by Barbara Ingle